Racism, Xenophobia, Antisemitism, and Islamophobia in European Football

This book examines the prevalence of racism, xenophobia, antisemitism, and Islamophobia in European football. It provides critical assessments of selected policies, strategies, campaigns, and initiatives that have been developed by various stakeholders aimed at combating these discriminatory practices.

Bringing together leading football researchers, this book opens with a discussion of the historical context for racism, xenophobia, antisemitism, and Islamophobia in European football and outlines the key terms and core concepts that frame the study of this topic. The book then offers ten in-depth case studies of European countries, including England, France, Germany, Italy, the Netherlands, Poland, Portugal, Scotland, Spain, and Sweden. Each chapter describes and analyses the various manifestations of racism, xenophobia, antisemitism, and/or Islamophobia against the specific socio-historical, demographic, political, and cultural contexts of the country before engaging with the responses of selected stakeholders. The case studies are followed by a critical account of supra-national responses, including the involvement of UEFA, the European Union, the Council of Europe, and Football Against Racism in Europe (FARE). The book is rounded off by a cross-cultural, comparative analysis drawing out the key themes that define the problem of racism and discrimination in European football today.

The most up-to-date study of one of football's most disconcerting and enduring issues, this book is fascinating reading for any student, researcher, policymaker, or practitioner with interest in the sociology of sport, football and its fan cultures, issues of inclusion and exclusion in modern societies, European football, and the relationships between sport and wider society.

Udo Merkel is a German social scientist who spent most of his life working at HE institutions in England, UK. He has a keen interest in the political economy of football, politics and sociology of sport, mega sports events as a foreign policy and diplomatic tools, globalisation, comparative European sport studies, and fan cultures. Now semi-retired, Udo is based in Spain and works as a consultant and independent critical scholar.

Critical Research in Football

Series Editors:
Pete Millward
Liverpool John Moores University, UK
Jamie Cleland
University of Southern Australia
Dan Parnell
University of Liverpool, UK
Stacey Pope
Durham University, UK
Paul Widdop
Manchester Metropolitan University, UK

The *Critical Research in Football* book series was launched in 2017 to showcase the inter- and multi-disciplinary breadth of debate relating to 'football'. The series defines 'football' as broader than association football, with research on rugby, Gaelic, and gridiron codes also featured. Including monographs, edited collections, short books, and textbooks, books in the series are written and/or edited by leading experts in the field whilst consciously also affording space to emerging voices in the area and are designed to appeal to students, postgraduate students, and scholars who are interested in the range of disciplines in which critical research in football connects. The series is published in association with the Football Collective, @FB_Collective.

Antisemitism in Football: International Perspectives
Edited by Emma Poulton

Politics, Social Issues and the 2023 FIFA Women's World Cup
Edited by Danielle Sarver Coombs and Molly Yanity

Football, Community and Social Responsibility: Everton's 'Blue Family' and Sport at the Service of Humanity
Chris Stone

Racism, Xenophobia, Antisemitism, and Islamophobia in European Football: Symptoms, Sources, and Solutions
Edited by Udo Merkel

For more information about this series, please visit: https://www.routledge.com/Critical-Research-in-Football/book-series/CFSFC

Racism, Xenophobia, Antisemitism, and Islamophobia in European Football

Symptoms, Sources, and Solutions

Edited by Udo Merkel

LONDON AND NEW YORK

First published 2025
by Routledge
4 Park Square, Milton Park, Abingdon, Oxon OX14 4RN

and by Routledge
605 Third Avenue, New York, NY 10158

Routledge is an imprint of the Taylor & Francis Group, an informa business

© 2025 selection and editorial matter, Udo Merkel; individual chapters, the contributors

The right of Udo Merkel to be identified as the author of the editorial material, and of the authors for their individual chapters, has been asserted in accordance with sections 77 and 78 of the Copyright, Designs and Patents Act 1988.

The Open Access version of this book, available at www.taylorfrancis.com, has been made available under a Creative Commons Attribution-Non Commercial-No Derivatives (CC-BY-NC-ND) 4.0 International license.

Any third party material in this book is not included in the OA Creative Commons license, unless indicated otherwise in a credit line to the material. Please direct any permissions enquiries to the original rightsholder.

An electronic version of this book is freely available, thanks to the support of libraries working with Knowledge Unlatched (KU). KU is a collaborative initiative designed to make high quality books Open Access for the public good. The Open Access ISBN for this book is 9781003495970. More information about the initiative and links to the Open Access version can be found at www.knowledgeunlatched.org.

Trademark notice: Product or corporate names may be trademarks or registered trademarks, and are used only for identification and explanation without intent to infringe.

British Library Cataloguing-in-Publication Data
A catalogue record for this book is available from the British Library

ISBN: 978-1-032-80205-3 (hbk)
ISBN: 978-1-032-80206-0 (pbk)
ISBN: 978-1-003-49597-0 (ebk)

DOI: 10.4324/9781003495970

Typeset in Optima
by Apex CoVantage, LLC

Contents

List of contributors	*vii*
Foreword	*xii*

1 Introduction: Key contexts, terms and nomenclature 1
   UDO MERKEL

2 Conceptual and theoretical considerations: Racism, xenophobia, antisemitism and Islamophobia 19
   SCOTT FLEMING

3 England: Islamophobia in English professional and amateur football: A blind spot 36
   TOM TAYLOR

4 France: *Les Bleus* and the Republic: Diversity, difference and discrimination 54
   JONATHAN ERVINE

5 Germany: Tensions and contradictions in football: Integration versus discrimination 71
   LASSE MÜLLER

6 Italy: Racism, xenophobia, and the North-South divide in football 92
   ALESSIO NORRITO

7 The Netherlands: Racism and policy responses in Dutch football: A critical evaluation 108
   RENS CREMERS, ARNE VAN LIENDEN, AGNES ELLING AND JACCO VAN STERKENBURG

8 Poland: Nationalism, racism, xenophobia and football
   fan sub-cultures: Historical developments and
   contemporary issues   125
   RADOSŁAW KOSSAKOWSKI

9 Portugal: Making sense of and tackling racism in football   141
   SOFIA NEVES, JOANA TOPA, JANETE BORGES, ESTEFÂNIA SILVA,
   ARIANA CORREIA AND MAFALDA FERREIRA

10 Scotland: Sectarianism as racism in football? The cut and
   thrust of an ongoing debate   158
   ALAN BAIRNER AND STUART WHIGHAM

11 Spain: Understanding and fighting racism in football:
   A story of ignorance and half-heartedness   173
   RAMÓN LLOPIS-GOIG

12 Sweden: Swedish society and football at odds with each
   other – So open, yet so closed   188
   KATARZYNA HERD

13 Europe (I): Supranational political and policy responses
   to racism and discrimination in football   206
   CHRISTOS KASSIMERIS

14 Europe (II): Comparative observations: Commonalities
   and differences   222
   UDO MERKEL

   Index   *242*

Contributors

Alan Bairner is Professor of Sport and Social Theory at Loughborough University in England. He studied Politics at the University of Edinburgh, gained a PGCE in History and Modern Studies at Moray House College of Education, and was awarded a PhD by the University of Hull. Prior to his arrival in Loughborough in 2013, he was Professor of Sport Studies at the University of Ulster, where he had worked for 25 years. His main research interest is in the relationship between sport and politics with a specific focus on nations, nationalism, and national identities. He is co-editor (with Mariann Vaczi) of *Sport and Secessionism* (2021) and (with Tzu-hsuan Chen and Ying Chiang) *Sport in Taiwan. History, Culture, Policy* (2023).

Janete Borges earned a PhD in Interdisciplinary Sciences at the University of Porto. She is Assistant Professor at the School of Health, Polytechnic of Porto, and a researcher at the Centre for Health Studies and Research, University of Coimbra, and the Associated Laboratory for Green Chemistry of the Network of Chemistry and Technology, Portugal. Currently, she is a member of the Portuguese National Observatory of Violence against Athletes team. She also participates in other research projects related to the study of violence and discrimination. Her work focuses mainly on the statistical treatment and analysis of data.

Ariana Correia earned a PhD in Psychology at the University of Porto. Since 2011, she has been involved in several academic and field projects, all covering gender violence, domestic violence, intimate partner femicide, and the social construction of crime. She is also recognized as a specialist in gender equality, domestic violence, and violence against women by the Gender Equality and Citizenship Commission. She is a researcher at the Interdisciplinary Centre for Gender Studies, Institute of Social and Political Sciences, University of Lisbon. She is also a co-founder of *Associação Plano i*, an NGO based in Porto that promotes human rights under an intersectional matrix.

Rens Cremers is a researcher at the Mulier Institute in Utrecht and a PhD candidate at Erasmus University Rotterdam. Trained as an interdisciplinary social scientist, he has a keen interest in issues surrounding social inequality and diversity in sport. His quantitative and qualitative research focuses particularly on social inclusion and exclusion related to 'race'/ethnicity, gender, and sexual orientation.

Agnes Elling is a senior researcher at the Mulier Institute in Utrecht and an internationally highly respected academic in the field of social inequalities in and through sport. She pays particular attention to gender, ethnicity, and sexual orientation and the intersections between them.

Jonathan Ervine is Senior Lecturer in French and Francophone Studies at Bangor University in Wales. Originally from Scotland, he joined Bangor University in 2007 after earning a PhD at Leeds University in Northern England. His areas of expertise and research interest are French popular culture as well as debates about identity and belonging in contemporary France. He is the author of two books: *Humour in Contemporary France: Controversy, Consensus and Contradictions* (2019) and *Cinema and the Republic: Filming on the Margins in Contemporary France* (2013). He has also published several articles and book chapters about debates on French national identity in sport, music, and comedy, and he also has written several articles about videogames in France.

Mafalda Ferreira is a criminologist with a master's degree in forensic medicine from the Institute of Biomedical Sciences and a PhD in forensic sciences from the Faculty of Medicine, both at the University of Porto. She is president of *Associação Plano i*, an NGO based in Porto, that advocates for human rights in an intersectional manner. She is also a member of the Interdisciplinary Centre for Gender Studies in the Institute of Social and Political Sciences, University of Lisbon. Furthermore, the Commission for Citizenship and Equality recognizes her as a specialist in the areas of gender equality, violence against women, domestic violence, sexual orientation, gender identity, and others. She is also a member of the research team of the EU-funded project Uni4Equity that intends to strengthen universities response to sexual harassment.

Scott Fleming is Emeritus Professor of Sport and Leisure Studies. He has a long-standing interest in 'race relations' and youth studies, which form part of his wider portfolio of research linked to equality and diversity. His work embraces the social sciences and humanities, and some recent projects have been concerned with organisational cultures and aspects of sport development linked to public health. A former Chair of the Leisure Studies Association (2004–2009), Scott was Managing Editor of *Leisure Studies* (2010–2016) and is a member of the Editorial Board of *The Sport Psychologist*.

Katarzyna Herd is Associate Professor (Senior Lecturer) in the Department of Arts and Cultural Sciences at Lund University in Sweden. She earned a PhD about the rituals of producing history in Swedish football clubs in 2018. Since then, she has worked on several projects that deal with socio-historical developments in football, transfer patterns, Swedish-speaking clubs in Finland, and others. She is particularly interested in the political economy of sport and tensions and contradictions of Scandinavian football fandom and has published several papers in this field.

Christos Kassimeris is Professor at the European University Cyprus and the coordinator of the local MPA Public Administration programme. He is the author of *European Football in Black and White: Tackling Racism in Football* (2007), *Football Comes Home: Symbolic Identities in European Football* (2010), *Discrimination in Football* (2021), and *The Politics of Football* (2023). He is also the editor of *Anti-racism in European Football: Fair Play for All* (2009) and co-editor of *Exploring the Cultural, Ideological and Economic Legacies of Euro 2012* (2025) and *Football, Racism(s) and Digital Media* (2022, special issue). He has several publications in political science journals and has contributed book chapters to edited collections.

Radosław Kossakowski is Associate Professor of Sociology and Dean for Research and International Cooperation in the Social Sciences Department at Gdańsk University in Northern Poland. His areas of expertise and research interest are the sociology of sport and culture, in particular football and fandom, qualitative methodology and methods, and identity and masculinity studies. He has published several books on football fandom as well as papers in many international journals, such as the *International Review for the Sociology of Sport*; *Soccer & Society*; *Sport in Society*; *Sociology of Sport Journal*; *Men and Masculinities*; *Identities*; and *Media, Culture and Society*.

Ramón Llopis-Goig is Full Professor of Sociology at the University of Valencia in Spain. He has been Vice Dean of Academic Planning of the Faculty of Social Sciences at the same university and President of the Spanish Association of Social Research Applied to Sport. His sociological research interests include sport, health, and organizational issues, and he has published widely in these areas. In 2015, he published a monograph titled *Spanish Football and Social Change* that draws on his extensive research into the development of Spanish football. Currently, he is particularly interested in issues such as the cultural and structural determinants of sport participation and the influence of social change on the construction of subjectivity and mental health.

Lasse Müller has a keen academic and research interest in discrimination in sport. He earned a master's degree in the social sciences of sports at the Institute of Sport Sciences at the Goethe University in Frankfurt. Subsequently, he worked as a research assistant examining the impact of migration on German sports clubs. His PhD dissertation focused on antisemitism in amateur football. Formerly, the Deputy Project Leader of an initiative combating antisemitism in sports (*Zusammen1/MAKKABI Germany*), he now works as a research associate at the University of Wuppertal. He is also member of the Human Rights Advisory Council of the German National Olympic Sports Federation (DOSB).

Sofia Neves has a bachelor's degree in psychology (1999) and a PhD in social psychology (2005), both from the University of Minho. She is Associate Professor at the University of Maia and the Coordinator of the Branch of the Interdisciplinary Centre for Gender Studies, hosted by the Institute of Social and Political Sciences, University of Lisbon. Her research interests and areas of expertise are domestic and gender-based violence, discrimination, violence based on sexual orientation, and identity and/or gender expression. Since September 2024, she has been a member of the Technical-Scientific Group of the Advisory Council of the Commission for Citizenship and Gender Equality. Currently, she is in charge of the Portuguese team that contributes to the EU-funded research project Uni4Equity that intends to strengthen universities' responses to sexual harassment.

Alessio Norrito earned an MSc at the University of Edinburgh and a PhD at Loughborough University. He is currently Lecturer in Sociology and Management of Sport at Manchester Metropolitan University in England, where he teaches undergraduate and postgraduate students. He is an expert in the field of sport for development and peace, and he also is interested in applying philosophy and cultural sociology to the organizational and informal contexts of sport and leisure. His investigative work seeks to improve the well-being of marginalized communities and places through sport and leisure. His research has been featured in different media outlets, such as Sky Sports, The Conversation, and different Italian newspapers.

Estefânia Silva earned a PhD in social psychology at the University of Minho. She is Assistant Professor at the University of Maia, a researcher at the Interdisciplinary Centre for Gender Studies at the Institute of Social and Political Sciences of the University of Lisbon, and a specialist in gender equality recognized by the Commission for Citizenship and Gender Equality. Currently, she participates in research projects related to the study of gender-based violence, inequalities, and migration. Her research focuses mainly on gender studies, migration, gender-based violence, discrimination, work–family balance, and human rights.

Tom Taylor has a keen interest in the critical, social-scientific analysis of sport and sports mega-events as socio-cultural and political phenomena that produce both positive and negative impacts. He sees them as phenomena that help us to understand wider social issues, problems, and developments in the context of ongoing globalisation processes and changes, such as racism and Islamophobia. In 2025, he earned a PhD at the University of

Brighton that explored football fans' multi-layered experiences of Muslims and Islam in the context of the 2022 FIFA Men's World Cup in Qatar.

Joana Topa earned a bachelor's degree in psychology and a PhD in social psychology, both at the University of Minho. She is Assistant Professor at the University of Maia, a researcher at the Interdisciplinary Centre for Gender Studies hosted by the Institute of Social and Political Sciences, University of Lisbon, and at the Centre for Psychology at the University of Porto. Currently, she participates in research projects on gender-based violence, inequalities, and discrimination. Her main research interests are migration issues, gender-based violence, maternal health, diversity, and discrimination, which she examines through a feminist, decolonial, and critical lens.

Arne Van Lienden is a post-doctoral researcher at the Radboud University Nijmegen and Erasmus University Rotterdam. His research uses a critical sociological lens on sport and sports media. In his PhD research, he focused on representations of ethnicity in sports media in Poland. In addition, he was involved in a similar research project in other European countries, including the Netherlands. He has also conducted research on female football coaches from ethnic minority backgrounds. In his current position, he is involved in the Re/presenting Europe project that focuses on representations of athletes from the Caribbean part of the Dutch Kingdom.

Jacco Van Sterkenburg holds an endowed Chair/Professorship ('Race', Inclusion and Communication, specifically in relation to Football and Media) in the Department of Media and Communication at the Erasmus University Rotterdam. His research mainly focuses on football and racism, in a broad sense, including media, leadership, and professional and recreational sports/football. His research portfolio has gained recognition inside and outside academia.

Stuart Whigham is Senior Lecturer in Sport, Coaching and Physical Education in the Department of Sport, Health Sciences and Social Work at Oxford Brookes University. There, he is also a Co-Lead of the Sport, Exercise and Physical Activity Research Group. Furthermore, he is a fellow of the Higher Education Academy and Associate Editor for the renowned *Sport and Society* journal. Stuart's research interests in the sociology and politics of sport focus on national identity, nationalism and sport, the politics of the Commonwealth Games, and the sociology and politics of Scottish sport. He has published widely in these areas.

Foreword

Sport is a complex, multi-layered socio-economic, cultural, and political phenomenon. It can also be controversial and contradictory. While sport is often celebrated for its potential to offer equal opportunities, integration, and social inclusion, too often it also reflects and reinforces major divisions in society, in particular those based on class, gender, and 'race'/ethnicity.

This book takes as its focus examples of intolerance, bigotry, and hatred in European football, which is often caused by the 'race' and ethnicity of players of all genders. It is written for all those who are interested in the relationship between football, society, and culture in Europe, in particular, the discriminatory treatment of ethnic minority players, and particularly those from Black and Muslim communities. As such, this book is firmly committed to the critical, social-scientific study of racism, xenophobia, antisemitism, and Islamophobia in European football. It offers a diverse range of interesting case studies – all of them with a clear focus and dealing with the same set of issues and themes – and draws on the expertise of internationally renowned football scholars, who describe and analyse the manifestations of discriminatory attitudes in football grounds, on and off the pitch, in public narratives, in board rooms and online spaces, the various media, and public policies. In addition, the authors also critically evaluate selected strategies, campaigns, initiatives, and measures that have been developed and taken by different stakeholders to combat these problems.

This edited collection offers unique insights into ten European countries, complementing existing scholarly publications in the field. Each chapter is written in an accessible way so that no prior knowledge is required. This book will be of interest to students of sport, discrimination, and wider social issues, football fans, practitioners working in the football industry, and governmental and non-governmental organisations, which have a professional interest in addressing the widespread discriminatory behaviour explored in this book.

This edited collection accomplishes a number of important and diverse tasks, and it is a pleasure to see the benefits of bringing together experts from different countries to examine the same issue in a comparative perspective. Such an approach is essential to confront and tackle a common problem in

Europe's most popular team sport. Furthermore, this book is both a timely reminder and also issues an important challenge to those in powerful positions to confront discrimination so that football becomes a truly democratic and genuinely inclusive sport.

Elizabeth Pike
Professor of Sport, Health, and Exercise
University of Hertfordshire

Chapter 1

Introduction

Key contexts, terms and nomenclature

Udo Merkel

Over the last few decades, the European continent has undergone, and continues to experience, major socio-economic, political and cultural changes. Many of these are the result of, or at least linked to, significant demographic changes. They are the outcome of increasing levels of human mobility across national boundaries. In addition to the free movement of people within the European Union (EU), which currently hosts 27 member states with several more waiting to join, there are a large number of migrants arriving from former colonial territories. There are also millions of asylum seekers and refugees who fled violence in war zones or tried to escape poverty in their home countries. Consequently, in the first quarter of the second millennium, Europe has become a culturally and ethnically more diverse continent than ever before. That is clearly reflected in, and frequently spearheaded by, the world of sport. Football, in particular, has become one of the most ethnically diverse segments of European society and culture. That applies to the whole and complex continuum of this sport, ranging from the grassroots and recreational level to the professional game, and involves girls and boys, women and men, players, referees, fans, the media and sponsors. And yet, various forms of discrimination such as racism, xenophobia, antisemitism and Islamophobia continue to constitute serious issues in the world of recreational, amateur and professional football, as the following four examples illustrate:

In July 2021, Italy and England met in the final of UEFA's Euro 2020. The English team was defeated in a penalty shootout and Italy claimed the European crown at Wembley Stadium in London. The backlash of the loss was heavily felt by three of the team's Black players, Marcus Rashford, Jordan Sancho and Bukayo Saka. They missed their penalties and, subsequently, received a flood of, primarily online, vicious racist comments, slurs and abuse and became the scapegoats of the English team.

In 2023, in Spain, the image of an effigy with a rope tied around the neck of Real Madrid's Vinícius (José Paixão de Oliveira) Júnior hanging from a motorway bridge in Spain's capital became one of the most repulsive manifestations

DOI: 10.4324/9781003495970-1

This chapter has been made available under a CC-BY-NC-SA 4.0 license.

of racism in Spanish football. This incident marked the abhorrent climax of racist taunts since Vinícius arrived in Spain in 2018 from Brazil. Two weeks before, the 22-year-old was reduced to tears during a match after confronting a fan who had called him a monkey and made monkey gestures towards him.

In March 2024, various newspapers reported the display of fascist salutes and chanting of "Duce", hailing Benito Mussolini, the founder of the National Fascist Party (PNF) in Italy and the country's dictatorial Prime Minister from 1922 to 1943, that a group of Lazio Rome fans performed in a Munich beer hall before the Champions League match against Bayern Munich. Five years prior, a similar scene had been witnessed in Glasgow's city centre before Lazio's Europa League match against Celtic.

The increasing visibility of Muslims in professional football, such as Nicolas Anelka, Karim Benzema, Ousmane Dembélé, Ilkay Gündoğan, N'Golo Kante, Riyad Mahrez, Sadio Mane, Paul Pogba, Mesut Özil, Franck Ribéry, Antonio Rüdiger and Mohamed Salah, constitutes another tier of the diversity of this sport. However, their presence has also added another layer to the complexity of discriminatory practices. General comments and chants such as "Pakis shouldn't be allowed to play football" and "Burn the Quran" or referring to individuals as "Taliban", "terrorist" or "bomber" can nowadays be heard in various football environments. Mesut Özil ended his international career in 2018 when he quit Germany's national team stating that he had faced racism and a lack of respect for his Turkish ancestry. More recently, in March 2024, at the beginning of Ramadan, which requires Muslims to fast for one month, Antonio Rüdiger posted a photo on Instagram that showed him kneeling on a prayer mat in a white robe with his right index finger pointing upward. Subsequently, the former editor of a German tabloid paper accused Rüdiger to support the terrorist organisation Islamic State (IS) due to his raised finger as he considered the gesture to be a symbol of Islamist radicalisation.

It is these various forms and manifestations of discrimination that constitute the first thematic focus of this book and its individual chapters that offer detailed country case studies. All contributors have been asked to address the following two sets of questions:

(I) What are the manifestations of racism, xenophobia, antisemitism and Islamophobia in the world of football? Who are the perpetrators? Who are the targets and victims? How can we explain these phenomena?
(II) What is done to tackle racism, xenophobia, antisemitism and Islamophobia? Who is involved in fighting these issues? What do different stakeholders do? What are their key strategies and measures? How successful are they?

The second thematic focus is naturally and closely linked to the first theme. It is, of course, about the fundamental question what has been done to solve the aforementioned problems that affect the world of football at various levels and in different disguises? In other words: How did and do the various stakeholders in the world of football such as players, fans, clubs, officials, governing bodies as well as local, regional and national state authorities react and respond? What has been, and is currently, done to tackle these problems? Have their policies, strategies, methods, schemes, initiatives and measures been successful (or not)?

In addition to the ten country case studies (England, France, Germany, Italy, the Netherlands, Poland, Portugal, Scotland, Spain and Sweden), the last two chapters will take a broader, bird's eye perspective. Chapter 13 will examine how supra-national European organisations respond to the various forms of discrimination and evaluate their contributions to the elimination of these problems in football. The final chapter will then offer some critical, cross-cultural, comparative observations. It will contrast the findings of the individual country case studies in order to identify, explain and evaluate commonalities and differences. This book offers a distinctive European perspective and as such complements and, on some occasions, updates the valuable contributions previously made by, for example, Awan and Zempi (2023), Bradbury, Lusted and Sterkenburg (2020), Brunssen and Schüler-Springorum (2021), Burdsey (2021), Cashmore and Cleland (2014), Carrington and McDonald (2001), Crabbe, Solomos and Back (2001), Doidge, Kossakowski and Mintert (2022), Garland and Rowe (2001), Harris (2021), Hassan (2013), Kassimeris (2007, 2009, 2021), Kearns, Sinclair, Black et al. (2022), Kilvington and Price (2018), Llopis-Goig (2015), Rowe (2004) and Sterkenburg, Peeters and Amsterdam (2019). Due to the limited scope of this book, vertical comparisons have to be ignored, although some chapters offer a developmental account. However, the more seasoned readers may recall a book that my colleague, Walter Tokarski, and I put together and published almost three decades ago (Merkel and Tokarski, 1996) that had a similar European approach, structure and rationale. As this book is now almost 30 years old, it may be a useful point of reference to identify and analyse some interesting historical developments.

Although this book is not concerned with the respective legal frameworks that regulate these different forms of discriminatory practices and how criminal law authorities deal with these issues, it is noteworthy that discriminatory practices based on, or linked to, racism, xenophobia, antisemitism and Islamophobia constitute hate crimes in Europe. Although Anastassia Tsoukala's book (2009) focuses on the way national and supranational lawmakers and enforcers have defined football hooliganism, there is also a wealth of information on the legal aspects of the issues this book addresses.

Nomenclature, orthography and the use of language

In order to avoid repetition throughout this book, some of the key terms, which will be frequently used in the subsequent chapters, will now be considered. The subsequent chapter will expand on these introductory comments and clarifications. It is dedicated to a more detailed discussion of key concepts and theories that frame, underpin and inform the sociological analysis that this publication offers.

Sociologically, this book is primarily concerned with analysing and critically evaluating the causes and consequences of the socially constructed divisions of social groups according to their so-called 'race' as well as other characteristics. Through the use of inverted commas, we wish to indicate that this categorisation of individuals and groups is not based on any biologically valid distinctions between the genetic composition of different 'races'. The process of racially categorising people tends to draw on phenotypical differences such as skin colour, facial characteristics or hair type. However, these do not necessarily correlate to differences in their genetic makeup. For the same reason, it makes sense to avoid the term "Caucasian". Both terms originate from 18th-century European (pseudo-) *science* of 'racial' classification that suggested that there are innate differences of character traits, intelligence, personality and other individual propensities.

Having said this, we do not wish to question or downplay the degree to which individuals form distinct ethnic groups through explicitly acknowledging their historical, geographical, national and/or cultural roots, share a sense of identity, engage in similar cultural and/or religious practices and/or life styles, which differentiate them from other social and/or ethnic groups in society. Both concepts, 'race' and ethnicity, are obviously central to this book as they form the basis for, and frequently trigger dislike, prejudice, bias, intolerance, discrimination, opposition and even hatred that the subsequent chapters will be examining. Therefore, the term 'race' is purely used as an analytical tool, despite the lack of any genetic validity.

The capitalisation of the "B" in Black in this book stresses that this adjective does not only refer to a colour but implies a distinct history and ethnic identity of the people it tries to (linguistically) capture. Depending on the context, white may or may not be capitalised. Although derogatory, disrespectful, discriminatory and offensive, "White trash" is a useful example. It is one of those terms that require capitalisation of the "W" since it refers to a very distinct group of (impoverished and uneducated) US citizens (primarily, but not exclusively, in the country's southern states). Capitalising White does not only acknowledge that White people also constitute a distinctive ethnic group; in some cases, it also indirectly touches on the role and functions of Whiteness in social and political institutions and communities.

The terms "people of colour" and "non-white" are also used in this book. "People of colour" has its roots in political circles and social justice environments but has slowly become mainstream and spread to academia. It is, however, not an unproblematic label. It was initially used in the United States and Canada to describe any person who is not white, did/does not exclusively refer to African-Americans but encompasses all non-white groups and emphasises the common experiences of systemic racism. In contrast, "people of colour" at least describes people with their own attributes as opposed to what they are not, for example, "non-white".

The unhyphenated spelling of antisemitism in this book intends to dispel the idea that there is an entity "Semitism" which "anti-Semitism" opposes. Antisemitism needs to be understood as a unified term which refers to, and succinctly summarises, modern Jew-hatred.

Xenophobia and Islamophobia contain the term "phobia", which generally refers to an inexplicable and irrational fear, extreme dislike and/or aversion to something. In medical terms, it is an individual and usually rather specific anxiety disorder. Therefore, its use in this book is not unproblematic either. When we use these terms, it does not mean that the problems they refer to are medical conditions of individuals that require cure. Quite the opposite, we are, of course, much more concerned with, and interested in, the underlying socio-economic, cultural and political conditions that cause the collective dislike, discrimination and hatred of foreigners and Muslims (and those perceived as such).

Racism

For the purpose of this book, the term "racism" refers to the belief that members of different 'races' possess distinctively different characteristics, abilities and qualities that are specific and unique to that 'race', especially so as to distinguish it as inferior or superior to another 'race'. Prejudice, discrimination and/or antagonism directed against someone of a different 'race' are usually rooted in the belief that one's own 'race' is superior. While originally this sense of superiority was based on the assumption of fundamental biological differences, there has been a significant shift to cultural differences that are, apparently, most obvious in the realm of people's norms, values, beliefs, behaviour, cultural traditions and practices. Any analysis of this phenomenon therefore needs to take into consideration the socio-economic conditions and cultural configurations as these are the realms in which 'racial' and ethnic identities are constructed. Cultural racism (Alcoff, 2023) is closely linked to the concept of ethnocentrism which involves using one's own culture as a yardstick when judging other cultures and usually leads to the belief that one's own culture is superior to other people's way of life.

However, in the world of sport racist attitudes do not necessarily imply or express a sense of White superiority. There has been a popular but highly questionable myth that Black athletes are actually superior to White athletes due to their genetically determined physique. The most infamous book written about this myth is certainly Jon Entine's publication *Taboo: Why Black Athletes Dominate Sports and Why We're Afraid to Talk About It* (2000). Over 300 pages long, this book tries to show – rather unconvincingly – that Black people possess innate physical advantages and where these come from.

While Entine's arguments are generally discarded, there are still plenty of obvious traces of this kind of thinking around, particularly in the world of sports commentators (Campbell and Bebb, 2022). They often tend to emphasise Black athletes' *natural* athleticism such as strength, speed and endurance rather than their strategic or tactical thinking, hard work, decision-making and leadership skills. Scott Fleming will discuss this in greater detail in the following chapter. Needless to say, there is plenty of evidence that the idea that Black people are naturally better equipped for top-level achievements in sport is rather distorted, misleading and an inaccurate reflection of reality. It is just one of the many racist stereotypes alongside many others such as their pronounced aggressiveness, simple-mindedness, natural sense of rhythm and proneness to crime, to name just a few, that continue to linger around in the public imagination and frequently come to the forefront in the context of racist slurs, insults and attacks.

The aforementioned succinct definition of racism constitutes a useful starting point but requires further differentiation as it does not capture the complexity of the phenomenon and the wide variety of its manifestations. Racism expresses itself in various forms and operates at different levels. In the world of sport, for example, it includes intolerance, discrimination, harassment, vilification and/or hatred by athletes directed at their opponents; by spectators directed at players; or racist behaviour among rival fan groups. It also includes the actions of sporting officials, administrators and coaches, as well as the aforementioned journalists and media commentators.

Xenophobia

There is a fine line between xenophobia and racism. In comparison to the latter, xenophobia is a very distinct phenomenon. It is also multi-layered, has a long history and frequently overlaps with each other. Xenophobia is best understood as the immense dislike, fear or hatred of foreigners. The term denotes behaviour and cultural practices that people perceive to be the result of somebody being from a different country, society and/or culture and thus an outsider and not a member of the native community or one's nation. In fact, manifestations of xenophobia frequently occur against people of identical physical characteristics, sometimes even of shared ancestry, when such people arrive, return or migrate to countries where occupants consider them to be outsiders. Both concepts, racism and xenophobia, share a key defining characteristic, the hostile attitude towards the other in a given large-scale group or population.

While xenophobia and racism do converge in some areas, xenophobia is not necessarily motivated by other people's physical features or membership in a specific ethnic group. Xenophobia tends to divide people into two groups, insiders and outsiders. The latter are presumed to constitute a threat to the insiders, in many cases the existing inhabitants of a country, and the sheer existence of large groups of outsiders often sparks insecurities and fears.

Although xenophobia is not by any means a new phenomenon, the rapid globalisation over the last decades has meant that national boundaries have become more porous and permeable. This, in turn, has led to increased migration, particularly to rich and developed countries, by people in search of a better life. The large-scale arrival of immigrants has caused an increased sense of fear and anxiety by the native residents to lose their way of life, social status, identity, jobs and ultimately their economic security. Today's xenophobia in Europe primarily targets migrants and asylum seekers. The latter's influx, particularly since 2015, has constituted a serious challenge for the countries of the European Union.

Although there have been some notable demographic shifts in various European countries, the often-exaggerated fear of far-reaching socio-economic and cultural changes combined with disinformation and negative stereotyping that frequently dehumanise and criminalise immigrants and asylum seekers and their portrayal as inherently threatening has considerably fuelled xenophobia. That is clearly reflected in the growing popularity of several far-right political parties that draw on, exploit and leverage social anxieties. In recent years, even mainstream and traditionally more moderate political forces have embraced this dangerous rhetoric.

Antisemitism

Historically, antisemitism is most frequently associated with the Holocaust of Nazi Germany (1933–1945), when approximately six million European Jews were systematically murdered in Hitler's concentration camps. Jews refer to it as "Shoah", which means "catastrophe" in Hebrew. The Holocaust did not happen surprisingly and unexpectedly. Hitler did not make a secret of his hatred of Jews in *Mein Kampf*, which was first published in 1925. However, the termination of the Jewish people in Germany as part of his political project developed much later. Initially, the Nazis planned to remove all Jews from Germany and pressurised them to emigrate through systematic discrimination, exclusion, withdrawal of citizenship rights, theft and violence. Deportation to other countries in Eastern Europe was also considered. One plan proposed to relocate them to the island of Madagascar, located off the south-eastern coast of Africa. Ultimately, the Nazis opted for the systematic genocide of the Jewish population in Germany. Against this context, chants in football stadia referring to the gas chambers in the concentration camps and Nazi salutes as well as symbols such as the swastika on banners are particularly distasteful.

However, antisemitism did not commence or finish with the Holocaust. The hatred of Jews, which the term antisemitism describes, has a long history in Europe as Jews have been discriminated against and persecuted for several hundreds of years. In medieval times, they were often forced to live outside the local communities in separate areas or ghettos, were systematically excluded from guilds and some professions, and often barred from holding posts in governmental organisations and the military. In the context of economic upheaval and unrest, Jews were regularly identified as the scapegoats.

As a consequence of the racially inspired ideologies in the 19th century, Jews were also considered to be members of a distinct 'race' with innate characteristics, attributes and traits, frequently excluded from the nation of a state and often regarded as inferior. The pseudo-scientific ideas about the existence of distinct 'races' made antisemitism more respectable and popular. Since then, antisemitism needs to be understood as discrimination of, and hostility towards, Jewish people as both a religious and 'racial' group.

Although antisemitism has historically been most prominent in Europe, over the last century there has been a steep increase in anti-Jewish sentiment in the Arab world. This is largely due to a considerable growth of anti-Semitic conspiracy theories that often claim that Israel is waging a war against Islam. In Europe, the far-right spreads and promotes antisemitism by disseminating conspiracies that directly name Jews either as a dangerous threat or more subtly through historical comparisons and analogies. These narratives frequently describe Jews as affluent, powerful and influential, and therefore able to manipulate and control governments, the financial sector and the media to the detriment of humanity.

Manifestations of antisemitism may include the targeting of the state of Israel, that is frequently conceived as a representation of a Jewish collectivity. However, criticism of Israel due to its political or military actions similar to that directed at other nation-states should not necessarily be regarded as antisemitic.

Islamophobia

Islamophobia is literally translated as the fear of Islam, has its roots in, and is a form of, racism that aims at Muslims, expressions of Muslimness or perceived Muslimness. In essence, Islamophobia is anti-Muslim racism. This dislike, prejudice, discrimination and hatred towards Muslims tend to be caused by the perception that Islam does not share any norms and values with other cultures, is inferior to the West and constitutes a violent political ideology rather than a religion. The Runnymede Trust Institute offers a helpful definition of Islamophobia and describes it

> any distinction, exclusion, or restriction towards, or preference against, Muslims (or those perceived to be Muslims) that has the purpose or effect of nullifying or impairing the recognition, enjoyment or exercise, on an equal footing, of human rights and fundamental freedoms in the political, economic, social, cultural or any other field of public life.
>
> (2017, p. 7)

Islamophobia has existed for centuries but came into more prominent usage after the attacks on the Twin Towers in New York in September 2001. Although Muslims are a rather heterogeneous religious group rather than a 'race', many scholars argue that Muslims have been racialised into one entity. They are identified and labelled through a 'racial' differentiation process that draws on cultural characteristics, such as their dress code or culinary conventions. As such, racialisation is a process in which racist assumptions of ethnic and 'racial' groups, in this case Arabs, are placed onto groups such as Muslim communities (Garner and Selod, 2015, pp. 9–19). Islamophobia tends to have a greater impact on visibly identifiable Muslims such as women wearing head coverings or *hijabs*.

The Islamophobia of politicians of the far-right is fairly obvious despite their attempts to hide it behind smokescreens. In December 2023, Anna Maria Cisint, the mayor of Monfalcone, a small town in Northern Italy not far from the Slovenian border, decided to ban Muslim worship at the town's Islamic cultural centres and the wearing of burkinis at the local beaches. Cisint, from the far-right League Party in Italy, argued that the use of burkinis was unacceptable and raised serious concerns about health, hygiene and modesty. Her justification for banning Muslim prayers in the town's cultural centres referred to urban planning regulations, in particular the designated use of the centres, as well as health and safety concerns due to the attendance of large groups of people (Kazmin, 2024).

The presence of Muslims in Europe and Islamophobia are not new phenomena. Both have been around for a long time. In Spain, for example, Muslims have been present since the beginning of the eighth century. The Emirate of Granada, in the south of Spain, used to be a vibrant place of Islamic culture and civilisation and lasted until the end of the 15th century. It was not until after the Second World War that large numbers of Muslims returned to Europe. They were needed due to severe labour shortages in many countries and were usually recruited from ex-colonies or countries that historically had political ties. During the 1950s and 1960s, hundreds of thousands of North Africans went to France; Pakistanis and Indians emigrated to the United Kingdom. The Netherlands attracted people from Indonesia and Surinam; Kurdish and Turkish labour migrants came to Germany.

Not all of these migrants were Muslims, but most of them were. More importantly, the vast majority did not necessarily plan to settle permanently in Europe. In Germany, they were referred to as *Gastarbeiter* (guest workers). They intended to support their families back home and accumulate sufficient funds to eventually start a business in their native country. Until the early 1970s, neither migration nor Muslims were perceived as problematic. Quite the opposite, these migrants were seen as vital contributors to the economic reconstruction, development and boom of many European countries. Furthermore, as these migrants did not intend to stay, they did not have any specific demands related to their religious preferences.

All of that changed with the economic crises of the 1970s. In several European countries, laws restricting further immigration were enacted. At the same time, family reunification was made possible and many immigrants managed to reunite with their families. That led to a considerable increase and feminisation of the migrant population. The birth of children also marked the inauguration of a second generation of migrants. These changes impacted in several ways on the daily life of the migrants. There was now a need to provide places for religious worship. They became more visible in public spaces and congregated in ethnically fairly homogenous residential areas where they could draw on familiar social networks and find support structures of like-minded people.

Subsequently, during the 1980s, these developments, in particular the emergence of mosques, the visibility of *hijabs* in everyday life, and the mushrooming of foreign shops and restaurants started to become issues of public concern and causes for anxiety. It is against this context that the first far-right political parties emerged who denounced migration as a threat to the host community, its traditions, customs, values, norms and identity.

These fears continued to exist and have turned into a substantial sentiment that Europe is currently invaded by a growing number of Muslims who do not wish to integrate but take over Europe. Ten years ago, the various PEGIDA (Patriotic Europeans Against the Islamisation of the West) demonstrations in Germany had the motto "Against the Islamisation of Europe". Since then, the public discourse about Muslims also claims that they are culturally so different that it is impossible to integrate them. They are perceived to be not only unwilling but also unable to adjust to European norms, values, principles and secular ways of living. In a nutshell, Islam is incompatible with Western ideas and culture, and the belief system of Muslims makes it impossible to integrate them. Therefore, Islam is the main problem.

Intersectionality

Despite the relatively straightforward analytical differentiation between different forms of discrimination, the reality is as always more complex, often blurred and frequently multi-layered and overlapping. The latter is referred to as intersectionality. The term was originally coined by Kimberlé Crenshaw in the early 1990s to come to terms with the multi-dimensionality of Black women identities and the corresponding systems of prejudices, discrimination and disadvantage (Crenshaw, 1991). It looks at the way that, for example, racism (or any other form of discrimination) interacts, and is sometimes combined, with xenophobia, antisemitism, sexism, classism, Islamophobia and other discriminatory practices.

Shortly before the 2024 Summer Olympics in Paris, a vicious discussion about who would be appropriate (or not) to headline the Olympic opening ceremony emerged. It was triggered by the rumour that Aya Nakamura, one of the best-known and most popular French singers in the world, will feature prominently in the opening ceremony. Nakamura is France's biggest popstar and is well known for her unique French music style shaped by Afro beats and Caribbean rhythms. The public debate, initiated by right-wing politicians and TV commentators, revealed deeply ingrained racist attitudes combined with class prejudice. It focused on the question whether Nakamura was genuinely and truly French. After all, she is Black, was born in Mali, grew up on a poor housing estate in the northern suburbs, *banlieue*, of Paris and the lyrics of her songs often integrate the slang and colloquialisms of young people.

However, there is a third layer to the resistance and lack of respect for Nakamura frequently in France. Nakamura is rather unique because she is a Black *female* artist, comes across as very authentic and appears not to have modified or adjusted herself to meet and please White bourgeois expectations in France. Her public persona is unapologetic, full of confidence, pride and self-assurance. That, of course, constitutes a serious challenge, perhaps even provocation, for a country that usually expects gratitude from minorities and modesty from women.

But that debate also revealed a high level of misogynoir in France. This term, initially put forward by Moya Bailey in 2010, acknowledges the frequent and very specific connection between gender and 'race' in the context of prejudice, discrimination and hatred. It is best understood as anti-Black misogyny as it describes black women being the targets of both racism and misogyny (Bailey, 2021).

The European context: Fortress Europe, migration and the changing political landscapes

All the aforementioned forms of discrimination are an ugly element of European society, culture and everyday life in the 21st century. Although in the last seven decades, internal barriers to the free movement of people, capital and goods have all but disappeared in the EU, external barriers continue to exist. While the influx of capital and goods from outside the EU has also become relatively easy, the obstacles for the migration of people from outside the EU remain rather high and are in many cases insurmountable. Those who reach the European shores and, eventually, countries of their destination frequently face racism, xenophobia and Islamophobia. Particularly vulnerable to, and often the targets of, hostilities, discrimination and abuse are irregular or unauthorised migrants.

Most of the aforementioned forms of bias and intolerance are clearly reflected in various public and political discourses about migration such as the treatment of irregular migrants, asylum seekers, political refugees and minority groups, the concept of socio-cultural integration and allocation of citizenship rights to migrants. These issues also constitute the core of the political programmes of various far-right political groups, movements and parties that promote racist, xenophobic, antisemitic and anti-Muslim views. They systematically exploit the widespread anxieties and insecurities to gain political capital and advance their anti-immigrant, nationalist, anti-democratic and often reactionary agendas. Framing migration as an invasion has become a standard practice and pointing to it as the single source of all the European continent's problems has made migration a toxic subject. Of course, these discourses offer a distorted sense of reality that, indeed, without migrants the European economy would seriously struggle and the continent's cultural life would miss out on diversity and variety. The negative narratives about, and frequent demonisation of, migrants usually involve portraying them as a hostile and dangerous army that requires turning Europe into a fortress. Economic insecurity in times of scarce resources is certainly one reason for the widespread anti-migrant backlash, but one should not underestimate the significance of old plain racist and xenophobic attitudes.

This is even more surprising when considering that not too long ago millions of Europeans left their native countries to escape various forms of hardship, in particular poverty, in search of a new and better life. Several hundred thousand Irish people left their home for America in the 19th century. So did many Scandinavians and Italians, with the latter heading to Argentina, where 85% of the total population are estimated to be of European descent. Approximately one million Italians and 250,000 Germans settled in Brazil. Three-quarters of the Australian population has European origins, the vast majority coming from the British Isles. Although Europe's socio-historical development is also a history of migration, treating it as a major problem and threat to prosperity and national cultures these days, is hypocritical, dishonest and dangerous as the rapidly changing political landscapes in various countries clearly indicate.

At the end of 2023, the French government under Emmanuel Macron finalised the draft of a new immigration law that is so repressive that even the far-right's leader, Marine Le Pen, welcomed it. She and her fellow 87 members of parliament from the *Rassemblement National* (National Rally, RN), formerly known as the *Front National*, even voted for it. They claimed that the essence of the new law was mirroring fundamental principles of their demands for "national preference" and putting "the French first". That may be partly true, but the reality and details of the new immigration bill went nowhere near the kind of discriminatory, anti-migrant policies Le Pen and her supporters wish to implement. Their proposals include, for example, reserving employment opportunities for French citizens and the introduction of fees for foreign children attending state schools. The French left, however, was outraged and described the immigration bill as oppressive and the most racist legislation the country had seen for a long time. What this randomly chosen example clearly shows is the tendency of conservative political forces to veer further to the right in order to take the wind out of the sails of the far-right's popular anti-immigration propaganda. However, that strategy appears to be backfiring as it actually legitimises the hard-line approach of the far-right.

Marine Le Pen's ideological counterpart in Italy is Giorgia Meloni, who became the country's prime minister in October 2022 after promising strict measures to contain and reduce the influx of migrants from across the Mediterranean. She does not hide her admiration for Benito Mussolini, Italy's fascist dictator from 1925 to 1945. Meloni tends to present herself as an honest, patriotic girl-next-door type, who is not part of the political cast, and the friendly but tough-speaking face of Italy's far-right. She makes no secret of her dislike of migrants and is well-known for her tough rhetoric on immigration, abortion access, LGBTQ rights, Euro-scepticism and admiration of Margaret Thatcher. She seems to share the latter with the previous British Prime Minister, Rishi Sunak. Both politicians also believe and argue that without any firm action, Europe may be overwhelmed and destabilised by immigration. They are also very keen to stop migrant boats arriving on their country's respective shores and pursue policies that have sparked widespread criticism such as Meloni's attempts to restrict the activities of rescue ships in the Mediterranean and send men intercepted in international water to centres in Albania while their asylum applications are being processed. Sunak's deportation bill, which became law in April 2023, legalised the deportation of asylum seekers, who had arrived in the UK illegally, to Rwanda.

In the UK, "Stop the Boats" is one of the most casual messages trivialising the desperation of people trying to escape persecution or seeking work. But it is also a message that has hijacked the public discourse, although the number of unauthorised arrivals (approximately 30,000 in 2023) constitutes a rather small minority in the bigger picture of migratory flows. And yet, politicians in the UK have embraced the slogan in order to express their outrage and often integrate it into their alarmist anti-immigration rhetoric.

Although the number of irregular migrants and refugees landing on the Spanish coast (approximately 45,000 in 2023) is considerably higher, immigration has not become a central issue in Spain's political debates and does not appear to be a major public concern. This is partly due to the Spanish government's more realistic and calmer assessment of the overall situation. In his speech to the Spanish parliament, in October 2024, Spanish Prime Minister, Pedro Sánchez, defended migration for economic and humanitarian reasons. His stance largely reflects that of many other European governments, who also oppose, for example, the plans of the previous UK government and Italy to deport asylum seekers to centres in third countries such as Rwanda and Albania, respectively. In Spain, only VOX, an extremely right-wing, political party, declared migration to be a serious problem and threat to national integrity and the party's manifesto contains some highly controversial measures to curb irregular immigration. There is little doubt that VOX's anti-immigration stance appears to be deeply rooted in Islamophobia. In October 2023, VOX's leader, Santiago Abascal, defended immigration from Latin America while reiterating his hard-line resistance to the migration of people from Muslim countries.

VOX's German counterpart, the *Alternative für Deutschland* (Alternative for Germany, AfD), is considerably more radical and openly racist, xenophobic and anti-Muslim. Its vicious political positions even fuelled a debate whether the party should be banned. At the beginning of 2024, hundreds of thousands of Germans in several cities demonstrated against right-wing extremism, in general, and the AfD, in particular, after some of their senior officials had taken part in a secret meeting with other far-right extremists at the end of 2023. It was investigative journalists form the news outlet CORRECTIV who revealed that the discussions at this meeting had focused on a sinister "remigration masterplan" that proposes to forcefully deport migrants, asylum seekers and "non-assimilated" Germans to their countries of origin. It would also affect German citizens with a migratory background who, apparently, live in aggressive parallel societies. There was also mention of deportations to an unnamed North African country that would accommodate up to two million people. Germans fighting for the rights of refugees would also be sent there (Bensmann, von Daniels, Dowideit et al., 2024). This draft scheme was presented by Martin Sellner, the founder and leader of Austria's Identitarian Movement. They favour the "great replacement theory" that claims there is a conspiracy by non-white migrants to replace Europe's "native" population who they consider to be the superior ethnic group.

Among the participants at the talks outside Potsdam were also CDU (Christian Democratic Union) members who belong to an extremely conservative branch of the party, that is one of the major political forces in Germany. The presence of AfD representatives did not come as a surprise. The party was established in 2013 and became initially known for its Euroscepticism. However, its focus quickly shifted to immigration and Islam, which the party claims are irreconcilable with German society and culture. The AfD's rhetoric has overt racist undertones and frequently uses terms and phrases that originated in the country's Nazi past. Some years ago, Alexander Gauland, a prominent figure of the AfD, claimed that Germans generally like Jérôme Boateng, a well-known German footballer who was born in Berlin to a Ghanaian father but would not want to have him as a neighbour. The AfD frequently manages to attract considerable numbers of voters and has become a powerful and influential political force in Germany. Its election strategies and campaigns are openly Islamophobic, tapping into anxieties over the perceived Islamisation of the West, in general, and the large number of Muslims and the influence of Islam in Germany, in particular.

The AfD shares its fundamental right-wing political views with the *Rassemblement National* in France, the FPÖ (Freedom Party) in Austria, the anti-Islam Freedom Party (PVV) of Geert Wilders in the Netherlands, which is in favour of banning the Koran and mosques, the *Fratelli d'Italia* (Brothers of Italy), Poland's Law and Justice Party (PiS), the Sweden Democrats (SD) and the Norwegian Progress Party (FrP), to name just a few. They are not identical but comparable as they show a large number of ideological parallels and offer the electorate hard-line views on societal, in particular demographic, and cultural issues. They promote explicit anti-Islam discourses, anti-immigrant agendas and propose strict immigration policies. They claim that immigration has been disadvantageous for their respective countries, the coexistence of different cultures does not work, Islam is a threat, and the EU does more harm than good and undermines the sovereignty of the nation-states in Europe. They do not explicitly view the nation as an ethnically homogenous community, based on shared blood and ancestry, but draw on civic nationalist discourses (Halikiopoulou, Mock and Vasilopoulou, 2013, pp. 107–127), which partly explains why many voters consider them to be respectable political parties. Needless to say, these far-right organisations favour the interests of the "native" population over the needs of outsiders, particularly in areas such as work and social welfare. That, in turn, is the bases for and justifies all their socio-economic and cultural policy positions. The sheer presence and, even more so, the growing popularity of the far-right in several European countries emboldens racist and xenophobic football fans, justifies their discriminatory attitudes, legitimises their grievances and normalises their attitudes as they share very conservative, anti-democratic, nation-first and anti-immigration positions.

The aforementioned shift to the political right of established and traditionally more moderate parties in various European countries can also be observed at the supra-national level. In April 2024, the European Parliament voted on a large package of new rules, policies and measures that are intended to reform the EU's existing immigration and asylum laws. It particularly affects the processing of irregular arrivals of asylum seekers and migrants. Although this new system had been in the making for eight years, even after its approval it continued to be contested as it contains a large number of highly controversial measures. While the far-right argued that the new laws were not going far enough and would increase migration, many non-governmental organisations criticised the new scheme for its disregard of human rights and the likelihood that it would cause more human suffering.

> Ahead of European elections in June [2024], in which rightwing populist parties are predicted to make significant gains, the pact's centrist supporters have hailed the legislative package as a victory for the traditional EU values of compromise and moderation. Yet with a heavy focus on security screening and the removal of migrants deemed undeserving, the pact highlights how far Europe's centre has already shifted to the right on migration – and risks further empowering the radical right it aims to neutralise.
> (Trilling, 2024, p. 20)

In June 2024, the aforementioned prediction became true as Europe's far-right, particularly those parties in core member states of the EU, made significant electoral gains. For many observers, this success was the logical culmination of a trend that started two decades ago. The combined vote for these parties across the EU means that in terms of the allocated seats they are more or less on par with the largest group in the European parliament, the EPP (European People's Party) block. There is a strong likelihood that the far-right will manoeuvre the EU further to the right from inside. This will involve much stricter immigration policies, a weakening of those measures fighting climate change and, of course, clawing back national control from the EU. After all, what all these different far-right parties share is their core belief in the priority of nationalist interests.

The following chapters focusing on racism, xenophobia, antisemitism and Islamophobia in football in different European countries need to be located in this tense socio-political climate, in which this sport is embedded. However, it needs to be stressed that the world of football is neither a passive reflection nor a small-scale mirror image of the aforementioned developments. The intense and often hostile debates about migration, the changing demographic compositions of many European societies and the dramatic rise of far-right ideas and organisations have a very dynamic, interactive relationship with the world of European football. That happens on several platforms: First, sport, in general, and football due its simplicity and global appeal, in particular, are widely considered to be useful integration tools that offer a wide array of opportunities for informal learning, personal development, mixing with other people, helping to bridge social divisions, identity-formation processes, development of healthy lifestyles, promoting inclusivity and so on. Second, after the French president, Emmanuel Macron called for a snap parliamentary election in June 2024, Ousmane Dembélé, Jules Koundé, Kylian Mbappé and Marcus Thuram spoke out about their fears caused by the rise of the *Rassemblement National* and urged voters to prevent Marine Le Pen's party to gain a majority in the French parliament. Whether their intervention had any impact on the French parliamentary elections remains to be seen. However, the results of the second round were a severe blow to Marine Le Pen and her party as they came in third, although they had been predicted to win most seats. Third, Merih Demiral, the highly versatile Turkish centre-back, celebrated his second goal against Austria during UEFA's EURO 2024 with a display of a symbol that is associated with the far-right Grey Wolves, a violent ultra-nationalist organisation in Turkey. Fourth, in Hungary, ethnic homogeneity is top of the political agenda of the country's prime minister, Viktor Orban, who is an outspoken opponent of multi-culturalism, ethnic and religious heterogeneity and immigration. Despite Orban's dogmatic commitment to ethnic-nationalist ideas, when it comes to sport and, in particular, to success in international sports competitions, foreign athletes are welcome with open arms and given Hungarian citizenship fairly swiftly. The team sent to the EURO 2024 in Germany was headed by an Italian manager, Marco Rossi, who was responsible for several players who were born abroad and did not even speak Hungarian. Several others had been through development programmes and spent most of their careers in Austria, England and Germany. Recruiting players with any kind of Hungarian roots and naturalising the outstanding performers of Hungary's top flight of the football league system, appear to be key elements of the country's football policy. That, of course, is rather contradictory to Viktor Orban's far-right anti-migration and nationalist rhetoric. Fifth, the Middle East conflict fuelled antisemitic and Islamophobic abuse and attacks in the Netherland's capital at the beginning of November 2024, when fans of Ajax Amsterdam clashed with supporters of Israel's Maccabi Tel Aviv in the context of a Europa League match. While Maccabi fans chanted anti-Arab slogans, demonstrators defied a ban of their pro-Palestine demonstration outside the Johan Cruyff Arena.

The following chapters offer, of course, more detailed accounts of these kinds of incidents and broader issues related to racism, xenophobia, antisemitism and Islamophobia in their respective national football environments. What all these countries have in common is the popularity of this sport. Indeed, in many European countries, football is the national sport, and this continent hosts more clubs than any other part of the world. And yet, there is a fundamental paradox at the heart of this game. On the one hand, football is ethnically one of the most diverse segments of European culture and able to unite people with very different socio-economic, ethnic, cultural and national backgrounds. On the other hand, racism, xenophobia, antisemitism and Islamophobia continue to constitute serious issues in the world of recreational, amateur and professional football.

References

Alcoff, L.M. (2023) "The persistent power of cultural racism", *Philosophy*, 98(3), pp. 249–271.
Awan, I. and Zempi, I. (Eds.) (2023) *Hate crime in football: how Racism is destroying the beautiful game*, Bristol: Bristol University Press.
Bailey, M. (2021) *Misogynoir transformed: black women's digital resistance*, New York: NYU Press.
Bensmann, M., von Daniels, J., Dowideit, A., Peters, J. and Keller, G. (2024) "Secret plan against Germany", *Correctiv*, 15th January. Available: <https://correctiv.org/en/latest-stories/2024/01/15/secret-plan-against-germany/ [accessed on 25th March 2024].
Bradbury, S., Lusted, J. and Sterkenburg, J. (Eds.) (2020) *'Race', ethnicity and racism in sports coaching*, London: Routledge.
Brunssen, P. and Schüler-Springorum, S. (Eds.) (2021) *Football and discrimination: antisemitism and beyond*, London: Routledge.
Burdsey, D. (2021) *Racism and English football: for club and country*, London: Routledge.
Campbell, P. I. and Bebb, L. (2022) "'He is like a Gazelle (when he runs)' (re)constructing race and nation in match-day commentary at the men's 2018 FIFA World Cup", *Sport in Society*, 25(1), pp. 144–162.
Carrington, B. and McDonald, I. (2001) *'Race', sport and British society*, London: Routledge.
Cashmore, E. and Cleland, J. (2014) *Football's dark side: corruption, homophobia, violence and racism in the beautiful game*, Basingstoke: Palgrave Macmillan.

Crabbe, T., Solomos, J. and Back, L. (2001) *The changing face of football: racism, multiculturalism and identity in the English game*, Oxford: Berg.

Crenshaw, K. (1991) "Mapping the margins: intersectionality, identity politics, and violence against women of color", *Stanford Law Review*, 43(6), pp. 1241–1299.

Doidge, M., Kossakowski, R. and Mintert, S.M. (2022) *Ultras: the passion and performance of contemporary football fandom*, Manchester: Manchester University Press.

Entine, J. (2000) *Taboo: why Black athletes dominate sports and why we're afraid to talk about it*, New York: PublicAffairs.

Garland, J. and Rowe, M. (2001) *Racism and anti-racism in football*, Basingstoke: Palgrave Macmillan.

Garner, S. and Selod, S. (2015) "The racialization of Muslims: empirical studies of islamophobia", *Critical Sociology*, 41(1), pp. 9–19.

Halikiopoulou, D., Mock, S. and Vasilopoulou, S. (2013) "The civic zeitgeist: nationalism and liberal values in the European radical right", *Nations and Nationalism*, 19(1), pp. 107–127.

Harris, H. (2021) *Red card to racism: the fight for equality in football*, Woodbridge: Ad Lib Publishers.

Hassan, D. (2013) *Ethnicity and race in association football: case study analyses in Europe, Africa and the USA*, London: Routledge.

Kassimeris, C. (2007) *European football in Black and White: tackling racism in football*, London: Lexington Books.

Kassimeris, C. (2021) *Discrimination in football*, London: Routledge.

Kassimeris, C. (Ed.) (2009) *Anti-racism in European football: fair play for all*, London: Lexington Books.

Kazmin, A. (2024) "The Italian town where tensions are flaring over migrant workers", *The Financial Times*, 6th February. Available: <https://www.ft.com/content/45d12b10-1485-4f30-a7c5-1718a11022aa> [accessed on 10th March 2024].

Kearns, C., Sinclair, G., Black, J., Doidge, M., Fletcher, T., Kilvington, D., Liston, K., Lynn, T. and Rosati, P. (2022) "A scoping review of research on online hate and sport", *Communication & Sport*, 11(2), pp. 402–430.

Kilvington, D. and Price, J. (Eds.) (2018) *Sport and discrimination*, London: Routledge.

Llopis-Goig, R. (2015) *Spanish football and social change: sociological investigations*, Basingstoke: Palgrave Macmillan.

Merkel, U. and Tokarski, W. (1996) *Racism and xenophobia in European football*, Aachen: Meyer and Meyer.

Rowe, M. (2004) *Policing race and racism*, London: Routledge.

Runnymede Trust (2017) *Islamophobia: still a challenge for us all*, London. Available: <https://www.runnymedetrust.org/publications/islamophobia-still-a-challenge-for-us-all> [accessed on 10th April 2024].

Sterkenburg, J., Peeters, R. and Amsterdam, N. (2019) "Everyday racism and constructions of racial/ethnic difference in and through football talk", *European Journal of Cultural Studies*, 22(2), pp. 195–212.

Trilling, D. (2024) "The EU's new migration pact is intended to neutralise the far right – it risks empowering it", *The Guardian*, 16th April. Available: <https://www.theguardian.com/commentisfree/2024/apr/16/eu-migration-pact-intended-neutralise-far-right-europe> [accessed on 20th April 2024].

Tsoukala, A. (2009) *Football hooliganism in Europe – security and civil liberties in the balance*, Basingstoke: Palgrave Macmillan.

Chapter 2

Conceptual and theoretical considerations

Racism, xenophobia, antisemitism and Islamophobia

Scott Fleming

The chapters of this volume provide a series of case studies that analyse racism and other forms of discrimination in various European countries. Each has a theoretical perspective – some more explicit than others. The purpose of this chapter is to offer a conceptual framework to contextualise them collectively. It draws quite deliberately upon discourses about racisms from different disciplinary traditions (e.g. anthropology, geography, history, philosophy, psychology, sociology), a variety of subject fields (e.g. education, health, media, medicine, politics, sport), and scholars and practitioners from several countries (e.g. Austria, Cyprus, France, Hungary, Spain, Switzerland). Despite this wide range of sources, empirical examples to illustrate conceptual and theoretical points are drawn primarily from men's football, reflecting the main focus of researchers' attention and the relative scarcity of women's (and non-binary) voices in the public domain on themes associated with racisms. Material is also drawn from sources available in the English language which may also indicate an implicit Anglocentrism.

It is almost 30 years since *Racism and Xenophobia in European Football* was published. In it, drawing especially on the work of Robert Miles (1982), Mike Cole (1996) offered a clear and uncomplicated conceptual account of the fundamentally problematic concept of 'race' and how it was the basis for racism. Those themes remain in this chapter, followed by a brief account of 'racial science' and 'scientific racism'. A conceptual framework for understanding racisms signalled in the previous chapter is then linked to a lexicon of related terms, followed by an overview of some of the key perspectives that inform other chapters and the particular prominence of Critical Race Theory (CRT). Finally, there is a short summary section.

'Race'

The concept of 'race' does not provide a meaningful depiction of human biological variation, and as Fuentes, Ackermann, Athreya et al. (2019, p. 400) make unambiguously clear in the American Association of Physical Anthropology's statement on 'race' and racism, "it was never accurate in the past,

DOI: 10.4324/9781003495970-2

This chapter has been made available under a CC-BY-NC-SA 4.0 license.

and it remains inaccurate when referencing contemporary human populations". Yet 'race' became and continues to be a profoundly important building block for the flawed logic of racisms.

As a form of classification grounded in European colonialism (and hence domination, exploitation and discrimination), 'race' has been used to differentiate humankind into groups based on inherited biological characteristics manifest in physical appearance (phenotype) and linked genealogically to geographical origin (James and Burgos, 2024). Throughout the history of its use, 'race' has had various meanings – as a 'group' of shared common descent, as a 'type' for the purposes of classification, as a 'sub-species' and within political rhetoric and other contemporary debates (Banton, 2004a). It has also become a signifier of cultural difference and 'otherness' in discourse analysis (van den Berghe, 2004).

There are, at least, five fundamental problems with the concept of 'race'. First, as UNESCO (1965, p. 8) made plain, "pure races – in the sense of genetically homogeneous populations – do not exist in the human species". Hence, the description of 'races' is inevitably blurred, and it would be impossible to categorise every individual according to 'race' (Howells, 1974). Second, all humans have 99.9% of their DNA in common, yet there is significant variability in the observable characteristics of people that result from the interaction between their genetic composition and environmental factors. Natural selection and adaptation to local environments have shaped the physical characteristics of populations (Fuentes, Ackermann, Athreya et al., 2019). Third, the movement of people – first through colonisation, commerce, slavery, and later through globalisation, industrialisation and migration – has made discrete 'racial' categories unsustainable and hence meaningless (Spracklen, 2008). Geographic distance, topography and socio-political influences have also affected patterns of population dispersal and distribution (Fuentes, Ackermann, Athreya et al., 2019). Fourth, as Farb (1978, p. 276) concedes, "the genetic difference *between* two different (geographical) populations is very much the same as the difference *within* a single population" [original emphasis], and the phenotypic differences within a 'race' are at least as great as the differences between 'races' (Fleming, 2007). Fifth, variation within a population has given rise to claims for 'sub-races' with descriptions to match (e.g. Tobias, 1972 [1961]), but these have been discredited as lacking a strong evidential basis. There remains, therefore, a simple and irresolvable problem about an operational definition of 'races' which has a confounding effect on claims for empirical precision about them (Hirschman, 2004).

As John Rex (1994, p. 537) concluded, "there is no justification in biological science for the popular use of the term race", and biological accounts of 'race' as sub-species have been rejected by most biologists and anthropologists (Williams, 2001). However, the social construct of 'race' remains important for the understanding of 'race' and ethnic relations amongst sociologists, psychologists, geographers, economists, epidemiologists and others.

Racisms

Like the concept of 'race', the term 'racism' has also been used at different times and in several contexts for various purposes, for example, as an ideology, a discourse, an analytical tool and a political label (Farrington, Kilvington, Price et al., 2012). Racism is multi-faceted and complex (Solomos and Back, 1994); it has occurred and continues to occur in different socio-economic structures and cultural contexts (Jarvie, 1991); it has many historical manifestations (Banton, 2004b) and may have a changing prime target (Long and Spracklen, 2011). New forms of racism have emerged over time (Small, 1994), and there is a growing interest in the intersectionality with gender and class (Lewis, Hagerman and Forman, 2019) as well as sexual orientation. There are also different modes of opposition and resistance to it (Ellefsen, Banafsheh and Sandberg, 2022). As a result, the term 'racisms' is often preferred.

Broadly, racisms are the consequence of ideas and policies that produce and normalise inequalities based on 'races' (Kendi, 2019), and often emphasise how (false) theories of 'race' are used to deny or unjustly distribute social and economic opportunities and political rights (e.g. Lemert, 2006), as well as creating unfair privilege and oppression (Sumerau and Denise, 2018). Accounts of racisms often refer to prejudice and discrimination on the basis of their membership or assumed membership of a particular ethnic group – usually one that is marginalised through an imbalance in power relations (e.g. Australian Human Rights Commission, n.d.).

In a systematic review of the meanings attached to racisms in over 1,000 articles in sociology journals between 1995 and 2015, Shiao and Woody (2021) emphasised the deep, wide-ranging and nuanced complexity of a sociological understanding of racisms by identifying four sets of constructs: individual attitudes, cultural schema, pre-existing consequential inequalities (e.g. 'racial' dominance) and processes that create or maintain 'racial' dominance. Attempts to interrogate, understand and tackle racisms are complex owing, in part, to the use of vocabulary and the professional practice community and academic discipline from which they are made. Distinctive forms of racism first delineated between individual or personally mediated racism and institutionalised racism (Bowser, 2017). Later, when cultural markers, context and embedded stereotypes and prejudices were acknowledged as key determinants of racist dispositions, cultural racism was adopted (Jones, 2000). Most recently, recognising the difference between *intra*-institution racism and wider societal and political racism (Lander, 2021), as well as the *inter*-connectedness of institutions (Dean and Thorpe, 2022), a fourth conceptualisation was added – structural or systemic racism (e.g. Lewis, Hagerman and Forman, 2019). This overview provides an inclusive platform for interpreting and analysing racisms.

There are, however, some important caveats about adopting and applying this framework. First, it should not be inferred that the disambiguation above means that forms of racism are mutually exclusive – there is overlap (Small, 1994). Second, forms of racism are not fixed, and new meanings are created (Farrington, Kilvington, Price et al., 2012). Third, the terms used are fluid and flexible (Banton, 2004b). Fourth, forms of racism do not operate in isolation from each other, and they are often encountered in combination (Cole, 2019). Fifth, some typologies of racisms focus on a particular field of professional practice – for example, in health studies (Jones, 2000) or psychology (Brogaard and Gatzia, 2020). Nevertheless, this framework provides a conceptual point of departure for understanding racisms in their various instantiations and enables linkages with other descriptors linked to racisms to be explored (see Table 2.1).

In the context of sports performance (see Wiggins and Nauright, 2017; Adair, 2023), stereotypes about athletes from marginalised groups have been explored through the lens of 'racial' science or 'scientific racism'. An early example was Martin Kane's (1971) article *An assessment of black is best*, in which he argued that anatomical and physiological differences between 'races' bestowed performance advantages on Black athletes. Inevitably, the article attracted compelling critique – notably by Edwards (1972) and Cashmore (1982) – but also resonated with some latent racist perceptions and

Table 2.1 A lexicon of 'racisms'

Concept	Characteristics	Linked to other . . . 'racisms'
Individual	• Perceptions, attitudes, behaviours • Overt or covert • Explicit or inadvertent (conscious or unconscious) • Through action and inaction	• *Discursive* – how people are spoken to or talked about ('racial' jokes, hate speech) • *Explicit* – behaviour that is consistent with personal racist values of superiority/inferiority • *Habitual* – unquestioning, unreflective and unconscious ingrained behaviour • *Interactional* – how people interact with each other (e.g. non-verbal communication) • *Internalised* – acceptance of racialised perceptions (negative or positive) • *Interpersonal* – beliefs/biases influencing interaction (e.g. tokenism) • *Linguistic* – written or spoken, individual or collective discrimination based language • *Personally mediated* – behaviour based on prejudicial/discriminatory assumptions • *Relational* – the context of everyday human relationships

(*Continued*)

Table 2.1 (Continued)

Concept	Characteristics	Linked to other . . . 'racisms'
Institutional	• Policies, procedures, practices and administrative structures • Within an institution or organisation • Often anonymous discrimination with undetectable causes • Focus on outcomes/consequences (e.g. under-representation)	• *AI* – existing biases perpetuated through generative artificial intelligence • *Colour-blind* – discriminatory outcomes in spite of attempts to disregard 'race' or ethnicity • *Techno* – fallibilities in facial recognition software disadvantage some marginalised groups • *Unconscious* – where individual racism affects institutional policies, procedures and practices
Cultural	• Normalised views and beliefs embedded as 'common sense' • Negative stereotypes and symbolic portrayal • Biological determinism • Extended to aspects of culture (e.g. nationality, religion)	• *Accidental* – racist behaviour/actions not intended to be racist • *Epistemic* – domination of knowledge (e.g. Eurocentrism) • *Epistemological* – Eurocentric bias in qualitative research • *Ideological* – everyday 'common sense' ways of thinking • *Inferential* – forms of media from which racism can be deduced or presumed • *Laissez-faire* – blaming marginalised groups for their disadvantage • *New* – a departure from biological (old) racism • *Representational* – depictions of 'racial' stereotypes (e.g. in popular culture) • *Reverse/White* – prejudice/discrimination by people of colour to Whites • *Scientific* – conceptual commitment biological 'races' and to 'race science' • *Sexual* – discrimination or bigotry in the selection of sexual partners • *Symbolic* – support for principles of equality but no commitment to implementation of change • *Unwitting* – a lack of understanding, ignorance or mistaken beliefs

(Continued)

Table 2.1 (Continued)

Concept	Characteristics	Linked to other . . . 'racisms'
Structural/ systemic	• Embedded societal reproduction of stratification and discrimination • Rationalisation of inequalities in prejudices, stereotypes and ideologies • Reflected in power imbalances with spatial and temporal dimensions • Leads to patterns of resistance	• *Colonial* – domination and exploitation of people and resources through subjugation • *Environmental* – disadvantage/discrimination in relation to the built environment • *Overt* – favourable coverage in support of an openly racist view or policy • *Xeno* – xenophobic discrimination (e.g. concerns about community conflict and national security)

Sources: adapted from Anderson (2020); Ashwini (2024); Back, Crabbe and Solomos (2001); Bowser (2017); Brogaard and Gatzia (2020); Carrington (2008); Cashmore (2004); Cole (2019); Farrington, Kilvington, Price et al. (2012); Jones (2000); Kendi (2019); Long and Mc-Namee (2004); Long and Spracklen (2011); Loppie, Reading and de Leeuw (2014); Malcolm (2008), Müller, van Zoonen and de Roode (2007); Patel (2023); Ramadan (2024).

affirmed some views that had begun to surface about Black footballers in the UK and elsewhere.

In *Taboo: Why Black athletes dominate sports and why we're afraid to talk about it*, Jon Entine (2000) was forthright and unconvincing in an argument about the links between 'races' and sports performance. The work was controversial (e.g. St Louis, 2003, 2004; Darda, 2024) and addressed football in particular with some "crude and inaccurate caricatures" (Back, Crabbe and Solomos, 2001, p. 282). Individual racism has also been prevalent in the words and actions of fellow players, coaches, managers and supporters (Fleming and Tomlinson, 1996) as well as media pundits (Boyle and Haynes, 2000). Players' experiences of racisms were documented in biographies (e.g. Hill, 1989; Longmore, 1988), in autobiographies (e.g. Ferdinand, 1998; Wright and McCarthy, 1996) and through the institutional impact of stereotyped perceptions that became established and most visible through the disproportionate over-representation of Black players in specific playing positions (e.g. Maguire, 1991; Nobis and Lazaridou, 2023). Dominant discourses became embedded as cultural racism and resulted in negative consequences for Black players in captaincy roles within teams and in career opportunities, progression and retention in coaching, management and administration leadership roles (Holding with Hawkins, 2021; Howell, 2022) – even for highly successful international players (Thuram, 2020).

There may be several reasons to explain why the victims of racisms did not pursue redress through whatever channels were available to them, not least the power relations and hierarchies within professional sport. However, since retiring from playing, some Black players have been very candid about perceptions of structural racism encountered (Barnes, 2021). The exposure of high-profile cases of discursive racism has also shone a light on behaviour and opinions that may be habitual and/or internalised and/or representational and/or unwitting – see, for example, the widespread condemnation of former player, manager and popular pundit, Ron Atkinson, following unmistakably racist remarks about Marcel Desailly in what he thought was a private conversation that was actually being broadcast (Carrington, 2011).

Related conceptual considerations

Driven by expressions of difference (Bhugra, Smith, Liebrenz et al., 2023), a common feature of racisms is the racialised *Other* along with the related construct of *Otherness* and the process of *Othering*. These are based on binaries and stem from philosophical explorations of identity, in particular the differences between the same and the Other (Nederveen Pieterse, 2004), or 'us' and 'them' (Udah, 2023). To paraphrase Goldberg (2000), differences linked to 'race' are identified by the dominant group, and knowledge is constructed based on their evaluation, invariably negative. Even ostensibly positive stereotypes about the athletic prowess of Black footballers are offset by the pernicious corollary about assumed laziness and decision-making capability (see Harris, 2017; Barnes, 2021). Voices of the Other are neglected or ignored, and power differential is perpetuated within the dominant group which then confirms policies, practices and behaviours that reinforce and maintain the subjugation of the Other. This 'otherism' is a versatile and adaptable conceptual tool for investigating and understanding the social and political inequalities of marginalised or oppressed groups (Bhugra, Smith, Liebrenz et al., 2023).

As an ideology, the fundamental premise of **nationalism** is that nation-states are the basis of social life (Kumar, 2006) and that national identity should align with political recognition (Walz, 1995). This means that the world is divided into nations, each with unique characteristics and cultural markers, and with the right to self-determination (Miles, 2004). As a concept, nationalism embraces several forms of national attachment (Mylonas and Tudor, 2021) – including, in particular, 'ethnic nationalism' and 'civic nationalism'. The former is characterised by a shared sense of heritage, culture and language; the latter is based on democratic legitimacy, voluntary engagement and citizenship (Roshwald, 2015).

Sport is closely linked to displays of nationalism through economic and diplomatic propaganda (Bairner, 2008b); the history of the modern Olympic Games is a narrative of global politics (Cottrell and Nelson, 2010; Grix, 2013). Through international competition especially, sport provides a platform for celebrations of national identity and ethnic pride, and also for discourses about the Other.

Manifestations of racisms are historically grounded and situationally sensitive. They are also experienced differently by marginalised groups depending on their circumstances. For instance, **anti-Black racism** exists in different parts of the world, but unique iterations can be found in national and regional contexts (Showers, 2015). These are influenced by specific institutionally racist immigration policies and practices leading to structural racism of exclusion, oppression and disadvantage. To illustrate, with origins in slavery and colonialism, discriminatory racist legislation in South Africa (i.e. Apartheid) and the USA (i.e. the Jim Crow laws in the southern states) enforced segregation and subordination of Black people in different ways. Both of these were also different from the anti-Black racisms experienced by the diverse groups of migrant and refugee Africans in Australia (Udah, 2023). It is anti-Black racism that is seen most frequently in football, especially in Europe.

In the context of European football fandom, anti-Other racism has been well documented. For example, in relation to verbal abuse directed at Romani Hungarians (Földesi, 1996), the perceptions in Austria of 'foreign' players, especially Turks and Yugoslavs (Horak and Marschik, 1996), the racism-hooligan couplet and the rise of the far right in Germany, especially in the east (Kassimeris, 2010), and extremist views and Fascist salutes amongst Lazio's supporters in Italy (Kassimeris, 2011).

In its broadest sense, **sectarianism** refers to the relationship between two groups through which harm is caused, or perceived to be caused, by one to the other. It is applied most often to religious groups and their political differences (Bairner, 2008a). As a specific form of racism (McVeigh, 2019), sectarianism exists in various ways and in different contexts (e.g. India, Lebanon). It, too, creates and reinforces social inequality and can be understood as a labelling process and an ideological justification (Sugden and Bairner, 1993). Unlike some other forms of racism, however, as Brewer (1992, p. 352) notes, sectarianism's "social markers are more opaque, less deterministic . . . more context bound". In Scotland, one such marker is football allegiance (Rosie, Clegg, Morrow et al., 2015), and although the recent history of conflict is different (Hassan, McCullough and Moreland, 2010), football fandom also symbolises religion, culture and politics in Northern Ireland (Boyle and Haynes, 2000; Cronin, 2002).

Xenophobia is predicated on Otherism in relation to people or things that are foreign or unfamiliar. Etymologically, the term reflects fear, dislike or aversion, and involves stigmatisation and rejection of those who are, or are perceived to be migrants, refugees, asylum-seekers, displaced persons and non-nationals (International Labour Office et al., 2001). A distinction between racisms and xenophobia is made explicit by Banton (2004c, p. 455): "racism can be seen as relying on ideas of inferiority, whereas xenophobia relies on ideas of fundamental differences between cultures". For analytical purposes, however, xenophobia is often treated as a form of racism and finds expression in many of the same ways (Llopis-Goig, 2009).

A specific form of xenophobic prejudice and hostility directed at Muslims as a religious-cultural group is **Islamophobia**. The concept is contested, and a precise definition has proved elusive (López, 2011). The associated bigotry includes negative anti-Muslim attitudes and emotions (Bleich, 2011), but Islamophobia is more than a particular religious intolerance and may be better considered as a form of cultural racism. More widely, Islamophobia is often the basis for perceptions of geopolitical threats and terrorism from Islamic states (Hedges, 2021).

Sport is often seen as a site for displays of cultural conflict, especially amongst football spectators in Europe (see Doidge, 2017). Interestingly, however, Alrababa'h, Marble, Mousa et al. (2021) have reported research findings that support the parasocial contact hypothesis in relation to Islamophobia. Described as 'visibly Muslim', Mohammed Salah has been a key player in the successes of Liverpool F.C. men's team since he joined the club in 2017. His popularity is thought to have reduced Islamophobia amongst fans and is supported by hate crime data, analysis of social media and a fan survey.

The alignment of Islamophobia with cultural racism has prompted some commentators to draw a comparison with **antisemitism**, but that, too, is contested (López, 2011). The term Jew is a signifier of religion but as Dart (2021, p. 678) makes clear, Jewish identity is "intersectional and a dynamic set of social relations" and includes ethnicity, community and the secular. As a form of Othering, antisemitism has a 2,000-year history and recognised as institutional and/or structural since 1870 (Bonnett, 2004). It has also been connected to ideas of 'race' and therefore, as a concept, is more than being 'anti-Jewish'.

There is a crude stereotype that 'Jews don't play sport' (Dart, 2021) and examples of antisemitism from supporters include songs and chants on the terraces (Tamsut, 2021). There is also the profoundly offensive hissing to mimic the sound of gas entering the chambers at Nazi concentration camps at games involving Tottenham Hotspur FC (Back, Crabbe and Solomos, 2001), especially against neighbouring London clubs (Poulton, 2013). In addition, antisemitic language was reported in text messages between club officials at Cardiff City FC (Doidge, 2017); and on the field, in 2013, Nicolas Anelka celebrated a goal with the *quenelle* gesture, thought by many to be antisemitic (BBC Sport, 2014).

Racisms and xenophobia do not exist in isolation from other forms of prejudice and discrimination. Pioneering work by bell hooks (2014), first published in 1981, explored the interfaces of ethnicity, gender and class, and the term **intersectionality** was adopted in the late 1980s as an analytical construct to recognise combinations of power imbalances and socio-political disadvantage (Crenshaw, 1991). However, multiple social and political identities also include, for example, age, disability and sexuality. Together, in different ways and to varying extents depending on the circumstances, these shape day-to-day experiences and influence the life chances of individuals and groups sharing common characteristics. Furthermore, the failure to accommodate intersectionality risks simplistic reductionism and assumes mistaken homogeneity of monolithic groups.

In sport, racisms are often co-articulated with sexism and homophobia (Carrington, 2011), and intersectionality is still emerging as an explicit research domain (Sherry, Bowell, Symons et al., 2024), for example, in sport psychology (Bennett, Owens and Prewitt-White, 2022). Although there have been important contributions to debates about sport, ethnicity and gender (e.g. Corbett and Johnson, 1993; Lovell, 1991; Scraton, 2001; Borish, 2002; Kay, 2006; Sutherland, 2017), relatively little attention has been paid directly to the gender-ethnicity dynamic in European football – Scraton, Caudwell and Holland (2005), Caudwell (2022) and Leslie-Walker, Taylor and Jones Russell (2023) are notable exceptions.

A prevailing theoretical account

Although theoretical insights inform many of the concepts in the earlier sections of this chapter, in relation to the dynamics and social relations between different ethnic groups in and through sport and leisure, a dominant theoretical account has surfaced. In a systematic review of research outputs addressing the themes of 'race', Whiteness and sport in academic journals between 2009 and 2015, Fletcher and Hylton (2017) report that Critical Race Theory (CRT) was the primary theoretical theme.

Developed as a theoretical approach to examining systemic and institutional racism with analytical and practical applications (e.g. Hylton, 2011; Lawrence and Hylton, 2022), CRT has become a controversial focus in educational policy discourses in Australia and the USA (López, Molnar, Johnson et al., 2021). Different interpretations of CRT have emerged since its development in the 1970s, but crucially, as Hylton (2005, p. 81) makes plain, its use is

> likely to lead towards a resistance to a passive reproduction of the established practices, knowledge and resources, that make up the social conditions that marginalize 'race' as a core factor in the way we manage and experience our sport and leisure.

There are five precepts, CRT

(i) "[centralises] 'race' and racism at the same time as recognising their connection with other forms of subordination and oppression";
(ii) "challenges traditional dominant ideologies around objectivity, meritocracy, colour-blindness, 'race'-neutrality and equal opportunity";
(iii) "has a clear commitment to social justice that incorporates elements of liberation and transformation";

(iv) makes a significant contribution by centralising marginalised voices; and
(v) is transdisciplinary.

(distilled from Hylton, 2005, pp. 84–85)

In addition to the work on theorising the nexus between sport and CRT already cited earlier (e.g. Hylton, 2005, 2011; Fletcher and Hylton, 2017), there is a body of research explicitly linking CRT to football in the UK. Led in particular by scholars associated with Leeds Beckett University and the University of Brighton, studies have addressed, amongst other things, British Asians in football cultures (Burdsey, 2007), the failure of liberal approaches to 'race' equality and anti-discriminatory policies (Lawrence, 2017), the fandom experiences of marginalised groups (Lawrence and Davis, 2019), the criminalisation of football spectator behaviour (Gardiner and Welch, 2011), professional football (Burdsey, 2011) and the men's English Premier League (Lawrence, 2017).

Summary

There are key messages from this chapter that apply to later chapters:

- Although the biological concept of 'race' has been discredited and almost completely discarded, the social construct of 'race' remains an influential element in the enduring perceptions of (false) 'racial' distinctions.
- Racisms exist in different but overlapping and linked forms. The 'individual – institutional – cultural – structural' typology provides a very useful framework for interpretation and analysis.
- There is some inconsistency in the use of vocabulary associated with racisms that does not always add clarity to discussion and debate.
- Concepts linked to the Other underpin forms of discrimination, oppression and subordination experienced by various groups for different reasons.
- Intersectionality is an important construct for understanding the multiple, and frequently overlapping, power imbalances and socio-political disadvantages experienced by members of marginalised groups.
- CRT has emerged as an influential theoretical lens for understanding the dynamics and social relations of minoritised groups in sport and is applicable to European football.

References

Adair, D. (2023) "Sport, race and ethnicity", in Wenner, L.A. (Ed.), *The Oxford handbook of sport and society*, Oxford: Oxford University Press.

Alrababa'h, A., Marble, W., Mousa, S. and Siegel, A.A. (2021) "Can exposure to celebrities reduce prejudice? The effect of Mohamed Salah on Islamophobic behaviors and attitudes", *American Political Science Review*, 115(4), pp. 1111–1128.

Anderson, R. (2020) "Sexual racism – romantic bigotry in the 21st century", *Psychology Today*, 23rd December. Available: <https://www.psychologytoday.com/us/blog/

the-mating-game/202012/sexual-racism?msockid=0d3b5b9cc06c64243eda4f6dc1
8c65ca> [accessed on 1st October 2024].

Ashwini, K.P. (2024) "Contemporary forms of racism, racial discrimination, xenophobia and related intolerance", Human Rights Council, fifty-sixth session 18, Agenda item 9. Available: <https://documents.un.org/doc/undoc/gen/g24/084/20/pdf/g2408 420.pdf> [accessed on 1st October 2024].

Australian Human Rights Commission (n.d.) "What is racism?" Available: <https://humanrights.gov.au/our-work/race-discrimination/what-racism> [accessed on 1st October 2024].

Back, L., Crabbe, T. and Solomos, J. (2001) *The changing face of football – racism, identity and multiculture in the English game*, Oxford: Berg.

Bairner, A. (2008a) "Sectarianism", in Malcolm, D. (Ed.), *The SAGE dictionary of sport studies*, London: SAGE.

Bairner, A. (2008b) "Nationalism", in Malcolm, D. (Ed.), *The SAGE dictionary of sport studies*, London: SAGE.

Banton, M. (2004a) "Race: as classification", in Cashmore, E. (Ed.), *Encyclopedia of race and ethnic studies*, London: Routledge.

Banton, M. (2004b) "Racism", in Cashmore, E. (Ed.), *Encyclopedia of race and ethnic studies*, London: Routledge.

Banton, M. (2004c) "Xenophobia", in Cashmore, E. (Ed.), *Encyclopedia of race and ethnic studies*, London: Routledge.

Barnes, J. (2021) *The uncomfortable truth about racism*, London: Headline Publishing.

BBC Sport (2014) "Nicolas Anelka banned and fined £80,000 for 'quenelle' gesture". Available: <https://www.bbc.co.uk/sport/football/26326484> [accessed on 1st October 2024].

Bennett, H., Owens, R. and Prewitt-White, T. (2022) "Living and embracing intersectionality in sport: introduction to the special issue", *Journal of Clinical Sport Psychology*, 16, pp. 297–301.

Bhugra, D., Smith, A., Liebrenz, M., Ventriglioc, A., Nishanth Gnanapragasam, S., Buadzee, A., Pemberton, M. and Poulter, M. (2023) "'Otherness', otherism, discrimination, and health inequalities: entrenched challenges for modern psychiatric disciplines", *International Review of Psychiatry*, 35(3–4), pp. 234–241.

Bleich, E. (2011) "What is Islamophobia and how much is there? theorizing and measuring an emerging comparative concept", *American Behavioral Scientist*, 55(12), pp. 1581–1600.

Bonnett, A. (2004) "Anti-semitism", in Cashmore, E. (Ed.), *Encyclopedia of race and ethnic studies*, London: Routledge.

Borish, L.J. (2002) "Women, sport and Jewish identity in the late nineteenth and early twentieth centuries", in Magdalinski, T. and Chandler, T.J.L. (Eds.), *With god on their side – sport in the service of religion*, London: Routledge.

Bowser, B.P. (2017) "Racism: origin and theory", *Journal of Black Studies*, 48(6), pp. 572–590.

Boyle, R. and Haynes, R. (2000) *Power play – sport, media and popular culture*, Harlow: Pearson Education.

Brewer, J.D. (1992) "Sectarianism and racism, and their parallels and differences", *Ethnic and Racial Studies*, 15(3), pp. 352–364.

Brogaard, B. and Gatzia, D.E. (2020) "The many faces of racism", *Psychology Today*, 27th December. Available: <https://www.psychologytoday.com/us/blog/the-superhuman-mind/202012/the-many-faces-racism#:~:text=The%20Many%20Faces%20of%20Racism%20There%20is%20not%20one%20or?msockid=0d3b5b9cc06c64243 eda4f6dc18c65ca> [accessed on 1st October 2024].

Burdsey, D. (2007) *British Asians and football: culture, identity, exclusion*, Abingdon: Routledge.

Burdsey, D. (2011) "Applying a CRT lens to sport in the UK: the case of professional football", in Hylton, K., Pilkington, A., Warmington, P. and Housee, S. (Eds.) *Atlantic crossings: international dialogues on critical race theory*, Birmingham: C-SAP.

Carrington, B. (2008) "Race", in Malcolm, D. (Ed.), *The SAGE dictionary of sport studies*, London: SAGE.

Carrington, B. (2011) "'What I said was racist, but I'm not a racist': anti-racism and the White sports/media complex", in Long, J. and Spracklen, K. (Eds.), *Sport and challenges to racism*, Basingstoke: Palgrave Macmillan.

Cashmore, E. (1982) *Black sportsmen*, London: Routledge and Kegan Paul.

Cashmore, E. (2004) *Encyclopedia of race and ethnic studies*, London: Routledge.

Caudwell, J. (2022) "For women's Euro 2022 to have a meaningful legacy, football must do more to tackle racism and sexism", *The Conversation*, 11th August. Available: <https://theconversation.com/for-womens-euro-2022-to-have-a-meaningful-legacy-football-must-do-more-to-tackle-racism-and-sexism-188084> [accessed on 1st October 2024].

Cole, M. (1996) "'Race', racism and nomenclature: a conceptual analysis", in Merkel, U. and Tokarski, W. (Eds.), *Racism and xenophobia in European football*, Aachen: Meyer and Meyer Verlag.

Cole, N.L. (2019) "Defining racism beyond its dictionary meaning", *ThoughtCo*, 31st July 2021. Available: <https://www.thoughtco.com/racism-definition-3026511> [accessed on 1st October 2024].

Corbett, D. and Johnson, W. (1993) "The African-American female in collegiate sport: sexism and racism", in Brooks, D. and Althouse, R. (Eds.), *Racism in college athletics: the African-American athlete's experience*, Morgantown, WV: Fitness Information Technology.

Cottrell, M.P. and Nelson, T. (2010) "Not just the games? power, protest and politics at the Olympics", *European Journal of International Relations*, 17(4), pp. 729–753.

Crenshaw, K. (1991) "Mapping the margins: intersectionality, identity politics, and violence against women of color", *Stanford Law Review*, 43(6), pp. 1241–1299.

Cronin, M. (2002) "Catholics and sport in Northern Ireland", in Magdalinski, T. and Chandler, T.J.L. (Eds.), *With God on their side – sport the service of religion*, London: Routledge.

Darda, J. (2024) "The mismeasure of sport: race and the science of athletic performance", *Differences*, 35(1), pp. 43–73.

Dart, J. (2021) "Sport and British Jewish identity", *International Review for the Sociology of Sport*, 56(5), pp. 677–694.

Dean, L.T. and Thorpe, R.J. (2022) "What structural racism is (or is not) and how to measure it: clarity for public health and medical researchers", *American Journal of Epidemiology*, 191(9), pp. 1521–1526.

Doidge, M. (2017) "Racism and European football", in Nauright, J. and Wiggins, D.K. (Eds.), *Routledge handbook of sport, race and ethnicity*, London: Routledge.

Edwards, H. (1972) "The myth of the racially superior athlete", *Intellectual Digest*, 2, pp. 58–60.

Ellefsen, R., Banafsheh, A. and Sandberg, S. (2022) "Resisting racism in everyday life: from ignoring to confrontation and protest", *Ethnic and Racial Studies*, 45(16), pp. 435–457.

Entine, J. (2000) *Taboo: why Black athletes dominate sports and why we're afraid to talk about it*, New York: Public Affairs.

Farb, P. (1978) *Humankind – a history of the development of man*, London: Jonathan Cape.

Farrington, N., Kilvington, D., Price, J. and Saeed, A. (2012) *Race, racism and sports journalism*, London: Routledge.

Ferdinand, L. (1998) *Sir Les: autobiography of Les Ferdinand*, London: Hardline Publishing.

Fleming, S. (2007) "Sport, science and the problems of 'race'", *Paideia – Philosophical E-journal of Charles University*, 1–2(iv), pp. 1–9.

Fleming, S. and Tomlinson, A. (1996) "Football, racism and xenophobia in England (I): Europe and the old England", in Merkel, U. and Tokarski, W. (Eds.), *Racism and xenophobia in European football*, Aachen: Meyer and Meyer Verlag.

Fletcher, T. and Hylton, K. (2017) "'Race', whiteness and sport", in Nauright, J. and Wiggins, D.K. (Eds.), *Routledge handbook of sport, race and ethnicity*, London: Routledge.

Földesi, G.S. (1996) "Football, racism and xenophobia in Hungary: racist and xenophobic behaviour of football spectators", in Merkel, U. and Tokarski, W. (Eds.), *Racism and xenophobia in European football*, Aachen: Meyer and Meyer Verlag.

Fuentes, A., Ackermann, R.R., Athreya, S., Bolnick, D., Lasisi, T., Lee, S.-H., McLean, S.-A. and Nelson, R. (2019) "AAPA statement on race and racism", *American Journal of Physical Anthropology*, 169(3), pp. 400–402.

Gardiner, S. and Welch, R. (2011) "Football, racism and the limits of 'colour blind' law", in Burdsey, D. (Ed.), *Race, ethnicity and football – persisting debates and emergent issues*, London: Routledge.

Goldberg, D.T. (2000) "Racial knowledge", in Back, L. and Solomos, J. (Eds.), *Theories of race and racism – a reader*, London: Routledge.

Grix, J. (2013) "Sport, politics and the Olympics", *Political Studies Review*, 11, pp. 15–25.

Harris, L.J. (2017) "Britain", in Nauright, J. and Wiggins, D.K. (Eds.), *Routledge handbook of sport, race and ethnicity*, London: Routledge.

Hassan, D., McCullough, S. and Moreland, E. (2010) "North or south? Darron Gibson and the issue of player eligibility in Irish soccer", in Bandyopadhyay, K. (Ed.), *Why minorities play or don't play soccer*, London: Routledge.

Hedges, P. (2021) *Religious hatred: prejudice, Islamophobia and Antisemitism in global context*, London: Bloomsbury Academic.

Hill, D. (1989) *'Out of his skin': the John Barnes phenomenon*, London: Faber and Faber.

Hirschman, C. (2004) "The origins and demise of the concept of race", *Population and Development Review*, 30(3), pp. 385–415.

Holding, M. with Hawkins, E. (2021) *Why we kneel, how we rise*, London: Simon and Schuster.

hooks, b. (2014) *Ain't I a woman – Black women and feminism*, 2nd edition, New York: Routledge.

Horak, R. and Marschik, M. (1996) "Football, racism and xenophobia in Austria: 'if you let them, they behave like the Mafia'", in Merkel, U. and Tokarski (Eds.), *Racism and xenophobia in European football*, Aachen: Meyer and Meyer Verlag.

Howell, A. (2022) "Les Ferdinand: FA diversity code 'made no difference' in helping black players get jobs in football", *BBC Sport*, 19th October. Available: <https://www.bbc.co.uk/sport/football/63307161> [accessed on 1st October 2024].

Howells, W.W. (1974) "The meaning of race", *New Community*, III(1–2), pp. 26–30.

Hylton, K. (2005) "'Race', sport and leisure: lessons from critical race theory", *Leisure Studies*, 24(1), pp. 81–98.

Hylton, K. (2011) "Too radical? critical race theory and sport against racism in Ireland", in Long, J. and Spracklen, K. (Eds.), *Sport and challenges to racism*, Basingstoke: Palgrave Macmillan.

International Labour Office, International Organization for Migration and Office of the United Nations High Commissioner for Human Rights (2001) *International migration, racism, discrimination and xenophobia*, Geneva. Available: <https://www2.ohchr.org/english/issues/migration/taskforce/docs/wcar.pdf> [accessed on 1st October 2024].

James, M. and Burgos, A. (2024) "Race", in Zalta, E.N. and Nodelman, U. (Eds.), *The Stanford encyclopedia of philosophy* (Spring Edition). Available: <https://plato.stanford.edu/archives/spr2024/entries/race> [accessed on 1st October 2024].

Jarvie, G. (1991) "Introduction", in Jarvie, G. (Ed.), *Sport, racism and ethnicity*, London: Falmer.

Jones, C.P. (2000) "Levels of racism – a theoretical framework and a gardener's tale", *American Journal of Public Health*, 90(8), pp. 1189–1328.

Kane, M. (1971) "An assessment of black is best", *Sports Illustrated*, 34(3), pp. 78–83.

Kassimeris, C. (2010) "Deutschland über Alles: discrimination in German football", in Bandyopadhyay, K. (Ed.), *Why minorities play or don't play soccer*, London: Routledge.

Kassimeris, C. (2011) "Fascism, separatism and the ultràs: discrimination in Italian football", *Soccer and Society*, 12(5), pp. 677–688.

Kay, T. (2006) "Daughters of Islam – family influences on Muslim young women's participation in sport", *International Review for the Sociology of Sport*, 41(3), pp. 357–373.

Kendi, I.X. (2019) *How to be an antiracist*, London: The Bodley Head.

Kumar, K. (2006) "Nationalism", in Turner, B.S. (Ed.), *The Cambridge dictionary of sociology*, Cambridge: Cambridge University Press.

Lander, V. (2021) "Structural racism: what it is and how it works", *The Conversation*, 30th June. Available: <https://theconversation.com/structural-racism-what-it-is-and-how-it-works-158822> [accessed on 1st October 2024].

Lawrence, S. (2017) "A critical race theory analysis of the English Premier League – confronting the declining significance of 'race' and racism myth", in Elliott, R. (Ed.), *The English Premier League – A socio-cultural analysis*, London: Routledge.

Lawrence, S. and Davis, C. (2019) "Fans for diversity? a critical race theory analysis of black, Asian and minority ethnic (BAME) supporters' experiences of football fandom", *International Journal of Sport Policy and Politics*, 11(4), pp. 701–713.

Lawrence, S. and Hylton, K. (2022) "Critical race theory, methodology, and semiotics: the analytical utility of a "race" conscious approach for visual qualitative research", *Cultural Studies ↔ Critical Methodologies*, 22(3), pp. 255–265.

Lemert, C. (2006) "Racism", in Turner, B.S. (Ed.), *The Cambridge dictionary of sociology*, Cambridge: Cambridge University Press.

Leslie-Walker, A., Taylor, K. and Jones Russell, E. (2023) "'Inclusivity for who'? an analysis of 'race' and female fandom at the 2022 UEFA European Women's Championships", *International Review for the Sociology of Sport*, 59(3), pp. 459–475.

Lewis, A.E., Hagerman, M.A. and Forman, T.A. (2019) "The sociology of race and racism: key concepts, contributions and debates", *Equity and Excellence in Education*, 52(1), pp. 29–46.

Llopis-Goig, R. (2009) "Racism and xenophobia in Spanish football: facts, reactions and policies", *Physical Culture and Sport Studies and Research*, XLVII, pp. 35–43.

Long, J. and McNamee, M. (2004) "On the moral economy of racism and racist rationalizations in sport", *International Review for the Sociology of Sport*, 39(4), pp. 405–420.

Long, J. and Spracklen, K. (Eds.) (2011) *Sport and challenges to racism*, Basingstoke: Palgrave Macmillan.

Longmore, A. (1988) *Viv Anderson*, London: Heinemann Kingswood.

López, F., Molnar, A., Johnson, R., Patterson, A., Ward, L. and Kumashiro, K. (2021) *Understanding the attacks on critical race theory*, Boulder, CO: National Education Policy Center. Available: <http://nepc.colorado.edu/publication/crt> [accessed on 1st October 2024].

López, F.B. (2011) "Towards a definition of Islamophobia: approximations of the early twentieth century", *Ethnic and Racial Studies*, 34(4), pp. 556–573.

Loppie, S., Reading, C. and de Leeuw, S. (2014) "Indigenous experiences with racism and its impact", *National Collaborating Centre for Indigenous Health*. Available: <https://www.nccih.ca/495/Indigenous_experiences_with_racism_and_its_impacts.nccih?id=131> [accessed on 1st October 2024].

Lovell, T. (1991) "Sport, racism and young women", in Jarvie, G. (Ed.), *Sport, racism and ethnicity*, London: Falmer.

Maguire, J. (1991) "Sport, racism and British society: a sociological study of England's élite male Afro-Caribbean soccer and rugby union players", in Jarvie, G. (Ed.), *Sport, racism and ethnicity*, London: Falmer.

Malcolm, D. (Ed.) (2008) *The SAGE dictionary of sport studies*, London: SAGE.

McVeigh, R. (2019) *Sectarianism: the key facts*, Belfast: Equality Coalition/Committee of the Administration of Justice/Unison. Available: <https://www.equalitycoalition.net/wp-content/uploads/2020/02/Secatrianism-The-Key-Facts-FINAL-LOW-RES.pdf> [accessed on 1st October 2024].

Miles, R. (1982) *Racism and migrant labour*, London: Routledge and Kegan Paul.

Miles, R. (2004) "Nationalism", in Cashmore, E. (Ed.), *Encyclopedia of race and ethnic studies*, London: Routledge.

Müller, F., van Zoonen, L. and de Roode, L. (2007) "Accidental racists: experiences and contradictions of racism in local Amsterdam soccer fan culture", *Soccer and Society*, 8(2–3), pp. 35–350.

Mylonas, H. and Tudor, M. (2021) "Nationalism: what we know and what we still need to know", *Annual Review of Political Science*, 24, pp. 109–132.

Nederveen Pieterse, J. (2004) "Other", in Cashmore, E. (Ed.), *Encyclopedia of race and ethnic studies*, London: Routledge.

Nobis, T. and Lazaridou, F. (2023) "Racist stacking in professional soccer in Germany", *International Review for the Sociology of Sport*, 58(1), pp. 23–42.

Patel, T.G. (2023) *Race, ethnicity and society*, London: SAGE.

Poulton, E. (2013) "Tackle antisemitism, not the 'Yid Army' chants", *The Conversation*, 20th September. Available: <https://theconversation.com/tackle-antisemitism-not-the-yid-army-chants-18491> [accessed on 1st October 2024].

Ramadan, I. (2024) "Resisting epistemic racism in UK academia? challenges and risks in the age of Islamophobia: the voices of Muslim academics", *Whiteness and Education*, online first, DOI: 10.1080/23793406.2024.2409633.

Rex, J. (1994) "Race", in Outhwaite, W. and Bottomore, T. (Eds.), *The Blackwell dictionary of twentieth-century social thought*, London: Blackwell.

Roshwald, A. (2015) "Civic and ethnic nationalism", in Smith, A.D., Hou, X., Stone, J., Dennis, R. and Rizova, P. (Eds.), *The Wiley Blackwell encyclopedia of race, ethnicity, and nationalism*, online first, DOI: 10.1002/9781118663202.wberen436.

Rosie, M., Clegg, C., Morrow, D., Lynch, M. and Galloway, I. (2015) *Tackling sectarianism and its consequences in Scotland: final report of the advisory group on tackling sectarianism in Scotland*, Scottish Government. Available: <https://www.pure.ed.ac.uk/ws/portalfiles/portal/25458071/00477619.pdf> [accessed on 1st October 2024].

Scraton, S. (2001) "Reconceptualizing race, gender and sport: the contribution of black feminism", in Carrington, B. and McDonald, I. (Eds.), *Race, sport and British society*, London: Routledge.

Scraton, S., Caudwell, J. and Holland, S. (2005) "'Bend it like Patel' – centring 'race', ethnicity and gender in feminist analysis of women's football in England", *International Review for the Sociology of Sport*, 40(1), pp. 71–88.

Sherry, E., Bowell, P., Symons, K. and Pankowiak, A. (2024) "Researching women in sport development: an intersectional approach", *Sport in Society*, 27(5), pp. 820–842.

Shiao, J. and Woody, A. (2021) "The meaning of 'racism'", *Sociological Perspectives*, 64(4), pp. 495–517.

Showers, F. (2015) "Being black, foreign and woman: African immigrant identities in the United States", *Ethnic and Racial Studies*, 38(10), pp. 1815–1830.

Small, S. (1994) *The Black experience in the United States and England in the 1980s*, London: Routledge.

Solomos, J. and Back, L. (1994) "Conceptualising racisms: social theory, politics and research", *Sociology*, 28(1), pp. 143–161.

Spracklen, K. (2008) "The holy blood and the holy grail: myths of scientific racism and the pursuit of excellence in sport", *Leisure Studies*, 27(2), pp. 221–227.

St Louis, B. (2003) "Sport, genetics, and the 'natural athlete': the resurgence of racial science", *Body and Society*, 9(2), pp. 75–95.

St Louis, B. (2004) "Sport and common sense racial science", *Leisure Studies*, 23(1), pp. 31–46.

Sugden, J. and Bairner, A. (1993) *Sport, sectarianism and society in a divided Ireland*, Leicester: Leicester University Press.

Sumerau, J.E. and Denise, E.J. (2018) "Obscuring oppression: racism, cissexism, and the persistence of social inequality", *Sociology of Race and Ethnicity*, 4(3), pp. 322–337.

Sutherland, S. (2017) "Intersections of race and gender in sport", in Nauright, J. and Wiggins, D.K. (Eds.), *Routledge handbook of sport, race and ethnicity*, London: Routledge.

Tamsut, F. (2021) "European football clubs tackle antisemitism", *DW*. Available: <https://www.dw.com/en/antisemitism-in-european-football-time-to-change-the-chants/a-59106242> [accessed on 1st October 2024].

Thuram, L. (2020) *White thinking – behind the mask of racial identity*, London: Legend Times Group.

Tobias, P. V. (1972 [1961]) "The meaning of race", in Baxter, P. and Sansom, B. (Eds.), *Race and social difference*, Harmondsworth: Penguin.

Udah, H. (2023) "Anti-black racism and othering: an exploration of the lived experience of black Africans who live in Australia", *Social Identities*, 29(2), pp. 185–204.

UNESCO (1965) "Biological aspects of race – a document of paramount importance", *The UNESCO Courier*, April. Available: <https://unesdoc.unesco.org/ark:/48223/pf0000078423> [accessed on 1st October 2024].

Van den Berghe, P. L. (2004) "Race: as synonym", in Cashmore, E. (Ed.), *Encyclopedia of race and ethnic studies*, London: Routledge.

Walz, M. (1995) "Nationalism", in Honderich, T. (Ed.), *The Oxford companion to philosophy*, Oxford: Oxford University Press.

Wiggins, D.K. and Nauright, J. (2017) "History of race and ethnicity in sports", in Nauright, J. and Wiggins, D.K. (Eds.), *Routledge handbook of sport, race and ethnicity*, London: Routledge.

Williams, J. (2001) *Cricket and race*, Oxford: Berg.

Wright, I. and McCarthy, P. (1996) *Mr Wright: the explosive autobiography of Ian Wright*, London: Harper Collins.

Chapter 3

England

Islamophobia in English professional and amateur football: A blind spot

Tom Taylor

English football has a problem that can no longer be ignored: Islamophobia. The hostility, prejudice and discrimination towards Muslims have become an integral part of the social fabric of English football culture and another blemish on its precarious reputation. The 2023/24 season represented a troubling milestone as the anti-discrimination organisation *Kick it Out* reported a 138% increase in Islamophobic incidents across English football compared to the previous season (Kick it Out, 2024a). Therefore, this chapter examines the emergence, development and manifestations of Islamophobia in English football with particular reference to its fan cultures. It will also deal with selected measures that have been, and need to be, taken to tackle the issue.

As a microcosm of society and a popular cultural sphere, football has long reflected wider social, cultural and political processes. It is an arena in which discourses and ideologies are reinforced and challenged (Burdsey, 2021). In Britain, Muslims and the religion of Islam have been positioned as an 'ultimate Other' (Said, 2003), especially over the previous three decades. In the aftermath of the World Trade Centre attacks in New York in September 2001, also known as the 9/11 attacks, and the 2005 bombings across numerous modes of London's transport, Muslims from a complex myriad of cultural and religious backgrounds have been cast as terrorists: their real and perceived religious and cultural practices have been constructed as a threat to, and as incompatible with, the British way of life (Hope Not Hate, 2018; Jones and Unsworth, 2022; Selod, Islam and Garner, 2024). A recent report further revealed how Muslim communities within British society are considered the 'second least' liked group (Jones and Unsworth, 2022).

Influential media discourses have exacerbated this scenario. Research has consistently highlighted how the British media often reduce Muslims and Islam to a coherent single entity and frame as something negative (Poole, 2002; Kabir, Huda Alkaff and Bourk, 2018). In December 2024, the Centre for Media Monitoring (CFMM) released the results from a two-year study on the right-wing news broadcasters, *GB News* (CFMM, 2024). The key findings showed that the organisation was 'overwhelmingly negative' towards Muslims and Islam, and that they fail to represent the heterogeneity of Muslim

DOI: 10.4324/9781003495970-3

This chapter has been made available under a CC-BY-NC-SA 4.0 license.

communities in Britain. Undoubtedly, these constructions influence public perceptions and consciousness as they digest and interpret top-down discourses. It is against this backdrop that the rise of Islamophobia in English football needs to be understood.

Islamophobia in football has so far received limited academic attention from sport sociologists and academics with a keen interest in this sport. Scholarly attention has justifiably focused on the experiences of British Asians at the grassroots level of the game and the discriminatory barriers that inhibit their progression to the higher echelons of professional football in England (Burdsey, 2007; Kilvington, 2016, 2019). British Asians are people of Asian descent, for example, from Bangladesh, India, Nepal, Pakistan and Sri Lanka, who hold British passports. A large proportion are Muslims. Kilvington (2016) noted how Islamophobia and anti-Muslim sentiment is widespread in grassroots football. Players are frequently subjected to derogatory language and 'racial' abuse by opposing players and managers, with the perpetrators often going unpunished. Yet, we know little about Islamophobic attitudes among football fans and how Islamophobia shapes discourses of other stakeholders.

This chapter is complemented by a select number of findings from my recent PhD thesis, which investigated England football fans' perceptions of, contact and experiences with Muslims, Islam and the Arabian Peninsula in the context of the 2022 FIFA Men's World Cup in Qatar. My research focused on the fans' constructions of Muslims and Islam, paying particular attention to how their experiences and attitudes reinforce or challenge wider Islamophobic discourses. To begin, however, the chapter examines the term and concept of Islamophobia by locating it within broader discussions of racialisation and Orientalism. After that, the chapter considers the manifestations of Islamophobia in English football and fan cultures.

Islamophobia, racialisation and Orientalism

The race equality and civil rights think tank *Runnymede Trust* is often credited with popularising the term Islamophobia. In 1997, in a report highlighting the British media's negative framing of Muslims and Islam, the think tank defined Islamophobia as the "unfounded hostility towards Islam. It also refers to the practical consequences of such hostility in unfair discrimination against Muslim individuals and communities" (Runnymede Trust, 1997, p. 4). As discussed within the introduction of this edited collection, *Runnymede Trust* has since developed their definition and continued their activism in tackling Islamophobia in Britain.

However, since Islamophobia has become infused within the public consciousness, debated on radio and television talk shows, features frequently on the news and social media, differing interpretations of the term have emerged. Anecdotally, a common argument perpetuated on social media, often by Islamophobes and right-wing commentators, is that a person cannot be Islamophobic because the suffix 'phobia' implies that an individual has a phobia towards Muslims and Islam based upon an irrational fear. Their assertion is that being suspicious, critical of, and fearing, Muslims and Islam is entirely rational, logical and justifiable, and therefore it is not a 'phobia'. Others claim that Islamophobia is not racism, does not exist and/or is a fictional term. Discursively, these objections function as a denial of prejudices, discriminatory attitudes, and/or 'racial' hostility towards Muslims and Islam.

Inextricably, Islamophobia cannot be detached or separated from the concept of 'race'. As Saha (2021) points out, ideas of 'race', particularly ideas of physical, cultural and religious differences, are ascribed to being or 'looking Muslim'. This is the racialisation process whereby perceived Muslim and Islamic practices acquire 'racial' meaning, a modus operandi that does not necessarily rely upon biological and somatic characteristics such as skin colour. In essence, it reduces a heterogeneous group of people, who engage in different cultural practices and have different religious preferences to a singular entity (Meer, 2013; Selod, Islam and Garner, 2024). Naber (2008) argued that in the aftermath of the 9/11 attacks in New York, the racialisation of Muslims and Islam was characterised by a myriad of 'racial' signifiers that were associated with *being* Muslim. This involved names, for example, Mohammed, or having dark skin, dress codes, for example, wearing a headscarf or *hijab* and suspected nations of origin, for example, Syria, Iraq or Pakistan. This is an evolving and dynamic process that is not fixed and contributes to the presence of Islamophobic racism across society.

Moreover, whilst 'race' has been embedded within many of the academic debates on Islamophobia and anti-Muslim prejudice, some scholars have argued that a distinction should be made between the two. The latter specifically denotes a hostility towards Muslims (Halliday, 2003) and implies it is less about Islam. But as Saha (2021) asserts, it positions Islamophobia also as something more acceptable, as a critique of Islam, rather than a prejudice towards Muslims. Another argument is that Islamophobia should be viewed as a contemporary phenomenon, a modern form of racism that emerged in the aftermath of the 9/11 attacks in New York (Allen, 2020). However, this approach ignores how Islamophobia today is shaped by the racialisation of Muslims at different times and in various contexts (Meer, 2013; Saha, 2021; Selod, Islam and Garner, 2024). Indeed, Islamophobia is not new, anti-Muslim and Islamic sentiment significantly pre-date our current understanding of discrimination towards Muslims.

Edward Said's formative text on Orientalism (2003), that was first published in 1978, provides a salient starting point to situate contemporary manifestations of Islamophobia. For Said (2003), Orientalism concerned how Britain, and the Western world more broadly, constructed knowledge on, what the author referred to, as the 'Orient' comprising initially of Arabs and Muslims. Later, in 1981, in his book Covering Islam (1997), he also included Islam.

Said (2003) convincingly demonstrated how the textual and visual representation of the Orient, especially during the colonial period, via literature and academia, compressed millions of different people, places and cultures into a homogenous entity. This construction further served to justify political and cultural domination (colonialism) of the Orient (Kumar, 2021). Ultimately, this produced an entire way of thinking within Britain and the West that is marked by the dichotomisation of the Orient and Britain/the West, with the former positioned as inferior to the latter.

For Said (2003), the construct of the Orient as a homogenous single entity had little ontological stability, rather, the author argued, the Orient was a figment of the imagination of Britain and the West. However, it became an ideological and 'racial' framework, in which Britain and the West viewed themselves as a dominant and civilised 'race' and ascribed ideas of physical and cultural differences to the Orient as backwards, exotic and inferior (Kumar, 2021; Saha, 2021). Several global events in the 1970s, such as the 1973 oil crises, the Iranian revolution in 1979, and the subsequent Iranian hostage crises led Said to develop his critique of Orientalism further. He specifically focused on how Britain and the West constructed and modified knowledge on Islam and the Islamic world. The Orient and Islam became situated as a threat to the Western world, depicted as oppressive, most visible in the treatment of women, considered irrational, lacking reason and logic, and were perceived to be the cause of worldwide conflicts, and as Said (1997) noted, Muslim men were portrayed as terrorists. These constructions have persisted and are embedded within contemporary manifestations of Islamophobia.

Muslims in Britain

Orientalism provided a salient foundation for the ideological, 'racial' and discursive nature of Islamophobia today. However, constructions of the Orient and Islam have changed over time. Several global and domestic events have reshaped and reconstructed how Islamophobia is understood. In Britain, Islamophobia arguably stems from, and is closely linked to, debates on Muslim migration into the country and their integration. The Honeyford Affair in 1985, for example, generated a heated public debate after a head teacher at a secondary school in Bradford criticised multicultural educational policies and the Muslim communities. A few years later, the Rushdie Affair in 1989, witnessed British Muslims take to the streets to oppose the publication of the Satanic Verses for its perceived blasphemy of Islam. The author, Salmon Rushdie, was issued a *fatwah*, a death sentence, by the Iranian Ayatollah Khomeini (Saha, 2021). Both events acted as a catalyst for 'race' relations as forms of a specific Islamophobia started to emerge. Discourses of an ethnic Other, for example, Asians or Pakistanis, were replaced by a discernible religious and Muslim Other.

More recently, the integration debate has been shaped by the Trojan Horse Affair in 2014, which involved an alleged Islamist plot to underpin school curriculums in Birmingham by an Islamist ethos, anti-LGBT protests by Muslims outside primary schools where teaching material touches upon LGBT stories, and Shamima Begum, whose British citizenship was revoked due to national security grounds based on her previous link to ISIS. In particular, ongoing narratives of 'Muslim grooming gangs' have led to the demonisation of Muslim communities. These narratives are loaded with 'racial' meaning as the issue, the organised sexual abuse and exploitation of children, is blamed on Muslims and Islam as if it is an exclusive cultural and religious practice (Cockbain and Tufail, 2020). Nonetheless, the above events have fuelled Islamophobic sentiment and promoted a suspicion of Muslim communities within Britain. Moreover, terror-related domestic incidents including the London bombings in 2005, the Manchester Arena bombing in 2016, and the Westminster Bridge attack in 2017, resulted in a spate of attacks on Muslim communities and significantly shaped how Muslims are nowadays constructed in British society (Selod, Islam and Garner, 2024).

It appears that the media have fuelled Islamophobia and anti-Muslim prejudice within Britain. Kabir, Huda Alkaff and Bourk (2018) highlighted how the print press, for example, *The Daily Mail* and *The Telegraph*, use negative language to describe Muslims and Islam, and position them as both a cultural threat to British culture and a physical threat to life itself. Furthermore, right-wing politicians and commentators often decry a loss of British identity and sensationalise the threat of an 'Islamic invasion'. This has led to some commentators sarcastically referring to the UK's capital city, London, as 'Londinistan' due to the city's Muslim population and Mayor, Sadiq Khan (Phillips, 2007). Selod, Islam and Garner (2024) note, this informs public sentiment and consciousness, and in the context of terror-related incidents gives rise to racialised state policies, such as the increased surveillance and suspicion of Muslim communities, that position Muslims outside of the nation-states imaginary.

In Britain, a significant manifestation of Islamophobia is gendered, as numerous narratives view Muslim men as terrorists, and Muslim women as oppressed victims of their Islamic faith (Selod, Islam and Garner, 2024). Wearing a *hijab* or veil is perceived as forced, but, paradoxically, as Ahmad (2011, p. 104) argued, the visible expression of women wearing a *hijab* has also become a symbol and evidence of "Muslims' unwillingness to integrate" into British society. This gendered discourse was also detectable in the language of former British Prime Minister, Boris Johnson. Writing in 2018 as Secretary of State for Foreign Affairs and Commonwealth Affairs for the Telegraph, Boris Johnson argued, he felt 'entitled' to expect women to remove face coverings when talking to him and that Muslim women looked like 'bank robbers' (Sa'di, 2021). Although these comments were criticised at the time, he did not face condemnation from his Conservative peers, with the comments seemingly acting as a green light for Islamophobia. In the weeks following

Boris Johnson's article, reports of Islamophobic attacks increased by 375% (TellMAMA, 2019).

However, as the Muslim population has developed within Britain, a slightly more complex but value-laden demographic has emerged (Selod, Islam and Garner, 2024). In the wake of terror-related incidents such as the aforementioned 9/11 attacks on the World Trade Centre, political and media discourses presented a dichotomous dualism between 'good' and 'bad' Muslims. Modood (2005) referred to the former as 'corporate Muslims'. They are perceived to represent British values and characterised by liberal views, tolerance and inclusivity. Some of them, British Muslims as well as non-British Muslims, are widely celebrated and often appear on our television screens. For example, Mo Farah, a Somali-born British Muslim was considered a symbol of British multiculturalism following his Olympic successes as a long-distance runner and has since appeared on numerous television shows. In politics, Sadiq Kahn, the mayor of London, was successfully elected with overwhelming majorities on three occasions in 2016, 2021 and 2024. What this begins to illustrate is that public sentiments, as Hall (1980) argued, are subject to interpretation and negotiation. Moderate portrayals of both Muslims and Islam indeed exist and begin to challenge the assumptions that Muslims represent a cultural and physical threat to the British way of life (Selod, Islam and Garner, 2024).

Despite this complex picture and framing of Muslims and Islam within Britain, the varying communities are still positioned as an ultimate Other. TellMama, an organisation that measures Islamophobia in society and supports those who experience anti-Muslim hate, shared with *The Guardian* that between 7 October 2023 and 30 September 2024, they recorded 4,971 incidents of anti-Muslims attacks – the highest in the past 14 years (Gohil, 2024). The organisation further suggested that the ongoing conflict between Israel and Palestine since the Hamas-led attack on Israel on 7 October 2023 may be an explanation for a rise in anti-Islamic sentiment. It is within these developments that I situate discussions of Islamophobia within English football and fan culture.

Manifestations of Islamophobia in English football

Discrimination and the Othering of Muslims and Muslim communities in sport is nothing new. Williams (2020), for example, described how members of the Men's Pakistani cricket team and Pakistan itself was Othered by the British media throughout the 1980s and 1990s when the England cricket team toured the country. Pakistani players were labelled as cheats and painted as villains, while Pakistan was constructed as a backwards and unpalatable place to visit. However, how Islamophobia manifests in sport and football, in particular, has so far escaped significant academic attention. In addition, those at the heart of this sport, particularly football's governing body, the

Football Association (FA), have ignored and downplayed the prevalence of Islamophobia. Yunus Lunat, the first British Muslim to sit on the FA Council, for example, comments, "football seems to have a blind spot when it comes to Islamophobia" (Sky Sports, 2024a).

One reason that may explain the existence of this 'blind spot' is the absence of critical media, reporting mechanisms and researchers in the lower echelons of the game, that is in grassroots football (Kilvington, 2016, 2019; Awan and Zempi, 2021). In this context, Islamophobic racism reflects wider patterns of racism in that it is more entrenched at this level of the game compared to professional football (Lusted, 2009). Primarily this is because at the highest levels of the game a set of specific safeguards is in place that often protects players and fans within football stadiums. Various surveillance measures, stewards and the presence of police officers in and around grounds on match days also act as deterrents. As the problem fails to generate attention in the grassroots sphere, public consciousness is very limited, especially in comparison with identifiable incidents of racism towards Black players and fans within professional football.

Research that has explored issues of discrimination at grassroots football has often focused on the experiences of British Asians, many of whom identify as Muslims. Despite the popular appeal of football amongst the British Asian community, they face considerable barriers just to participate and are underrepresented at the professional level (Burdsey, 2007; Kilvington, 2019). Kilvington (2016) argued British Asians are often overlooked by scouting systems who wrongly perceive British Asians and their bodies to be incompatible with the physical demands of football. These are, of course, prejudicial and stereotypical views, which Burdsey (2007) has comprehensively challenged. However, more importantly, Kilvington (2019) considers them to be a form of covert racism towards Muslims.

The continued presence and extent of Islamophobia in grassroots football was laid out in a report by researchers from Birmingham City University. Awan and Zempi (2021) revealed how players experienced Islamophobic abuse from members of the public, opposing players, managers and coaches. They recalled being targeted due to their perceived religious and cultural identities and being called 'Paki bombers' and 'fucking Muslims'. Similarly, in 2019, the former Arsenal and Queens Park Rangers youth academy player Taff Rahman discussed abuse he received in the aftermath of the 9/11 attacks in New York. Speaking to Sky Sports News, Rahman noted how opposing players would see his name on the team sheet, and, in the tunnel before the game, announced "let's get the Taliban" (Trehan, 2019). Such references to terrorism reinforce derogatory stereotypes about Muslim men, which associate their perceived Muslimness with terrorism.

As in wider society, Islamophobia at the grassroots level is also gendered. In 2024, Iqra Ismail, the former captain of Somalia's national football team, was prevented from participating in a Greater London Women's football league match for wearing tracksuit bottoms. She was informed by the referee that it was a requirement to wear shorts to participate. Ismail refused on religious grounds, and subsequently became ineligible. The FA's official guidelines are ambivalent on this matter. On the one hand, they stipulate tracksuit bottoms can only be worn by goalkeepers, but on the other, suggest leniency and flexibility in how the guidelines are interpreted. Nonetheless, this is a befitting example of gendered Islamophobia. It follows trends over the past two decades of governing Muslim women's bodies, like FIFA's *hijab* ban from 2007 to 2014, a policy Ahmad (2011, p. 108) rightly described as "Islamophobia in action". Muslim women are thus, Othered and positioned as incompatible with English footballing culture. It is noteworthy that the FA later issued an apology to Iqra Ismail stressing its commitment to diversity and inclusivity, and emphasising that players are allowed to wear sports clothes that accommodate their religious preferences.

Returning briefly to Awan and Zempi's (2021) report, the Muslim players interviewed alluded to a lack of professional Muslim players as one reason for the existence of Islamophobia at the grassroots level. In recent years, there has been a noticeable shift of Muslim professional football players applying their trade across Europe's top divisions. In the English Premier League, Hylton, Kilvington, Long et al. (2024) observed that there are now far more Muslim professional players than ever before. During the 2024/25 season, most clubs employed at least one player who identified as Muslim. Players such as Mohamed Salah, Thomas Partey, Idrissa Gueye, Noussair Mazraoui and Rayan Alt Nouri have all been celebrated by supporters and heard their name reverberate around the stands. Nevertheless, professional English football and fan culture has been a site for the expression of overt Islamophobia. Burdsey (2021) reminds us in relation to Black, male footballers that "the consumption of their sporting prowess occurs equally within invidious, discriminatory and exploitive forms" (p. 39). This also applies to the complexity and contradictions of Islamophobia within fan cultures: on one hand, fans celebrate Muslim players, but on the other, they use discriminatory language towards them. Therefore, it is a site where 'racial' and ideological discourses are reinforced both in the stands and online.

Ahmad (2011) characterised the 'Mido Affair' in 2007 as a pivotal event that brought the concept of Islamophobia (briefly) into the spotlight of football and fan culture. In a match between Middlesbrough and rivals Newcastle United, fans of the latter directed a chant towards the formers Egyptian forward Ahmed Hossam Hussaein Abdelhamid, also known as Mido, referring to him as a 'terrorist bomber'. Following the incident, Millward (2008) explored how fans of both teams responded to it online. He revealed that both sets of fans used Islamophobic slurs and dismissed the choice of words as nothing more than friendly banter between rival fan groups. Notably, Newcastle United FC failed to comment or condemn the incident and the supporters went unpunished. For Ahmad (2011), the muteness of the club and football's governing body exemplified how Islamophobia is often shrugged off and not dealt with in the same severity as racism or antisemitism.

The intertwining of Muslim players with terrorism is a particularly insidious Islamophobic chant used by fans. Like in wider socio-political and media discourses, reducing all Muslim men to a terrorist frame serves to position them as violent individuals and a physical threat based on their religious identities (Kumar, 2021). Liverpool's Mohamed Salah, an Egyptian born Muslim and widely celebrated as one of the top professional players of his generation, has persistently been subjected to this frame. In 2019, three Chelsea FC supporters were denied entry to watch Slavia Praha versus Chelsea after a 19-second video emerged on social media showing the young men chanting "Salah is a bomber" (Fifield, 2019). A few months earlier, a West Ham supporter was recorded chanting "Salah, you fucking Muslim, you fucking Muslim cunt" (Steiner, 2019). More recently, as reported by the BBC, an Everton fan was handed a three-year banning order from football for racially abusing Salah during the local derby between Liverpool and Everton in 2023 (BBC, 2024). Within these examples, Salah's faith, identity and perceived Muslimness are condensed by supporters who take an essentialised view on Muslims.

Although one study claims Salah's arrival in Liverpool has helped to reduce anti-Muslim hate crimes (Alrababa'h, Marble, Mousa et al., 2021), it is noteworthy that Liverpool fans' themselves have been accused of legitimising Islamophobic racism and Othering Muslims. In a chant that can be heard around the stands of Anfield football stadium on a match day, Liverpool fans sing,

> Mo Salah, Mo Salah, if he's good enough for you, he's good enough for me, if he scores another few, then I'll be Muslim too, he's sitting in the mosque, that's where I want to be.

Fans and other commentators have widely praised this chant, claiming that it is an example of inclusivity, multiculturalism and a challenge to Islamophobic assumptions. However, a more critical interpretation suggests it underscores a cynical and deep-seated hatred towards Muslims. Selod, Islam and Garner (2024) argue the chant implies "sitting in a mosque is constructed as an extreme act that fans are willing to do, if Salah continues to perform well" (p. 31). It suggests, Salah can only ever be tolerated, as long as wider Oriental and 'racial' structures remain unchallenged. He will never truly be accepted as one of *them*: Salah's perceived Muslimness still positions him as Other and inferior, and is something *they* can only temporarily overlook, if he continues to score goals. It is also contextual as the earlier examples illustrate, as some opposing fans reject Salah and are openly Islamophobic towards him.

In another example, two Middlesbrough supporters were found guilty of ripping pages out of a Qur'an and pretending to set it alight during a game against Birmingham City in 2014. One of the supporters received a fine, while the other was banned from every football ground in the country for three years (BBC, 2014). Although the perpetrators were punished, and the incident widely condemned by the footballing authorities, anti-racism organisations and other fans, this example underscores the presence and severity of anti-Muslim and Islamic hostility in fan cultures. Fans can thus be seen rejecting Islam and Muslims, which suggests that in some corners of English footballing culture, Muslims, including Salah, are considered to be a "threat to football's hegemonic whiteness" (Kilvington, 2016, p. 65).

With the notable exceptions of Millward (2008) and Alrababa'h, Marble, Mousa et al. (2021), research into football fans' perceptions of, and attitudes towards, Muslims and Islam remains scarce. It is critical to develop a detailed and thorough understanding of the role of Islamophobia in the world of fans. Not only does this complement scholarship on British Asian Muslim experiences in grassroots football, but also it additionally illustrates how socio-political and ideological frames are constructed, reproduced or challenged within fan discourses. For example, most of the England fans I interviewed for my doctoral research were very aware that the 2022 FIFA Men's World Cup was to be staged within a non-secular Islamic society for the first time. Their responses simultaneously reinforced wider Islamophobic discourses and challenged them,

> I'm not particular for or against [Islam]. I mean, there has been an anti-Islamic undercurrent in this country, probably since the bombings in London. I worked for an American firm, albeit in this country, when the Twin Towers [of the World Trade Centre in New York] got done. So clearly, the Americans didn't like Islam very much. Um, then we got the London bombings, so that became [pause] I mean, the country became anti-Islamic, didn't it? Um, you get things like 'oh, Islam is the religion of peace,' so why are you putting bombs everywhere?
>
> (Ken, 9 March 2023)

Although the participant claims that he is not anti-Islamic, his discourse is loaded with Islamophobic sentiment and frames. For example, Ken, associates Islam with violence, that is the 9/11 attacks and the London bombings, and challenges the belief that Islam is a religion of peace. Not only does this reinforce wider socio-political Islamophobic discourses, but it also reflects the language used by football fans who have targeted Muslim players like Mo Salah. However, fan culture is not static, it can also serve as a site of contestation, as Peter, another England fan, argued,

> Having worked in that community [Muslim], they get a raw deal. Islam gets a raw deal in the British press. You know, it's a peaceful religion; it's a good religion; it's a religion for good, but that's not the way it's painted in the British press.
>
> (Peter, 27 April 2023)

Peter is defensive of Islam and critical of the way the British media frame Muslims and Islam, as he acknowledges that they are portrayed negatively. Based on his lived experiences, Peter strongly rejects the idea that Islam is inherently violent and takes an 'oppositional reading' to dominant media constructions (Hall, 1980). Not only does this indicate a level of sympathy, but it highlights the complex nature of the integration debate in Britain as differing White voices show solidarity and support for Muslim communities. English fan culture can provide a rich and significant site to investigate how Islamophobia is understood and how it manifests within English football. It permits a lens into how discursive socio-political and ideological processes operate at a micro level amongst fan discourses but may also show that people's understanding and framing of differences is inherently complex, subjective and context specific.

Islamophobia on social media

Islamophobia in English football is not limited to the grassroots game or the fans in the stands of football stadiums; it manifests and intersects with the online world of football fandom. Millward's (2008) analysis of online forum responses to the 'Mido Affair' was an important (early) contribution in highlighting this intersection. However, the growth and development of social media sites, such as Facebook, X (formally known as Twitter) and Instagram, have arguably assisted and exacerbated, anti-Muslim discrimination in football and wider society (Kilvington, Hylton, Long et al., 2022). For example, despite a paucity of high-profile incidents of media coverage of online Islamophobia within the professional game, online manifestations of Islamophobia accounted for 66% of reported Islamophobic incidents in the 2023/2024 season in *Kick it Out's* latest report (Kick it Out, 2024a).

Awan and Zempi's (2020) report of online Islamophobia in British society more generally and found that a rise in anti-Muslim online discrimination often coincides with 'trigger events'. These are characterised by local, national and international incidents such as the Manchester Arena bombings in 2016, that can instantly evoke an anti-Muslim and anti-Islamic response online, as well as offline. In football, Hylton, Kilvington, Long et al.'s study (2024) highlights how trigger events can occur when professional clubs show support for cultural events or campaigns on their social media platforms, such as Eid Mubarak – a religious festival marking the end of one month's fasting, Ramadan, that is celebrated by Muslims around the world. They observed how club support is swiftly followed by two or three days of online abuse and backlash. It can also manifest between rival fans in response to the on-field action during matches. For example, in 2019, Leicester City's midfielder Hamza Choudhury, a practicing Muslim, received online 'racial' abuse following a dangerous challenge on Liverpool's Mo Salah, which left Salah with a minor injury (The Guardian, 2019).

Quite recently, in December 2024, a Conservative MP, Robert Jenrick, used his social media platform, X, to respond to a controversy involving Ipswich Town's Sam Morsy and Crystal Palace's Marc Guehi. The former refused to wear a captain's armband in support of the Premier Leagues Rainbow Laces LGBT campaign based on his religious beliefs as a Muslim, while the latter displayed "I love Jesus" and "Jesus loves you" messages. Morsy's decision was supported by Ipswich Town, whereas Guehi received warnings on two separate occasions by the FA for displaying a religious symbol on his shirt as it constituted an act that is banned by the sport's governing body. In response, Jenrick posted "Why is a Christian player being treated differently to a Muslim player?" (Rumsby and Holl-Allen, 2024). This arguably represents a not-so-subtle manifestation of online Islamophobia. Not only does he purposely ignore the FA's rules and regulations, Jenrick uses divisive rhetoric that reinforces the idea that Britain is somehow losing its identity and is being replaced by Muslims and Islam, thus posing a threat to the British way of life.

Interrelated to the above point, supporters also use social media and other platforms to discuss and debate the very nature and existence of Islamophobia within professional football. Like Millward (2008), Kilvington, Hylton, Long et al. (2022) found that fans "fail to comprehend the complexity of racism and Islamophobia" (p. 855). They tend to deny and downplay racism and Islamophobia in football and often characterise incidents as non-racist. Doidge (2015) found that it is often the case that football fans' online contributions, responses and engagements with social media forums replicate their offline biases. A player care consultant, who is responsible for many of the non-sporting and non-medical aspects of a player's time at a club, at Burnley FC, for example, was recently issued a warning by the FA for liking several offensive and Islamophobic social media posts shortly after the Hamas-led attacks on Israel in October 2023 (Sky Sports, 2024b). These examples suggest that any attempt to understand and address Islamophobia within English football requires acknowledging not only its presence offline but also its online manifestations.

Tackling Islamophobia in English football: challenges and opportunities

The profile and scope of anti-racism campaigns over the past two decades have grown exponentially (Burdsey, 2021). Campaigns such as the Premier League's *No Room for Racism* initiative and the FA's *Love Football, Protect the Game* campaign are now an integral part of the fabric of English football and have unquestionably helped to raise awareness of racist discrimination within the game. However, Islamophobia presents another challenge to the various stakeholders of the football industry. There are claims that the authorities do not take it as seriously as racism and are not doing enough to tackle this problem (Awan and Zempi, 2021). Furthermore, the football authorities' reliance upon grouping Islamophobia under the rubric of wider anti-racism initiatives and institutional policies fundamentally fails to acknowledge the distinctiveness, idiosyncrasies and specific manifestations of it. Therefore, it is necessary to take three important initial steps and also reconsider existing strategies that aim to increase diversity.

First, as a distinct form of racism (Saha, 2021), it has become increasingly important to distinguish the practices, manifestations and underlying processes of Islamophobia in order to address the problem. Islamophobia needs to be explicitly positioned within the institutional discourses and policies of the footballing authorities.

Second, it is strategically vital to adopt a comprehensive and user-friendly definition of the term. *Kick it Out* and the *Islamophobia Working Group* (IWG), chaired by the former Conservative politician Baroness Sayeeda Warsi, lobbied football's governing bodies in March 2024 to adopt the *All-Party Parliamentary Group on British Muslims* 2018 definition. It acknowledges that Islamophobia is "rooted in racism and is a type of racism that targets expressions of Muslimness or perceived Muslimness" (2018, p. 11). *Kick it Out* and the IWG argue it will "enable them to deal effectively with any anti-Muslim hate directed at its clubs, personnel and participants" and will "make day-to-day assessments of whether certain behaviour is racially aggravated or not" (Kick it Out, 2024b). This definition advocated for by *Kick it Out* already has parliamentary and governmental support in Britain, with several political parties, like the ruling Labour Party and Liberal Democrats, adopting the definition within their policies. Whether the FA include a working definition in their forthcoming strategy remains to be seen. However, it would serve to empower Muslims within English football, providing them with a newfound confidence that their concerns are taken seriously. Likewise, it would represent a significant step in challenging the 'racial' prejudices and stereotypes operating at the grassroots and professional levels of the game.

Third, another challenge associated with tackling Islamophobia is characterised by an inconsistency between professional English football and the grassroots game. In the higher echelons, fans and managers recently witnessed the drastic consequences of being Islamophobic. In 2023, John Yems, the former Crawley Town manager, was banned from football for three years after using offensive, racist and Islamophobic language. However, participants of Awan and Zempi's study argue that not enough attention is paid by the FA to combat anti-Muslim discrimination and Islamophobia at the amateur level. One participant commented, "you need a campaign alongside racism because that is working, and they take that seriously unlike Islamophobia" (2021, p. 8). There is, thus, a view amongst British Muslims that their experiences at the lower levels of football are ignored.

In addition to these three key measures that lay the foundations for more differentiated and focused awareness-raising and other initiatives, the FA needs to rethink and adjust its policies that aim to make football more inclusive and diverse. So far, the FA's institutional approach has centred primarily upon representation and inclusion of British Asians at all levels of the game. In 2015, football's governing body in England launched *Bringing Opportunities to Communities: Asian Inclusion Strategy*. It was the first initiative dedicated to promoting equal opportunities for 'Asians' in English football and promoting diversity more broadly (Kilvington, 2019; Football Association, 2023). However, a cursory glance at the latest evaluation report of this strategy suggests the approach has had a limited impact on increasing participation. For example, in 2019, the FA reported that 12.9 per cent of known players within men's grassroots football were from an 'Asian' background but in 2023 that figure had dropped to 10 per cent. For women, the statistics are slightly more optimistic: during the same time period, the FA reported a 2.3 per cent increase in participation. Homogenously grouping 'Asians' obscures the challenges faced by differing communities and effectively relegates Islamophobic concerns and incidents at the grassroots level. Further, diversity and inclusion campaigns, as Burdsey (2021) has argued, simply serve to acknowledge structural 'racial' inequalities within football, without addressing and challenging the root causes of racism or discrimination. Not adopting a definition of Islamophobia provides an example of this, as the footballing authorities are *seen* to be pro-active but have yet to critically challenge the Islamophobia grassroots players experience.

A recent development within the European footballing industry more generally, and within England in particular, that can act as a site of contestation where dominant and discriminatory discourses can be tentatively challenged or reinforced, relates to the growing influence of Arabian Peninsula states in professional football (Taylor, Burdsey and Jarvis, 2023). Millward (2011) argued supporters of Manchester City embraced the investment from an Abu Dhabi backed consortium in 2009. To date, the success and longevity of the ownership has helped to develop and stimulate intergroup engagements between the fans and their non-secular owners. Similarly, since Newcastle United were acquired by a Saudi-led consortium in 2021, which was financially supported by the state's Public Investment Fund (PIF), fans have been seen waving Saudi Arabia flags and wearing white *thawbs*, traditional long-sleeved, ankle-length Saudi dresses, accompanied by *Keffiyeh* scarfs at matches (Brown, 2021). Of course, both takeovers have been justifiably scrutinised and are inherently problematic. However, these symbolic gestures and growing ties can temporarily act as a site within fan culture for an awareness and understanding of different Muslim people and cultures.

Interrelated to the above point is the presence and popularity of outstanding Muslim professional players in the Premier League. Although he was subjected to Islamophobic abuse from opposing supporters on several occasions, Mo Salah, for example, also provides a sense of optimism. Preliminary findings drawing on hate crime statistics by Alrababa'h, Marble, Mousa et al. (2021) suggest the player's arrival in Liverpool had a positive impact on fans' attitudes towards Muslims and may have contributed to a reduction of faith-based hate crimes in the city. This claim, however, is not unproblematic as I discussed earlier in relation to some chants from Liverpool fans that featured Mo Salah. Rather, it can potentially provide a complex lens into better understanding and reducing anti-Muslim or Islamophobic racism in fan culture by engaging with players and developing relations with club owners.

Conclusion

This chapter has identified various manifestations of Islamophobia within English football and fan culture in the context of Orientalism and racialisation. This phenomenon is not new and appears to be growing. It can only be fully understood against the socio-demographic composition of English society and the widespread treatment of the complex and multi-layered Muslim communities as a single entity combined with the vilification of Muslim men. The chapter has also touched upon England football fans' constructions of Muslims and Islam and outlined selected approaches that have been and need to be taken to reduce Islamophobia in football. As Islamophobia in English football remains under-researched, only cautious conclusions can be drawn. Firstly, Islamophobia appears to be prevalent and deeply rooted at all levels of the game since it has emerged and grown over the past two decades. Secondly, it appears to be particularly widespread in grassroots football as British Asian Muslims face numerous structural barriers to participate in the recreational game and are severely underrepresented in professional football. There is also a gendered element as Muslim women's bodies are governed by Western liberal values, and Muslim women are often Othered, due to their conspicuous dress code. Thirdly, Islamophobia is becoming more common and noticeable in professional football, both offline and online, as selected players are racialised by some fans. They use 'racial' and religious stereotypes that associate Muslim players with violent extremism and thereby conflating their perceived 'Muslimness' with terror. Finally, discussions with England fans confirm that fan culture is a complex site where top-down stereotypes and prejudicial discourses are both reinforced and challenged. This suggests that Islamophobia in fan culture is not static but rather subjective, dynamic and context-specific. There is an urgent need for the footballing authorities and other stakeholders to take Islamophobia seriously, and reconsider and modify current initiatives and campaigns as they fall short of challenging dominant 'racial' structures and ideologies. As a starting point, the FA would be well advised to implement the definition of Islamophobia developed by *Kick it Out* and the parliamentary *Islamophobia Working Group*. That would give the victims of Islamophobic abuse, at least, a sense of recognition, although much more has to follow.

References

Ahmad, A. (2011) "British Muslim female experiences in football: Islam, identity and the *Hijab*", in Burdsey, D. (Ed.), *Race, ethnicity and football: persisting debates and emerging issues*, Oxon: Routledge.

All Party Parliamentary Group on British Muslims (APPG) (2018) *Islamophobia defined: the inquiry into a working definition of Islamophobia*, London: APPG. Available: <https://static1.squarespace.com/static/599c3d2febbd1a90cffdd8a9/t/5bfd1ea3352f531a6170ceee/1543315109493/Islamophobia+Defined.pdf> [accessed on 19th December 2024].

Allen, C. (2020) *Reconfiguring Islamophobia: a radical rethinking of a contested concept*, Leicester: Palgrave Macmillan.

Alrababa'h, A., Marble, W., Mousa, S. and Siegel, A. (2021) "Can exposure to celebrities reduce prejudice? The effect of Mohamed Salah on Islamophobic behaviors and attitudes", *American Political Science Review*, 115(4), pp. 1111–1128.

Awan, I. and Zempi, I. (2020) *Offline and online experiences of anti-Muslim crime. Special rapporteur on freedom of religion or belief*, TellMaMA. Available: <https://tellmamauk.org/wp-content/uploads/2017/05/We-Fear-For-Our-Lives.pdf> [accessed on 19th December 2024].

Awan, I. and Zempi, I. (2021) *How the 'beautiful game' turned to hate: why Islamophobia has creeped into grassroots football*, Birmingham: Birmingham City University. Available: <https://bcuassets.blob.core.windows.net/docs/awan-and-zempi-report-11-feb-2021-132593302460533798.pdf> [accessed on 15th November 2024].

BBC (2024) *Football fan banned for Mohamed Salah abuse and disaster taunts*. Available: <https://www.bbc.co.uk/news/uk-england-merseyside-68288991> [accessed on 20th November 2024].

Brown, M. (2021) "Newcastle urge fans to avoid 'culturally inappropriate' clothing at games", *The Guardian*. Available: <https://www.theguardian.com/football/2021/oct/20/newcastle-urge-fans-to-avoid-culturally-inappropriate-clothing-at-games> [accessed on 20th September 2022].

Burdsey, D. (2007) *British Asians and football: culture, identity, exclusion*, Oxon: Routledge.

Burdsey, D. (2021) *Racism and English football: for club and country*, Oxon: Routledge.

Centre for Media Monitoring (CFMM) (2024) "GB news a snapshot of anti-Muslim hate". Available: <https://cfmm.org.uk/gbnews-report-2024/> [accessed on 13th December 2024].

Cockbain, E. and Tufail, W. (2020) "Failing victims, fuelling hate: challenging the harms of the 'Muslim grooming gangs' narrative", *Race & Class*, 61(3), pp. 3–32.

Doidge, M. (2015) "'If you jump up and down, Balotelli dies': racism and player abuse in Italian football", *International Review for the Sociology of Sport*, 50(3), pp. 249–264.

Fifield, D. (2019) "Chelsea fans barred from game after 'bomber' chants against Mohamed Salah", *The Guardian*. Available: <https://www.theguardian.com/football/2019/apr/11/chelsea-fans-barred-bomber-chants-mo-salah> [accessed on 20th November 2024].

Football Association (2023) *Bringing opportunities to communities (phase 2): the FA Asian inclusion plan – progress report, year 3*, London: Football Association.

Gohil, N. (2024) "Record amounts of anti-Muslim abuse reported in UK since 7 October attacks", *The Guardian*. Available: <https://www.theguardian.com/news/2024/oct/04/record-amount-of-anti-muslim-abuse-reported-in-uk-since-7-october-attacks> [accessed on 9th November 2024].

The Guardian (2019) "Leicester contact police over racist abuse aimed at Hamza Choudhury", *The Guardian*. Available: <https://www.theguardian.com/football/2019/oct/05/leicester-contact-police-racist-abuse-choudhury> [accessed on 19th December 2024].

Hall, S. (1980) "Encoding/decoding", in Hall, S. Dobson, D., Lowe, A. and Willis, P. (Eds.), *Culture, media, language*, London: Routledge.

Halliday, F. (2003) *Islam and the myth of confrontation: religion and politics in the Middle East*, London: Tauris.

Hope Not Hate (2018) *Britain divided*, London. Available: <https://www.hopenothate.org.uk/wp-content/uploads/2018/04/Britain-Divided-50-years-on.pdf> [accessed on 5th February 2021].

Hylton, K., Kilvington, D., Long, J., Bond, A. and Chaudry, I. (2024) "Dear prime minister, Mr Musk and Mr Zuckerberg! the challenge of social media and platformed racism in the English premier league and football league", *International Review for the Sociology of Sport*, pp. 1–24. Available:<https://journals.sagepub.com/doi/pdf/10.1177/10126902241234282> [accessed on 4th December 2024].

Jones, S. and Unsworth, A. (2022) *The dinner table prejudice: Islamophobia in contemporary Britain*, Birmingham: University of Birmingham. Available: <https://www.birmingham.ac.uk/documents/college-artslaw/ptr/90172-univ73-islamophobia-in-the-uk-report-final.pdf> [accessed on 4th December 2022].

Kabir, S., Huda Alkaff, S. and Bourk, M. (2018) "Iconizing "Muslim terrorism" in a British newspaper and public perception", *Journal of Muslim Minority Affairs*, 38(2), pp. 179–197.

Kick it Out (2024a) 2023/2024 incident reporting, London: Kick it Out. Available: <https://www.kickitout.org/sites/default/files/2024-07/2023-24_Incident%20Reporting_2307_FINAL.pdf> [accessed on 15th November 2024].

Kick it Out (2024b) *Kick it Out calls on football to adopt working definition of Islamophobia*. Available: <https://www.kickitout.org/news-media/kick-it-out-calls-football-adopt-working-definition-islamophobia#:~:text=The%20definition%20sets%20out%20how,of%20Muslimness%20or%20perceived%20Muslimness> [accessed on 9th November 2024].

Kilvington, D. (2016) *British Asians, exclusion, and the football industry*, Oxon: Routledge.

Kilvington, D. (2019) "Two decades and little change: British Asians, football and calls for action", *Soccer & Society*, 20(4), pp. 584–601.

Kilvington, D., Hylton, K., Long, J. and Bond, A. (2022) "Investigating online football forums: a critical examination of participants' responses to football related racism and Islamophobia", *Soccer & Society*, 23(8), pp. 849–864.

Kumar, D. (2021) *Islamophobia and the politics of empire: 20 years after 9/11*, London: Verson Books.

Lusted, J. (2009) "Playing games with 'race': understanding resistance to 'race' equality initiatives in English local football governance", *Soccer & Society*, 10(6), pp. 722–739.

Meer, N. (2013) "Racialization and religion: race, culture and difference in the study of antisemitism and Islamophobia", *Ethnic and Racial Studies*, 36(3), pp. 385–398.

Millward, P. (2008) "Rivalries and racisms: 'closed' and 'open' Islamophobic dispositions amongst football supporters", *Sociological Research Online*, 13(6), pp. 14–30.

Millward, P. (2011) *The global football league*, Basingstoke: Palgrave Macmillan.

Modood, T. (2005) *Multicultural politics: racism, ethnicity, and Muslims in Britain*, Edinburgh: Edinburgh University Press.

Naber, N. (2008) "'Look, Mohammed the terrorist is coming!' Cultural racism, nation-based racism, and the intersectionality of oppressions after 9/11", in Jamel,

A. and Naber, N. (Eds.), *Race and Arab Americans before and after 9/11: from invisible citizens to visible subjects*, New York: Syracuse University Press.

Phillips, H. (2007) *Londonistan*, New York: Encounter.

Poole, E. (2002) *Reporting Islam: media representation of British Muslims*, London: Tauris.

Rumsby, B. and Holl-Allen, G. (2024) "FA accused of 'two-tier response' as MPs weigh in on Guehi-Morsy armband row", *The Telegraph*. Available: <https://www.telegraph.co.uk/football/2024/12/04/marc-guehi-escapes-fa-punishment-breaking-rules-armband/> [accessed on 19th December 2024].

Runnymede Trust (1997) *Islamophobia: a challenge for us all*, Report for the Runnymede Trust Commission on British Muslims and Islamophobia.

Sa'di, A. (2021) "Orientalism in a globalised world: said in the twenty-first century", *Third World Quarterly*, 42(11), pp. 2505–2520.

Saha, A. (2021) *Race, culture and media*, London: SAGE.

Said, E. (1997) *Covering Islam: how the media and experts determine how we see the rest of the world*, London: Vintage.

Said, E. (2003) *Orientalism*, London: Penguin Books.

Selod, S., Islam, I. and Garner, S. (2024) *A global racial enemy: Muslims and 21st-century racism*, Cambridge: Polity Press.

Sky Sports (2024a) *Football has a blind spot when it comes to Islamophobia, says first Muslim FA council member Yunus Lunat*. Available: <https://www.skysports.com/football/news/11095/13147737/football-has-a-blind-spot-when-it-comes-to-islamophobia-says-first-muslim-fa-council-member-yunus-lunat> [accessed on 19th November 2024].

Sky Sports (2024b) *FA issues warning to Burnley player care consultant for liking Islamophobic posts on social media*. Available: <https://www.skysports.com/football/news/11708/13145221/fa-issues-warning-to-burnley-player-care-consultant-for-liking-islamophobic-posts-on-social-media> [accessed on 9th November 2024].

Steiner, J. (2019) "West Ham and police investigate Islamophobic abuse of Mohamed Salah", *The Guardian*. Available: <https://www.theguardian.com/football/2019/feb/06/west-ham-police-investigating-alleged-islamophobic-abuse-mo-salah> [accessed on 9th November 2024].

Taylor, T., Burdsey, D. and Jarvis, N. (2023) "A critical review on sport and the Arabian Peninsula – the current state of play and future directions", *International Journal of Sport Policy and Politics*, 15(2), pp. 367–383.

TellMAMA (2019) *Islamophobic attacks in the UK rose 'significantly' after Boris Johnson's controversial comments comparing veiled Muslim women to letterboxes, watchdog reveals*. Available: <https://tellmamauk.org/press/islamophobic-attacks-in-uk-rose-significantly-after-boris-johnsons-controversial-comments-comparing-veiled-muslim-women-to-letterboxes-watchdog-reveals/> [accessed on 19th November 2024].

Trehan, D. (2019) *Taff Rahman opens up on Islamophobia and racist abuse suffered as a player*. Available: <https://www.skysports.com/football/news/11095/11797278/taff-rahman-opens-up-on-islamophobia-and-racist-abuse-suffered-as-a-player> [accessed on 15th November 2024].

Williams, J. (2020) "'Paki Cheats!' postcolonial tensions in England-Pakistan cricket", in Bale, J. and Cronin, M. (Eds.), *Sport and postcolonialism*, Oxon: Routledge.

Chapter 4

France

Les Bleus and the Republic: Diversity, difference and discrimination

Jonathan Ervine

France's constitution and political culture

Recent decades have seen football in France praised as a symbol of a country that is inclusive and tolerant, yet it has also featured in highly discriminatory discourses. When seeking to understand how sport and discrimination, in particular racism, are discussed in a French context, one must first make sense of how such debates are often shaped by France's constitution and political culture. This chapter will begin by mapping out how key elements of the French model of citizenship shape discussions of equality and diversity, and the impact this has on combatting discrimination. Having explored this conceptual framework, it will then examine several key events during a period of just over a quarter of a century. This will begin in 1998, the year when France hosted and won the FIFA Men's World Cup, an event portrayed as being of great socio-political significance. As we will see in the first of three main parts of this chapter, the diverse composition of the French playing squad was viewed by many observers as symbolising a modern tolerant country and the success of the French model of integration. However, it will also be shown that the triumph obscured a more complex and potentially troubling reality that provided a very different vision of social cohesion in France. The second main part of this chapter will demonstrate that the last decade and a half has seen a shift in the nature of political discourses which have been evoked in discussions of the French men's national football team. Most notably, there has been an increase in the use of discriminatory rhetoric. The third and final main part of this chapter will explore socio-political reasons why France's 2018 World Cup winning squad was not celebrated in the same way as the team of 1998 and what this tells us about contemporary French society. Although the focus of this chapter is on the relationship between French society and its national football team, it should be remembered that many of the aspects of discrimination addressed can also be found at other levels of French football. This includes amateur and local leagues and affects both men and women.

The constitution of the French Fifth Republic, founded in 1958, establishes a legal and theoretical framework that provides the key principles and

DOI: 10.4324/9781003495970-4

This chapter has been made available under a CC-BY-NC-SA 4.0 license.

vocabulary that is used when discussing discrimination. Within this context, the concept of universalism is crucial. France has long prided itself on being a single and indivisible nation which cannot, at least in theory, be broken down into a series of constituent parts, and whose inhabitants are to be treated as individual citizens rather than members of groups. Although this approach aims to ensure equality, some argue that it fails to reflect the diversity of French society and can even obscure various forms of inequality (see Hayward, 1983, p. xii; Jennings, 2000, p. 575; Knapp and Wright, 2001, p. 22; Lentin, 2004, p. 116).

French political culture has not always been adequately acknowledged within discussions of football and discrimination in France. In the introduction to *Anti-racism in European Football: Fair Play for All*, Christos Kassimeris provides a succinct description of France that is in some respects accurate in demographic terms but does not fully reflect how French political culture shapes discourses about discrimination:

> Similar to the composition of the population in Britain, France is yet another west European state that features a strong sense of multiculturalism. Except for the Basque, Breton, Catalan, Corsican and Roma national minorities, French society has long been receiving migrants from third countries.
> (Kassimeris, 2009, p. 13)

Here, the notion that multiculturalism is prevalent in the country is problematic. The political theorist Jeremy Jennings has suggested that the concept of multiculturalism is actually "un-French" since it "places culture before politics, groups before individuals" (2000, p. 589). Under the French model of citizenship, individuals play a more important role than groups. Therefore, France does not perceive itself as a nation-state within which there are minority groups.

Another key principle written into France's constitution that is highly relevant to discrimination, especially Islamophobia, and diversity is that of *laïcité* or secularism. The strict separation between the state and religion has existed in France since 1905, and this principle is referred to in the first article of the French constitution. French secularism has significant implications for everyday life. It means, for example, that it is not permissible for pupils to wear ostentatious religions symbols in state schools as it would highlight group membership and thus go against the universalist ethos of the French Republic. In a footballing context secularism is sometimes evoked within discussions of how to maintain a harmonious and inclusive environment (Vilas, 2014, p. 19). State-owned sporting spaces such as public playing fields or gyms are also affected as they are regarded as places of neutrality where, for example, religious markers, expressions or practices are prohibited.

1998 and celebrating *l'équipe black-blanc-beur*

When France hosted and won the 1998 FIFA Men's World Cup, a mood of exuberant national celebration that was about more than just sport ensued. France had previously won the Men's European Championship and Olympic Football titles in 1984, but the 1998 World Cup surpassed these successes on several levels. The 1998 team was described as being *black-blanc-beur*, a nickname that referenced the presence of players who were Black, White, and of North African descent. Their roots could be traced from different regions of mainland France, the French Caribbean, and places such as North Africa, West Africa and the Indian Ocean. For example, the World Cup winning captain, Didier Deschamps, was from the Basque region of South West France. It was Zinedine Zidane, born in Marseille and the son of Algerian parents, who scored twice in the 3–0 win against Brazil in the final. In the semi-final against Croatia, defender Lilian Thuram, originally from Guadeloupe in the French Caribbean, had scored both of France's goals.

The focus on the squad's diversity was somewhat paradoxical given the previously mentioned universalist ethos of the French Republic, which sees itself as a single and indivisible nation supposedly composed of individual citizens rather than an accumulation of groups. Political opportunism goes a long way to explaining why the 1998 team's success was heralded in this manner. Discussing sport in general, Marjoribanks and Farquharson's argue that "for supporters, any success achieved by their national team is understood to be a more general reflection of the status of the nation itself" (2012, p. 76). French politicians were quick to portray the World Cup victory as representing a modern, tolerant and inclusive France (Hare, 2003, p. 134). President Jacques Chirac described the team as "simultaneously tricolour and multicoloured" (Tévanian, 2001, p. 109), evoking both tradition and diversity. Prime Minister Lionel Jospin branded the triumph the "best example of our unity and diversity" (Buob, 1998). These public declarations illustrate how politicians on both the centre-right and centre-left used France's footballing success to counter the discriminatory rhetoric of the far-right *Front National* and its leader Jean-Marie Le Pen, as they had also done earlier in the 1990s (Fière, 1996). Le Pen had suggested that the diverse composition of the French squad made it less French (Vilas, 2018, p. 36) and accused the majority of the team of not singing the *Marseillaise*, the French national anthem, before matches (Thompson, 2015, pp. 101–103). The celebratory declarations by mainstream politicians such as Chirac and Jospin can be read as suggesting that the *Front National's* brand of nationalism was out of phase with the national mood and outdated. However, as we will see later, this did not mean that the far-right was about to begin a lasting decline.

In many ways, the 1998 World Cup victory provided a means for French politicians to deflect attention away from more complex and less positive realities. Ten years on, the historian Yvan Gastaut argued that "without displaying any critical analysis, the entire [French] political class identified with the French team via a form of fashionable unanimity" (2008, p. 88). The Uruguayan writer and journalist Eduardo Galeano suggested that this mood of euphoria helped to obscure the political class's failings as the French World Cup squad was significantly more diverse than the French political classes:

> Zidane, the most acclaimed [of France's 1998 World Cup winners], is the son of Algerians. "Zidane for president" wrote an anonymous hand on the Arc de Triomphe on the day of the victory celebration. President? There are many Arabs and children of Arabs in France, but not a single one is a member of parliament, much less a minister.
>
> (2013, p. 251)

It is in part this lack of representation and recognition experienced by people of North African descent in France that explains why a match at the *Stade de France* in Paris between France and Algeria in October 2001 produced a very different image of French society (Vilas, 2018, p. 257). The title of an article by Philip Dine (2010) suggested that the so-called friendly between the two nations marked "the end of an idyll". This sporting encounter was supposed to symbolise reconciliation between the two nations, almost 40 years after the Algerian War led to Algeria's independence from France. Many Algerian supporters in the *Stade de France* lived in the Parisian *banlieues*, housing estates on the periphery of the French capital, which included the area immediately surrounding the stadium. Many of them booed the *Marseillaise* before the match and whistled when French players touched the ball (Dine, 2002, p. 503). In the 76th minute, with France winning 4–1, Algerian fans started to invade the pitch, and several of them brandished the Algerian flag. The match's subsequent abandonment meant that it had failed to fulfil its intended role of helping to foster reconciliation between the two countries. As Dine argued, "this wholly unexpected outcome was quickly and broadly perceived as an indication that at troubled colonial past still weighed to heavily to permit 'normal' sporting relations between the two nations" (2002, p. 503).

A further reminder that French society was not as cohesive as had been suggested amidst the euphoria of 1998 came at the ballot box as France prepared to defend the World Cup trophy in 2002. Jean-Marie Le Pen, a far-right candidate and the founder of the *Front National*, unexpectedly came second in the 2002 Presidential Elections. Three and a half years later, a dramatic and tragic event provided a powerful reminder that football does not necessarily provide an exit route or distraction from the challenges of living in areas such as the aforementioned underprivileged housing estates in major French cities. On 27 October 2005, two teenagers, Zyed Benna and Bouna Traoré, died in Clichy-sous-Bois after they were chased by police on their way home from playing football with friends and sought refuge in an electrical substation. The fact that Zyed Benna was of Tunisian descent and Bouna Traoré of

Mauritanian heritage raised questions about the policing of the *banlieues* and led to a period of protests and unrest in the face of what many demonstrators felt was institutionalized police discrimination.

Forgetting about *l'équipe black-blanc-beur?*

Writing in 2013, the French sports journalist Daniel Riolo said that "France 98 and the *black-blanc-beur* idea represents a past which we barely remember" (2013, p. 189). This owes much to events on and off the field, in the period that has followed France's initial World Cup victory in 1998. Although France was crowned European Champions in 2000, their performances in major tournaments in the rest of the first decade of the new millennium was – with the exception of unexpectedly being runners-up in the 2006 World Cup – largely underwhelming. Furthermore, the period from 1998 to 2010 saw football in France shift from being celebrated in order to project positive visions of French society to becoming the focus of increasingly discriminatory and divisive rhetoric. Patrick Vieira, who played for France over a hundred times between 1997 and 2009, summarizes that change succinctly:

> When everything was going well, people talked about the concept of *black-blanc-beur*. Today, things have turned on their head. People try to tell us that the problems stem from us coming from housing estates and lacking principles or an education.
> (Quoted in Jeudy and Nedjari, 2010, p. 50)

Vieira was born in Dakar (Senegal) before moving to France with his family at the age of eight. His family moved to Dreux, a town approximately 50 miles west of Paris where the far-right *Front National* managed to get their first-ever councillor elected in 1983. The blame and denunciations to which Vieira alludes were particularly vociferous following the 2010 World Cup in South Africa. At this time, several leading French politicians and intellectuals discussed football and footballers using discriminatory rhetoric. France was eliminated after the first round despite finding themselves in what had appeared to be a far from tough group. They managed a goalless draw against Uruguay before losing to Mexico and South Africa. In addition the disappointing performances and results, it was the players' behaviour off the pitch that led to criticism. France attacker Nicolas Anelka was a particular target after he was sent home for allegedly swearing at the national team's coach, Raymond Domenech, during half-time of the match against Mexico. Subsequently, Anelka refused to make a public apology. The French team then decided to go on strike rather than participate in a training session prior to their final game against South Africa following Anelka's expulsion. Consequently, the critics' anger intensified and increasingly focused on the squad as a whole.

Much criticism of the 2010 French World Cup squad was based on the idea that the players were overly individualistic and featured a particular degree of hostility towards players from France's *banlieues*. Roselyne Bachelot, the centre-right Minister for Health and Sports, blamed the team's failure on players who she compared to "urban gang leaders" (Beaud, 2011, p. 18). This type of emotive denunciation ignored the fact that one of the key initiators of the players' strike in South Africa was Jérémy Toulalan, who is White, not of foreign descent but of Breton origins and was brought up in Nantes. Beaud thus argues that Toulalan's background means that "skin colour and ethnic origins consequently do not provide an adequate explanation for the strike" (2011, p. 89).

Given that a significant proportion of those who live in *banlieues* denounced by public figures in France in summer 2010 are of foreign descent, it could potentially be argued that these statements had racial undertones. As John Marks notes, intellectuals such as Alain Finkielkraut "focus[ed] on what they saw as the unbalanced and fragmented 'ethnic' composition of the team, which was in turn seen as a reflection of a fragmented nation" (2104, p. 14). Christopher Thompson argues that the presence of a large contingent of non-White players of foreign descent in the 2010 World Cup squad meant that many of the alarmist reactions to the players' behaviour in South Africa took on racist undertones:

> Such conduct by the nation's athletic representatives implicitly evoked earlier colonial stereotypes of ungrateful, immature, disobedient "savages": violent, oversexed, undisciplined Arabs and lazy, simple-minded, childlike blacks had dominated French media depictions and colonial propaganda in the late nineteenth and early twentieth centuries.
>
> (Thompson, 2015, p. 107)

The hostile reactions to France's failures on and off the pitch at the 2010 World Cup led to an even more explicitly racist backlash after the team's elimination. Dubois mentions that "a small group of protestors entered the FFF [French Football Federation] headquarters, demanding that it create a team that was 'white and Christian' by 'firing' the 'blacks and Arabs'". He adds that "such sentiments have long been expressed by the far right – most prominently by Jean-Marie Le Pen" (2014, p. 113). This provided a further reminder that the far-right and its divisive and discriminatory visions had not been permanently confined to the past by France's 1998 World Cup victory.

The way in which the 2010 World Cup unfolded provoked a period of high-profile soul-searching within French football. Thierry Henry, who retired from the French national team after the 2010 World Cup, was even summoned to meet the French president, Nicholas Sarkozy (Marks, 2014, p. 15; see also Grynbaum and Schneider, 2010, pp. 27–30). France played their first match after the 2010 World Cup under a new national coach, Laurent

Blanc, and without many of the players who were perceived as having been responsible for the players' strike in South Africa. Although the FFF appeared keen for the men's national team to make a fresh start, it was not long before the French governing body became embroiled in further controversy at an institutional level.

In April 2011, the French investigative website *Mediapart* published an article based on covert recordings of FFF meetings in which senior figures, including Laurent Blanc, participated. It revealed a discussion about introducing limits on the numbers of players with dual nationality at academies run by the FFF and France's leading clubs. A key reason for this proposal was that players with dual nationality could, potentially, play international football for another country after benefitting from several years of high-quality training in France (Thompson, 2015, p. 108; Dubois, 2014, pp. 113–115). The ensuing scandal became known as the "Quotas Affair" and particular controversy stemmed from Laurent Blanc and other senior members of the FFF also talking about introducing limits on the numbers of Black and Arab players (Thompson, 2015, p. 109; Dubois, 2014, p. 113). Due to key principles of the egalitarian French model of citizenship, it is clear that such an approach would have been fundamentally problematic on a variety of levels. As Dubois rightly observes, the French model of citizenship has "for years strongly opposed 'quotas' that would instigate 'positive discrimination' (i.e. affirmative action) in order to help diversify universities and other institutions" (2014, p. 113). Words like "quotas", "affirmative action", and "positive discrimination" are strongly associated with an American model of managing diversity that philosopher and academic Régis Debray described as being alien to France's Republican model in a famous 1989 article in a weekly news magazine. Laurent Blanc was one of several figures at the meeting of which *Mediapart* obtained the recording that revealed highly racialised ideas concerning the supposed strengths and weaknesses of players in France. He notably contrasted the supposed strength and power of Black and Arab players with the supposedly greater "tactical ability" of White players (Dubois, 2014, p. 113). Although the discriminatory quotas discussed were never actually introduced, Dubois argues that the recorded discussions "suggested that racist ideas had become normalized at the highest levels of the French Football Federation" and that they "constituted not only a striking violation of the principles of equality that supposedly form the basis of French political life, but also the principles of sport" (2014, p. 111).

In the aftermath of the 2010 World Cup in South Africa, the French media continued to focus on players' behaviour on and off the pitch. This led the French Football Federation's president, Noël Le Graët, to say prior to the 2012 European Championship that a key objective was to "qualify from the group stage and show positive behaviour", adding that "being well-mannered is the least one can do" (Guillou, 2012). However, Samir Nasri's perceived disrespectful and inappropriate behaviour attracted considerable media attention.

Nasri grew up in an urban area north of Marseille and is the grandson of Algerian immigrants. He aimed a "be quiet" gesture in the direction of journalists after scoring against England in the first phase of the tournament and swore at a journalist after France's elimination against Sweden in the quarter-finals. As I have mentioned elsewhere (Ervine, 2014a, p. 77), this led to some commentators in France again employing highly emotive and denunciatory rhetoric as they had done in response to the team's participation in the 2010 World Cup in South Africa (Ervine, 2014a, p. 77).

Although there were fewer negative headlines concerning French players during the 2014 FIFA Men's World Cup in Brazil, 'race' and discrimination were brought back into the limelight following comments made by Cameroon defender Benoît Assou-Ekotto. Assou-Ekotto was born in the French city of Arras to a Cameroonian father and a French mother but opted to play international football for Cameroon. He claimed he had never considered playing for France due to the discriminatory scapegoating that he said takes place when the French national team is not successful. He argued that "when the national team get a bad result, they start to say there is a little bit too many Black people, Muslim people and this kind of stuff", adding "there is no point for me to play for this kind of country" (Anonymous, 2014a). Although Assou-Ekotto's comments focus specifically on football, they point towards the existence of a socio-political climate which makes some people who are of foreign descent question the extent to which the realities of contemporary France match with the inclusive rhetoric of its constitution.

In a sporting context, the existence of such a climate stems, in part, from some key figures within French football failing to learn lessons from the "Quotas Affair" of 2011. In November 2014, Willy Sagnol – then manager of Bordeaux and a member of the France team that reached the 2006 World Cup Final – made comments about African footballers that were described as "uninhibited anti-Black racism" by French anti-racism group *SOS-Racisme* (Okeleji, 2014). In a question-and-answer session hosted by the French regional newspaper *Sud Ouest*, Sagnol talked about his reluctance to sign a lot of African players. He initially explained that this was due to being unable to play them in club matches during the African Cup of Nations, which takes place every other year. Subsequently, he employed similar stereotypes to the ones which were evoked in the meeting that led to the "Quotas Affair" (Ervine, 2014b). Sagnol stated that "the advantage of what I would call the typical African player is that they are cheap, ready to fight". He then added, "but football is not just about that, it is about technique, intelligence, discipline, so you need everything" (Okeleji, 2014). Bordeaux's president Jean-Louis Triaud sought to excuse Sagnol by describing him as "anything but racist" before echoing Sagnol's view that African footballers lack sophistication and skill. Triaud talked about how "African players arrive in France at a young age" before adding "they obviously work hard physically but they lack a tactical level, tactical intelligence" (Okeleji, 2014). FFF President Noël Le

Graët argued that looking at the players Sagnol had selected for Bordeaux was enough to prove he was not racist (Anonymous, 2014b), but the Chad-born football agent, director and journalist Pape Diouf argued that African players in France should respond to Sagnol's comments by refusing to play in a round of league matches. Diouf was also critical of Thierry Braillard, the French Secretary of State for Sport, who described Sagnol's comments as "a simple slip-of-the-tongue" (Diouf, 2014).

When France hosted the 2016 Men's European Championship, the composition of Didier Deschamps' French squad attracted much discussion. The former France and Manchester United player Eric Cantona suggested that Deschamps may have left out Karim Benzema and Hatem Ben Arfa, two players of North African descent who grew up in the *banlieues* of major French cities, due to their ethnic background (Gibson, 2016). In a Spanish newspaper, Benzema said that Deschamps had "given into pressure from a racist part of France" by not including him in his squad (Polo, 2016). Following these comments, the *Front National's* Marion Maréchal questioned Benzema's Frenchness by referencing comments Benzema had made in a radio interview as an 18-year-old and suggested that he "should go to play in 'his country' [that is Algeria] if he's not happy" (Chrisafis and Aarons, 2016). In December 2006, Benzema was asked about playing international football for France rather than Algeria and responded as follows:

> Algeria is the country of my parents, it's in my heart. But then, in sporting terms, it's true that I will play for the French team. . . . It's more for the sporting aspect because Algeria is my country, my parents are from there, so really France is a sporting choice.
> (Quoted in Masson, 2020, p. 172)

Both at the time of the interview and subsequently, some, especially those on the right or far-right in France, suggested Benzema's motivation for representing France was based on self-interest and financial considerations rather than any sense of national belonging. Dufy and Laure argue that these criticisms of Benzema ignore the many moments since 2006 when he expressed his attachment to France (2016, p. 75).

One of the main reasons why Benzema had not played regularly for France in the build-up to the 2016 European Championships and the subsequent years was that he was under investigation for his alleged role in blackmailing his international teammate Mathieu Valbuena. This occurred after an intimate video of Valbuena and his partner found its way into the hands of a group of individuals who persuaded Benzema to talk to Valbuena about the tape. Benzema's discussion with Valbuena about the video initially took place at a French team get-together in October 2015. Six years later, in October 2021, Benzema was given a ten-month suspended prison sentence and a €75,000 fine for his involvement in the scandal. The media's treatment of Benzema's role in the so-called "Sex Tape Affair" cannot be entirely explained by 'racial' prejudice. However, the former Auxerre manager and television analyst Guy Roux suggested that Benzema would be less likely to find himself at the heart of press storms if his surname was Dupont (Dufy and Laure, 2016, p. 72). By using the stereotypically French surname of "Dupont", Roux seemed to imply that Benzema would have been treated differently if he had been White and/or not of foreign descent.

The 2018 World Cup and beyond: the evolving relationship between sport, politics and Frenchness

Prior to the 2018 FIFA Men's World Cup in Russia, French President Emmanuel Macron expressed his belief in the unifying power of football when visiting the FFF's national training centre at Clairefontaine:

> The World Cup is important for our country, for our young people. . . . Sport provides models, examples to follow. Where parents are not up to scratch, when situations are difficult, it is sometimes sport that people hold onto. Having a team that defends our colours is good for national cohesion.
> (Quoted in Pernia and Guégan, 2022, p. 281)

These sentiments place a high level of responsibility on athletes and also appear to be based on a contested, or at least dated, premise. When France won the FIFA Men's World Cup for a second time in 2018, they again did so with a highly diverse group of players. In the final, they beat Croatia 4–2. One of their goalscorers in this match was the teenage attacker Kylian Mbappé, born in Paris to a father from Cameroon and a mother whose parents arrived in France from Algeria. Mbappé scored only minutes after France's third goal had been added by Paul Pogba, a player born to parents from Guinea who also grew up on the fringe of Paris. In the first half, Antoine Griezmann, the son of a French-born father of distant German descent and a mother of Portuguese parentage, had converted a penalty. France was captained by Hugo Lloris, born in Nice to White, upper-middle-class parents.

Given that the diversity of the 2018 World Cup winning squad mirrored that of its 1998 predecessors, their triumph could, theoretically, have been situated within the same type of celebratory discourse. However, a survey conducted by the polling agency IFOP in the aftermath of the 2018 World Cup showed that French people were much less prepared to see the result as a symbol of unity, national cohesion, patriotism, and optimism than before. In 1998, 88% of French people polled had felt that winning the World Cup "developed a climate of understanding between French people", but in 2018, this figure dropped to 51%. In 1998, 57% of people surveyed believed that the World Cup win "reinforced [their] patriotism and attachment to France" but 20 years later only 39% agreed. The change in mind-set between 1998 and 2018 was further reinforced by the fall in the proportion of respondents who felt that the World Cup win "increased French people's confidence in their future" from 70% (1998) to 35% in 2018 (Jeudy, 2018). These survey results demonstrated that France in 2018 was a very different place from France in 1998. This was also reflected in the considerably changing political landscape of France. Four years after the country's first World Cup victory, the presence of the far-right *Front National's* Jean-Marie Le Pen in the second round of the 2002 French Presidential Elections had caused shockwaves. In 2017, the year before France's second World Cup win, the participation of his daughter Marine Le Pen in the second round of the French Presidential Elections was a widely expected outcome. Although the *Front National* were again defeated, the margin was significantly slimmer than it had been 15 years previously when the centre-right's Jacques Chirac secured 82% of the second-round vote and Jean-Marie Le Pen only 18%. In 2017, the centrist Emmanuel Macron scored 66% and Marine Le Pen 34%. Five years later, the gap narrowed further when Emmanuel Macron's second-round victory against Marine Le Pen was 59%–41%. Between 1998 and 2018, the far-right had capitalised on the growing divisions within French society during a time when there was significant unrest in many *banlieues* in the autumn of 2005 and a series of fatal terrorist attacks such as the one which took place at the offices of the satirical publication *Charlie Hebdo* in January 2015.

After Kylian Mbappé's penalty was saved in a shootout against Switzerland in the second round of the 2020 European Championships, the French star, who had played a key role in his country's 2018 World Cup victory, considered quitting the national team. The fact that this was primarily due to racist abuse he received on social media was, however, only part of the story. What was just as significant was that Mbappé himself took to social media to criticise French Football Federation president Noël Le Graët for suggesting that his desire to quit the national team was due to frustration at his penalty miss rather than being a victim of racism (Hay, 2022). This provided a further example of Le Graët standing accused of ignoring or downplaying racism within French football and French society more broadly.

However, the FFF more rapidly and publicly denounced racism directed at its players following France's 2022 World Cup Final defeat against Argentina in Qatar. Black French players singled out for racist abuse on social media on this occasion included Aurélien Tchouameni and Kinglsey Coman, who failed to score in the crucial penalty shootout, as well as Randal Kolo Muani, who was unable to take advantage of a late opportunity in extra time to score what would almost certainly have been a winning goal for France (Nestler, 2022).

Tensions within French society again emerged during the 2024 Men's European Championships in Germany. While the tournament was taking place, the French nation was also preparing for legislative elections, which had been unexpectedly called by Emmanuel Macron. The prospect of France having its first ever far-right Prime Minister appeared more realistic than ever before. It led to several members of the French squad, notably Kylian Mbappé, Jules Koundé, and Marcus Thuram, encouraging people to vote and, most importantly, reject the extremism of Marine Le Pen's *Rassemblement National* (National Rally), formerly known as the *Front National*. They followed in the footsteps of Marcel Desailly and some of his national teammates, who, in 2002, publicly condemned the racism and exclusion promoted by the *Front National* under the leadership of her father. In 2024, this created an awkward situation for the French Football Federation, which sought to defend its players' freedom of expression while, at the same time, insisting on its own need to remain politically neutral as a sporting organisation. Its president, Philippe Diallo, expressed his desire to "avoid any form of pressure and political exploitation of the French national team" (Duluc, 2024). Diallo's comments about not wanting the French team to be politically exploited seemed somewhat ironic, given that its appropriation for positive ends in 1998 had not seemed to pose any problems for the FFF. This stance was potentially awkward as the FFF's desire to remain politically neutral could also be read as a failure to endorse leading players' explicit rejection of extreme ideologies. Furthermore, it should be remembered that these ideologies emanated from a political grouping that has long faced accusations of racism and scapegoating footballers – and others – of foreign descent.

Conclusions: continuing challenges on and off the pitch

In this chapter, we have seen that France has a theoretical framework, which is supposed to ensure equality. However, the "Quotas Affair" of 2011, which involved the French Football Federation, was largely about the potential introduction of discriminatory practices, which contravened key elements of these egalitarian principles. Furthermore, Noël Le Graët's presidency of the FFF between 2011 and 2023 was marred by several declarations, which did little to inspire confidence in his ability to either acknowledge the existence of discrimination or tackle it. During a television interview, in 2020, in the aftermath of a tense match between Paris Saint-Germain and Marseille, during which a player was alleged to have made racist comments to an opponent, Le Graët sought to downplay the existence of racism within French football. He stated that "when a Black player scores a goal, the whole stadium gets to its feet" before being adamant that "the phenomenon of racism in sport and in particular football does not exist or hardly exists" (Ricotta, 2020). This led to criticism from former professional players and amateur players alike, as well as protest outside the FFF headquarters. Former France international Olivier Dacourt accused Le Graët of being "in denial" about the existence of racism in French football (Le Gall, 2020).

Just over a year earlier, Le Graët had also been the subject of criticism and protests for saying that he believed racist chanting in a stadium provided a valid reason for stopping a game but homophobic chanting did not (Pretot, 2019). These comments seemed surprising given that footballing authorities in France such as *La Ligue de Football Professionnel* (Professional Football League, LFP) have organised annual initiatives to combat homophobia. However, some players refused to wear specially designed shirts featuring their number and name in rainbow colours, covered anti-homophobia logos on their shirts or tried to avoid appearing in a team photograph next to anti-homophobia banners (Danjon, 2024; Millar, 2024; Maes, 2024). Some of these players were concerned that the campaign would promote homosexuality or claimed that it was incompatible with their personal and/or religious beliefs. Faced with this kind of reluctance, the *Ligue de Football Professional* needed to rethink its approach to tackling discrimination, in particular racism. In response to suggestions from players, it developed a new awareness-raising initiative, *Dégageons le racisme!* (Let's get rid of racism!), that was introduced in March 2024.

Although some of the challenges mentioned earlier could potentially be blamed on the institutional culture of the FFF under Le Graët's leadership, there are broader and more systemic issues facing sport in France that are closely linked to the country's constitution. As mentioned earlier, French secularism is a strict and far-reaching principle which has a significant impact on what is considered to be acceptable in public life. It has, among other things, resulted in France's footballing authorities not following guidelines from international football's governing body, FIFA (*Fédération Internationale de Football Association*), to allow female players to wear the *hijab*.

Furthermore, *laïcité* is also the reason why the French *Ligue de Football Professional* has not followed the example of other European countries (and professional North American sports leagues) to allow referees to briefly interrupt games so that Muslim players taking part in Ramadan can break their fast. As Wolfeys has noted, a French government report on secularism in 2022 described the wearing of the *hijab*, praying and consuming halal food at sports venues as being incompatible with France's Republican values, in particular the strict separation of state and church. He also referenced a previous report of 2017 that associated such practices with radicalisation (Wolfreys, 2023, pp. 172–173). As Wolfreys also observes, this attitude can have a negative impact on how comfortable some French Muslims feel about participating in sport. Furthermore, it is part of a mindset that whereby French secularism is "part of a set of values distinguishing those who are 'really' French from those who are not" (Wolfreys, 2023, pp. 173–174). From the French government's perspective, in certain contexts it is legitimate to discriminate against people who do not adhere to its secular norms. However, there have long been debates about what the practical implications of French secularism should be in settings such as educational and sporting establishments. In addition, the way in which wearing a *hijab*, praying and consuming halal food have been associated with radicalisation could be seen as somewhat alarmist and out-of-step with many other countries in Europe where such practices do not create a potential barrier to sporting participation.

As has been shown in this chapter, France seems increasingly willing to acknowledge that sport cannot be as much of a symbol or driver of integration and tolerance as appeared to be suggested by many public figures in 1998. However, this shift has certainly not been accompanied by a universal refusal to either associate sport with social problems or seek to exploit it for political purposes. During 2023, several politicians on the French right and far-right made unsubstantiated allegations that Karim Benzema had links with radical Islam (Williams, 2023). Silverstein (2018) has referred to such events as being part of a process whereby:

> football ... has become an anxious national spectacle, in which rituals of social and cultural renewal are subject to commercialization, radicalization, and politicalization to the profit of some and the exclusion of others. It is a preeminent stage on which national loyalty and adhesion are performed and scrutinized, and in which passions of identification are felt, expressed, and evaluated.
>
> (p. 100)

This process of cultural and national renewal is closely shaped, and sometimes restricted, by the French constitution and model of citizenship, although this supposedly egalitarian and inclusive model has at times been ignored when it has been politically opportune to do so. Furthermore, we have seen that practical implications of key elements of the French constitution have had a negative impact on the extent to which sports such as football are open to all. The fact that liberty, equality and fraternity are the three values that form France's national motto certainly has not meant that footballers – and others – have been protected from highly prejudiced attitudes and abuse from people within football and public life in France.

References

Anonymous (2014a) "World Cup 2014: Benoît Assou-Ekotto: no point playing for France", *BBC Sport*, 17th June. Available: <https://www.bbc.co.uk/sport/football/27895655> [accessed on 29th September 2024].

Anonymous (2014b) "Le Graët: "Mauvais procès"" ["Le Graët: 'unfounded allegations'"], *L'Équipe*, 5th November. Available: <https://www.lequipe.fr/Football/Actualites/Le-graet-mauvais-proces/512470> [accessed on 29th September 2024].

Beaud, S. (2011) *Traîtres à la nation? Un autre regard sur la grève des Bleus en Afrique du Sud* [*Traitors to the nation? A different perspective on the French team's strike in South Africa*], Paris: La Découverte.

Buob, J. (1998) "La France voit la vie en bleu" ["France sees life in Blue"], *Le Monde*, 11th July. Available: <https://www.lemonde.fr/archives/article/1998/07/11/la-france-voit-la-vie-en-bleu_3678585_1819218.html> [accessed on 17th September 2009].

Chrisafis, A. and Aarons, E. (2016) "Marine Le Pen: Karim Benzema 'hides wickedness' behind accusations of racism", *The Guardian*, 2nd June. Available: <https://www.theguardian.com/football/2016/jun/02/marine-le-pen-karim-benzema-wickedness-racism-france> [accessed on 30th September 2024].

Danjon, A. (2024) "Racisme, homophobie: comment la LFP a repensé sa lutte contre les discriminations" ["Racism, homophobie: how the LFP has rethought its fight against discrimination"], *L'Équipe*, 27th March. Available: <https://www.lequipe.fr/Football/Article/Racisme-homophobie-comment-la-lfp-a-repense-sa-lutte-contre-les-discriminations/1457109?utm> [accessed on 1st October 2024].

Debray, R. (1989) "Êtes-vous démocrate ou républicain?" ["Are you a democrat or a republican?"], *Le Nouvel Observateur*, 1308, pp. 115–121.

Dine, P. (2002) "France, Algeria and sport: from colonisation to globalisation", *Modern and Contemporary France*, 10(4), pp. 495–505.

Dine, P. (2010) "The end of an idyll? sport and society in France, 1998–2002", *Modern and Contemporary France*, 11(1), pp. 33–43.

Diouf, P. (2014) "Pape Diouf appelle les joueurs africains à boycotter la Ligue 1", *Le Monde*, 5th November. Available: <https://www.lemonde.fr/football/article/2014/11/05/pape-diouf-appelle-les-joueurs-africains-a-boycotter-la-ligue-1_4518703_1616938.html> [accessed on 29th September 2024].

Dubois, L. (2014) "Racism and the specter of 'dual nationality' in French football", *Contemporary French Civilization*, 39(1), pp. 111–131.

Dufy, G. and Laure, R. (2016) *Les Très sales gosses: ces champions au-dessus des lois* [*The very bad kids: champions who are above the law*], Paris: Robert Laffont.

Duluc, V. (2024) "Diallo entre deux chaises" ["Diallo sitting on the fence"], *L'Équipe*, 19th June, p. 8.

Ervine, J. (2014a) "*Les banlieues* and *Les Bleus*: political and media discourse about sport and society in France", *French Cultural Studies*, 25(1), pp. 70–81.

Ervine, J. (2014b) "French football caught offside in new race controversy", *The Conversation*, 7th November. Available: <https://theconversation.com/french-football-caught-offside-in-new-race-controversy-33952> [accessed on 29th September 2024].

Fière, R. (1996) "Bleus de France: union multicolore contre les discriminations de Le Pen" ["France's Blues: a multicoloured union against Le Pen's discrimination"], *Libération*, 25th June. Available: <https://www.liberation.fr/evenement/1996/06/25/bleus-de-france-union-multicolore-contre-les-discriminations-de-le-pen_172937/> [accessed on 17th September 2024].

Galeano, E. (2013) *Soccer in sun and shadow* (trans. by Mark Fried), New York: Nation Books.

Gastaut, Y. (2008) *Le Métissage par le foot. L'intégraton, mais jusqu'où?* [*Diversity via football. Integration, but to what extent?*], Paris: Éditions Autrement.

Gibson, O. (2016) "Eric Cantona believes Didier Deschamps may have left out France players on racial grounds", *The Guardian*, 26th May. Available: <https://www.theguardian.com/football/2016/may/26/eric-cantona-didier-deschamps-may-left-out-players-racial-grounds> [accessed on 29th September 2024].

Grynbaum, A. and Schneider, R. (2010) *Foot et politique: liaisons dangereuses* [*Football and politics: dangerous Liaisons*], Paris: Jean-Claude Gawsewitch.

Guillou, C. (2012) "Non, L'Equipe n'a pas "été très méchant" avec Nasri" ["No, L'Équipe has not "been very mean" to Nasri"], *Rue89*, 12th June. Available: <https://www.nouvelobs.com/rue89/rue89-euro-2012/20120612.RUE0591/non-]2l-equipe-n-a-pas-ete-tres-mechant-avec-nasri.html> [accessed on 29th September 2024].

Hare, G. (2003) *Football in France: a cultural history*, Oxford: Berg.

Hay, A. (2022) "Kylian Mbappe: I wanted to quit France national team due to racist abuse after penalty miss", *The Athletic*, 19th June. Available: <https://www.

nytimes.com/athletic/3489869/2022/06/19/kylian-mbappe-i-wanted-to-quit-france-national-team-due-to-racist-abuse-after-penalty-miss/> [accessed on 5th November 2024].

Hayward, J. (1983) *Governing France: the one and indivisible republic*, London: Weidenfield and Nicholson.

Jennings, J. (2000) "Citizenship, republicanism and multiculturalism in contemporary France", *British Journal of Political Science*, 30(4), pp. 575–598.

Jeudy, B. (2018) "Sondage Ifop: les Bleus de 2018 face à ceux de 1998" ["Ifop survey: the blues of 2018 compared to those of 1998"], *Paris Match*, 25th July. Available: <https://www.parismatch.com/Actu/Sport/Sondage-Ifop-les-Bleus-de-2018-face-a-ceux-de-1998-1565470> [accessed on 27th July 2024].

Jeudy, B. and Nedjari, K. (2010) *Sarkozy côté vestiaires* [*Sarkozy in the changing rooms*], Paris: Plon.

Kassimeris, C. (2009) *Anti-racism in European football: fair play for all*, Plymouth: Lexington Books.

Knapp, A. and Wright, V. (2001) *The politics and government of France* (4th Edition), London: Routledge.

Le Gall, A. (2020) "'Il y a une vraie omerta sur le sujet ' . . . Le football est-il encore gangrené par les problèmes de racisme?" ["'There's a real code of silence about the subject '". . . Is football still contaminated by a problem with racism?"], *20 Minutes*, 8th December. Available: <https://www.20minutes.fr/sport/football/2864403-20200918-vraie-omerta-sujet-football-encore-gangrene-problemes-racisme> [accessed on 1st October 2024].

Lentin, A. (2004) *Racism and anti-racism in Europe*, London: Pluto Press.

Maes, A. (2024) "Homophobie: une plainte déposée contre Nabil Bentaleb et le LOSC" ["Homophobia: legal action taken against Nabil Bentaleb and Lille"], *La Voix du Nord*, 5th June. Available: <https://www.lavoixdunord.fr/1469386/article/2024-06-05/homophobie-une-plainte-deposee-contre-nabil-bentaleb-et-le-losc> [accessed on 1st October 2024].

Marjoribanks, T. and Farquharson, K. (2012) *Sport and society in the global age*, Basingstoke: Palgrave Macmillan.

Marks, J. (2014) "Public discourse and the conceptualization of football in France since 1998", *Contemporary French Civilization*, 39(1), pp. 11–34.

Masson, M. (2020) *1987, Génération sacrifiée?* [*The sacrificed generation*], Péronas: Exuvie Éditions.

Millar, C. (2024) "Monaco's Mohamed Camara given four-game suspension for covering LGBTQ+ badge", *The Athletic*, 31st May. Available: <https://www.nytimes.com/athletic/5531488/2024/05/31/monaco-camara-ban/> [accessed on 1st October 2024].

Nestler, S. (2022) "Post-World Cup ugliness between Argentina and France", *Deutsche Welle*, 22nd December. Available: <https://www.dw.com/en/post-world-cup-ugliness-between-argentina-and-france/a-64190360> [accessed on 5th November 2024].

Okeleji, O. (2014) "Willy Sagnol: Bordeaux coach criticised over 'African' remark", *BBC Sport*, 5th November. Available: <http://www.theguardian.com/football/2014/nov/05/bordeaux-willy-sagnol-african-players> [accessed on 29th September 2024].

Pernia, C. and Guégan, J.-B. (2022) *La République du foot: pas le même parti, mais la même passion* [*The Republic of football: not the same game, but the same passion*], Paris: Amphora.

Polo, P. (2016) "Benzema: "Deschamps se pliega a la presión de una parte racista de Francia" "["Benzema: "Deschamps bows to pressure from a racist part of France""], *Marca*, 1st June. Available: <https://www.marca.com/futbol/real-madrid/2016/06/01/574dfc86e2704e5c1d8b463c.html> [accessed on 29th September 2024].

Pretot, J. (2019) "French federation head: stop games over racist chants – but not homophobic ones", *The Independent*, 10th September. Available: <www.independent.co.uk/sport/football/european/ligue-1-french-football-federation-noel-le-graet-racist-homophobic-a9099371.html> [accessed on 1st October 2024].

Ricotta, J. (2020) "Selon Noël Le Graët, 'le racisme dans le foot n'existe pas ou peu'" ["According to Noël Le Graët, 'racism in football is inexistant or barely exists'"], *Europe 1*, 15th September. Available: <https://www.europe1.fr/sport/selon-noel-le-graet-le-racisme-dans-le-foot-nexiste-pas-ou-peu-3992121> [accessed on 1st October 2024].

Riolo, D. (2013) *Racaille football club: fantasmes et réalités du foot français* [*Lowlife scum football club: fantasies and realities in French football*], Paris: Hugo et compagnie.

Silverstein, P. (2018) *Postcolonial France: race, Islam and the future of the Republic*, London: Pluto Book.

Tévanian, P. (2001) *Le Racisme républicain: réflexions sur le modèle français de discrimination* [*Republican racism: reflections on the French model of discrimination*], Paris: Esprit frappeur.

Thompson, C. (2015) "From Black-Blanc-Beur to Black-Black-Black? 'L'Affaire des Quotas' and the shattered 'image of 1998' in twenty-first-century France", *French Politics, Culture and Society*, 33(1), pp. 101–121.

Vilas, N. (2014) *Dieu Football Club* [*God football club*], Paris: Hugo Sport.

Vilas, N. (2018) *Enquête sur le racisme dans le football* [*Investigation into racism in football*], Vannes: Marabout.

Williams, T. (2023) "Explained: Karim Benzema and the extraordinary attacks on him from French politicians", *The Athletic*, 30th October. Available: <https://www.nytimes.com/athletic/5004730/2023/10/30/explained-karim-benzema-and-the-extraordinary-attacks-on-him-from-french-politicians/> [accessed on 3rd October 2024]

Wolfreys, J. (2023) "'Avec Vous?' Islamophobia and the Macron presidency", *Modern & Contemporary France*, 31(2), pp. 165–182.

Chapter 5

Germany

Tensions and contradictions in football: Integration versus discrimination

Lasse Müller

In Germany, the characterisation of sport, in general, as a "vehicle for integration" is often taken for granted in the public discourses (Braun and Finke, 2010). This is most notable in organised football, where the notion of integration can be regarded as a key element of this sport's brand identity (Blecking, 2015, p. 152). The diversity of the German national football team has repeatedly been cited as a positive and convincing example, illustrating "how football effortlessly connects people and cultures" (Niersbach, 2011, p. 2). Over seven million individuals are organised under the umbrella of the German Football Association (DFB) – as players, coaches, referees, in voluntary roles, or as passive members such as fans (DFB, 2023a). This represents an organisational rate of almost 10% of the German population. Both the amateur and professional levels share the narrative that football is an integrative force and non-exclusionary sport, often referencing supposedly inherent sporting values such as fair play, respect, and tolerance. It is simply assumed that these implicit and unwritten values result in equal opportunities and equal treatment irrespective of characteristics such as class, religion, or gender (Delto and Zick, 2022, p. 226). And yet, as this chapter will show, discriminatory practices of various kinds are widespread, have a long history and can be found at various levels and in different environments.

Having said this, over the last few decades, increased awareness of discriminatory practices, intervention concepts, and strategies such as publicly rejecting right-wing ideologies appear to have considerably reduced those discriminatory manifestations in most stadiums (Schubert, 2019). Nevertheless, football crowds in Germany continue to consist primarily of white, male, heterosexual spectators, with discriminatory incidents being deeply embedded and occurring regularly (MeDiF-NRW, 2023). So, an ambivalent and contradictory picture emerges that Degele and Janz (2011, p. 8) succinctly summarise:

> Football connects – but always through exclusion. The feeling of togetherness and community arises by delineating boundaries against others: We understand who we are when we recognise those whom we differ

from. Football provides numerous opportunities for this. Village clubs form through distinguishing themselves from neighbouring village teams, nations through the stylisation and staging of the distinctiveness of national team opponents, heterosexual male bastions through the exclusion of women and gays, well-trained key players through the invisibility of those with depression, and well-off VIPs through the ridicule of the penniless and ultras.

This chapter outlines the integration debates and paradigms that continue to shape German sport, in general, and football, in particular, and, subsequently, shift to the contradictory features, that is selected forms of discrimination. There is no doubt that German football continues to be marred by racism and other forms of discrimination. This chapter will briefly address the issue of racism to convey its complexity, then explore the intricate interplay between integration expectations and anti-Muslim stereotypes through the case of Mesut Özil, followed by a more detailed discussion of antisemitism in various football contexts. The main focus will be on antisemitism due to the country's infamous 20th-century history and its still-persistent, ambiguous relationship with the subject.

Integration through sport in Germany

The late 1990s marked a significant turning point in Germany's history, as decades of ignoring and/or denying the realities of immigration came to an end. Legally, politically, and socially, Germany's simple and blunt response to the existence of a large migrant community transitioned from an integration-through-assimilation paradigm to acknowledging societal accountability for the development of a much more differentiated and nuanced integration philosophy (Sauer and Brinkmann, 2016). Before, migration and integration were not perceived as long-term issues, as evidenced by the prevalent term *Gastarbeiter*, guest workers, which suggested that foreign labour migrants would eventually return home (Meier-Braun, 2017, p. 15). In the 1960s, West Germany began recruiting foreign workers, particularly from Italy and Turkey, to address labour shortages that the *Wirtschaftswunder*, the economic miracle, of the 1950s had caused. However, in the 1970s, structural shifts and economic crises led to a considerable downscaling of this recruitment. Despite several fundamental (immigration) policy changes, the foreign resident population gradually rose to nearly five million by 1989, challenging unrealistic expectations of "migration control", especially due to family reunification (Oltmer, 2016, pp. 80–81). Additionally, in the reunited Germany of the 1990s, large numbers of refugees and migrants arrived from Eastern Europe and the Middle East (Kogan, 2011, pp. 93–94).

The German government only began implementing systematic integration policies at the turn of the millennium. Measures such as the introduction of a multi-layered "National Integration Plan", which focused on education, training, employment, as well as cultural issues, were initiated (Bendel and Borkowski, 2016, p. 112). Since 2013, integration efforts that once focused on labour migrants have also been targeting refugees (Bendel and Borkowski, 2016, pp. 105–106). However, the significantly increased numbers of refugees from the mid-2010s onwards had profound political implications in Germany. The "Alternative for Germany" (AfD), initially known for its Euroscepticism in the context of the European banking crisis, swiftly rebranded itself as a right-wing populist force with an outspoken anti-migration agenda. It opposed the government's migration policies, rallied against "asylum chaos", and promoted anti-Islam sentiments. By exploiting the increasing polarisation of German society, the AfD entered the *Bundestag*, the federal parliament, in 2017 as the first far-right party in post-war Germany (Geiges, 2018). Particularly in the eastern regions, it emerged as the strongest force in polls for state elections in 2024. But not only in this geographical area, far-right political positions resonate within society; in the 2023 edition of the population-representative *Mitte*-survey, nearly 28% of the respondents agreed with the statement that Germany is "dangerously overforeignised" due to migration – while an additional 22% gave a mixed response, indicating partial agreement (Zick and Mokros, 2023, pp. 64–65).

These socio-political developments over the last 70 years can also be observed in the microcosm of sport. There were early signs that the integration-through-assimilation approach did not work in the world of sport as, for example, members of the large Turkish migrant community in Germany founded their own clubs rather than joining existing "German" clubs. They were "very popular among Turkish migrants, attracting large audiences and having financial backing from Turkish businesses" (Merkel, Sombert and Tokarski, 1996, p. 161). These so-called ethnic sports clubs questioned and undermined the expectation of individual membership in "regular" German clubs. Nevertheless, during the period from 1955 to 1973, these (football) clubs offered migrant workers opportunities for integration into their new environment by facilitating initial contacts with the local population and strengthening self-confidence – thus also contributing to changing perceptions within the majority society. Whether and what kind of strategies the DFB pursued during this period remains speculative (Baumann, 2022, pp. 84–86).

During the 1990s, extensive debates arose about the potentially sectarian effects of ethnic sports clubs, particularly in response to increased migration. Additionally, there was consistent reporting of discriminatory incidents against and between those clubs (Stahl, 2011). Heitmeyer (1998, p. 29) expressed concerns about whether organised football is indeed able to resolve existing social and ethnic divisions and conflicts. Instead, he proposed that clubs are adept at delineating social identities and can serve as platforms for displaying political power and dominance. Other voices portrayed the development as a more open process with integration potentials from a pluralistic and non-assimilative viewpoint (Blecking, 2008, pp. 124–125). On the sports policy level, this perspective prevailed as the "German Olympic Sports Confederation" (DOSB), the governing body of German sport, eventually recognised "ethnic" clubs as a form of cultural enrichment in 2010 (Blecking, 2015, p. 157).

In this context, it is notable that the DOSB has recently taken a clear stance against "anti-democratic, right-wing populist, and extremist parties, groups, and actors" urging its member organisations to do the same. A joint statement with the association's youth organisation (dsj) specifically mentions the AfD: "It is evident that the dsj's humanistic outlook on non-profit, organised sports is broader and more comprehensive than the limited perspective of right-wing populist parties such as the AfD" (DOSB and DSJ, 2020).

Regarding the entire German sports sector, various associations and governing bodies started to implement specific integration policies at the end of the 1980s targeting underrepresented groups such as migrants, women, and seniors. Since 2015, the largest program of the DOSB, "Integration through Sport" also formally addresses refugees (Verweyen, 2019, p. 560). In sports science and policy, the understanding of (migration-related) integration now predominantly refers to the mutual adaptation required in an intercultural process, relying on the involvement and contributions of both sides, thus including the majority society (Thiel, Seiberth and Mayer, 2023, p. 383). While there are numerous different integration concepts, three essential overarching objectives regarding integration in (and through) the world of German sport can be identified (Derecik and Tiemann, 2021):

1. Integration *into* sports involves providing access to organised sports for individuals with a migration history.
2. Integration *in* sport demands the actual involvement of individuals with a migration history in the sporting community, fostering competencies within sporting contexts.
3. Integration *through* sport refers to the integration process extending beyond the world of sport, encompassing competency-related transfer effects and attitudes towards society.

Whether these goals have been achieved is questionable. From a simple quantitative perspective, approximately 20% of the DFB members have a migration background, roughly mirroring the current demographics of the country (DFB, 2021). However, integration into sports, namely increasing migrant participation, does not inevitably ensure that subsequent policy objectives are achieved. The limited existing research, especially for sports clubs, suggests that further integrative processes are not necessarily initiated. Instead, targeted, continuous, and pedagogically underpinned integration work is required (Derecik and Tiemann, 2021; Thiel, Seiberth and Mayer, 2023).

Discourses on discrimination in German sports and social sciences

The formal definitions of discrimination in the respective statutes and regulations of various sports organisations have been largely harmonised across the German sports sector. The DOSB, currently comprising more than 101 member organisations, adopted a distinct human rights policy in 2023. In the "Anti-Discrimination" section, it stipulated:

> Every individual should have the opportunity to engage in sports and develop their own abilities in all areas and functions of sports without experiencing discrimination, be it racial discrimination or discrimination based on actual or ascribed nationality or migration history, social origin, social status, religion, worldview, age, gender, and/or gender identity, sexual identity, or disability. For this purpose, the DOSB and the DSJ [German Sports Youth] actively engage while considering intersectionality.
> (DOSB, 2023, p. 6)

The DFB's (2023b, pp. 32–33) approach is quite similar:

> Who violates the human dignity of an individual or a group of individuals through derogatory, discriminatory, or defamatory statements or actions related to origin, skin colour, language, religion, disability, age, gender, or sexual identity, or behaves in a racist and/or contemptuous manner toward others, will be suspended for a minimum of five weeks.

In German social sciences and public discourses, racism has now become widely recognised as a general social problem, whilst in the second half of the 20th century, it was primarily associated with, and limited to, right-wing extremism (Alexopoulou, 2023, p. 35). German historians who used the term racism confined it to the prejudice and intolerance of Black people (Alexopoulou, 2023, p. 44). In recent years, common definitions of racism have expanded to include aspects of culture or religion. Racism is now widely understood as a system of discourses and practices that legitimise and perpetuate power dynamics rooted in history as well as contemporary contexts. In this system, people are grouped into apparently homogeneous categories, presenting others as fundamentally different and incompatible with the "host society", ultimately resulting in the establishment of a hierarchy (Rommelspacher, 2011, p. 29). Different perspectives arise when, for example, further exploring the subtle differences between "Islam hostility" and "anti-Muslim racism". Attia (2013) argues that the concept of "Islam hostility" solely focuses on hostility towards Muslims rather than the process, the Muslimisation. "Anti-Muslim racism", according to his understanding, assumes that religion and culture are unalterable distinguishing features. Consequently, it no longer matters whether a person is religious. What is crucial is solely that the majority of society labels the individual as a Muslim. In this context, he refers to and applies the concept of "Othering", which is often seen as either the underlying mechanism of exclusion behind different forms of discrimination or an unintended precursor to discrimination by excessively highlighting cultural differences (Nobis and El-Kayed, 2022). It describes practices of constructing "Others" and the consequent creation of a positive and powerful "Us" self-image (Thomas-Olalde and Velho, 2011). Particularly in settings that are usually shaped by unity and conflict between groups, as frequently seen in sports environments (Dolan and Connolly, 2016), this concept seems very useful and highly applicable. Especially in football, the creation and reinforcement of "us" versus "them" often leads to the devaluation of the opposing team as part of the game or even the objective itself. Derogatory actions tend to derive from markers of distinction against the respective group, such as in racist slurs against "ethnic" clubs. However, this is not always the case; provocation may still be effective without targeting actual or attributed characteristics of the opposition. It is more of a (football-cultural) code of devaluation, for example, when queer hostile slurs are used to doubt the opponents' perceptions of masculinity (Sülzle, 2011).

Discrimination (I): manifestations of racism and countermeasures

Racist incidents in German amateur and professional football have been regularly documented in the post-Nazi era (Schubert, 2021), although there are no reliable data regarding the quantity and intensity over time. This remains the case until today. Although the DFB annually releases a "Situation Report on Amateur Football", these statistics are not very insightful as they only draw on match reports from referees. During the 2022/23 season, there were 2,679 reported incidents of discrimination, which constituted 0.21% of approximately 1.4 million matches (DFB, 2023c). Detailed data on the proportion of racist incidents are not available. The monitoring conducted by a reporting centre for discriminatory incidents in football in the federal state of North Rhine-Westphalia (MeDiF-NRW), however, clearly shows that racism remains a significant issue. From July to November 2022, a total of 543 incidents reported to MeDIF in both amateur and professional football were examined. Racist incidents made up the second largest share at 26%, following sexism at 28%. In addition to racist remarks made in stadiums, social media play a significant role in the context of racist incidents, with over half of the documented cases (56%) occurring on these platforms (MeDiF-NRW, 2023, p. 33).

Instances of racism that have come to public attention in recent years illustrate the breadth of this phenomenon. They seem to occur across all levels of play, in various regions and involve different actors. Furthermore, they encompass manifestations of anti-Black and anti-Muslim racism, as the following examples show.

In 2019, Clemens Tönnies, then chairman of the supervisory board of the then *Bundesliga* club Schalke 04, stated at a conference on climate change that it would be preferable "to finance 20 power plants in Africa annually". His reasoning was as follows: "This would lead Africans to stop cutting down trees, and they would stop producing children when it's dark". After Tönnies convincingly distanced himself from the aforementioned statements in a hearing, the Ethics Commission of the DFB decided not to initiate further proceedings (DFB, 2019).

In 2020, the then-third division football club Türkgücü Munich was targeted by a nationwide campaign by the far-right fringe party *Der Dritte Weg* (the third way). The party labelled the club's promotion to professional football as a sign of increasing 'foreign infiltration' of the sport. The campaign intertwined racist and anti-Muslim narratives with criticism of the commercialisation of football, targeting the Turkish club patron (Bayerische Informationsstelle gegen Extremismus, 2020).

Even the players from the DFB's national teams, who are frequently referred to as role models for integration, are subjected to (racist) discrimination, as evidenced by the recent case during the 2023 UEFA European Under-21 Championship. After a preliminary match, *Bundesliga* players Youssoufa Moukoko and Jessic Ngankam faced racist backlash on social media for missing penalties (der Spiegel, 2023).

In March 2024, a regional amateur match in Saxony-Anhalt, eastern Germany, had to be abandoned after a Black player was subjected to derogatory racist remarks. He was called a "monkey" and told to "go back to where he came from" by an opposing player (Mitteldeutscher Rundfunk, 2024). The regional association in Saxony-Anhalt has repeatedly been under public scrutiny: in 2023, it expelled the ninth-division club Eintracht Gladau from participating in competitive matches. A prominent neo-Nazi figure is a leading member of the club, and some players are listed as extremists by the State Ministry of the Interior. However, in 2024, courts overturned this decision, citing insufficient evidence that the football club was promoting far-right and neo-fascist ideas (Rieger and Trepper, 2024).

Given that racist attitudes are prevalent across all social strata (Rommelspacher, 2011), at least in fragmented elements, it is not surprising that they surface in various football settings. Racist abuse and other similar incidents that reflect a far-right extremist worldview are more likely to occur in regions where such attitudes are more deeply rooted and widespread. Hence, these reported incidents are more common in eastern Germany, particularly in rural areas and amateur leagues. The DFB appears to be aware of this, as shown by its launch of an anti-racism project in collaboration with the Northeast German Football Association (NOFV) in 2024, which targets amateur football in this pilot region. The project includes anti-racism training for players, coaches, officials, and club boards. The overarching goal is to develop and implement preventive and interventionist strategies in collaboration with individuals in clubs and associations who are already actively involved in combating racism (Nordostdeutscher Fußballverband, 2024). It aligns with a series of existing initiatives, programs, and projects aiming to fight racism in German football, such as:

- The "Schalke Fan Initiative", which already in 1994 advocated for the inclusion of an anti-racism clause in the statutes of FC Schalke 04 (https://www.fan-ini.com);
- Annual awareness-raising campaigns like themed match days in German professional football during the "International Weeks Against Racism" (https://bundesliga-wirkt.dfl.de/iwgr23);
- Member organisations of *Lernort Stadion*, learning location stadium, situated in 26 football grounds or club museums across Germany, offer anti-racism workshops aimed at students (https://www.lernort-stadion.de/);
- "Fan projects" of professional clubs that operate as autonomous youth welfare organisations employ social pedagogy with supporters to tackle instances of violence and racism, while also providing support to those affected (https://www.kos-fanprojekte.de/);
- The network *Bündnis Aktiver Fußballfans*, alliance of active football fans (BAFF), acts as a lobbying organisation for football supporters and actively combats racism within fan communities, for example, by participating in public forums with football associations and/or organising issue-specific demonstrations (https://www.aktive-fans.de).

Overall, fans and fan organisations stand out as pioneers and a major driving force of anti-racism campaigns and initiatives. A growing number of professional clubs have adopted these initiatives in recent years and integrated them into their membership management and corporate social responsibility agendas (Zengel, 2021; Müller, Haut and Heim, 2024). However, there are hardly any critical evaluations of these efforts available and little is known about the success and impact of these measures. In amateur football, occasional actions and sporadic messages are noticeable. Signs bearing messages like "No Place for Racism" are nowadays widespread in football venues all over Germany. Yet, it is questionable whether they alone without any additional substantive measures have an impact or if they might even inhibit a deeper, self-reflective examination of racist structures and attitudes in the clubs.

Discrimination (II): Islamophobia (?), Mesut Özil and the Turkish president

In May 2018, German national players Mesut Özil and İlkay Gündoğan, both Germans of Turkish descent, appeared for a photo opportunity with Turkish

President Recep Tayyip Erdoğan, which ignited an interesting controversy in Germany. The photo was interpreted as a gesture of support for Erdoğan, who is not very popular in Germany due to, among other reasons, his autocratic leadership style, and raised questions about their "loyalty to Germany". Criticism escalated after Germany's disappointing World Cup performance in 2018 in Russia, with Özil bearing much of the media backlash. On 22 July 2018, Özil resigned from the national team, citing racism and disrespect as his main reasons (Waas, 2021). The incident sheds light on broader issues of integration and anti-Muslim racism in German society.

Various discourse analyses of the media coverage (Waas, 2021; Möllering and Schmidt, 2022) suggest that the "Özil case" was often publicly framed as a symbol of failed integration in Germany, rather than as an example of widespread racism. In contrast to other footballers with migrant backgrounds, such as Lukas Podolski and Miroslav Klose, both have Polish roots, Özil was more frequently discussed in the context of integration and ethnicity. This indicates that individuals of Turkish descent (and/or Muslims) face greater pressure to meet biased or one-sided integration expectations (Möllering and Schmidt, 2022). Despite being celebrated before the 2018 World Cup as the "poster child for integration" (Waas, 2021, p. 151), Özil's loyalty and sense of belonging to German society were repeatedly questioned, often in conjunction with his decision not to sing the national anthem before matches (Zambon, 2022).

Gündoğan was able to quickly put the controversy surrounding the Erdoğan photo behind him and later even became captain of the German national team. Özil's actions, however, following his resignation from the German national team, such as having Erdoğan as his best man, were mostly interpreted as a gradual distancing from Germany. Özil later moved to Turkey, where he continues to live after retiring from professional football. During the recent EURO 2024 quarter-final match in Germany between Turkey and the Netherlands, Özil accompanied Erdoğan as part of his entourage. The game in Berlin was politically highly charged, with additional tension caused by the controversy surrounding the "Grey Wolves Salute", a symbolic hand gesture associated with the Turkish far-right movement. Turkish player Merih Demiral, along with numerous fans in the stands, made the gesture during his goal celebration in the Round of 16 against Austria, which resulted in a two-game suspension by UEFA. The incident even sparked diplomatic tensions, leading both Germany and Turkey to summon each other's ambassadors. Özil further involved himself in the debate by posting a photo on Instagram of Demiral's controversial celebration, accompanied by a message of support for Turkey (Der Spiegel, 2024).

The "Özil case", which can only be briefly summarised here without exploring all its nuances, serves as a prime example of the complex and emotionally charged discussions surrounding "successful" integration in German football and society. Double standards fuelled by anti-Muslim racism and Islamophobia contrast sharply with a factual yet critical examination of Özil's behaviour.

Discrimination (III): from subtle insinuations to overt hatred – Antisemitism as a constant in football

As antisemitism was a core tenet of the Nazi ideology during the "Third Reich" (1933–45) and, ultimately, led to the Holocaust, it has been a highly sensitive issue and topic in German politics, society, and social research ever since (Müller, Haut and Heim, 2023, p. 552). This extends to football as well. Jews were important pioneers as players and club officials in the early stages of football's history in Germany, that is from the late 19th century onwards. "However, in 1933, this changed abruptly: Shortly after the NSDAP's seizure of power, many clubs, in anticipatory obedience, began to exclude their Jewish members and erase their former teammates from the collective club memory" (Peiffer and Wahlig, 2020, p. 40). Jewish clubs, serving as refuges for footballers excluded from "German" clubs, endured persistent harassment, preceding their complete disenfranchisement and persecution by 1938 (Müller and Haut, 2021, p. 31). The DFB and most of its clubs "turned a blind eye to the increasingly relentless treatment of their former Jewish sports companions, thereby making themselves complicit in the murder of Jews" (Havemann, 2006). For several decades after the Second World War, representing the history of most clubs during the Nazi era was considered taboo, and club chronicles between 1933 and 1945 were conspicuously absent. Primarily, initiatives by fan organisations and individuals have independently examined the role of their clubs (Berger and Engelhardt, 2023, p. 118). Today, according to Wahlig, there is no sports association worldwide "that is as dedicated to commemorative culture as the DFB" (DFB, 2023d).

The majority of antisemitic incidents in post-Nazi German football are not necessarily directed at genuine Jews (Brunssen, 2023, p. 65). As previously highlighted, the dynamics of in-groups and out-groups in football tend to foster an "us versus them" mentality (Degele and Janz, 2011). The use of antisemitic rhetoric as a taboo-breaking strategy to provoke the opposing team appears to be particularly effective. In 2019, German sociologist Florian Schubert suggested that "Jew is the biggest insult in football" (Scheler, 2019). Professional and semi-professional German football have repeatedly witnessed various expressions of antisemitism, ranging from fan chants to banners or stickers referencing crimes of the Nazi era. Manifestations of this "antisemitism without Jews" (Brunssen, 2023) carry, of course, the risk of trivialisation of a much larger issue. For instance, antisemitic chants by fans are downplayed as casual language or banter rather than a reproduction of Jew hatred. This strengthens the externalisation of "dangerous" antisemitism, portraying it as an issue solely present within the context of right-wing extremism and Islamism, and thereby underestimating and neglecting its prevalence in society as a whole (Brunssen and Müller, 2024, p. 147).

Another facet is the dissemination of conspiracy theories drawing on antisemitic arguments and story-lines (Müller, 2021). Antisemitic conspiracy narratives often employ global economic crises or pandemics. The identification of alleged culprits and scapegoats works quite effectively in football, too, even in the absence of Jewish individuals. This is particularly evident in the case of referees, who are often labelled as a "Jew" in conjunction with allegations of corruption, as "the complexities of the game are projected onto the decisions of an individual" (Brunssen, 2023, p. 65). This can be understood as coping with contingency, which involves reducing uncertainties for which one has no explanation. Football matches comprise a series of random situations, and the final result cannot be entirely attributed to individual factors or situations. This sense of overwhelm and perplexity can be managed and simplified through the creation of conspiracy narratives, such as claims of bias by referees or sports authorities (Brunssen and Müller, 2024, p. 150).

Before further discussing football-related antisemitism directed specifically at Jews, it is worthwhile to examine the rather complex composition of the Jewish community in Germany. Between 1990 and 2004, an estimated 220,000 Jews from the former Soviet states migrated to Germany. They constitute the largest group among the Jewish population in the country today (Botmann, 2023, p. 17). Particularly, younger generations of Jews are a highly diverse social group, although they mainly comprise post-Soviets. In addition, there is a large contingent of Jews raised in Germany as descendants of Holocaust survivors and migrants from Israel. The majority appears to be secular but continue to engage with some religious elements as cultural practices (Brankovic and Kranz, 2022, pp. 151–154). Irrespective of whether they individually have a migration history (or not), Jews frequently recount experiences of Othering, being constructed as essential outsiders through attributions and symbolic exclusions (Zick, Hövermann, Jensen et al., 2017, p. 43). This may also be linked to the portrayal of Jews in the media who tends to be framed by the triad of antisemitism, the Holocaust, and the conflict in the Middle East (Ott, 2022, p. 4), or they are, stereotypically, depicted as orthodox-religious (Brankovic and Kranz, 2022, p. 154). The creation of otherness inevitably leads to the expectation of integration, which subsequently appears even more paradoxical: "The Jews" are often perceived as "highly capable and willing to integrate". However, even when performing a kind of "cultural assimilation" (e.g. by not publicly practicing their religion), they still become targets of antisemitism (Zick, Hövermann, Jensen et al., 2017, p. 60). Furthermore, current monitoring points to an intertwining of antisemitism and anti-Slavic racism, as Jewish individuals and communities report antisemitic atmospheres, feeling stigmatised as "migrants" and targeted for being Jewish, due to social markers like language (Feldmann and Steinitz, 2019, p. 20). However, they are often being excluded from anti-racist initiatives and intersectional concepts due to the blanket categorisation as "White" (Ott, 2022, p. 6).

Müller's quantitative study (2021) offers insights into the prevalence of antisemitic incidents affecting German Maccabi sports clubs. Maccabi is a Jewish sports movement with associations and clubs in over 80 countries. Currently, there are 41 German Maccabi clubs, comprising approximately 6,000 Jewish and non-Jewish members. These clubs were (re)founded from the 1960s onwards, following the break-up of the Jewish sports movement in Germany during the Nazi era (Müller and Haut, 2021). 39% of the 309 members surveyed in 2021 had encountered antisemitism due to their Maccabi membership at least once. When focusing on footballers, this percentage increases to 68% (Müller, Haut and Heim, 2023, p. 559). These incidents affected both Jewish and non-Jewish athletes and occurred within and beyond sports facilities. Crude verbal insults or subtle insinuations constituted the most common forms, while notably, physical assaults were more frequent compared to antisemitic incidents in other societal contexts. Incidents ranged from antisemitic conspiracy myths ("You Jews did Corona") to slurs and threats related to the Holocaust ("You will eventually be gassed") or Israel-related antisemitism. In this context, nearly half of the respondents stated that Maccabi members are often perceived as representatives of Israeli politics (Müller, 2021, p. 43). Previous research documented similar statements from officials of Jewish Maccabi sports clubs in Germany. It appears that escalations in the Middle East conflict often result in heightened antisemitic incidents against Maccabi organisations and its members (Schubert, 2019, p. 267). The Hamas attacks on Israel in October 2023 and subsequent antisemitic sentiments in Germany led to the suspension of several sporting activities by Maccabi clubs due to security concerns (Norddeutscher Rundfunk, 2023).

The perception and labelling of non-Jewish members as Jewish reveals a specific and peculiar set of discrimination dynamics. Muslim members, in particular, are stigmatised as "traitors", as their affiliation with Maccabi aligns them with Judaism, which excludes them from an imagined Muslim community (Schubert, 2019). Additionally, there is also an example of a Black footballer who reports being subjected to insults such as "Shit black Jew" – illustrating the intersectionality of antisemitic insults with racism (Müller, 2021, p. 35).

The overlap between antisemitism and other forms of discrimination in football can also be found outside the Maccabi sphere (Brunssen and Müller, 2024, pp. 150–153). For instance, antisemitic hostilities in fan chants are sometimes fused with anti-Romani sentiment. Occasionally, antisemitic banners also carry sexist messages that serve to reinforce a traditional sense of masculinity and uphold the "male grammar" in football fan culture (Sülzle, 2011). The link between ideologies of inequality, such as sexism, queerphobia, and antisemitism, is apparent, as they have always been framed by the propagation of "weak" body images. Unsurprisingly, these ideologies are frequently communicated in the context of football, which is inherently physical. Until now, research into football-related discrimination has mostly focused on individual phenomena which reveal a high degree of complexity. There is an urgent need to fully understand their origins and develop recommendations for action. Even when solely examining antisemitic discrimination, great diversity among offenders, victims, and types of incidents can be observed (Brunssen and Müller, 2024, p. 157).

Preventive and interventionist efforts – countermeasures by football organisations

Since the 1980s, key stakeholders in German football have paid increased attention to the complex issue of discrimination and subsequently introduced and progressively expanded countermeasures. However, different forms of discrimination have not received equal attention over time. While initially, the emphasis was on racism, projects, and campaigns against queer hostility and sexism only experienced heightened attention from the mid-2000s onwards. Degele and Janz (2011, p. 27) note a "boom in initiatives" addressing these two forms of discrimination, nearly paralleling the number of projects against racism during the same period.

However, endeavours to address discrimination in professional German football are now firmly institutionalised. In the 2019/2020 season alone, first and second-division clubs implemented over 1,100 social and educational projects. Antidiscrimination was recognised as their primary focus, with other themes and activities including "support for children" and "environment and ecology" following (Zengel, 2021, p. 7). Club activities in this context vary considerably. For instance, clubs provide workshops either independently or in collaboration with non-governmental organisations, focusing on topics like discrimination and democratic values. Alongside these educational initiatives, there are recurring efforts to raise awareness during match days. The target audiences typically include the general public, fans, or youth groups (Hedderich and Krümmel, 2017). The increase of many clubs' social engagement can be explained by a combination of intrinsic values and external pressure. Much like the competitive dynamics inherent in sports, a contest for social legitimacy appears to have unfolded (Raimo, Vitolla, Nicolò et al., 2021). This implies that effective preventive projects introduced by one club are frequently replicated or adjusted by others. In addition to the requests from fans and members, expectations for socially responsible actions come from various sources, such as sponsors, political institutions, or even mandates by the associations (Reuter, 2023, pp. 14–15).

In the context of monitoring discriminatory incidents in amateur football, the pivotal role of referees has been stressed. However, Germany has been contending with a shortage of referees for several years, which can be partly attributed to violence and discrimination directed at them (Süddeutsche Zeitung,

2024). This shortage creates pressures for those involved. Clubs, for example, face penalties if the prescribed quota of referees is not met, and associations risk negative public relations due to an increasing number of cancelled matches. It can be presumed that this situation also results in the appointment of referees who may not be suitable for the task, which, in turn, affects the quality of the match officials. Football associations are aware of this challenge and address it in various ways. One structural approach involves supplementing referees through additional reporting mechanisms: In recent years, "Contact points for incidents of violence and discrimination" were established by the regional associations: "The goal is that every person – whether affected individuals, teammates, coaches, officials, or spectators – can report incidents to the regional association, and these will be processed appropriately" (Steinrücke, 2023, p. 109). Additionally, the DFB has intensified its effort to promote awareness of how to deal with genuine discrimination during games. In collaboration with partners, the DFB produced the instructional video "Referees Against Discrimination" in 2023, featuring FIFA referees Deniz Aytekin and Katrin Rafalski. The video educates referees on how to differentiate between "regular" insults, such as "asshole", which warrant a red card but do not target personal characteristics or social power dynamics, and those that contain discriminatory content. The video also offers guidance on appropriate responses and post-incident procedures (DFB, 2023e).

Criticism on the handling of incidents also extends to the sports judiciary level, as only a minimal fraction is legally adjudicated as discrimination under sports law (Vester, 2023, p. 91). In addition to the renewed confusion between non-discriminatory and discriminatory insults at this level, legal challenges arise from some regional associations who hastily and simply adopted the exact wording of the corresponding DFB norm. This results in disproportionately high mandatory fines of €18,000 that potentially endanger the existence of amateur clubs. Consequently, sports judges may consciously downgrade the discriminations to "regular" insults (Vester and Reif, 2022). In recent years, efforts have been made to establish a new catalogue containing a more constructive set of sanctions. Such "alternative sanction measures" aim to induce behavioural change through educational interventions, including workshops that address discrimination. These measures target individual players, teams, or even entire clubs. They are carried out in collaboration with expert organisations or facilitated by football conflict managers within the association (Steinrücke, 2023, p. 109). However, there is currently a lack of data on the success of this instrument.

Conclusion

This chapter has focused on the tense and contradictory relationship between socio-cultural integration and various forms of discrimination in the complex and multi-layered world of football in Germany. There appears to be a very visible gulf between expectations and reality, which is particularly challenging as both German society and the world of German football are ethnically very diverse entities. Nonetheless, it should be noted that the long-standing integration-through-assimilation paradigm, despite recent political developments, no longer dictates the actions of key actors in the associations and major clubs. This is also reflected in the changed communication and more refined messages: In 1993, prompted by a right-wing terrorist murder in Solingen and responding to a large number of racist incidents in the Bundesliga, a charity match was organised featuring the German national team against a selection of foreign *Bundesliga* players under the motto "My friend is a foreigner". On the occasion of its 30th anniversary, the DFB revisited the theme and changed it to "My friend is no longer a foreigner" in order to stress its commitment to "integration and diversity" (DFB-Stiftungen, 2023). The balancing act between leveraging integration potentials and recognising and addressing discrimination continues to represent a challenge for football's key stakeholders.

It is obvious that in German football various forms of discrimination persist, at both the amateur and professional levels. A reliable assessment of whether the quantity and intensity of these phenomena have changed over the past decades proves challenging due to the absence of longitudinal data. Nevertheless, there is no doubt that awareness among key stakeholders has grown. Progress in establishing reporting systems has also been made, albeit with plenty of room for further improvement. Particularly in the context of monitoring and evaluation, it would be advisable to coordinate the efforts of sports organisations, policymakers, and civil society actors to avoid a potential duplication of structures and efforts. Despite these advancements, significant research gaps persist, particularly concerning intersectionality of different forms of discrimination. The diversity of approaches to analytically separate different forms of discrimination and their empirical measurability remains a challenge but also serves as an indicator of ongoing developments in research that responds to societal changes.

Concerning prevention, the predominant focus of anti-discrimination initiatives in German football lies in primary prevention. This approach accentuates the empowerment of individuals and groups, as well as the establishment of conditions mitigating discrimination. According to Pilz (2016, pp. 670–671), football authorities such as the DFB and DFL (German Football League, which manages, organises and controls the top two divisions of German football) must also assume responsibility for secondary prevention and should establish targeted efforts with at-risk populations, such as youth leaning towards right-wing extremism. In this context, socio-educational fan projects funded by the football authorities, as well as fan representatives of clubs, play a pivotal role (Pilz, 2016, pp. 670–671).

Reluctance to openly confront issues related to discrimination still stems from uncertainties in managing it and anxieties about potential harm to the sport's public image, leading to an emphasis on the affirmative aspects of diversity in football (Lazar, 2020, pp. 18–19). While promoting diversity is commendable, it cannot replace the explicit sensitisation to discriminatory practices. As crucial elements, it is necessary to include further relevant qualifications for key individuals within the associations and, at the very least, the clubs with the appropriate resources, as well as clear (advisory) structures, unambiguous guidance, and a culture of openness that recognises the pervasive nature of discrimination in all segments of German society – not solely in the context of right-wing extremism.

References

Alexopoulou, M. (2023) "Rassismus als Leerstelle der deutschen Zeitgeschichte" [Racism as a blank space in German contemporary history], in Polat, S. (Ed.), *Rassismusforschung* [Racism Research], Bielefeld: Transcript Verlag.

Attia, I. (2013) "Privilegien sichern, nationale Identität revitalisieren. Gesellschafts-und handlungstheoretische Dimensionen der Theorie des antimuslimischen Rassismus im Unterschied zu Modellen von Islamophobie und Islamfeindlichkeit" [Securing privileges, revitalizing national identity: sociological and action-theoretical dimensions of the theory of anti-Muslim racism compared to models of Islamophobia and anti-Islam sentiment], *Journal für Psychologie*, 21(1), pp. 1–31.

Baumann, A. (2022) "Mehr integration? Fußball und Arbeitsmigranten in der Bundesrepublik Deutschland 1955 bis 1973" [More integration? Football and labour migrants in the Federal Republic of Germany from 1955 to 1973], *Vierteljahrshefte für Zeitgeschichte*, 70(1), pp. 63–86.

Bayerische Informationsstelle gegen Extremismus (2020) "'Türkgücü München nicht willkommen': der Dritte Weg agitiert gegen Fußballverein" ['Türkgücü Munich not welcome': the third way agitates football club], *Bayerische Informationsstelle gegen Extremismus*. Available: <https://www.bige.bayern.de/infos_zu_extremismus/aktuelle_meldungen/turkgucu-munchen-nicht-willkommen-der-dritte-weg-agitiert-gegen-fussballverein/> [accessed on 1st March 2024].

Bendel, P. and Borkowski, A. (2016) "Entwicklung der Integrationspolitik" [Development of integration policy], in Brinkmann, H.U. and Sauer, M. (Eds.), *Einwanderungsgesellschaft Deutschland. Entwicklung und Stand der Integration* [Immigration society Germany: development and state of integration], Wiesbaden: Springer VS.

Berger, M. and Engelhardt, L. (2023) "Bekämpfung von Antisemitismus im Sport: der multiperspektivische Ansatz von Zusammen1" [Combating antisemitism in sport: the multiperspective approach of Zusammen1], in Zentralrat der Juden in Deutschland (Ed.), *Strafraum. Die (Un-)Sichtbarkeit von Antisemitismus im Fußball* [Penalty area: the (in)visibility of antisemitism in football], Leipzig: Hentrich & Hentrich.

Blecking, D. (2008) "Diachroner Vergleich und aktuelle Integrationsdiskurse im Sport" [Diachronic comparison and current integration discourses in sport], in Gieß-Stüber, P. and Blecking, D. (Eds.), *Sport – Integration – Europa: Neue Horizonte für interkulturelle Bildung* [Sport – Integration – Europe: new horizons for intercultural education] Baltmannsweiler: Schneider.

Blecking, D. (2015) "Vielheit statt Integration. Wie Migranten den deutschen Fußball aufbauen" [Diversity instead of integration: how migrants build German football], in Endemann, M., Claus, R., Dembowski, G. and Gabler, J. (Eds.), *Zurück am Tatort Stadion: Diskriminierung und Antidiskriminierung in Fußball-Fankulturen* [Back at the crime scene stadium: discrimination and anti-discrimination in football fan cultures], Göttingen: Die Werkstatt.

Botmann, D. (2023) "Antisemitismusbekämpfung aus jüdischer Perspektive" [Combating antisemitism from a Jewish perspective], in Zentralrat der Juden in Deutschland (Ed.), *Strafraum. Die (Un-)Sichtbarkeit von Antisemitismus im Fußbal* [Penalty area: the (in)visibility of antisemitism in football], Leipzig: Hentrich & Hentrich.

Brankovic, C. and Kranz, D. (2022) "Mehr als Antisemitismus und Exotenzirkus" [More than antisemitism and an exotic circus], in Bundeszentrale für politische Bildung (Ed.), *Jüdisches Leben in Deutschland* [Jewish life in Germany], Bonn: Bundeszentrale für politische Bildung.

Braun, S. and Finke, S. (2010) "Integrationsmotor Sportverein: ergebnisse zum Modellprojekt 'spin – Sport interkulturell'" [Sport club as an engine for integration: results of the model project 'spin – Intercultural sport'], in Braun, S. and Nobis, T. (Eds.), *Migration, integration und sport. Zivilgesellschaft vor Ort* [Migration, integration, and sport: civil society on the ground], Wiesbaden: Springer VS.

Brunssen, P. (2023) "Zwischen den Zeilen: antisemitismus ohne Juden im Fußball" [Between the lines: antisemitism without Jews in football], in Zentralrat der Juden in Deutschland (Ed.), *Strafraum. Die (Un-)Sichtbarkeit von Antisemitismus im Fußball* [Penalty area: the (in)visibility of antisemitism in football], Leipzig: Hentrich & Hentrich.

Brunssen, P. and Müller, L. (2024) "Ziemlich unsportlich. Antisemitismus, Intersektionalität und Mehrfachdiskriminierungen im Sport" [Quite unfair: antisemitism, intersectionality, and multiple discrimination in sport], in Initiative Interdisziplinäre Antisemitismusforschung (Ed.), *Antisemitismus in der postnazistischen Migrationsgesellschaft* [*Antisemitism in the post-Nazi migration society*], Trier: Barbara Budrich.

Degele, N. and Janz, C. (2011) *Hetero, weiß und männlich? Fußball ist viel mehr!* [Hetero, white, and male? Football is much more!], Berlin: Friedrich-Ebert-Stiftung.

Delto, H. and Zick, A. (2022) "Antisemitismus und fußballaffine Jugendliche im Verein: ausprägungen, Differenzen und Strategien für einen zivilen Umgang" [Antisemitism and football-affiliated youth in clubs: forms, differences, and strategies for civil approaches], in Baier, J. and Grimm, M. (Eds.), *Antisemitismus in Jugendkulturen: Erscheinungsformen und Gegenstrategien* [Antisemitism in youth cultures: manifestations and counter-strategies], Schwalbach am Taunus: Wochenschau Verlag.

Der Spiegel (2023) "Moukoko wehrt sich gegen Rassismus auf Instagram" [Moukoko takes a stand against racism on Instagram], *Der Spiegel*, 23rd June 2023. Available: <https://www.spiegel.de/sport/fussball/u21-em-2023-youssoufa-moukoko-wehrt-sich-gegen-rassistische-beleidigungen-a-e48c033c-d305-4eb4-8fa5-0f7e094c122f> [accessed on 27th February 2024].

Der Spiegel (2024) "Mesut Özil in Erdoğans Entourage beim Spiel gegen die Niederlande" [Mesut Özil in Erdoğan's Entourage at the match against the Netherlands], *Der Spiegel*, 6th July 2024. Available: <https://www.spiegel.de/sport/fussball/em-2024-tuerkei-vs-niederlande-mesut-oezil-in-der-entourage-von-recep-tayyip-erdogan-a-5462a7af-e2f4-46b7-a1b4-1c4eb98a570b> [accessed on 14th September 2024].

Derecik, A. and Tiemann, H. (2021) "Integration im Sport – Inklusion im Sport – Diskurse und Perspektiven" [Integration in sport – Inclusion in sport – Discourses and perspectives], in Güllich, A. and Krüger, M. (Eds.), *Sport in Kultur und Gesellschaft* [*Sport in culture and society*], Berlin: Springer Spektrum.

Deutscher Fußball-Bund (2019) Fall Clemens Tönnies: Erklärung Der Unabhängigen Ethik-Kommission [The Clemens Tönnies case: statement of the independent ethics commission]. Available: <https://www.dfb.de/news/detail/fall-clemens-toennies-erklaerung-der-unabhaengigen-ethik-kommission-206724/> [accessed on 27th February 2024].

Deutscher Fußball-Bund (2021) *Integration.* Available: <https://www.dfb.de/vielfaltanti-diskriminierung/herkunft/integration/> [accessed on 27th February 2024].

Deutscher Fußball-Bund (2023a) *Mitglieder Statistik 2023* [Membership statistics 2023]. Available: <https://www.dfb.de/fileadmin/_dfbdam/286387-DFB-Statistik_2023_%281%29.pdf> [accessed on 27th February 2024].

Deutscher Fußball-Bund (2023b) *Rechts-und Verfahrensordnung. Ethik-Kodex* [Rules and procedures: code of ethics]. Available: <https://www.dfb.de/fileadmin/_dfbdam/292214-Heft_07_Rechts-Verfahrensordnung_Ethik-Kodex_20231001.pdf> [accessed on 27th February 2024].

Deutscher Fußball-Bund (2023c) *DFB veröffentlicht 9. Lagebild des Amateurfußballs* [DFB publishes 9th report on amateur football]. Available: <https://www.dfb.de/news/detail/dfb-veroeffentlicht-9-lagebild-des-amateurfussballs-254303/> [accessed on 27th February 2024].

Deutscher Fußball-Bund (2023d) Neues geschichtsbuch über jüdischen fussball in der ns-zeit [New history book on Jewish football in the Nazi era]. Available: <https://www.dfb.de/vielfaltanti-diskriminierung/news/news-detail/full/1/?tx_news_pi1%5Bnews%5D=140160&cHash=00321bac51a56a92c1b95e13b433ab37> [accessed on 27th February 2024].

Deutscher Fußball-Bund (2023e) *Aytekin und rafalski starten aufruf "schiris gegen diskriminierung"* [Aytekin and Rafalski launch call to action 'refs against discrimination']. Available: <https://www.dfb.de/news/detail/aytekin-und-rafalski-starten-aufruf-schiris-gegen-diskriminierung-250120/> [accessed on 27th February 2024].

Deutscher Olympischer Sportbund (2023) *Menschenrechtspolicy des Deutschen Olympischen Sportbunds und der Deutschen Sportjugend* [Human rights policy of the German Olympic sports confederation and the German sports youth]. Available: <https://cdn.dosb.de/user_upload/www.dosb.de/uber_uns/Menschenrechte/DOSB-23004_Menschenrechts_Policy_WEB.pdf> [accessed on 27th February 2024].

Deutscher Olympischer Sportbund und Deutsche Sportjugend (2020) *Klare Haltung für eine offene, vielfältige und demokratische Gesellschaft* [Clear stance for an open, diverse, and democratic society]. Available: <https://static-dsj-de.s3.amazonaws.com/Deutsche_Sportjugend/Positionen/Gemeinsame_Positionierung_gegen_Rechtspopulismus_DOSB_dsj.pdf> [accessed on 27th February 2024].

DFB-Stiftungen (2023) *"mein freund ist kein ausländer mehr" – DFB-stiftungen und lothar matthäus senden zeichen für integration und vielfalt* ['My friend is no longer a foreigner' – DFB foundations and Lothar Matthäus send a message for integration and diversity]. Available: <https://www.dfb-stiftungen.de/news/mein-freund-ist-kein-auslander-mehr-dfb-stiftungen-und-lothar-matthaus-senden-zeichen-fur-integration-und-vielfalt> [accessed on 27th February 2024].

Dolan, P. and Connolly, J. (2016) "Sport, unity and conflict: an enduring social dynamic", *European Journal for Sport and Society*, 13(2), pp. 189–196.

Feldmann, D. and Steinitz, B. (2019) *Antisemitismus in Brandenburg. Problembeschreibung* [Antisemitism in Brandenburg: problem description], Berlin: Bundesverband der Recherche-und Informationsstellen Antisemitismus.

Geiges, L. (2018) "Wie die AfD im Kontext der "Flüchtlingskrise" mobilisierte. Eine empirisch-qualitative Untersuchung der "Herbstoffensive 2015"" [How the AfD mobilized in the context of the 'refugee crisis': an empirical-qualitative study of the 'autumn offensive 2015'], *Zeitschrift für Politikwissenschaft*, 28, pp. 49–69.

Havemann, N. (2006) *Fußball unterm Hakenkreuz* [Football under the Swastika]. Available: <https://www.bpb.de/shop/zeitschriften/apuz/29769/fussball-unterm-hakenkreuz/> [accessed on 27th February 2024].

Hedderich, F. and Krümmel, M. (2017) *Zweite Studie zum freiwilligen gesellschaftlichen Engagement des Profifussballs. Saison 2015/16* [Second study on voluntary social engagement in professional football: season 2015/16], Frankfurt am Main: Bundesliga-Stiftung.

Heitmeyer, W. (1998) "Gesellschaftliche Desintegration und ethnisch-kulturelle Konflikte" [Social disintegration and ethno-cultural conflicts], in Klein, M.L. and Kothy, J. (Eds.), *Ethnisch-kulturelle Konflikte im Sport* [Ethno-cultural conflicts in sport], Hamburg: Czwalina.

Kogan, I. (2011) "New immigrants: old disadvantage patterns? Labour market integration of recent immigrants into Germany", *International Migration*, 49, pp. 91–117.

Lazar, R. (2020) *Handlungsempfehlungen zum Vorgehen gegen Antisemitismus im Fußball* [Recommendations for action against antisemitism in football]. Available: <https://www.stiftung-ng.de/fileadmin/dateien/Stiftung/ueber_uns/Projekte/Handlungsempfehlungen_zum_Vorgehen_gegen_Antisemitismus_im_Fussball.pdf> [accessed on 27th February 2024].

MeDiF-NRW (2023) *1. Jahresbericht Meldestelle für Diskriminierung im Fussball in NRW* [1st annual report of the Reporting Office for Discrimination in Football in NRW], Bochum: Landesarbeitsgemeinschaft Fanprojekte NRW e. V.

Meier-Braun, K.H. (2017) "Einleitung: deutschland Einwanderungsland" [Introduction: Germany as a country of immigration], in Meier-Braun, K.H. and Reinhold, W. (Eds.), *Deutschland Einwanderungsland: Begriffe – Fakten – Kontroversen* [Germany as a country of immigration: terms – facts – controversies], Stuttgart: Kohlhammer.

Merkel, U., Sombert, K. and Tokarski, W. (1996) "Football, racism and Xenophobia in Germany: 50 years later – Here we go again?", in Merkel, U. and Tokarski, W. (Eds.), *Racism and Xenophobia in European football*, Aachen: Meyer & Meyer.

Mitteldeutscher Rundfunk (2024) "Rassismusvorwurf im Fußball: spielabbruch in Plötzkau" [Accusation of racism in football: match abandonment in Plötzkau], *Mitteldeutscher Rundfunk*. Available: <https://www.mdr.de/nachrichten/sachsen-anhalt/magdeburg/salzland/rassismus-fussball-landesklasse-ploetzkau-ottersleben–100.html> [accessed on 1st March 2024].

Möllering, M. and Schmidt, E. (2022) "The case of Mesut Özil: a symbol of (non-) integration? An analysis of German print media discourses on integration", *Discourse & Communication*, 16(3), pp. 326–345.

Müller, L. (2021) *Zwischen Akzeptanz und Anfeindung: antisemitismuserfahrungen jüdischer Sportvereine in Deutschland* [Between acceptance and hostility: experiences of antisemitism in Jewish sports clubs in Germany], Frankfurt am Main: Zusammen.

Müller, L. and Haut, J. (2021) "Jüdischer sport und antisemitismus: geschichte und Gegenwart" [Jewish sport and antisemitism: history and present], *Aus Politik und Zeitgeschichte*, 71(44–45), pp. 27–34.

Müller, L., Haut, J. and Heim, C. (2023) "Antisemitism as a football specific problem? The situation of Jewish clubs in German amateur sport", *International Review for the Sociology of Sport*, 58(3), pp. 550–569.

Müller, L., Haut, J. and Heim, C. (2024) "Combatting antisemitism in German football", *International Journal of Sport Policy and Politics*. Unpublished.

Niersbach, W. (2011) "Vorwort" [Foreword], in Deutscher Fußball-Bund (Ed.), *Tor! Integration fängt bei mir an!* [Goal! Integration starts with me!], Frankfurt am Main: Deutscher Fußball-Bund.

Nobis, T. and El-Kayed, N. (2022) "Othering in sport-related research: how research produces and reproduces images of 'the immigrant other'", *European Journal for Sport and Society*, 20(4), pp. 332–350.

Norddeutscher Rundfunk (2023) "Makkabi-Präsident Alon Meyer über Judenhass: 'Nie wieder ist jetzt'" [Maccabi president Alon Meyer on antisemitism: 'Never again is now'], *Norddeutscher Rundfunk*. Available: <https://www.ndr.de/sport/mehr_sport/

Makkabi-Praesident-Meyer-ueber-Judenhass-Nie-wieder-ist-jetzt,makkabi108. html> [accessed on 1st March 2024].

Nordostdeutscher Fußballverband (2024) "Fußballzeit ist die beste Zeit gegen Rassismus" [Football time is the best time against racism], *Nordostdeutscher Fußballverband*. Available: <https://nofv-online.de/index.php/aktuelles-leser/fussballzeit-ist-die-beste-zeit-gegen-rassismus.html> [accessed on 1st March 2024].

Oltmer, J. (2016) "Europäische und deutsche Migrationsverhältnisse im 19. und 20. Jahrhundert" [European and German migration relations in the 19th and 20th centuries], in Brinkmann, H.U. and Sauer, M. (Eds.), *Einwanderungsgesellschaft Deutschland. Entwicklung und Stand der Integration* [Immigration society Germany: development and state of integration], Wiesbaden: Springer VS.

Ott, M. (2022) "Intersektionale Betroffenheiten, analytische Leestellen und solidarische Strategien" [Intersectional concerns, analytical gaps, and solidarity strategies], *hinsehen, Halbjahresmagazin der Opferberatung Rheinland*, 4, pp. 3–6.

Peiffer, L. and Wahlig, H. (2020) "Verehrt, Verfolgt, Vergessen: Juden im deutschen Fußball und der lange Weg zur aktiven Erinnerungsarbeit" [Admired, persecuted, forgotten: Jews in German football and the long road to active remembrance], *Indes: Zeitschrift für Politik und Gesellschaft*, 1, pp. 40–50.

Pilz, G. (2016): "Rassismus und Fremdenfeindlichkeit im Fußballumfeld – Herausforderungen für die Prävention" [Racism and Xenophobia in football – Challenges for prevention], in Braun, S., Geisler, A. and Gerster, M. (Eds.), *Strategien der extremen Rechten* [Strategies of the far right], Wiesbaden: Springer VS.

Raimo, N., Vitolla, F., Nicolò, G. and Tartaglia Polcini, P. (2021) "CSR disclosure as a legitimation strategy: evidence from the football industry", *Measuring Business Excellence*, 25(4), pp. 493–508.

Reuter, S. (2023) "Übernahme gesellschaftlicher Verantwortung als zukunftsweisendes Grundverständnis von Profi-Fußballclubs" [Taking on social responsibility as a forward-looking principle for professional football clubs], in Reuter, S. and Thalmeier, P. (Eds.), *Mit mehr Nachhaltigkeit die Zukunft gestalten. Der deutsche Profi-Fußball im Wandel* [Shaping the future with more sustainability: German professional football in transition], Norderstedt: BoD.

Rieger, M. and Trepper, S. (2024) "Fußballmannschaft mit Rechtsextremen darf weiterspielen" [Football team with right-wing extremists allowed to continue playing], *Deutschlandfunk*. Available: <https://www.deutschlandfunk.de/dsg-gladau-faq-100.html> [accessed on 1st March 2024].

Rommelspacher, B. (2011) "Was ist eigentlich Rassismus?" [What is racism, really?], in Melter, C. and Mecheril, P. (Eds.), *Rassismuskritik. Band 1: Rassismustheorie und – forschung* [Critique of racism. Volume 1: racism theory and research], Schwalbach im Taunus: Wochenschau Verlag.

Sauer, M. and Brinkmann, H.U. (2016) "Einführung: integration in Deutschland" [Introduction: integration in Germany], in Brinkmann, H. and Sauer, M. (Eds.), *Einwanderungs-gesellschaft Deutschland* [Germany as an immigration society], Wiesbaden: Springer VS.

Scheler, F. (2019): "'Jude ist die größte Beleidigung im Fußball'" ['Jew' is the worst insult in football], *ZEIT Online*, 12th September 2019. Available: <https://www.zeit.de/sport/2019-09/antisemitismus-fussball-stadien-fans-florian-schubert> [accessed on 1st March 2024].

Schubert, F. (2019) *Antisemitismus im Fußball: tradition und Tabubruch* [Antisemitism in football: tradition and breaking Taboos], Göttingen: Wallstein Verlag.

Schubert, F. (2021) "Antisemitism in German football since the 1980s", in Brunssen, P. and Schüler-Springorum, S. (Eds.), *Football and discrimination: antisemitism and beyond*, London: Routledge.

Stahl, S. (2011) *Selbstorganisation von Migranten im deutschen Vereinssport: eine soziologische Annäherung* [Self-organization of migrants in German club sports: a sociological approach], Potsdam: Universitätsverlag Potsdam.

Steinrücke, K. (2023) "Die Anlaufstellen für Gewalt- und Diskriminierungsvorfälle in den Fußball-Landesverbänden" [The points of contact for violence and discrimination cases in Football State Associations], in Zentralrat der Juden in Deutschland (Ed.), *Strafraum. Die (Un-)Sichtbarkeit von Antisemitismus im Fußball* [Penalty area: the (in)visibility of antisemitism in football], Leipzig: Hentrich & Hentrich.

Süddeutsche Zeitung (2024) "Erstmals seit 20 Jahren: Zahl der Schiedsrichter steigt" [First time in 20 years: number of referees increases], *Süddeutsche Zeitung*. Available: <https://www.sueddeutsche.de/sport/fussball-erstmals-seit-20-jahren-zahl-der-schiedsrichter-steigt-dpa.urn-newsml-dpa-com-20090101-240126-99-767313> [accessed on 1st March 2024].

Sülzle, A. (2011) *Fußball, Frauen, Männlichkeiten: Eine ethnographische Studie im Fanblock* [Football, women, masculinities: an ethnographic study in the stands], Frankfurt: Campus-Verlag.

Thiel, A., Seiberth, K. and Mayer, J. (2023) *Sportsoziologie. Ein Lehrbuch in 13 Lektionen* [Sports sociology: a textbook in 13 lessons], Aachen: Meyer & Meyer.

Thomas-Olalde, O. and Velho, A. (2011) "Othering and its effects: exploring the concept", in Niedrig, H. and Ydesen, C. (Eds.), *Writing postcolonial histories of intercultural education*, Frankfurt: P. Lang.

Verweyen, L. (2019) "Ankommen im Sport: integrationsarbeit mit Geflüchteten und der Beitrag der Ethnologie" [Arriving in sport: integration work with refugees and the contribution of ethnology], in Klocke-Daffa, S. (Ed.), *Angewandte Ethnologie* [Applied ethnology], Wiesbaden: Springer VS.

Vester, T. (2023) "Antisemitismus – (k)ein Thema für die Sportgerichtsbarkeit?!" [Antisemitism: a topic for sports jurisdiction or not?!], in Zentralrat der Juden in Deutschland (Ed.), *Strafraum. Die (Un-)Sichtbarkeit von Antisemitismus im Fußball* [Penalty area: the (in)visibility of antisemitism in football], Leipzig: Hentrich & Hentrich.

Vester, T. and Reif, S. (2022) "Die Diskriminierungstatbestände der deutschen Fußball-Landesverbände – Nur gut gemeint oder auch gut gemacht?" [The discrimination offenses of the German Football State Associations: well-intentioned or well-executed?], *Sport und Recht*, 5, pp. 306–314.

Waas, S. (2021) "Failure of integration or symbol of racism: the case of soccer star Mesut Özil", *International Migration*, 61(4), pp. 141–153.

Zambon, K. (2022) "Controlling definitions: racism and German identity after Mesut Özil's national team resignation", in Heinsohn, B., Dawson, R., Knabe, O. and McDougall, A. (Eds.), *Football nation: the playing fields of German culture, history, and society*, Oxford: Berghahn Books.

Zengel, M. (2021) *Studie zum freiwilligen gesellschaftlichen Engagement des deutschen Profifußballs* [Study on voluntary social engagement in German professional football], Wiesbaden: ONE8Y.

Zick, A., Hövermann, A., Jensen, A. and Bernstein, J. (2017) *Jüdische Perspektiven auf Antisemitismus in Deutschland. Ein Studienbericht für den Expertenrat Antisemitismus* [Jewish perspectives on antisemitism in Germany: a study report for the expert council on antisemitism], Bielefeld: Institut für interdisziplinäre Konflikt-und Gewaltforschung.

Zick, A. and Mokros, N. (2023) "Rechtsextreme Einstellungen in der Mitte", in Zick, A., Küpper, B. and Mokros, N. (Eds.), *Die distanzierte Mitte: Rechtsextreme und demokratiegefährdende Einstellungen in Deutschland 2022/23*, Berlin: Dietz, pp. 53–89.

Chapter 6

Italy

Racism, xenophobia, and the North-South divide in football

Alessio Norrito

Football is full of tensions, opposites, contrasts, and dichotomies. That does not only succinctly characterize the events on the pitch but also the socio-political and cultural meanings that different groups attach to this modern spectacle. Inter Milan against Napoli, Francesco Acerbi against Juan Jesus, Italian against Brazilian – these binaries do not only refer to places and people but, more importantly, to very different identities and experiences. They will feature prominently in an episode I will describe and analyze in order to introduce this chapter's discussion of various forms of divisions and discrimination in the world of Italian football. In doing so, I draw on socio-ecological theories, particularly on the work of Bronfenbrenner (1979), whereby individuals are both shaped and shaping their environment in constant flux and are engaged in bi-directional relationships. When exploring divisions and discrimination within Italian society and its manifestation in football, this bi-directional relation is fundamentally represented by, and reduced to, two key oppositional actors, the discriminated and the discriminating, the victim and the perpetrator. The initial theory of Bronfenbrenner (1977) has evolved in contemporary sociology and forms the basis of what is commonly referred to as socio-ecological models. These models are often used to explain social scenarios and phenomena whereby multiple actors across different dimensions exist and interact with each other, which makes these theories apt and flexible tools within the sociology of sport (Hoekman, Breedveld and Kraaykamp, 2017; LaVoi and Dutove, 2012; Norrito, Michelini, Giulianotti et al., 2023; Schubring, Halltén, Barker-Ruchti et al., 2023). It is crucial to look at the individual interactions within a given socio-ecological model, as these interactions are the forces that shape the overall social environment of a given model. For the purpose of this chapter, we will call these bi-directional interactions "binaries'", to reflect their interconnectedness and inseparability. Other terms have also been used to characterize this relationship, such as "dyad", which was used by Bronfenbrenner (1979) himself, and 'binomial' within a socio-metric and quantitative context. Nonetheless, the term binary best expresses this reciprocal effect among interacting actors within a given socio-ecological system.

DOI: 10.4324/9781003495970-6

This chapter has been made available under a CC-BY-NC-SA 4.0 license.

Socio-ecological models are, for analytical purposes, traditionally divided into micro-, meso-, exo- and macro dimensions of a given environment. This chapter is less concerned with creating a socio-ecological model according to these dimensions but intends to dissect the interactions that occur within Italian football across different levels, horizontally as well as vertically. It does so through also accounting for changes overtime and acknowledging important socio-historical contexts that have shaped and continue to shape the current manifestations of discrimination. This exploration starts with a single symbolic, and, to some extent, representative, episode, that constitutes a catalyst to address three different forms and manifestations of discrimination in the Italian football system.

The day is 17 March 2024 and the match is Inter Milan vs. Napoli. During the 2023/24 season, Inter Milan is the dominating team of the league and will later win the *Serie A*. Napoli, who had just won the *scudetto*, in the year before, is unable to build on the success of the previous year and will only finish 10th in the table. Suddenly, Juan Jesus, Napoli's 32-year-old, Black, Brazilian defender, tries to get the attention of the referee. He points at his sleeve, where it is eloquently written "Respect". Juan Jesus reports that he has been racially insulted by one of the Inter Milan players. His name is Francesco Acerbi, a defender, 36-year-old, White, and Italian. The scenes are similar to what we often see in football matches, when, for example, a penalty has not been given or players insist on a red card for an opponent. And yet, something feels distinctively different and nebulous. It is only after the match that the incident is fully analysed and discussed, in great detail, by the many actors that populate the football environment. The first one to do that is Juan Jesus himself in a post-match interview. It appears that he is keen to move on as he says to the journalists that what happens on the field stays on the field. He also stresses that Francesco Acerbi is a good guy. However, when it is Francesco Acerbi's turn to comment on the incident, a day later, the Italian defender said it was Juan Jesus who misunderstood what he had said to him on the pitch. In the following days, Francesco Acerbi will stand trial being accused of racist behaviour during the Inter Milan-Napoli match. Eventually, the accusation will be dismissed. I am going to approach this contested issue from the perspective of the discriminated, that is the victim, and take the official declaration of Juan Jesus as the empirical basis for my analysis:

> I have read several times, with great regret, the decision with which the Sports Judge considered that there is no proof that I was the victim of racist insults during the Inter-Napoli match last March 17th. It is an assessment which, although respecting it, I struggle to understand and it leaves me with great bitterness.
>
> I am sincerely disheartened by the outcome of a serious matter, in which I am only guilty of having acted 'like a gentleman', avoiding the interruption of an important game with all the inconvenience that that would have

caused for the spectators, and trusting that my attitude would have been respected and taken, perhaps, as an example.

After this decision, those who find themselves in a similar situation will probably act in a very different way in order to protect themselves and to try and put a stop to the shame of racism, which, unfortunately, does not seem to be going away.

I do not feel protected in any way by this decision. I really don't understand how the phrase 'go away black man, you're just a n***o' can be classed as offensive, but not discriminatory.

In fact, I don't understand why there was so much fuss that evening if it had really been a 'simple offence', one that Acerbi felt obliged to apologise for and one that the referee felt he had to inform VAR. The match was interrupted for more than a minute and his teammates were struggling to talk to me.

I can't explain why, only the next day and ahead of the national team camp and not immediately after the match, Acerbi began a U-turn on his version of events. I didn't expect an ending of this kind, which, I fear, but hope that I'm wrong, could set a serious precedent. I sincerely hope that this sad story can help the entire football world to reflect on such a serious and urgent issue.

(Juan Jesus, 27 March 2024)

There are many ways to see, make sense, and reflect on this episode. I will focus on three different aspects and ramifications: xenophobia, racism, and territorial discrimination. These three forms of discrimination are intertwined and perfectly reflect three sources of discrimination in Italian football. Due to the qualitative nature of the analysis within this chapter, it is also important to provide the reader with a brief sense of my own identities and experiences, and my dual role as an insider and outsider. I am a White male who has lived for most of his life in places where White people have been the privileged majority. When it comes to xenophobia, I am a Southern Italian who has lived half of his whole life, and most of his adult life, in foreign environments.

Recent socio-demographic and political developments in Italy: migration, xenophobia, and moral panics

To explore the issues of xenophobia and racism, we have to reiterate that at the core of these two discriminatory attitudes and practices, there is another bi-directional relation, that of the insider and outsider (Nyamnjoh, 2006). This binary also relates to the concept of, and relationship between, discriminated and discriminating individuals, yet has more to do with the identities of the people involved rather than their experiences. This chapter will revolve around unveiling an important outsider-insider relation in the system, that of local-to-migrant, which is extremely significant to the Italian case.

To do so, however, we need to step back and examine the racist and xenophobic forces that currently shape Italian society and politics, and stem from the role of fascism in the development of Italian football (Kassimeris, 2011). At the time of writing this chapter, Italy is ruled by a far-right government whose political campaigns, among other things, promised to prevent more migrants from entering the country. They also tend to rail against the "Islamisation" of Europe. Their anti-migrant and anti-Islam stances were particularly pronounced in the run-up to the European parliamentary elections in June 2024. In May 2024, *the Camera dei Deputati*, the lower house of the Italian parliament, passed a law that legalizes the closure of praying spaces that are not explicitly referred to as mosques. The promises of Italy's far-right rulers and their ways of governing have often been dubbed as fascist, a term that is strongly rejected by the parties in power. Besides this contextual accusation, which needs to be seen as a useful way of framing the perception of the current government, the "issue" of migration is one of salience in the whole of Europe, not only in Italy.

Indeed, Italy has seen ongoing migration from the African continent, particularly due to many makeshift boat arrivals. The Mediterranean refugee crisis, also known as the "European migrant crisis", arguably started in 2013, when a very high number of migrants approached Europe in search of asylum and/or better quality of life. In 2013, almost 43,000 migrants reached Italy by sea (UNHCR, 2016). However, this humanitarian crisis reached a numerical peak in the years between 2014 and 2017, where the number of migrants arriving at the European shores has been consistently above 100,000, adding up to a total of more than 620,000 arrivals (UNHCR, 2024). The EU member states were not ready to face such a huge wave of migration (Buonanno, 2017), resulting in first-approach territories often being congested and unable to provide appropriate assistance to asylum seekers (Castelli Gattinara, 2017). Italy, along with Greece, was arguably one of the most affected countries by the European crisis. Indeed, Italy is now home to many reception centres due to its proximity to the North African region and needs to cope with the continuous influx of migrants from across the Mediterranean.

As Fontana (2020) points out, policies resulting from this crisis have shaped public discourses that feature two elements of the crime-migration nexus and foster negative labelling processes of migrants. She defines the key elements of this concatenation as the assumption that migrants cause an increase in crime rates, while, at the same time, illegal migration is a result of crimes such as smuggling and trafficking (Fontana, 2020). The crisis thus has led to the emergence of two interconnected narratives that feed into a moral panic (Goode, 2017) on the crime-migration nexus. These have been framed by the media accordingly and quickly endorsed by politicians (Colombo, 2018) in order to accumulate electoral support and, subsequently, political power. Consequently, when the stereotypical view of the migrant as a criminal is endorsed and spread, migrants are being transformed into subjects of fear in Italian society (Musarò and Parmiggiani, 2017).

In addition to fear related to the crime-migration nexus, sentiments of rejection and hate towards the migrant population have also emerged and grown. This is partly due to a decrease of low-skilled job opportunities since the refugee crisis (Planer, 2020). While the timeliness of the social issue endorses the populistic view that migrants are *ladri di lavoro*, job-thieves (Dalla Zuanna, 2016), research, on the contrary, suggests that finding regular employment as a migrant is much more complicated than as a well-established member of the local community (Fullin and Reyneri, 2011). This is generally due to discrimination (Krings and Olivares, 2007) and regulative barriers imposed by the anti-immigration political parties (Zaslove, 2004). The same barriers have also manifested themselves both in and through football in Italy (Norrito, 2024; Norrito, Michelini, Giulianotti et al., 2024). These restrictions often force migrants to accept unregulated jobs (Fullin and Reyneri, 2011) that do not contribute to the state economy, but instead to the "underground economy" (Mingione and Quassoli, 2000). In turn, this means that migrants, especially unregulated, rarely compete directly with Italians for low-skilled job opportunities.

This brief contextualization is essential in order to understand the connection between xenophobia and football in Italy. It is, however, noteworthy that Juan Jesus, of course, represents a very privileged, extremely skilful, well-paid, and highly respected migrant, as such is the status of footballers of his standing. Nevertheless, some aspects of the aforementioned incident provide interesting insights into the power dynamics between locals and migrants, particularly surrounding the discourse of the "misunderstanding" put forward by Francesco Acerbi in the interview after the match and the notion of otherness in Italian society.

"Another case of racism where no one is racist"? Charting racism from the pitch to the stands in Italy

Parts of the above subheading are borrowed from an opinion piece published in the independent Italian magazine *Ultimo Uomo*, written by Daniele Manusia in March 2024. His reading of the episode between Francesco Acerbi and Juan Jesus as a racist incident is by far the most frequent lens through which Italian and international news agencies have framed the episode. It is also convincingly expressed by the statement of Juan Jesus himself. Yet it is worth pointing out that juridically no racism has occurred in this episode, reducing all the "news" surrounding the case to unsubstantiated assumptions and misguided interpretations. However, this raises the disconcerting concern that the Italian Football Federation's decision may have created a dangerous precedent, as also mentioned in the statement by Juan Jesus, which would indeed be *another case of racism where no one is racist*.

The discriminatory component of the interaction within the aforementioned episode is the racist slur said by Francesco Acerbi to Juan Jesus during the match. Nonetheless, the cascading effect of such racism can be seen in multiple social environments and at different levels. These include the personal, club and institutional levels. However, while at both the personal and club levels, we have a contra-positional tension, that is Acerbi against Jesus and Inter Milan against Napoli, the same does not apply to the institutional level, where no two institutions (or organizations) of equal influence can be found in tension with each other. Indeed, the final judgment of the incident, which was deemed to be racist but without sufficient unequivocal evidence to prove it – whatever that means – was made by the Italian Football Federation (FIGC).

The FIGC is here to be seen as defining and shaping what racism is and means. It does not deny that racism has occurred, and, in a strange way, it even admits that racism occurred but decided not to punish Francesco Acerbi due to a lack of evidence. From a socio-ecological perspective, the lack of punishment has an enormous impact on shaping the responses to racism in the future. That is why both Juan Jesus and Napoli felt that justice was not served. One match after the publication of the verdict, Napoli players kneeled before kick-off. This gesture replicated Colin Kaepernick and other American Football players' silent and controversial protests during the national anthem to demonstrate their unity against all forms of racism.

The case of Juan Jesus and Francesco Acerbi represents a manifestation of racism involving two players, which is not as common and widespread as discriminatory chants and abuse from the terraces. This kind of interaction between players and fans is perhaps best exemplified in the racial abuses suffered by Italian striker Mario Balotelli, an Italian player born to Ghanian parents, who became a high-profile symbol of a generation of Italians born to immigrant parents (Mauro, 2016). Balotelli, was often racially abused by fans during his time in Italy, in opposition to his tenure playing in the English Premier League (Doidge, 2015a).

To better understand this kind of abusive behaviour of fans, we need to situate fans within the socio-ecological framework of this chapter. Indeed, organized fans in Italy, often referred to as *ultras*, have an important mediating role between clubs, players, ideologies, and political entities. Scalia (2009) points this out showing how both political figures and football clubs have used *ultras* for their purposes, effectively legitimizing their mediating role within football culture. Therefore, in the interaction between football and society, *ultras* are significant actors who have the power to affect both club-level decision-making and wider decision-making in society.

Guschwan (2013) reported that *ultras* interrupted the 2004 Rome derby, AS Roma vs SS Lazio. They demanded to speak with the captains of both teams, with the then captain of Roma, Francesco Totti, telling the referee to call the match off to avoid fan riots. This incident was connected to the anti-police sentiment of Italian *ultras* in the early 2000s (Guschwan, 2013; Testa, 2018). Therefore, when the political dimension is added to the interactions of *ultras* within a football context, we see a strong connectedness with both racism and anti-racism.

Whether one "ultra" group aligns with racism or anti-racism obviously depends on the broader political orientation of their members. While existing literature has largely focused on the issue of racism and racist fan behaviour, it is important to acknowledge that left-wing *ultras* support anti-racist ideologies in Italian football (Doidge, 2014; Sterchele and Saint-Blancat, 2015). Nonetheless, most of the current knowledge of racism within the Italian football stands links its causes to the historical influence that fascism had on the country (Kassimeris, 2011; Martin, 2018; Testa and Armstrong, 2008). Sometimes this link is very direct and undeniable.

On 26 December 2024, the right-back of Juve Stabia, a Serie B club, Romano Floriani Mussolini, scored his first goal. He is the great-grandson of Italy's fascist dictator Benito Mussolini (1922–1943). Fans of the local team celebrated with a fascist salute as the speaker asked them to chant the player's surname. This is another example showing how fascist sentiments are still latent and persist among Italian football fans, while far-right extremism and populism continue to rise off the pitch. Despite explicit assurances from Juve Stabia that there was no connection between its fans' gestures and fascism, the Italian football federation announced the opening of an investigation.

Despite the well-established links between fascism and antisemitism, episodes of antisemitic abuse on Italian football grounds are rather rare, with the notable exception of the Roman football rivalry (Stratton, 2015). For example, in 2018, SS Lazio used the image of Anne Frank to mock their rivals AS Roma. However, the act was strongly condemned and both the club and the FIGC took immediate actions, which included reading excerpts from the Diary of Anne Frank in the next football match, observing a minute of silence, and the players wearing images of Anne Frank on their jerseys, among other initiatives (Curtis, 2019).

Discussions about racism in the context of football fandom in Italy need to be located in the wider context of xenophobia, as racism is one of the forms in which a fear or rejection of the other is manifested. Numerato (2015) corroborates this point in his analysis of the rejection of modern, hyper-commercialized football by Italian supporters. Indeed, he finds that while the idea of modern football supports neoliberal ideologies, some advocates of modern football may be less welcoming to campaigns against racism, or against discrimination, in general (Numerato, 2015). After all, they would have to admit that their commodity, modern football, has ugly, structural flaws that need to be remedied.

Episodes of racism in Italy do not only involve Black players but also players originating from Eastern Europe who are often racialized. Eastern European players who have received racial slurs included, for example, the Juventus striker Dusan Vlahovic, who is originally from Serbia. In May 2023, during the Atalanta vs. Juventus match, he called the attention of the referee, who temporarily suspended the game and warned the fans through the speakers in the stadium. Once the match restarted, the insults continued. When Vlahovic scored a goal and celebrated in front of the fans who had racially abused him, the referee punished Vlahovic with his second yellow card and sent him off. One month earlier, something very similar had happened to Inter Milan's Black striker Romelu Lukaku, originally from Belgian. After he converted a penalty, his finger touched his lips in front of Juventus fans who had previously abused him. The referee deemed his behaviour to be provocative and showed him a second yellow card. However, his automatic one-match ban was later overturned by the Italian Football Federation to set a sign against racism.

In both situations, fans were the perpetrators of the racial insults and players the victims. And yet, the referees punished the players for reacting to the crowd. The referee represents and symbolizes the moral and legal authority on the football pitch. His/her task is to make sure that the rules of the game are enforced. The rules and procedures state that a player is punished with a yellow card if they taunt the fans, yet the fans are only served with a general verbal warning when they taunt the players in a discriminatory manner. The discriminated-discriminating binary is turned on its head through the severe punishment of the abused player, while the perpetrators receive a mild warning. While Doidge (2015a) has explained how Italy can tackle racism through a better understanding of inter-club rivalries, the exemplary impurities within the rules of the game suggest that we need a broader approach. Doidge also states that "when allegations of corruption are fined more severely than racist chanting, there is much to be done by the federation" (2015a, p. 261). While first written about 10 years ago, this statement still holds true today.

Territorial discrimination: the north-south divide in Italian football

There is another layer to the Francesco Acerbi and Juan Jesus incident, which takes us to Italy's geography and the positioning of the cities of Napoli and Milan. They represent a geographical division that has been in existence since the unification of Italy in 1861. To better understand the issue of territorial discrimination, it is important to briefly outline its historical roots. Southern Italians have, for a long time, been the targets of xenophobic sentiments of a vast portion of Northern Italians, based on a wide variety of stereotypes (Bullaro, 2010; Capussotti, 2010), that continue to exist (Musolino, 2018). One of these stereotypes is that of the "mafioso", whereby Southern Italians are stereotypically associated with organized crime and therefore labelled as criminals. These stereotypes come from the domination of the mafia, particularly within Sicily, which has caused suffering and underdevelopment across the region, as well as the popularity of the mafia phenomenon within pop culture (Schneider and Schneider, 2005). Another stereotype is that of the Southern Italians as lazy, which research attributes to counterproductive economic policies that undermined the motivation to work hard, invest, and innovate in the South (Bigoni, Bortolotti, Casari et al., 2016).

Gramsci (1926) believed that the socio-economic underdevelopment of the southern regions had to be related to, and can be explained with, the way the territories were administered before Italy's unification in 1861, as the paternalistic way of the previous rulers did not favour the growth of a productive middle class. During the Second World War, there was an agreement between the Sicilian mafia and the United States to facilitate their mission to liberate Italy and receive military information. In exchange, the mafia demanded and achieved civil control over southern Italy (Lupo, 1997; Dalla Chiesa, 2010).

The aforementioned stereotypes of Southern Italians as unlawful and lazy align with the xenophobic discourse surrounding migrants. This should come as no surprise, as many Southern Italians have also been and continue to be migrants. As reported by Agnoli (2001), migration fluxes had a constant increase in southern Italy, although non-existent before the country's unification. It has been reported that between 1876 and 1900, more than 226,000 people had emigrated. Between 1901 and 1915, the number increased to 1,126,000 (Associazione Internet Emigrati Italiani, 2024). In post-war Italy, up until the 1960s, an average of 300,000 people per year left the country, with Sicily being the second most affected region after Calabria (e-migrantes, 2024). According to SVIMEZ (2019), in the period between 2002 and 2017, more than two million people left the south of Italy. Taking Sicily as an example, as of 2020, there were 784,817 Sicilians who are permanent residents in a foreign country and are registered as migrants with the Italian authorities (Migrantes-Aire, 2020).

This brief demographic context is necessary to understand the socio-ecological nature of the different types of discrimination we have discussed so far. Migration, racism, and geographical discrimination are all interacting with the concept of otherness and tied up in xenophobic fear. Indeed, as Kassimeris suggests (2011), Southern Italians were frequently abused with racist slurs during football matches even if, effectively, they belong to the same historical region, just due to the proximity of their region to the African continent.

Other examples include banners such as "Welcome to Italy", displayed in a match between Hellas Verona and Napoli in 1985, or the most recent in February 2024 against AC Milan, saying "Milan-Naples: No to the supporter's ID card, Yes to the passport".

The concept of geographical discrimination, or "territorial discrimination" as it is referred to in Italian, encapsulates both the discourse on migration and stereotypes, as well as the hindrance of social justice. Going back to our episode and focusing on Inter Milan and Napoli, the organizational response of both clubs is of key importance here. First, it needs to be noted that the statement of Juan Jesus was published through the official channels of Napoli's football club, who endorsed and disseminated the voice of their player. We have also narrated earlier how the team responded by bending the knee in the following match, demonstrating their solidarity and ant-racism stance. They are based in one of the most discriminated and excluded cities within Italy. Indeed, Napoli is one of the teams that receives the most hostile and aggressive insults from away fans (Martin, 2012), for example, invoking the eruption of Mount Vesuvius and the subsequent destruction of the city (Verde, 2020). While the concept of territorial discrimination among *ultras* is not widely and explicitly researched, Doidge (2015a) explains how team rivalry contributes to fostering discrimination in Italian football, particularly in relation to player abuse. Yet, the rivalry with, and vilification of, Napoli is one of a particular kind, rooted in a perceived superiority of the rest of Italy towards the city. So much so that the label *napoletano*, Napolitan, has been used with a discriminatory connotation for the purpose of insulting players (Testa and Armstrong, 2008). Indeed, this typical insult is often alternated with the word *terrone*, a specific slur directed towards Southern Italians, referring to a person with low hygienic standards who does not work (Testa and Armstrong, 2008).

Tackling discrimination in Italian football

A decade ago, Italy did not have any institutional or organized campaign to fight discrimination in football, particularly racism and xenophobia (Doidge, 2015a). Today, there is an institutional endorsement against discrimination, symbolized in the word 'Respect' printed on the shirt's sleeve. Italy has relied, and continues to rely, on punitive measures that include monetary and/or non-monetary sanctions. In January 2024, Udinese was punished with one game being played behind closed doors in an empty stadium after the club's supporters had target AC Milan's Black goalkeeper, Mike Maignan, with racist chants and monkey noises. Having said this, some of the incidents I summarized before have largely gone unpunished. Nonetheless, the Italian Football Federation and football leagues have made big steps forwards over the last decade, at the very least, from an organizational perspective. Every year, two match days are fully dedicated to the campaign 'Keep Racism Out', which is promoted by the *Lega Serie A*. The FIGC now has explicit anti-racism polices and strategic objectives that aim to eradicate any forms of racism within and beyond Italian stadiums by 2030.

While there are not many campaigns or initiatives organised by fans to fight racism directly in the *Lega Serie A*, the *Mondiali Antirazzisti*, the Anti-Racist World Cup, represents a significant exception (Sterchele, 2015, 2020; Sterchele and Saint-Blancat, 2015). It is a non-competitive football tournament combined with an intercultural festival that aims to celebrate diversity, promote the idea of sport as a tool for social inclusion and disseminate anti-discriminatory, in particular ant-racist, messages. Participants are usually football fans from all over Europe, members of the *ultras*, migrants, voluntary sector organizations and other groups. Its latest iteration took place in Florence on 25 May 2024 and involved more than 500 players, with 34 participating teams.

Furthermore, Italy is seeing the development of the *Calcio Popolare*, popular football, phenomenon, which rejects the neo-liberal logic of modern professional football with its hyper-commodification and commercialization. The *Calcio Popolare* movement emphasizes values such as diversity, inclusion, and respect, and promotes the idea that football should be owned by the people. Consequently, this alternative movement consists of fan-owned and fan-managed football teams that have a wider socio-cultural remit, including combating forms of discriminations. These include, for example, teams such as Liberi Nantes, Afro-Napoli, and the Centro Storico Lebowski, who has also helped organizing the latest Anti-Racist World Cup in Florence.

Another important blind spot in Italian football that will need to be monitored is gender discrimination, particularly when sexism intersects with other forms of discrimination, such as racism and xenophobia. While we do have exploratory studies of sexual preferences (Amodeo, Antuoni, Claysset et al., 2020), as well as on the current gender gap in professional football (Trequattrini, Cuozzo, Petrecca et al., 2022), there is currently a dearth of knowledge on discrimination per se, and the gendered experiences of playing football in Italy. To better and systematically understand the gender elements is crucially important, particularly as women's football continues its ongoing professionalization and growth (Valenti, Scelles and Morrow, 2018). Female athletes in other sports, who are currently more popular than in women's football, have been heavily discriminated. For example, the Italian Volleyball Federation questioned Paola Egonu, one of the most outstanding volleyball players, who had won multiple domestic and international awards, whether she was really Italian. Egonu was born in Italy to Nigerian parents, is Black, and is an outspoken advocate for inclusivity. She was vital in the Italian win of a gold medal in the Paris 2024 Olympic Games. In August 2024, a mural entitled "Italianness", by a street artist dedicated to Paola Egonu and her sporting achievements, was defaced only one day after it was unveiled in Rome. Overnight, her skin had turned pink and the anti-discriminatory message had been covered up. A year before, Roberto Vannacci, a member of *Lega*, had written about Paola Egonu that her physical features did not represent Italianness. Looking to the future, Italian football will need to protect women footballers from potential and, likely, overlapping forms of discrimination, learning from Egonu's example.

Several anti-racism initiatives in Italy operate at the grassroots level and use football as a tool for cultural exchange and empowerment of both men and women. ASD Balon Mundial, for example, is a non-profit organization and located in Turin. Its overall philosophy is about inclusion and participation and the various activities do not only focus on sportsmen and women but also on coaches and sports directors. Balon Mundial promotes a philosophy of "playing with", rather than "playing against" others, and does so by organizing multiple festivals of football centred around different themes. For example, their "Migrant World Cup" is similar to the format of the FIFA World Cup but hosts male and female teams of migrants residing in Turin.

There are several initiatives in Southern Italy that are aimed at refugees and displaced people, who often suffer overlapping forms of discrimination both in Italy and in their country of origin. One of these is ASD Don Bosco 2000, which incorporates their football initiatives into wider aspects of community building and place-making (Norrito, La Cara, Sella et al., 2023). Their fight against racism is not constrained to football per se, rather football is used as a strategic tool to expose refugees to the local community in a positive light and initiate a process of reciprocal understanding between migrants and local communities. Such a functionalist use of football to achieve wider social impacts, such as the reduction of discrimination and inequality, is characteristic of sport for development initiatives (Sterchele, 2015).

Initiatives at the grassroots level are not limited to independent organizations but occasionally stem from the FIGC itself. For example, they have introduced a trophy called "Junior Tim Cup/Keep Racism Out", consisting of a seven-a-side tournament for under 14-year-old players. The teams are made up of young-people affiliated with the 'oratories' in the 20 cities of the *Serie A* clubs. Oratories are effectively parish youth clubs, where young people, often underprivileged and disadvantaged, traditionally congregate to play football in Italy.

Conclusion: Italianness and discrimination in football

Having examined the manifestations of racism, xenophobia, and territorial discrimination in the Italian football system, the common thread reveals a nationalist conundrum between who is considered Italian and who is not. Looking at the three binaries that have dominated this chapter, we have the dualism of local and migrant, White and Black, and North and South. There are, of course, other binaries such as Christian and Muslim, or men and women that have not been addressed in this chapter.

Although a lot has been written about Islamophobic populism in Italian far-right politics, the concept of Islamophobia is largely absent from the academic literature about football in Italy. Foreign direct investment into Italian sport clubs has also only recently commenced with the acquisition of Palermo FC by the Emirates-linked City Football Group. In 2018, the Italian Cup final was played in Saudi Arabia for the very first time. Fans and the media heavily criticised the move as it constituted a deterritorialization of a cultural good (Bianco and Sons, 2023).

The disparity between men's and women's football is perhaps the most obvious example of such a binary, albeit not exclusive to Italian football (Trequattrini, Cuozzo, Petrecca et al., 2022). Due to the limited scope of this chapter, this disparity has not been entirely addressed.

Instead, this chapter has identified and analyzed the distinctive flavour of racism, xenophobia, and territorial discrimination in Italian football. All three discriminatory practices are driven by, and express, the contestation of the concepts of Italianness and inclusivity. Xenophobia is the one that, semantically, may feel the most logical and closely related to these two notions. Migrants, in general, are discriminated because they are geographically and culturally from other countries and because of a widespread and exaggerated fear towards the unknown and the different other. Within this anti-migrant sentiment, we also find racism and racialization, as the episode of Juan Jesus and Francesco Acerbi has exemplified here, encompassing both manifestations of discrimination across multiple dimensions. Juan Jesus is obviously the non-Italian and, therefore, the other, who had, allegedly, misunderstood what Francesco Acerbi had said, hinting at a language barrier, as well as the contents referring to the physical characteristics of Juan Jesus. Furthermore, there is the protection and paternalism of the national governing body, with the president hugging the player, a compatriot, after he was cleared of the allegations.

With regard to the North and South divide, this binary is subtler and rooted in socio-historical differences between distinct geographical regions in Italy. This complex set of tensions has been exemplified through the case of Napoli and its supporters and fans. Logically and semantically, the terminology Northern and Southern Italy both imply being part of the Italian peninsula and nation-state. Yet, as Doidge (2015b) explains, the anti-south rhetoric of political parties such as *Lega Nord* continues to flourish and manifest itself in football stadiums.

All of the above points to an overarching theme, "Italianness", that frames, underpins, and motivates the current discourse around, and manifestations of, discrimination in Italian football. Ultimately, Italian national identity is an exclusionary project (Mauro, 2020). However, these divisions exist way beyond the world of football and are deeply rooted in Italian history, society, culture, and politics. The narrowness of the concept of "Italianness", as expressed by fans in the world of football, clearly reflects narratives and discourses of exclusion present in wider Italian society. This inhibits the role that football may have in presenting an alternative sense of national identity that includes traditionally discriminated individuals in the national community (Mauro, 2016; Genovesi, 2024). Therefore, combatting racism, xenophobia, and territorial discrimination needs to be undertaken at a wider, societal level and has to be a concerted and coordinated effort, in which the world of football may be able to play an important role.

References

Agnoli, F.M. (2001) *La rivoluzione italiana: storia critica del Risorgimento* [The Italian revolution: a critical history of the Risorgimento], Roma: Il Minotauro.

Amodeo, A.L., Antuoni, S., Claysset, M. and Esposito, C. (2020) "Traditional male role norms and sexual prejudice in sport organizations: a focus on Italian sport directors and coaches", *Social Sciences*, 9(12), pp. 1–12.

Associazione Internet Emigrati Italiani (2024) *Emigrazione Italiana: Il Piu Grande Esodo Della Storia Moderna – Emigrati.it* [Italian emigration: the greatest exodus of modern history]. Available: <https://www.emigrati.it/Emigrazione/Esodo.asp> [accessed on 10th September 2024].

Bianco, C. and Sons, S. (2023) "More than a game: football and soft power in the gulf", *The International Spectator*, 58(2), pp. 92–106.

Bigoni, M., Bortolotti, S., Casari, M., Gambetta, D. and Pancotto, F. (2016) "Amoral familism, social capital, or trust? The behavioural foundations of the Italian North–South divide", *The Economic Journal*, 126(594), pp. 1318–1341.

Bronfenbrenner, U. (1977) "Toward an experimental ecology of human development", *American Psychologist*, 32(7), p. 513.

Bronfenbrenner, U. (1979) *The ecology of human development: experiments by nature and design*, Cambridge: Harvard University Press.

Bullaro, G.R. (Ed.) (2010) *From Terrone to Extracomunitario: new manifestations of racism in contemporary Italian cinema: shifting demographics and changing images in a multi-cultural globalized society*, Leicester: Troubador Publishing.

Buonanno, L. (2017) "The European migration crisis", in Dinan, D., Nugent, N. and Paterson, W.E. (Eds.), *The European union in crisis*, London: Palgrave.

Capussotti, E. (2010) "Nordisti contro Sudisti: internal migration and racism in Turin, Italy: 1950s and 1960s", *Italian Culture*, 28(2), pp. 121–138.

Castelli Gattinara, P. (2017) "The 'refugee crisis' in Italy as a crisis of legitimacy", *Contemporary Italian Politics*, 9(3), pp. 318–331.

Colombo, M. (2018) "The representation of the "European refugee crisis" in Italy: domopolitics, securitization, and humanitarian communication in political and media discourses", *Journal of Immigrant & Refugee Studies*, 16(1–2), pp. 161–178.

Curtis, M. (2019) "Antisemitism and European football", *Antisemitism Studies*, 3(2), pp. 273–290.

Dalla Chiesa, N. (2010) *La convergenza. Mafia e politica nella seconda repubblica* [The convergence: mafia and politics in the second republic], Milano: Melampo.

Dalla Zuanna, G. (2016) "Immigrazione e mercato del lavoro in Italia" [Immigration and the job market in Italy], *il Mulino, Rivista trimestrale di cultura e di politica*, 65(2), pp. 250–258.

Doidge, M. (2014) "'The birthplace of Italian communism': political identity and action amongst Livorno fans", in Kennedy, P. and Kennedy, D. (Eds.), *Fan culture in European football and the influence of left wing ideology*, London: Routledge.

Doidge, M. (2015a) "'If you jump up and down, Balotelli dies': racism and player abuse in Italian football", *International Review for the Sociology of Sport*, 50(3), pp. 249–264.

Doidge, M. (2015b) *Football Italia: Italian football in an age of globalization*, London: Bloomsbury Academic.

E-migrantes (2024) "Dal Secondo Dopoguerra Agli Anni '60 Del Novecento" [From the second Dopoguerra to the 1960s]. Available: <http://www.e-migrantes.it/dal-secondo-dopoguerra-agli-anni-60-del-novecento/> [accessed on 10th September 2024].

Fontana, I. (2020) "Migration crisis, organised crime and domestic politics in Italy: unfolding the interplay", *South European Society and Politics*, 25(1), pp. 49–74.

Fullin, G. and Reyneri, E. (2011) "Low unemployment and bad jobs for new immigrants in Italy", *International Migration*, 49(1), pp. 118–147.

Genovesi, F. (2024) "Spaces of football and belonging for people seeking asylum: resisting policy-imposed liminality in Italy", *International Review for the Sociology of Sport*, 59(1), pp. 82–100.

Goode, E. (2017) "Moral panic", in Schreck, C.J. (Ed.), *The encyclopedia of juvenile delinquency and justice*, Hoboken: Wiley-Blackwell.

Gramsci, A. (1926) "Alcuni temi della questione meridionale" [Some themes on the Southern Question]. Available: <https://www.nuovopci.it/classic/gramsci/questmer.htm> [accessed on 29th September 2024].

Guschwan, M. (2013) "Riot in the curve: soccer fans in twenty-first century Italy", in Brown, S. (Ed.), *Football fans around the world*, London: Routledge.

Hoekman, R., Breedveld, K. and Kraaykamp, G. (2017) "Sport participation and the social and physical environment: explaining differences between urban and rural areas in the Netherlands", *Leisure Studies*, 36(3), pp. 357–370.

Kassimeris, C. (2011) "Fascism, separatism and the ultràs: discrimination in Italian football", *Soccer & Society*, 12(5), pp. 677–688.

Krings, F. and Olivares, J. (2007) "At the doorstep to employment: discrimination against immigrants as a function of applicant ethnicity, job type, and raters' prejudice", *International Journal of Psychology*, 42(6), pp. 406–417.

LaVoi, N.M. and Dutove, J.K. (2012) "Barriers and supports for female coaches: an ecological model", *Sports Coaching Review*, 1(1), pp. 17–37.

Lupo, S. (1997) "The Allies and the mafia", *Journal of Modern Italian Studies*, 2(1), pp. 21–33.

Manusia, D. (2024) "Un altro caso di razzismo in cui nessuno è razzista" [Another case of racism where nobody is racist], *Ultimo Uomo*. Available: <https://www.ultimouomo.com/acerbi-juan-jesus-razzismo/> [accessed on 10th September 2024].

Martin, S. (2012) "Sport Italia: 150 years of disunited Italy", *Bulletin of Italian Politics*, 4(1), pp. 49–62.

Martin, S. (2018) "Football, fascism and fandom in modern Italy", *Revista Crítica de Ciências Sociais*, 116, pp. 111–134.

Mauro, M. (2016) *The Balotelli generation: issues of inclusion and belonging in Italian football and society*, Bristol: Peter Lang Publishing Group.

Mauro, M. (2020) "Media discourse, sport and the nation: narratives and counter-narratives in the digital age", *Media, Culture & Society*, 42(6), pp. 932–951.

Migrantes-Aire (2020) *Rapporto Italiani Nel Mondo 2020* [Report of Italians in the world 2020], *Fondazione Migrantes*. Available: <https://www.migrantes.it/wp-content/uploads/sites/50/2020/10/RIM-2020_allegatistatistici.pdf> [accessed on 10th September 2024].

Mingione, E. and Quassoli, F. (2000) "The participation of immigrants in the underground economy in Italy", in King, R., Lazaridis, G. and Tsardanidis, C. (Eds.), *Eldorado or fortress? Migration in southern Europe*, London: Palgrave Macmillan.

Musarò, P. and Parmiggiani, P. (2017) "Beyond black and white: the role of media in portraying and policing migration and asylum in Italy", *International Review of Sociology*, 27(2), pp. 241–260.

Musolino, D. (2018) "The north-south divide in Italy: reality or perception?", *European Spatial Research and Policy*, 25(1), pp. 29–53.

Norrito, A. (2024) "Between hope and cruel optimism? The dangers and possibilities of football in fostering hope for male refugees", *Leisure Studies (AOP)*, pp. 1–15.

Norrito, A., La Cara, R., Sella, A., Giulianotti, R. and Mason, C. (2023) "Building bridges in the Mediterranean: circular cooperation and sport for development and peace for refugees in Italy", *Journal of Sport for Development*, 12(1), pp. 1–11.

Norrito, A., Michelini, E., Giulianotti, R. and Mason, C. (2024) "'Refugee footballers': a socioecological exploration of forced migrants in the Italian and German elite football system", *International Review for the Sociology of Sport*, 59(1), pp. 119–138.

Numerato, D. (2015) "Who says "no to modern football?" Italian supporters, reflexivity, and neo-liberalism", *Journal of Sport and Social Issues*, 39(2), pp. 120–138.

Nyamnjoh, F.B. (2006) *Insiders and outsiders: citizenship and xenophobia in contemporary Southern Africa*, London: Zed Books.

Planer, T. (2020) *The effect of the 2014–17 refugee crisis on the Sicilian labor market*. Master Thesis. City University of New York. Available: <https://academicworks.cuny.edu/hc_sas_etds/558/> [accessed on 10th September 2024].

Scalia, V. (2009) "Just a few rogues? Football ultras, clubs and politics in contemporary Italy", *International Review for the Sociology of Sport*, 44(1), pp. 41–53.

Schneider, J. and Schneider, P. (2005) "Mafia, antimafia, and the plural cultures of Sicily", *Current Anthropology*, 46(4), pp. 501–520.

Schubring, A., Hallтén, M., Barker-Ruchti, N. and Post, A. (2023) "Balancing risk-taking and self-care: the ecology of athlete health behaviour during the Olympic qualification phase", *International Review for the Sociology of Sport*, 58(8), pp. 1326–1348.

Sterchele, D. (2015) "De-sportizing physical activity: from sport-for-development to play-for-development", *European Journal for Sport and Society*, 12(1), pp. 97–120.

Sterchele, D. (2020) "Memorable tourism experiences and their consequences: an interaction ritual (IR) theory approach", *Annals of Tourism Research*, 81, 102847.

Sterchele, D. and Saint-Blancat, C. (2015) "Keeping it liminal. The Mondiali Antirazzisti (anti-racist World Cup) as a multifocal interaction ritual", *Leisure Studies*, 34(2), pp. 182–196.

Stratton, J. (2015) "Playing the Jew: anti-semitism and football in the twenty-first century", *Jewish Culture and History*, 16(3), pp. 293–311.

SVIMEZ (2019) *Rapporto Svimez 2019 Sull'economia E La Societa' Del Mezzogiorno* [Svimez report 2019 on the economy and society of Southern Italy]. Available: <http://lnx.svimez.info/svimez/wp-content/uploads/2019/11/rapporto_svimez_2019_sintesi.pdf> [accessed on 10th September 2024].

Testa, A. (2018) "The all-seeing eye of state surveillance in the Italian football (soccer) terraces: the case study of the football fan card", *Surveillance and Society*, 16(1), pp. 69–83.

Testa, A. and Armstrong, G. (2008) "Words and actions: Italian ultras and neo-fascism", *Social Identities*, 14(4), pp. 473–490.

Trequattrini, R., Cuozzo, B., Petrecca, F. and Manzari, A. (2022) "Corporate governance and gender issues: the case of professional football companies in Italy", in Paoloni, P. and Lombardi, R. (Eds.), *Organizational resilience and female entrepreneurship during crises: emerging evidence and future agenda*, Cham: Springer International Publishing.

UNHCR (2016) *Italy sea arrivals dashboard: January to December 2016*. Available: <https://data.unhcr.org/en/documents/details/53356> [accessed on 10th September 2024].

UNHCR (2024) *Situation mediterranean situation*. Available: <https://data2.unhcr.org/en/situations/mediterranean/location/5205> [accessed on 10th September 2024].

Valenti, M., Scelles, N. and Morrow, S. (2018) "Women's football studies: an integrative review", *Sport, Business and Management: An International Journal*, 8(5), pp. 511–528.

Verde, M. (2020) "Discriminazione, hate crimes, Razzismo: la Questione Napolitana", *Revista Direito Civil*, 2(2), pp. 223–238.

Zaslove, A. (2004) "Closing the door? The ideology and impact of radical right populism on immigration policy in Austria and Italy", *Journal of Political Ideologies*, 9(1), pp. 99–118.

Chapter 7

The Netherlands

Racism and policy responses in Dutch football: A critical evaluation

Rens Cremers, Arne Van Lienden, Agnes Elling and Jacco Van Sterkenburg

On 17 November 2019, during the football match between FC Den Bosch and Excelsior Rotterdam in the Dutch 2nd league, Dutch footballer Ahmad Mendes Moreira, whose parents were born in Guinea-Bissau and Guinea, was subjected to noticeable racist abuse by fans. As a result, the match was temporarily suspended. This incident sparked far-reaching debates about racism in Dutch football, the media, and wider society and led to many high-profile players, coaches and other stakeholders involved in football to speak out against racism in football, including the Dutch national team.

Although research shows that racism and discrimination are not uncommon in Dutch society and culture, including football, the Dutch football world was nevertheless aghast: How could such an incident still occur in the Netherlands, a country generally regarded as a relatively open and progressive society (Ghorashi, 2023), and moreover, in football, a domain where social bonding and bridging across different (ethnic) groups are typically seen as central social functions of this sport (Janssens, 2005; Janssens and Verweel, 2014; Van Sterkenburg, 2011)?

This initial consternation in Dutch football reflects the self-perception of many Dutch people regarding racism and other forms of discrimination in Dutch society. Both professional and grassroots football are, not dissimilar to many other socio-cultural contexts, often lauded as great social equalisers, as meritocratic spaces and as useful tools for integration and the development of social cohesion. Football also displays far greater ethnic diversity than many other sports and sectors of society and therefore perceives itself as a space where bonding and bridging differences occur between individuals from different ethnic backgrounds (Lusted, 2009; Cleland and Cashmore, 2014).

Reality, however, often proves to be more ambivalent and complex. For several decades, critical scholars like Essed (1991) and, more recently, Wekker (2016) have analysed and paid detailed attention to a central discrepancy in Dutch society, namely, the parallel and contradictory existence of the passionate denial of racism, on one hand, and everyday racist micro aggressions towards individuals and even institutional racism, on the other. Sport, and football in particular, seem to reflect this contradiction.

DOI: 10.4324/9781003495970-7

This chapter has been made available under a CC-BY-NC-SA 4.0 license.

The fact that there was a sense of public bewilderment over the continued presence of racism in Dutch sports is significant. The governmental focus on minority groups in Dutch sports has largely been shaped by the policy objectives of participation in, and integration through, sports, especially since the turn of the century (Elling, 2017; Van Sterkenburg, 2011). The emphasis was primarily on the positive, functional aspects of sport. Policy papers did not explicitly address the ability of sport to (re)produce mechanisms of inequality and provide a stage for racism, sexism and other forms of discrimination. Emphasising the potential of sport as a tool for improving social relations aligns with the functionalist approach to sport, which has been the dominant governmental perspective on sport in Dutch and other (western) societies. This approach overlooks the key question of to what extent sport primarily serves the interests of privileged groups and, ultimately, reinforces existing inequalities and social structures (Coakley and Pike, 2014).

In response to the racist abuse of Mendes Moreira, the Royal Dutch Football Association (*Koninklijke Nederlandse Voetbalbond*, KNVB), together with the Dutch government, introduced an action plan against racism and discrimination in 2020: *"Our Football is for Everyone"* (OVIVI), which contains a comprehensive set of strategies and policies to tackle racism and discrimination in both professional and amateur football. As a result, policy attention in sports, previously centred on diversity and inclusion, broadened and also included explicit anti-racism and anti-discrimination measures. In this chapter, we will address the following questions and issues: How have Dutch anti-racism and anti-discrimination policies in football developed over time, and what key shifts in focus and strategy can be identified throughout these developments?

Considering the most frequent perpetrators and victims of discrimination in Dutch football, as well as how this discrimination relates to broader societal structures and patterns of inequality, we identify three frequently recognised forms of discrimination. They are, of course, interlinked and occasionally overlap. These include: Firstly, discrimination based on 'race', ethnicity, culture and religion. These range from individual acts of intentional or unintentional racism to institutional forms and systemic forms of racism (Bradbury, Van Sterkenburg and Mignon, 2014; Van Sterkenburg, Cremers, Longas Luque et al., 2023). Secondly, the discrimination of the LGBTQI+ (lesbian, gay, bisexual, transgender, queer and intersex) community, which is reflected in the high prevalence of homonegative acts and often expressed in jokes and comments in football (Elling and Cremers, 2022b, see also Smits, Knoppers and Elling-Machartzki, 2021) and, thirdly, antisemitic chants (Verhoeven and Wagenaar, 2021).

Since a racist incident was the trigger, and thereby anti-racism the underlying basis, for renewed policy attention to discrimination in Dutch football, this chapter will primarily focus on discrimination based on 'race,' ethnicity, culture and religion. The chapter commences with a brief overview of recent migration trends and 'racial'/ethnic diversity in the Netherlands. We will treat the concepts of 'race' and ethnicity as interwoven and will further explore the similarities and distinctions in subsequent sections. Subsequently, we will outline the prevalence of racism within Dutch sports and football. The chapter will then provide a brief history of Dutch football policy on racism before examining current policy developments in greater detail and assessing how they differ from earlier initiatives. Finally, we will analyse how sports and football policies align with broader social and political trends in the Netherlands.

'Race' and ethnicity in Dutch society: migration, socio-demographic developments, discourses and concepts

Until the mid-20th century, 'racial'/ethnic diversity in both Dutch society and football was minimal (Janssens, 2005). However, since the end of the Second World War, the Netherlands has evolved into a one of the most diverse societies in Europe through various so-called "migration waves" (Van Meeteren, Van de Pol, Dekker et al., 2013). The first major wave of migration followed Indonesia's independence in 1949, a former Dutch colony. This was followed by the arrival of "guest workers" in the 1960s, mainly from Morocco and Turkey. In 1975, Suriname's independence triggered further migration, and in the late 1980s, a wave from the (former) Dutch Antilles occurred. Up until then, the number of asylum seekers was relatively small, but it grew significantly from the 1990s, particularly from the former Soviet Union, the Middle East, and Africa (Van Meeteren, Van de Pol, Dekker et al., 2013). Additionally, since the 1970s, migration from Western-European countries has also risen.

Turkey, Morocco, Suriname, Indonesia, and the Dutch Caribbean islands are the countries of origin of the largest non-European migrant groups in the Netherlands (CBS, 2022). By 2022, a quarter of the Dutch population had a migration background, with 18% from non-European countries and 8% from Europe (CBS, 2022). Approximately half of the migrant population was born abroad and constitute first-generation migrants, while the other half are members of the second-generation and were born in the Netherlands. Over the past 80 years, the Netherlands has rapidly diversified, particularly in urban areas, reflecting significant 'racial'/ethnic diversity.

In the Netherlands, unlike in the American and British context, the term 'race' is less commonly used, with "ethnicity" being preferred (Van Sterkenburg, De Heer and Mashigo, 2021). Whereas in everyday discourses 'race' is typically associated with physical or somatic features such as skin colour, the term ethnicity is more often linked to cultural traits such as language, religion and traditions (Van Sterkenburg, De Heer and Mashigo, 2021). Although these terms can represent distinct forms of categorization, we use them conflated ('race'/ethnicity) to reflect how Dutch political and public discourses often employ 'racial' and ethnic markers interchangeably to define difference (Van Sterkenburg, Knoppers and De Leeuw, 2012; Wekker, 2016).

Although explicit invocations of 'race' are generally avoided in Dutch public and policy discourses, Wekker (2016) argues that discourses surrounding ethnicity and culture have become so hardened that they have become interchangeable with biological forms of racism. In the Dutch context, this is evident in hegemonic discourses surrounding Dutch Muslims, particularly those of Moroccan or Turkish descent. They are frequently constructed as essentially different from the dominant conception of Dutchness, which is implicitly linked to Whiteness and Christianity (Wekker, 2016). Van Sterkenburg (2011) notes that in Dutch sports policy discourses, too, different minority ethnic groups are often presented as undifferentiated and homogeneous entities, which might inadvertently reproduce the racialization of ethnicity. He also highlights how the Dutch social categorisations of "autochtonen" (literally translated "of the soil" and referring to White Dutch people) and "allochtonen" (meaning "from another soil" and frequently used for non-White groups) is reproduced in sports policy (Van Sterkenburg, 2011). Although officially removed from policy documents in 2016, these terms persist in everyday discussions about differences (Wekker, 2016). In official documents, they have largely been replaced with the categorisations of "without migration background", "Western-" and "non-Western migration background", which tend to be underpinned by the same implicit racialised logic (Wekker, 2016). Until 2022, "non-Western" commonly referred to migrants from Turkey, Morocco, Suriname, the Dutch Caribbean, and most African, Asian, and South American countries. While now outdated, these terms remain relevant due to their prevalence in past research and policy. The categories "Western" and "non-Western" reflect the racialisation of cultural and ethnic traits, a dynamic also evident in sports policy, that we will discuss further below.

'Racial'/ethnic representation, racism and antisemitism in Dutch football

From the mid-1950s, migrants from Suriname and South Africa began participating in Dutch football, with Humphrey Mijnals becoming the first Black Surinamese player in the national team in 1960. Despite this, Whiteness remained the norm, as evidenced by racist remarks from teammates and fans (Van der Gaag, 2022). The number of migrant players declined in the early 1960s, and was minimal by the 1970s (Janssens, 2005). It was not until 1979 that another player of colour played in the Dutch national team, and in the 1980s, this number increased considerably. Nonetheless, explicit racism remained widespread in Dutch football during this period (Van der Gaag, 2022).

Nevertheless, football became the most popular club sport among Dutch men with migrant backgrounds (Janssens, Elling and Verweel, 2010; Van Haaften, 2019), unlike many other sports that are less diverse (Elling and Cremers, 2022a). This popularity is attributed to football's prominence as a widely loved sport in both the Netherlands and migrants' countries of origin. Furthermore, the sport's professional nature and the visibility of elite male footballers in the media portray football as a pathway to improved socio-economic status (Janssens, Elling and Verweel, 2010).

However, a study among Dutch people with Turkish, Moroccan, Surinamese or Dutch Caribbean backgrounds found that between 2019 and 2021, 47% of team sports participants at sports clubs experienced racist comments during sports activities (Cremers, Anselma and Elling, 2022). Harmsen, Elling and Van Sterkenburg (2019, p. 8) convincingly illustrated that racist "jokes" were common in Dutch professional football:

> It was winter, so it got dark quickly. He needed our player pass. So, he took Jasper's pass and mine. . . . He gave Jasper's player pass back, but he still had mine. And he said: 'Who is this? I can't see him.' I had music in my ears, but my teammates started laughing. So I took my earbuds out, and he said, 'Guys, who is this? I can't see him.' . . . Not long after, I found a banana in my bag after showering.
> (Dutch male football player with a 'racial'/ethnic minority background)

Additionally, research among club administrators indicates that racist 'jokes' or comments appear to be more prevalent in football clubs (51%) than in other team sports (25%) or non-team sports clubs (17%) (Cremers, Anselma and Elling, 2022).

A study of football referees, both amateur and professional, revealed that nearly half (49%) witnessed racist remarks or abuse during the 2021/2022 season (Cremers and Visser, 2023). However, only 9% of those who observed manifestations of racism officially reported the incidents, despite the KNVB's requirements. Interestingly, nearly four in ten of the referees who had never filed a report of this kind indicated they would always report an incident, while almost two in ten claimed no incidents had occurred. Thus, over half indirectly implied that no discriminatory incidents had happened in their presence. Others played it down with sweeping comments such as "it wasn't a big deal". Additionally, reasons for not reporting incidents included the perceived insignificance of the incident and a preference for internal solutions.

The research highlights how widespread and common racist expressions have become in football and that referees often fail to (fully) recognise everyday racism, which results in a lack of reporting of such "incidents" (Cremers and Visser, 2023).

There is also plenty of evidence that racism is prevalent in professional football in the Netherlands. Four out of ten professional players report regular occurrences of racism and discrimination, with 14% having personally experienced it. This figure rises to 27% among those with a migrant background (Cremers and Elling, 2021). Additionally, 92% have observed discriminatory messages aimed at other players on social media, and 44% have received such messages, some daily, mostly of a racist nature (Verloove, Kros and Broekroelofs, 2022).

A survey conducted in 2022 among football fans revealed that a quarter of the respondents had encountered racist remarks in the previous three seasons (Elling, Anselma and Cremers, 2023). Among Dutch individuals with Turkish, Moroccan, Surinamese or Antillean backgrounds who attended professional matches, 51% witnessed racist comments, while 36% did so in amateur football (Elling, Anselma and Cremers, 2023).

Antisemitism is also a significant issue in Dutch professional football (Verhoeven and Wagenaar, 2021). Antisemitic chants in football stadiums have been a persistent problem, particularly in connection with Ajax Amsterdam, a club historically associated with the Jewish community. Ajax Amsterdam supporters have long embraced the epithet of "Jews", a label that frequently spurs antisemitic chants from rival fans. This form of racism appears particularly concentrated within the specific context of football fandom surrounding Ajax Amsterdam, although it has also been notorious in other contexts and is generally quite widespread in Dutch football stadiums. Seijbel, Van Sterkenburg and Oonk (2022) have recently offered a more detailed exploration of antisemitism in Dutch football.

Another, yet less often discussed form of institutional racism in Dutch football is the underrepresentation in coaching and governance positions. Dutch footballers with a visible migrant background are well represented on the playing field, in both amateur and professional men's football. However, their representation on executive boards and as coaches or managers remains limited – very similar to many other European leagues – with 90% of these positions in Dutch professional football taken up by White males (Elling and Cremers, 2022a; Van Sterkenburg, Cremers, Longas Luque et al., 2023).

In amateur sports, around half of those clubs who host sportsmen and women with a migrant background also have staff members with a migrant background. Apart from board positions, there is a clear link: the more migrant-background members a club has, the more coaches and staff reflect this diversity (Cremers, Anselma and Elling, 2022). Nearly all football clubs include members with a migrant background, but fewer than half have a coach from this group, and only six percent have a board member with a migration background.

In elite sports, the limited diversity in senior governance and operational positions can be attributed to the frequently closed recruitment processes. They tend to draw on socially homogeneous networks of men without migration backgrounds, coupled with a reluctance to discuss racism and discrimination (Bradbury, Van Sterkenburg and Mignon, 2014; Van Sterkenburg, Cremers, Longas Luque et al., 2023; De Kwaasteniet, Cremers and Elling, 2023).

The absence of 'racial'/ethnic diversity among top coaches may be linked to the stereotypes that explain positional stacking, as shown in various studies. Black players, particularly those of Sub-Saharan African descent, are often placed in peripheral rather than central roles, reflecting assumptions that underestimate their mental capabilities and football intelligence (Heim, Corthouts and Scheerder, 2020; Nobis and Lazaridou, 2023). The idea of "White Brain" (intellect) versus "Black Brawn" (physicality) is prevalent in Dutch society, with young people often associating Black players with speed and White players with mental skills (Van Sterkenburg, Peeters and Van Amsterdam, 2019). Dutch football media commentary tends to reinforce these stereotypes, despite some ambiguity in research findings (Kapelle, 2020; Van Meyel, 2022).

Data from the Netherlands shows positional segregation in professional football: three-quarters of White players occupy central positions, compared to less than half of Black players and two-thirds of other players with migration backgrounds. Additionally, the latter are less often chosen as captains (Makinde, 2021).

However, the evidence for positional segregation is frequently questioned in Dutch football (media). For example, the Dutch national team has, over the years, featured several "Black" players both in central positions and in the role of captain. In addition, many "Black" players occupy central positions at some of the top Dutch clubs, such as Ajax Amsterdam and PSV Eindhoven. As a result, many managers, coaches and journalists believe that positional segregation is not an issue.

Inclusion and anti-discrimination sport policies in the Netherlands

Initially, sports policies focused on mainstream sports as well as the self-organization of migrant groups, which aligned with the Dutch tradition of "pillarisation", where each socio-political group maintained its own facilities (Van Meeteren, Van de Pol, Dekker et al., 2013). It was not until the early 1990s that policy attention shifted and began to combat various forms of discrimination within sports (Janssens, 2005). In 1994, for example, the sports sector developed an anti-discrimination code and researchers paid more attention to countering interethnic tensions and violence in sports, especially in football.

Since the late 1990s, support for multiculturalism in the Netherlands has declined, with integration policies prioritising assimilation over diversity (Van Meeteren, Van de Pol, Dekker et al., 2013). This was reinforced by the attack on the World Trade Centre in New York in September 2001 and the assassination of the Dutch right-wing politician Pim Fortuyn in the subsequent year. As a result, Dutch society witnessed a rise of populist, Islamphobic, right-wing political parties (Ghorashi, 2023). There was a commitment to active citizenship and people with a migration background were required to adapt to the Dutch language and culture, arising from the public debate on the "integration", or rather assimilation, of Dutch citizens with a migration background.

This can also be seen in sports, where attention to discrimination was followed up by the national policy program *"Meedoen allochtone jeugd door sport"* (Participation of *allochthonous* youth through sport). As described by Van Sterkenburg (2011), the policy at that time clearly reflected a binary discourse of *autochthonous* versus *allochthonous* people, which reproduced the existing power hierarchy. This distinction clearly differentiates and essentialises the privileged 'racial'/ethnic group (autochthonous) from the underprivileged "other" (allochthonous).

The programme was later renamed and became *Participation of All Youth Through Sport*. This name change reflected the *zeitgeist*, as the development of policies for specific target groups had become undesirable. At the same time, the programme was a continuation of existing social policy objectives aimed at assimilating ethnic minorities. The rather instrumentalist perspective on sport saw it as an ideal means to pursue the desired policy goals. In this context, addressing racism, in the form of (micro)aggressions, exclusion and social inequality, was pushed to the background.

While support for social and cultural assimilation remained prevalent, the mid-2010s saw a resurgence of a public debate about racism in the Netherlands, which was clearly highlighted by the controversy over the Blackface figure *Zwarte Piet*. This "racially" charged folklore character, with his face painted black, a curly wig, and golden earrings, accompanies Saint Nicholas during the pre-Christmas season. Critics argue that the character perpetuates colonial-era stereotypes of Black people, while defenders insist it is merely a harmless cultural tradition. That debate, obviously, reveals fundamental tensions in Dutch society about 'race' and inclusivity.

Discrimination in sports received renewed policy attention in 2016 when the central government launched a *"National Action Program against Discrimination"*, addressing discriminatory chants in football stadiums. The government replaced the term *"allochtonen"* with "Dutch people with a migrant background," and also started to distinguish between "Western" and "non-Western" origins. Although this was an attempt to soften the division among Dutch individuals based on their migrant status, these categories remained de facto identical.

Nevertheless, the focus of sport policies continued to be on increasing the participation of underrepresented groups in, and through, sports, with limited attention paid to racism and discrimination. Only in 2019, 'race'/ethnicity and discrimination in sport shifted back into the policy limelight.

In 2018, the central government and various stakeholders launched *"The National Sports Agreement I"*, including sub-sections on *"Inclusive Sports and Movement"* and *"Positive Sports Culture"*, aimed at ensuring accessible, safe sports for all (VWS, VSG, VNG et al., 2018). The approach was less functionalist, emphasising the desire to increase sports participation across the population and reduce social inequalities. *"Inclusive Sports and Movement"* addresses financial, practical, and social accessibility to improve access and foster inclusion and diversity in sport. Additionally, it explicitly states that "exclusion and discrimination will be combated". The part on *"Positive Sports Culture"* stresses a commitment to an idealised vision of inclusivity, yet may overlook the complex realities and systemic issues that underpin exclusion and discrimination in sport:

> The basic philosophy of the present approach is founded on positivity. At the same time, parties do not close their eyes to abuses. Small in number, but big in impact. Therefore, the parties are explicitly committed to monitoring the bottom line.
>
> (VWS, VSG, VNG et al., 2018, p. 3)

This quote clearly reflects the self-perception of the Dutch sports world, which is generally positive. Furthermore, anti-racism and anti-discrimination were initially hardly addressed within *"Positive Sports Culture"*, which primarily focused on combating sexual misconduct. The targeted attention to racism and discrimination in the entire Sports Agreement is initially very limited. The two key terms, racism and discrimination, are either absent or mentioned once, respectively, in the 40-page document.

The racist football incident with Mendes Moreira's involvement in 2019, catalysed renewed attention to racism and discrimination in Dutch sports (Elling, Cremers, Stevens et al., 2021), leading to the launch of the anti-racism plan OVIVI, which was further propelled by the *Black Lives Matter* movement.

Inclusion and anti-discrimination policies in Dutch football

OVIVI, introduced by the KNVB and the national government, contained a three-year strategic plan (2020–2022) that included annual monitoring (KNVB, 2020a). The COVID-19 pandemic significantly delayed the smooth implementation of some parts of the scheme. As a result, it was extended by one year, and the successor action plan, OVIVI 2 (2023–2025), was introduced in 2023 (KNVB, 2023).

Both plans contain various measures along three substantive areas of intervention in collaboration with existing and new partners and networks: First, prevention; Second, identifying (including, reporting), and, finally, sanctioning. As previously mentioned, the programme addresses racism as well as other forms of discrimination.

Preventive measures include a media campaign and a training programme for clubs. The #OneLove campaign emerged as the most prominent element, partly because captains of several national men's teams wore the armband during the Nations League competition in September 2022, amid controversy during the men's FIFA World Cup in Qatar, where wearing this symbol was prohibited.

In the Netherlands, the captain's armband gained heightened visibility during *"Purple Friday"*, a day dedicated to foster LGBTQIA+ acceptance, when the captains in the two professional football divisions wore rainbow armbands. At the launch of the #OneLove campaign, this was replaced by the #OneLove armband, which features a heart with multi-coloured stripes and the number "1". Although the armband aimed to combat racism and discrimination and promote the message of inclusion, its primary association became LGBTQIA+ acceptance due to the contexts in which it was worn and its colourful design. While the campaign sparked significant discussions on LGBTQIA+ acceptance, it did little to raise awareness of efforts against racism.

Within the training programmes of clubs, however, anti-racism was one of the themes that received explicit attention. Initially, the plan was for associations to be given a variety of support on the themes of racism and discrimination, providing them with the opportunity to implement various forms of interventions. These interventions include a virtual reality (VR) game, a theatrical performance, and provision of an online game in a classroom setting, all accompanied by group discussions that were facilitated by a professional, addressing biases, prejudices, stereotypical beliefs, and racism.

There are high expectations for this set of preventive actions, which have now been adopted by 11 other sports federations and organisations. However, in practice, it proves challenging to engage clubs with this kind of socio-pedagogical work. Often, the educational programme seems to be limited to a workshop involving a few interested board members and other (team) members, with little follow-up at the club. Furthermore, the additional support from the responsible associations materialised rather infrequently. As in many other sports, a substantial number of amateur football clubs already face challenges in managing the basics of their clubs, leaving little room to address anti-racism as just one of the many "other" issues they need to tackle (Stuij, Hoeijmakers, Van Kalmthout et al., 2023).

The key action points under the heading of "identifying" aim to increase the willingness to report discrimination, thereby also raising the number of registered incidents (including those caused by spectators). Since the introduction of OVIVI, records are also kept on the grounds on which discrimination occurs, for example, skin colour or sexual preference. Additionally, closed-circuit television technology (CCTV) needs to be further developed to enable the unambiguous identification and subsequent prosecution of perpetrators of racism in football stadiums.

Despite the availability of an app designed to simplify the passing on of racist incidents, the number of reports remains low, with only 18 incidents registered during the 2022/2023 season. The willingness to relay such incidents appears to be relatively limited. Additionally, the reporting process for referees has been standardised in the match report form, making it easier for them to document racist manifestations. However, referees often struggle to recognise incidents or feel overwhelmed by the responsibility of addressing such issues alone, particularly since racism, including microaggressions, is prevalent in football culture (Cremers and Visser, 2023). In response, the KNVB nowadays focuses on enhancing referees' sensitivity and reducing their reluctance to act by providing additional training.

A low willingness to report discrimination can also be found in other areas of Dutch society, partly due to a lack of trust in follow-up actions (Walz and Fiere, 2023). This raises the question of how much potential there is to increase the willingness to relay discriminatory practices. From the perspective of victims and witnesses, it remains crucial to emphasise that reporting incidents is worthwhile and to make the monitoring process easier.

The use of cameras for identifying perpetrators of racism in stadiums has, so far, proven to be challenging, too. Not only is the privacy and data protection legislation complex, but it also raises questions about the suitability of this kind of evidence. The cameras appear to be successful tools for addressing physical misconduct in stadiums, but are now, partly due to the existing financial subsidies, being developed under the guise of combating racism. Whether they will ever prove effective for this purpose remains to be seen.

During the development of the second action plan, attention was also paid to identifying and combatting online racism, although the results of this initiative are not yet known. The key measures under the heading of "sanctioning" include the enhancement of criminal law, the appointment of special prosecutors, the toughening of penalties, the introduction of a (digital) reporting obligation, and the implementation of an educational penalty: the chanting project, in which (young) supporters receive lessons on the historical context of racism and antisemitism and the impact abusive chants can have on the victims.

The adjustments to criminal law, tougher penalties, and the appointment of special prosecutors have been successfully implemented. In the first Covid-free season (2022/2023), 272 cases were processed, but the lack of evidence resulted in half of the cases being dismissed. If the number of convictions for racist abuse remains low, this measure is likely to have relatively little impact on racism in football stadiums.

The development of a (digital) reporting obligation had already commenced prior to the launch of the OVIVI strategic plan. This is still in a pilot phase, and as such, no monitoring and evaluation results are yet available.

One major omission of all the aforementioned policies is that they do not contain strategies and measures that address social and ethnic diversity in senior management positions. Nor do they recognise the need to investigate the causes of institutional racism that may explain the limited progression of ethnic minorities, as well as women, to powerful and influential roles in football.

In response to criticism, the KNVB developed an internal diversity policy with target percentages for women and individuals with a "non-Western" migrant background to be achieved by 2030. The "Rooney Rule" was also introduced. It originates from American Football and requires sports organisations to invite at least one person from a minority group for an interview when filling a vacant position (Van Sterkenburg, Cremers, Longas Luque et al., 2023).

Additionally, the barriers faced by women and Dutch citizens with a "non-Western" migration background in accessing training programmes are examined and staff are undergoing inclusive-thinking training (KNVB, 2020b).

Although concrete figures are not yet available, diversity in high-profile leadership roles has improved, exemplified by the appointment of Nigel de Jong, a Black former footballer, as Director of Professional Football. Notably, 'racial'/ ethnic inequality within the football association is framed as an internal diversity issue, separate from, and unrelated to, the anti-discrimination programme. Racism is seen mainly as overt acts in stadiums and on the pitch, while exclusion within the organisation is surprisingly treated as a diversity issue.

It is noteworthy that although the OVIVI programme primarily targets professional football, clubs and players appear to be reluctant to publicly commit to and support anti-racism and anti-discrimination efforts. This hesitancy stems from concerns about reputational damage as clubs are concerned about conflicts with fans, while players are anxious about their career prospects (Kaufman, 2008; De Kwaasteniet, Cremers and Elling, 2023).

Furthermore, most initiatives originate from the KNVB and the government, with limited input from professional clubs. In OVIVI II, professional clubs are encouraged to take a more active role. After all, they have the potential to influence their supporters and local amateur associations.

Finally, the OVIVI-plan also turned out to be an inspiration for developing and implementing similar policies such as *"training programmes for clubs"* within the overall sports sector. For example, in the successor to "The National Sports Agreement I", "The National Sports Agreement II: 2022–2026" (VWS, VSG, VNG et al., 2022), racism is addressed more prominently.

Conclusion and recommendations

In the aftermath of the aforementioned racist incident in 2019, the KNVB and the national government launched the OVIVI initiative to combat discrimination. This effort, bolstered by the global *Black Lives Matter* movement, heightened awareness of racism in Dutch football and, also, other sports. Concrete measures have since then been further developed to fight racism, with OVIVI also inspiring broader policies in the sports sector.

Recent efforts to address discrimination in football follow decades of intermittent attention and respond to the growing sensitivity and the emergence of public debates in the Netherlands on diversity, multiculturalism, racism and discrimination (Elling, Cremers, Stevens et al., 2021). Media coverage has been inconsistent, typically peaking after overt racist incidents before fading again. The current attention given by football's governing bodies on anti-discrimination policies may herald a renewed and, hopefully, more sustained engagement with tackling racism in Dutch football.

Without wishing to undermine the potential impact of this renewed momentum, this chapter has highlighted some critical concerns regarding some of the underlying assumptions of the current anti-discrimination policies. Crucially, most anti-discrimination policies have adopted a rather narrow approach to tackling racism, framing the issue primarily as an explicit and immediately detectable phenomenon. Such an approach largely circumvents a deeper and more differentiated engagement with the ways that inequalities based on 'race'/ethnicity are manifested in Dutch football. Instead, underpinned by a functionalist way of thinking, policymakers often tend to focus on "positive" concepts and benefits like participation and integration of (ethnic) minority groups through sport.

As Wekker (2016) argues, inequalities based on 'race'/ethnicity are deeply embedded in Dutch discourses, often unnoticed by the White majority. Explicit racist incidents are publicly condemned, but there is little recognition of the subtler and everyday ways in which "racialised" hierarchies are constructed and maintained. In sport, particularly football, recognising and addressing hidden forms of racism can be seen as especially challenging. On the one hand, there is a powerful and persistent belief in the meritocracy and colour-blindness of sport, which offers equal opportunities to everyone. On the other hand, there is a common-sense assumption that 'racial'/ethnic differences exist and can even be beneficial, such as the supposed physical advantages attributed to Black athletes (Vorm, 2024). And while racist comments and chants are seen as the "real" racism that needs to be stopped, institutional and structural inequalities, such as the lack of 'racial'/ethnic diversity in coaching, governing and operational positions in Dutch football, are presented as a diversity and inclusion issue, with no one to blame.

This obviously leaves us with the question of what the future might hold for anti-discrimination policies and initiatives, and the role that scholarly work can play regarding the issue. A significant challenge is the current rise of the far-right in Dutch politics. As we have seen, policies in Dutch sport often reflect dominant societal debates, and today's hegemonic discourses around migration, asylum, and diversity have grown increasingly exclusionary and inward looking.

Currently, we can observe public and political discourses in the Netherlands that increasingly reduce and simplify complex issues to straightforward and uncomplicated narratives, creating the impression of two irreconcilable dichotomies. Progressive forces advocate for comprehensive approaches to tackle discrimination and promote diversity, while conservative groups reject such "woke" efforts, dismissing discrimination as a non-urgent issue (e.g. Wichgers, 2022). These groups often disparage minorities as threats to and/or incompatible with an "authentic" Dutch identity, framing such tensions as cultural conflicts. At the same time, skin colour remains a key marker of inclusion and exclusion, distinguishing White Dutch individuals from those perceived as outsiders (Essed and Trienekens, 2008).

Despite these stark narratives within the public and media domain, the more general reality "on the ground" seems more nuanced. Although polarisation was widely perceived to have grown in 2022, research shows differences of opinion had not significantly widened (Miltenburg, Geurkink, Tunderman et al., 2022). The perception of (an increasing) polarisation appeared to stem primarily from the hardening of public debates and the adoption of perceived radical positions. While the idea that Dutch society may be less polarised than it sometimes appears to be (Muis, 2024), offers some reassurance, we also observe how anti-discrimination measures (in sports) are perceived by some as "too extreme" (Cremers, Anselma, Visser et al., 2024).

Policy efforts to combat discrimination and racism in Dutch sport are at an all-time high. However, as demonstrated by the most recent election results, there is growing support for political parties that consider the focus on discrimination to be exaggerated (see Bol and Mulder, 2021). This raises concerns about the future success of anti-discrimination initiatives in football.

At the same time, we argue that the current political climate also provides a call for critical scholarship that takes seriously, and aims to challenge, the enduring role that racism plays in Dutch society and football at various levels. In the long run, this scholarship is likely to perturb the status quo and put pressure on Dutch football governing bodies to more firmly address the not-so-visible forms of racism. This may involve hiring practices within their own organisations and exploring the intersections with other social identities, such as gender and physical ability, in a more sustained and critical way.

A critical self-examination is necessary not only for football governing bodies but also for the Dutch scholarly community working on racism in football. For instance, all four authors of this chapter are White, able-bodied academics. In predominantly White societies, we risk being socialised into everyday hegemonic 'racial' discourses (Van Sterkenburg and Walder, 2021). While we aim to avoid replicating these discourses by engaging with critical 'race' studies (see, e.g. Hylton, 2009, and for a more elaborate reflection on positionality Van Lienden, 2024), increasing the visibility and participation of scholars from 'racial'/ethnic minority backgrounds are essential. Greater representation can further contribute to making Dutch football a space where differences are rendered as the norm rather than continuing to be sources of inequality.

References

Bol, R. and Mulder, V. (2021) *Zo denken én handelen politieke partijen als het gaat over racisme*, Amsterdam: De Correspondent.

Bradbury, S., Van Sterkenburg, J. and Mignon, P. (2014) *The glass ceiling in football in Europe: levels of representation of 'visible' ethnic minorities and women in leadership positions, and the experiences of elite level 'visible' ethnic minority coaches*, London: FARE/UEFA.

CBS (2022) *Integratie en samenleven 2022* [Integration and living together 2022], Den Haag/Heerlen: Centraal Bureau voor de Statistiek.

Cleland, J. and Cashmore, E. (2014) "Fans, racism and British football in the twenty-first century: the existence of a 'colour-blind' ideology", *Journal of Ethnic and Migration Studies*, 40(4), pp. 638–654.

Coakley, J. and Pike, E. (2014) *Sports in society: issues and controversies*, New York: McGraw-Hill.

Cremers, R., Anselma, M. and Elling, A. (2022) "Sportdeelname en ervaren racisme etnische minderheden" [Sports participation and experienced racism among ethnic minorities], in Stevens, V. and Steenbergen, J. (Eds.), *Samenwerking, dialoog en zelforganisatie als kiemen van een positieve sportcultuur* [Collaboration, dialogue, and self-organisation as seeds of a positive sports culture], Utrecht: Mulier Instituut.

Cremers, R., Anselma, M., Visser, T., De Kwaasteniet, R. and Elling, A. (2024) *Monitor OVIVI 2023*, Utrecht: Mulier Instituut.

Cremers, R. and Elling, A. (2021) *Racisme in het betaald mannenvoetbal. Veel draagvlak voor aanpak van expliciet racisme* [Racism in professional men's football: strong support for tackling explicit racism], Utrecht: Mulier Instituut.

Cremers, R. and Visser, T. (2023) *Discriminatie in het voetbal. Een perspectief vanuit de arbitrage* [Discrimination in football: a referees' perspective], Utrecht: Mulier Instituut.

De Kwaasteniet, R., Cremers, R. and Elling, A. (2023) *'Ons-kent-ons': Mechanismen van sociale in- en uitsluiting in het sporttechnisch topkader* [Birds of a feather flock together: mechanisms of social inclusion and exclusion in the high-performance sports framework], Utrecht: Mulier Instituut.

Elling, A. (2017) "Navigating 'in-betweenness' in studying sport in society", in Young, K. (Ed.), *Reflections on sociology of sport: ten questions, ten scholars, ten perspectives*, Leeds: Emerald Publishing Limited.

Elling, A., Anselma, M. and Cremers, R. (2023) *Monitor 'Ons voetbal is van iedereen'* [Monitor 'our football belongs to everyone'], Utrecht: Mulier Instituut.

Elling, A. and Cremers, R. (2022a) *Diversiteit in kaderfuncties sportbonden en clubs* [Diversity in leadership positions within sports associations and clubs], Utrecht: Mulier Instituut.

Elling, A. and Cremers, R. (2022b) "Monitoring 'inclusive masculinity' in sport in the Netherlands 2008–2021: no problems with gay men, but no gay-inclusive cultures", in Hartmann-Tews, I. (Ed.), *Sport, identity and inclusion in Europe*, Abingdon: Routledge.

Elling, A., Cremers, R., Stevens, V. and Anselma, M. (2021) *Monitor 'Ons voetbal is van iedereen'* [Monitor 'our football belongs to everyone'], Utrecht: Mulier Instituut.

Essed, P. (1991) *Understanding everyday racism: an interdisciplinary theory* (Vol. 2), London: Sage.

Essed, P. and Trienekens, S. (2008) "'Who wants to feel white?' race, Dutch culture and contested identities", *Ethnic and Racial Studies*, 31(1), pp. 52–72.

Ghorashi, H. (2023) "Taking racism beyond Dutch innocence", *European Journal of Women's Studies*, 30(1S), pp. 16S–21S.

Harmsen, F., Elling, A. and Van Sterkenburg, J. (2019) *Racisme, sociale kramp en innerlijke drijfkrachten in het betaald voetbal* [Racism, social tension, and inner drives in professional football], Amsterdam/Utrecht/Rotterdam: Be.People./Mulier Instituut/Erasmus Research Centre for Media, Communication and Culture.

Heim, C., Corthouts, J. and Scheerder, J. (2020) "Is there a glass ceiling or can racial and ethnic barriers be overcome?", in Bradbury, S., Lusted, J. and Van Sterkenburg, J. (Eds.), *'Race', ethnicity and racism in sports coaching*, London: Routledge.

Hylton, K. (2009) *"Race" and sport: critical race theory*, London: Routledge.

Janssens, J. (2005) "The Netherlands", in Van Sterkenburg, J., Janssens, J. and Rijnen, B. (Eds.), *Football and racism*, Nieuwegein: Arko Sports Media.

Janssens, J., Elling, A. and Verweel, P. (2010) "De Sport: een uitgelezen ontmoetingsplaats vooriedereen?" [Sport: an ideal meeting place for everyone?], in Kemper, F. (Ed.), *Interplay: studies on ethnicity, integration, and sport*, Werkendam: Avant.

Janssens, J. and Verweel, P. (2014) "The significance of sports clubs within multicultural society", *European Journal for Sport and Society*, 11(1), pp. 35–58.

Kapelle, T. (2020) *De representatie van etniciteit en huidskleur in het Nederlandse televisiecommentaar van voetbal en tennis* [The representation of ethnicity and skin colour in Dutch television commentary on football and tennis]. Master's Thesis. Erasmus University Rotterdam. Available: <https://thesis.eur.nl/pub/55310> [accessed on 14th November 2024].

Kaufman, P. (2008) "Boos, bans, and other backlash: the consequences of being an activist athlete", *Humanity & Society*, 32(3), pp. 215–237.

KNVB (2020a) *Ons voetbal is van iedereen. Plan van aanpak* [Our football belongs to everyone: action plan], Zeist: KNVB.

KNVB (2020b) *KNVB zet diverse en inclusieve organisatie kracht bij* [KNVB strengthens its commitment to a diverse and inclusive organisation], Zeist: KNVB. Available: <https://www.knvb.nl/nieuws/organisatie/berichten/62197/knvb-zet-diverse-en-inclusieve-organisatie-kracht-bij> [accessed on 21st September 2024].

KNVB (2023) *Ons voetbal is van iedereen. Plan van aanpak 2023–2025* [Our football belongs to everyone: action plan 2023–2025], Zeist: KNVB.

Lusted, J. (2009) "Playing games with 'race': understanding resistance to 'race' equality initiatives in English local football governance", *Soccer & Society*, 10(6), pp. 722–739.

Makinde, O. (2021) *Investigation of positional segregation in Dutch football caused by racial bias on black ethnic minorities*. Master's Thesis. Vrije Universiteit Amsterdam/ Mulier Instituut.

Miltenburg, E., Geurkink, B., Tunderman, S., Beekers, D. and Den Ridder, J. (2022) *Burgerperspectieven* [Citizen perspectives] 2022|2, Den Haag: Sociaal en Cultureel Planbureau.

Muis, Q. (2024) *"Who are those people?" Causes and consequences of polarization in the schooled society*. Doctoral Dissertation. Tilburg University.

Nobis, T. and Lazaridou, F. (2023) "Racist stacking in professional soccer in Germany", *International Review for the Sociology of Sport*, 58(1), pp. 23–42.

Seijbel, J., Van Sterkenburg, J. and Oonk, G. (2022) "Expressing rivalry online: antisemitic rhetoric among Dutch football supporters on Twitter", *Soccer & Society*, 23(8), pp. 834–848.

Smits, F., Knoppers, A. and Elling-Machartzki, A. (2021) "'Everything is said with a smile': homonegative speech acts in sport", *International Review for the Sociology of Sport*, 56(3), pp. 343–360.

Stuij, M., Hoeijmakers, R., Van Kalmthout, J., Cremers, R. and Slot-Heijs, J.J. (2023) *Sportverenigingen en hun uitdagingen: een analyse van oorzaken en verschillen tussen sportverenigingen* [Sports clubs and their challenges: an analysis of causes and differences between sports clubs], Utrecht: Mulier Instituut.

Van der Gaag, S. (2022) *Welke sporters strijden tegen racisme* [Which athletes are fighting against racism]?, Hilversum: NPO. Available: <www.npokennis.nl/longread/7468/welke-sporters-strijden-tegen-racisme> [accessed on 21st September 2024].

Van Haaften, A.F. (2019) "Ethnic participation in Dutch amateur football clubs", *European Journal for Sport and Society*, 16(4), pp. 301–322.

Van Lienden, A. (2024) *Between the lines: (re)constructions of race/ethnicity in Polish televised football*. Doctoral Thesis. Erasmus University Rotterdam.

Van Meeteren, M., Van de Pol, S., Dekker, R., Engbersen, G. and Snel, E. (2013) "Destination Netherlands: history of immigration and immigration policy in the Netherlands", in Ho, J. (Ed.), *Immigrants: acculturation, socio-economic challenges and cultural psychology*, New York: Nova Publishers.

Van Meyel, J. (2022) *The meaning of ethnicity in Dutch television commentary during matches of the Dutch national team*. Master's Thesis. Erasmus University Rotterdam. Available: <https://thesis.eur.nl/pub/65030> [accessed on 14th November 2024].

Van Sterkenburg, J. (2011) "Thinking 'race' and ethnicity in (Dutch) sports policy and research", in *Sport and challenges to racism*, London: Palgrave Macmillan UK.

Van Sterkenburg, J., Cremers, R., Longas Luque, C., Van Lienden, A. and Elling, A. (2023) *The governance index report: levels of gender and ethnic/racial representation in leadership positions in European football*, Amsterdam: Fare Network.

Van Sterkenburg, J., De Heer, M. and Mashigo, P. (2021) "Sports media professionals reflect on racial stereotypes and ethnic diversity in the organization", *Corporate Communications: An International Journal*, 26(5), pp. 31–46.

Van Sterkenburg, J., Knoppers, A. and de Leeuw, S. (2012) "Constructing racial/ethnic difference in and through Dutch televised soccer commentary", *Journal of Sport and Social Issues*, 36(4), pp. 422–442.

Van Sterkenburg, J., Peeters, R. and Van Amsterdam, N. (2019) "Everyday racism and constructions of racial/ethnic difference in and through football talk", *European Journal of Cultural Studies*, 22(2), pp. 195–212.

Van Sterkenburg, J. and Walder, M. (2021) "How do audiences of televised English football construct difference based on race/ethnicity?", *Language and Intercultural Communication*, 21(6), pp. 765–780.

Verhoeven, J. and Wagenaar, W. (2021) "Appealing to a common identity: the case of antisemitism in Dutch football", in Brunssen, P. and Schüler-Springorum, S. (Eds.), *Football and discrimination*, Abingdon: Routledge.

Verloove, J., Kros, K. and Broekroelofs, R. (2022) *Online discriminatie in het voetbal* [Online discrimination in football], Utrecht: Movisie.

Vorm, M. (2024) *'Holland no abi tifi maar ai beti'. Sport hereoes and the sense of belonging of young adult Surnamese and Dutch Caribbean athletes in the Netherlands*. Master's Report. Vrije Universiteit Amsterdam.

VWS, VSG, VNG and NOC*NSF (2018) *Nationaal Sportakkoord 2018–2022. Sport verenigt Nederland* [National sports agreement 2018–2022: sport unites the Netherlands], Den Haag: Ministerie van VWS.

VWS, VSG, VNG, NOC*NSF, and POS (2022) *Hoofdlijnen Sportakkoord II. Sport Versterkt* [Main points of sports agreement II: sport strengthens], Den Haag: Ministerie van VWS.

Walz, G. and Fiere, B. (2023) *Discriminatiecijfers in 2022* [Discrimination statistics in 2022], Rotterdam: Art. 1.

Wekker, G. (2016) *White innocence: paradoxes of colonialism and race*, Durham: Duke University Press.

Wichgers, L. (2022) *Hoezo mogen we van 'woke' 'niets meer zeggen'?!* [Why does 'woke' allow us to 'say nothing more'?!], Amsterdam: EW Podium. Available: <https://www.ewmagazine.nl/ingezonden-opinie/achtergrond/2022/09/hoezo-mogen-we-van-woke-niets-meer-zeggen-899727/> [accessed on 21st September 2024].

Chapter 8

Poland

Nationalism, racism, xenophobia and football fan sub-cultures: Historical developments and contemporary issues

Radosław Kossakowski

A warm evening in August 2024 sets the scene for a match in the Polish *Ekstraklasa*, the highest division of the country's football league system, between Lechia Gdańsk and Raków Częstochowa. The game marked Lechia's return to the top tier following a season in the *Pierwsza liga*, the country's second highest division, and they were pitted against the reigning Polish champion, Raków. Despite the traditional sport rivalry between these two clubs, the atmosphere was marked by a sense of camaraderie, as fans from both teams united in a display of shared passion, creating a mosaic of white-green and red-blue colours in the *ultras* sections of the stadium. Throughout the match, fans from both teams engaged in a variety of chants and pyrotechnic displays, leading to a brief interruption and some added time. Most of the chants were meant to support and encourage the players, reflecting the amicable relationship between the fan bases. However, this atmosphere of camaraderie, celebration and high spirits turned sour at the end of the match when the crowd started to chant nationalist slogans, including "Poland for the Poles" and "All of Poland sings with us; refugees get the fuck out". Despite the provocative nature of these chants, the referee did not intervene, and the stadium announcer merely urged the fans to refrain from such xenophobic slogans and focus on supporting their respective teams.

August 2024 also marked a period of intense discussion in the Polish media and among fans regarding Michael Ameyaw's potential call-up to the national team. At that time, Ameyaw was a player for Piast Gliwice. He now plays for Raków Częstochowa. He is a Polish citizen, born in Poland to a Ghanaian father who immigrated in the 1990s and a Polish mother. Ameyaw grew up in Poland and is fluent in Polish. However, he is Black and has faced racist comments online due to his skin colour. In response to these issues, Ameyaw stated: "I was born in Poland, my mother is Polish, and my father also holds Polish citizenship. Skin colour should not determine whether we can call someone a Pole" (interview for Canal+, 25.08.2024). A few months later, in October 2024, he made his debut in a match against Portugal.

The aforementioned examples underscore the persistence of racism, nationalism and xenophobia as social issues in Polish society, with significant

DOI: 10.4324/9781003495970-8
This chapter has been made available under a CC-BY-NC-SA 4.0 license.

implications for the world of football. Despite far-reaching historical and socio-cultural shifts, marginalised groups continue to face disproportionate levels of discrimination, abuse and violence, both overt and covert. Football's highly charged emotional atmosphere, often rooted in identity-based, national, and political affiliations, provides a fertile ground for expressing prejudices and aggression. This is exacerbated by the fact that football rivalries are frequently embedded in broader regional and historical narratives extending far beyond the pitch (Dmowski, 2013). Football's development in most countries is inextricably linked to the historical trajectories and socio-political contexts of specific regions and nations. Consequently, investigations into phenomena such as national identity or the discrimination of minorities necessitate a nuanced and multi-dimensional analytical framework. This endeavour becomes particularly challenging when the focus turns to the examination of highly problematic and socially unacceptable issues like racism and xenophobia.

This chapter focuses on racism and xenophobia within Polish football. Employing a sociological lens informed by historical analysis, it seeks to provide a comprehensive understanding of these phenomena. The historical perspective is indispensable for contextualising contemporary manifestations of these issues.

This chapter comprises several parts. Initially, I will provide a historical overview of football's development in Poland, focusing on ethnic and political dimensions. Subsequent parts will delve into more recent developments, beginning with the post-1989 period that witnessed a democratic transition of the country, leading to the emergence of the Third Polish Republic. These sections will examine the evolution of attitudes, behaviours and discourses related to racism and xenophobia within the rather complex fan culture of the country and broader socio-political visions. Additionally, the chapter will highlight selected initiatives to combat racism in Polish football. The concluding paragraphs will offer reflections on the future trajectory of ethnic diversity and dissonances in Polish football.

Football after regaining independence in 1918

Poland did not exist on the political map in the second half of the nineteenth and early twentieth centuries, when football was becoming institutionalised and grew rapidly in popularity, with clubs and football associations emerging all over Europe. It was only after regaining independence in 1918 that the new socio-political circumstances allowed for the formation of the Polish Football Association (*Polski Związek Piłki Nożnej*, PZPN), the governing body responsible for the organisation and supervision of all football-related issues in the newly unified country. The inaugural match of the Polish national team took place on 18 December 1921 against Hungary in Budapest.

In the interwar period, when football attracted a mass following, Poland was a diverse and multi-ethnic nation-state. In 1931, the population of Poland comprised 68.9% ethnic Poles, 13.9% Ukrainians, 8.7% Jews, 3.1% Belarusians and 2.3% Germans (Jałowiecki and Szczepański, 2007, p. 70). Political and social class divisions were frequently more crucial than national or ethnic identities. As elsewhere in Europe, antisemitic tensions were growing in Poland during the 1920s and 1930s, which also affected social relations in the world of football (Burski and Woźniak, 2021).

Many footballers of non-Polish ethnic background living in multi-ethnic regions of the country played for the Polish national team in the interwar period. For example, in the 1938 World Cup finals, Poland played a surprisingly close game against favoured Brazil, losing only 5–6 in extra time. Ernest Wilimowski scored four goals for Poland. Wilimowski's background and story were rather complex, yet not unusual for the region of Upper Silesia in the South of Poland and well-known for its heavy and mining industries. He received his Polish surname from his stepfather, who had married his German mother. He spoke German at home and used the Silesian dialect on the pitch and at school. To the dismay of the local German population, he chose to play for Ruch Chorzów, a Polish team. On 1 September 1939, the German army invaded Poland, bringing an end to Wilimowski's career as a Polish footballer. A German by birth, Wilimowski was automatically awarded German citizenship of the highest category. Sepp Herberger, the future coach of the 1954 World Cup winners, quickly called him up to the national team of the Third Reich. Willimowski's story perfectly illustrates the intricate, complex, dynamic and multifaceted nature of Poland's ethnic and national composition during that period.

The end of the Second World War saw Poland as a different country. The population had diminished substantially: almost six million Polish citizens lost their lives, including 90% of the Jewish population, and even more remained in those areas which were incorporated into the Soviet Union. During the communist rule that commenced in 1945, further attempts were made to unify the nation and generate a sense of national identity in order to limit the popular appeal of regional identities. This meant that the issue of footballers of non-Polish origins in the national team was non-existent during the communist period (1945–1989). The aforementioned factors contributed to a relative absence of racist and xenophobic manifestations within Polish football.

Subsequently, due to wartime upheavals, resettlements, and complex migration flows, Poland ceased to be ethnically diverse. Nowadays, it is one of the most homogenous European countries regarding a sense of belonging and identity. According to the 2021 National Census, 97.7% of the population share a sense of Polish national identity. However, over the last few years, the number of foreigners living in Poland has been steadily growing, primarily, but not exclusively, due to the war-related migration of Ukrainians.

Notably, Poland has witnessed a considerable increase in immigration from non-European cultural backgrounds, albeit the exact scale remains elusive.

Poland granted more than 500,000 work permits to non-EU nationals in 2021. 350,000 were given to people from Belarus and Ukraine, the rest from countries like India, Bangladesh, Philippines, Georgia, Nepal or Uzbekistan. The overall figure of about half a million immigrants signifies a 25% increase compared to 2020 and an eightfold increase compared to 2015 (Wójcik, 2023).

Poland has emerged as a significant hub for migration within the European Union, processing a quarter of all residence permit applications from non-EU citizens. This unprecedented development can be attributed to Poland's dynamic economy and its ongoing need for a skilled workforce.

The situation in Poland's football market presents a stark contrast. There are no restrictions on the number of foreign players who can participate in matches in the *Ekstraklasa*, Poland's top football league. However, the number of non-EU players is limited to two in the lower divisions. In women's football, the top league allows a maximum of four non-EU players on the pitch. Among foreign players in the Polish men's *Ekstraklasa*, Spaniards were the most numerous in the 2023/24 season, while Ukrainians dominated the lower divisions. Interestingly, due to financial considerations, Polish clubs often turn to foreign players, primarily Europeans. The transfer fees of Polish players are often prohibitively expensive, making it economically more viable to sign players from abroad. The hiring of foreign players is becoming almost a necessity, even for clubs with modest budgets. As the president of Puszcza Niepołomice, a club from a town with 16,000 inhabitants playing in the *Ekstraklasa* since 2023 in a stadium with a maximum capacity of 2,000 fans explains,

> I was also surprised in the past that clubs, after promotion to the Ekstraklasa, gradually change the structure of their squad, that they turn towards foreign players. And I did not expect Puszcza to go exactly in the same direction when promotion became our share. . . . It is simply financially very difficult to acquire a Polish player with skills that predispose him to play at the Ekstraklasa level. There is no magic here – economic factors decide.
>
> (Pawlak, 2024, p. 12)

Economic imperatives may foster fan acceptance of players with diverse ethnic or cultural backgrounds within Polish football, even when such inclusion is driven by necessity rather than choice. However, it is notable that the majority of these foreign players come from other European countries and usually share the same ethnic background as Poles. Despite potential differences in language, customs or religion, these players generally operate within a predominantly White cultural framework. As a result, they, more or less, fit in quite well and certainly do not fundamentally challenge the advantages afforded to White individuals within the sport, a phenomenon prevalent throughout European football (Doidge, 2017). Consequently, the acceptance of foreign players does not necessarily signify a commitment to inclusivity or anti-racism.

Given that 'race', as a social construct, is also a "floating signifier" (Ferriter, 2017), an analysis of the Polish context requires an examination of the social history of racism appearing in Polish stadiums. References to racist incidents can be compared with the help of existing data from longitudinal studies conducted in Poland for several decades that are dedicated to identifying changes and the persistence of factors defining attitudes of national inclusiveness in Poland (Łodziński and Nowicka, 2023). These empirical investigations, entitled "Poles and Others", repeated in 1988, 1998, and 2018, were primarily concerned with how national identity is perceived and constructed among Poles, and also, more importantly, in the context of this chapter, which characteristics a foreigner needs to display in order to be considered an integral part of the Polish community. The most important criteria for recognising a foreigner as Polish for the respondents have not changed significantly over the years. Frequently cited prerequisites include(d) Polish citizenship, a sense of Polishness, proficiency in the Polish language, knowledge of Polish culture and customs, and residency in Poland. While religious affiliation, specifically Catholicism, was considered less significant, the issue of ethnic identity proved more divisive. When asked whether a foreigner who meets all the above criteria but has a different skin colour could be considered Polish, 70% of the respondents in 1988, 80.6% in 1998, and 68% in 2018 answered affirmatively. This implies that a substantial minority, consistently exceeding 30%, maintained reservations about ethnic inclusivity. Given the significant increase in Poland's non-white population since 2018, one may wonder whether this has led to a change in attitudes.

The pathological 1990s: the emergence of racism as a post-transformative anomie

The collapse of the Soviet Union and Eastern bloc in 1989 was obviously a major turning point for Polish society and culture, including football and fandom. The systemic transformation process brought the opportunity to modernise and "civilise" all areas of socio-economic and political life. As such, this decade can be viewed as one of the most challenging periods in modern Polish history and will certainly be remembered for its economic "shock therapy", political chaos, social austerity and uncertainty. In those difficult times, the Polish government and elites struggled to achieve economic and political stability. As a result, many different aspects of social and cultural life were considered "less important" than others and remained underdeveloped. One such domain was the entire sphere of sport, which experienced severe problems due to systemic negligence. Sports clubs were primarily left alone, and many lost their financial and organisational stability. Some clubs collapsed quickly and disappeared from the country's sporting map. Additionally, the lack of government control in the field of sports resulted in many scandals, such as large-scale corruption in football (Kossakowski, Nosal and Woźniak, 2020). The existing sports infrastructure was falling into disrepair, and stadiums and sports halls became places only frequented by the most ardent fans.

The collapse of important industries and subsequent rise in unemployment, particularly among young people, significantly shaped the formation of fan groups and distinctive patterns of behaviours and attitudes. The 1990s witnessed unprecedented violence in stadiums, facilitated by law enforcement's inaction and legal loopholes. It was only in 1997 that the first law addressing stadium safety was introduced, which remained largely ineffective for many years. During this period, hooligan groups gained strength, perpetrating violence both inside and outside stadiums (Kossakowski, 2021). Concurrently, right-wing ideology became increasingly prevalent in football stadiums, fuelled by a lack of positive role models and a sense of marginalisation among young people who sought community and meaning in violence and extremism as the new capitalist order failed to provide them with meaningful opportunities.

Right-wing ideology provided a framework for making sense of the prevailing situation and identifying scapegoats while also offering a sense of belonging to a group of like-minded people. Particularly the first half of the 1990s witnessed a surge in incidents instigated by groups promoting Nazi ideology, coinciding with the peak of the skinhead subculture. While not always directly linked to football fans, football hooligans were an attractive recruitment field for skinheads due to their shared characteristics, such as youth, celebrating traditional forms of masculinity, a propensity for violence, and a willingness to engage in radical behaviour. During this period, there were many similarities in the attire of football hooligans and skinheads, including military boots, flight jackets, and their trademark, shaved heads. Some right-wing organisations actively recruited football fans. For example, the "National Rebirth of Poland" organisation invited ŁKS Łódź fans to join their street protests, distributing leaflets with slogans such as "Racist ŁKS, the pride of white Poland".

In many pictures from those times, one cannot ignore the prevalence of right-wing symbols. The most popular was the Celtic cross, but some symbols clearly related to Fascism, such as the swastika. At one point, Odra Opole supporters choreographed a "living" swastika symbol by lining up in the stands in such a pattern. One chant of Ruch Chorzów fans used at the time was "Adolf Hitler KS Ruch" ("KS" stands for *klub sportowy* – sports club). Fans of Victoria Jaworzno not only displayed flags with a skull but also used the symbols of the Ku Klux Klan; they were also responsible for the beating of a black footballer from Cracow. Some fan groups used slogans like "Our role model is Rudolf Hess" and "Barack 6, Zyklon B". Antisemitic chants, for example, "Jews, Jews – all of Poland is ashamed of you", were also very popular at the time, especially directed towards the fans of the two clubs from Łódź, Widzew and ŁKS. The most right-wing fans did not see the paradox in glorifying Nazism, which during the Second World War led to the murder of millions of Polish citizens. It is clear now that the extreme ideological perspective was taken without any profound understanding. Symbols and clothes were employed as signs of identity and belonging to a community, even if historical and ideological knowledge was very scarce.

Contemporary fans and their ideological preferences

In contrast to many Western European countries, the vast majority of Polish fans do not engage with left-wing symbols or the rhetoric of class struggle (Kossakowski, Szlendak and Antonowicz, 2018). There are no images of Che Guevara, the hammer and sickle or anti-capitalist slogans at Polish stadiums. Polish fans generally reject left-wing ideologies as a result of the disastrous reign of socialism in the country between 1945 and 1989. Indeed, many of them equate being left-wing with supporting communist ideas. As a consequence, in their attempts to express community experience and social discontent, many fan groups in Poland heavily rely on conservative-patriotic and religious ideas and symbols. Such an identity set is also associated with the specific structure of the fan movement: the hermetic, coherent, "militant" and non-democratic nature of fandom promotes identification with symbols referring to national(ist) and conservative ideas (Grodecki, 2023; Kossakowski, 2021). Progressive and liberal values are relegated to the margins, primarily in small, grassroots clubs operating outside the established modern football industry.

For a long time, the public display of fascist symbols, such as the swastika, went unpunished. Since 2009, they are prohibited and the Polish Criminal Code penalises the public promotion and dissemination of Nazi, communist, fascist, or other totalitarian ideas, messages and symbols with up to three years of imprisonment. Similar penalties apply to public insults against a group of people or individuals based on their nationality, ethnicity, religion, lack thereof or physical attacks motivated by such factors. Fans were not politically organised in the initial years following Poland's socio-economic and political transformation. While racist incidents occurred, it is important to note that due to the poor financial conditions of Polish clubs, the number of non-white players was relatively small. These racist manifestations were not the result of deliberate, organised, or institutionalised activities. More often than not, nationalist football fans clashed with members of other subcultures, particularly punks who had formed anti-fascist coalitions with other fan groups.

Ideologically, Polish football fans continue to subscribe to traditional, conservative and right-wing ideas, albeit these have evolved in tandem with broader social changes. Contemporary fan identities continue to be constructed around antagonisms, but the range of perceived enemies that threaten the collective "us" has expanded. Today, there are hardly any manifestations of racism. While the swastika has largely been abandoned as a visual prop in football grounds, flags exhibiting the Celtic cross can still sometimes be seen, mainly in smaller stadiums in lower leagues.

Before, in the 1990s, fans did not present themselves as defenders of any particular or coherent value system that reflected the prevailing anomie. Their right-wing ideology had an anarchic character, and they engaged in violent conflicts for their own sake rather than the construction of a nationalist order. In contrast, contemporary extremist content is often linked to the defence of Christian culture in response to the alleged Islamisation of Europe. For example, Christianity was mentioned in their anti-refugee campaigns when the *ultras* of Śląsk Wrocław presented a banner with the slogan "When Europe is flooded with the Islamic plague, let us stand up for Christianity". Polish fans proclaimed themselves to be the "Defenders of Europe" during the UEFA Euro 2016 tournament in France. Recent events at the Polish-Belarusian border have seen an influx of migrants from Arab countries, prompting varied reactions from Polish citizens. Notably, fans of Legia Warsaw expressed their views on this issue during a match against Zagłębie Lubin. They displayed a controversial banner reading "Refugees Welcome". It was accompanied by an image depicting two white men, one wielding a baseball bat and the other a hammer, alongside a white woman adorned with a crucifix and holding a plate with a pig's head. This imagery has been interpreted as a stark suggestion that only certain types of refugees are deemed acceptable in Poland, which does not include Muslims.

The ideological foundations and resulting attitudes, norms and values of Polish football fans extend beyond anti-migrant sentiments. The ongoing social changes in Poland have emboldened those fans who are ideologically unified in their opposition to what they perceive to be a "left-wing ideology". Quite frequently, supporters of various clubs in Poland display banners and flags displaying slogans such as "Good night, left side" accompanied by an image of a fighter kicking a reclining figure wearing a red star. Although, after the Russian invasion of Ukraine, fans displayed anti-Putin choreographies, the imagined, threatening enemy for the fans is not a foreign country, nation or culture but the "mainstream ideology" promoted by the European majority. As a consequence of their ideological stance, fans not only criticise liberal and progressive ideas, values and policies but also articulate traditionalist sentiments and promote, for example, traditional gender roles. After the mayor of Poznań declared its support for the organisation of the "Equality March" celebrating the rights of the LGBTQ community (in 2017), Lech Poznań fans declared on the banners that their stadium is "The last bastion of freedom in the city raddled with leftist paranoia".

As in many other countries, men dominate Poland's most active fan groups, creating a specific homosocial setting (Messner, 2004). For the cohesion of this homosociality, that has no sexual connotations, establishing relationships with women and other men (rivals and non-heteronormative), that explicitly reflect the unequal distribution of power, is crucial. Women are not antagonised, but their role is reduced to traditionally defined mother and wife responsibilities (Kossakowski, Antonowicz and Jakubowska, 2020). A more important element is the antagonism towards any non-heteronormativity. In the Polish context, homophobic chants serve as a tool of denigration for practically all enemies: rivals from opposite clubs, referees, police officers, politicians, journalists and so on. As a discursive tool, homophobic chants make a significant contribution to the construction of the gender identity of *ultras* as "real men". Polish *ultras* oppose the granting of equal rights to LGBT+ people and do not accept or tolerate formal or informal homosexual relationships. As previously noted, Polish football fans often present themselves as defenders of Christian values, a framing that is particularly salient in the context of their opposition to LGBT+ rights. This is exemplified by a banner displayed by Lechia Gdańsk fans during a period of intense public debate in Poland regarding the role of Pope John Paul II in the Church's handling of paedophilia scandals. The banner read, "Sodomy, faggots, and paedophiles from the LGBT community – keep your hands off John Paul II". Polish football fans have also been known to form patrols to protect churches during women's protests against the tightening of abortion laws in Poland. These actions were motivated by perceived attacks on the Roman Catholic Church, which was in favour of the new legislation.

Migrants, mainly from Islamic countries, along with LGBT+ individuals, have emerged as new targets for intolerant and abusive football fans, reflecting broader socio-political trends. While less frequent, antisemitic sentiments also persist in stadium-based narratives. *The Jew* is used as a symbolic figure of the "Other'", which can be used as an insult in an act of symbolic humiliation and degradation. This symbolic mechanism can be observed in Łódź, where supporters of the two rival local clubs, ŁKS and Widzew, call each other "Jews", and in Cracow, where the fans of Wisła are notorious for their malicious comments on the Jewish roots of Cracovia Club, which was co-founded in 1906 by members of the Jewish community.

A closer examination of the strategies employed in constructing fan-based ideological identities reveals a clear pattern of "eliminating" perceived enemies. By targeting migrants, representing different cultures and ethnic minorities, and left-wing values, these groups seek to create a "pure community". Such a collective should instead be free of left-wing ideology and committed to the glorification of the nuclear family and the Christian faith. Such an idealised community, even if only discursively constructed, can serve as fertile ground for exclusionary politics, racism and xenophobia.

Extremism in Polish football

The influx of foreign players in Polish football is a relatively recent phenomenon. After the post-1989 transformative changes, Polish clubs faced immense financial difficulties, rendering them unattractive for overseas players. This does not mean that there were no foreign players, as a considerable number of footballers from the former Soviet republics joined Polish teams. Black players also began appearing on the pitch. In the 1990s, Polish football witnessed several racist incidents. One of these occurred in Gdańsk in March 1998 during a match between Polonia Gdańsk and Śląsk Wrocław. When Morgan N'Kathazo, a player from Zimbabwe, entered the field, Śląsk fans invaded the pitch and forced the coach to change his decision. Fearing further escalation, the visiting team's manager substituted the player after just 15 minutes.

Fans of Śląsk Wrocław have long been among Poland's most right-wing supporters. For many years, their informal leader was Roman Zieliński, a right-wing journalist who openly expressed his admiration for Nazi ideology, authoring a book titled "Why I Fell in Love with Adolf Hitler". In 2013, Eric Mouloungui, a player from Gabon representing Śląsk Wrocław, received vicious racist comments on his Facebook account, where one post stated, "Fuck the nigger! Śląsk Wrocław – a White team". Due to the fans' radical views, Śląsk Wrocław rarely employed players of African descent. Ryszard Tarasiewicz, the team's coach from 2004 to 2006, admitted that he avoided signing Black players out of concern for his own safety (Antecki and Łuciów, 2013). Śląsk Wrocław fans have continued to make headlines in this context. In November 2022, during a Polish Cup match against Sandecja Nowy Sącz, after a penalty shootout, a Sandecja player was subjected to offensive verbal attacks from Śląsk fans seated behind the goal where the penalties were taken. He reported hearing monkey chants and racist slurs. After two rounds of penalties, the Sandecja players walked off the pitch in protest.

In 2023, Leandro, a Black player for Stal Mielec, became another victim of racism. He received a red card for allegedly arguing with fans of Ruch Chorzów, but it later emerged that he had responded to racist insults after being called a "Nigger" and told to "get the fuck out of Poland". The supporters from Ruch Chorzów are known for their extremist far-right views, having displayed Nazi symbols and sentiments as far back as the 1990s. It is important to note that Leandro, who has been living in Poland for many years, is married to a Polish woman and has family in Poland. As he emphasised in interviews, he has only experienced racist incidents from Ruch Chorzów fans. Generally, fans treated him kindly, and racist attacks were rather seldom. After the incident with Ruch Chorzów supporters, he received numerous expressions of support from other fans in Ruch Chorzów.

This case demonstrates that racist attacks are linked to the activities of a specific group: those fans who are strongly committed to far-right ideas, which involves an exaggerated and exclusionary sense of nationalism and often leads to humiliation and vilification of people with a different skin colour. This group, albeit a numerical minority, exerts a powerful influence in the stadium by leading, initiating and shaping the contents of chants. Other fans constitute a (not so) 'silent majority' that often cannot resist the group's vocal dominance and narratives. It is also worth noting that, in recent times, key individuals within the *ultras* scene have, occasionally, taken steps to suppress extreme messages and/or racist abuse. While conducting fieldwork at a Lechia Gdańsk away match, the author observed a small group of fans engaging in racist 'monkey chants' directed at a Black player from the opposing team. However, they were quickly reprimanded by one of the group leaders.

One of the most multi-layered cases of racism in Polish football's post-transformation history is that of Emmanuel Olisadebe, as it reveals the complex interplay of sport, ethnicity and nationality. A Nigerian-born footballer who arrived in Poland in 1997, Olisadebe quickly became a household name, particularly after his successful stint with Polonia Warsaw. His exceptional performances, which culminated in Polonia Warsaw winning the Polish championship in 1999/2000, brought him to the attention of the national team coach, Jerzy Engel. He pushed for Olisadebe's naturalisation as a Polish citizen, recognising his talent and potential contributions to Polish football on an international stage. In July 2000, Olisadebe was granted Polish citizenship, becoming the first Black player to represent Poland in international football. The naturalisation process was expedited despite Olisadebe not fully meeting the standard requirements. This decision proved pivotal for the Polish national team, as Olisadebe's exceptional performances, particularly his eight goals in the 2002 World Cup qualifiers, were instrumental in Poland's qualification for the tournament.

However, Olisadebe's naturalisation and subsequent inclusion in the national team caused mixed reactions. In May 2000, during a match in Lubin, fans of Zagłębie Lubin subjected Olisadebe to a variety of severe racist abuse, including being pelted with bananas. Following this event, Olisadebe even considered leaving the country. Although he admitted to experiencing racist abuse throughout his time in Poland, he also noted that it was not more prevalent or severe than in other countries where he had previously played. Early in his Polish career, during a trial with Ruch Chorzów, he was subjected to racist chants urging him to 'go back to Africa' (Kołodziej, 2022). Due to these experiences, Olisadebe became an ambassador for the "Kick Racism Out of the Stadiums" campaign organised by the "Never Again" association. The latter is a Polish anti-racism association, was founded in 1996 and runs many campaigns against chauvinism, neo-fascism and hatred towards foreigners in Polish society as well as in sports.

The case of Emmanuel Olisadebe, while unprecedented in the history of Polish football, is significant in several ways. In subsequent years, an increasing number of players not born in Poland have pursued Polish passports, triggering a range of emotions and discussions among fans and journalists. Roger

Guerreiro, born in 1982 and playing for Legia Warsaw, was also granted fast-track citizenship after the coach of the national team, Leo Beenhaker, recognised the Brazilian's potential for the national squad. He played at Euro 2008, co-hosted by Austria and Switzerland, scored the only goal for Poland there, and was indeed among the best Polish players. Initially, fans were unhappy with the Brazilian's presence in the national squad, booed him and made monkey noises in some stadiums. Jagiellonia Białystok fans even presented a banner with the words "Roger – you will never be a Pole". Olisadebe and Roger's spells in the national team were relatively short, and they left Poland soon after.

Tackling racism in Polish football

In Poland, the most deviant fans, *ultras* and hooligans, pose the most significant challenges as they promote extremist ideas and disseminate far-right messages in football stadiums. Physical violence against players of colour is relatively rare, confirming that extremist ideologies are primarily manifested in symbolic and discursive spaces. However, this does not diminish the significance of the problem, and with ongoing migration, these issues may become even more prominent.

In the post-transformation history of Poland, initiatives aimed at combating racism have been notably limited. Furthermore, there is a strong reluctance of Polish football fans to engage in anti-discrimination or pro-diversity campaigns, as fans often associate them with the promotion of a liberal, left-wing political agenda. Consequently, initiatives undertaken by European fan organisations such as FARE, Football Against Racism in Europe, and FSE, Football Supporters Europe, are frequently ignored by Polish supporters. An additional barrier arises from the fact that FARE and FSE work in collaboration with UEFA, which Polish fans perceive as a corrupt institution that enforces left-wing ideas as part of a larger, liberal and progressive project imposed by the so-called "spoiled West". In their choreographies and displays, fans often target UEFA, viewing it as a punitive force that penalises them for alleged misconduct or their political views.

For this reason, the activities of the Polish organisation "Never Again" struggle to reach these fans. This organisation has actively engaged with anti-racist initiatives for many years, reporting all instances of discriminatory behaviour and content in stadiums to UEFA. "Never Again" periodically publishes a report entitled the "Brown Book", which documents racist incidents in Poland, in and beyond football. Additionally, the organisation initiated the campaign "Let's Kick Racism out of the Stadiums", which received support from players of diverse ethnic backgrounds. However, this association does not have backing from the Polish Football Association, PZPN, or football clubs.

The PZPN does not undertake significant initiatives or campaigns to fight racism in Polish football grounds. As a member of UEFA, it does not boycott those campaigns implemented and promoted by the European governing body. Yet, it fails to show a wholehearted commitment and does not make any substantial efforts to support European policies. The behaviour of Polish officials is decidedly reactive rather than proactive. In many situations, PZPN attempts to maintain a non-aligned and apolitical position, creating an appearance of political neutrality. This was evident during the discussions surrounding the actions of Polish players before the match against England in 2021. Polish players did not kneel in solidarity with their English counterparts as part of the "Black Lives Matter" movement. Following the game, PZPN issued a press release clarifying the situation:

> The Polish Football Association informs that the players of the Poland national football team have taken a neutral and apolitical stance towards the "Black Lives Matter" initiative before the game against England at Wembley. At the same time, we emphasise that all representatives of Poland stand in solidarity against all manifestations of racism and intolerance. PZPN in its statutory activities and duties has always been guided by openness, respect for the principles of equality, tolerance and equal rights for all people, regardless of their nationality, skin colour, religion or political views.
>
> (PZPN, 2021)

The statement mentioned earlier encapsulates the approach taken by Polish football authorities regarding issues related to racism: they tend to avoid the topic until it becomes unavoidable. In other instances, PZPN makes only cursory references to statutory provisions, reiterating that – as a sports association – it is neutral regarding religion, ethnicity, and race and that any form of racial discrimination is prohibited under penalty of disciplinary sanctions.

It is important to emphasise that Polish clubs exhibit a similar approach; they do not initiate any campaigns related to combating discrimination and racism and avoid this topic for as long as possible. Despite the absence of public campaigns in Polish football, several ways of monitoring the phenomenon exist. One involves specifically trained observers who record discriminatory incidents. International organisations, such as UEFA, are also involved in monitoring efforts and collaborate with the "Never Again" association. The Ministry of the Interior also operates a monitoring system for these incidents, which extends beyond sports. Data regarding racist and antisemitic incidents is made available through the Polish Football Association's annual security reports. The actual numbers are relatively low and rarely exceed 10 per year, except for 2018/19 when 15 incidents were reported. However, these figures should be treated cautiously: Observers primarily report the most visible or audible elements in the football grounds and do not have access to fan behaviour en route to matches, outside the stadium, or in virtual spaces.

Consequently, the magnitude of the phenomenon appears to be significantly higher, as evidenced by the periodic publications from the "Never Again" association, which monitors xenophobic and racist incidents throughout Poland, not limited solely to those associated with sports.

The "Never Again" activities gained significant media attention in June 2023, when It submitted a letter to UEFA questioning the suitability of Polish referee Szymon Marciniak's officiating the Champions League final. Marciniak had participated in a conference organised by the members of a right-wing party called "Konfederacja". The latter promotes an explicit anti-migration programme. Following clarifications, Marciniak ultimately officiated the final. Notably, he is the only referee in Poland who has previously interrupted a match applying the so-called "anti-racist procedure". This incident occurred in 2019 during a game between Lechia Gdańsk and Piast Gliwice, where home fans directed racist insults at a Black player from Piast. After halting the game, the referee instructed the stadium speaker to read a statement which contained a warning that if the racist behaviour did not cease, the referee would terminate the match.

Conclusion

The history of Poland is marked by numerous far-reaching upheavals, which have profoundly influenced the nation's social fabric, socio-demographic structures and ethnic composition. Through several globally significant events, Poland transitioned from a diverse ethnic society to a predominantly mono-ethnic nation-state. This transformation had repercussions that affected reactions to migrants, mainly with cultural backgrounds that differ from – what is widely considered to be – the Polish norm. This phenomenon is also evident in football, as the sport reflects the processes occurring within the socio-political landscape. Incidents of a racist nature have repeatedly happened in stadiums. However, analysing the scale of these incidents presents significant challenges.

It must be stressed that Polish football is not particularly appealing to foreign players seeking European opportunities. Although the number of players from other countries has increased significantly in recent years, most have similar cultural and ethnic backgrounds. Consequently, their presence does not necessarily challenge the ideological status quo, as they, for example, do not differ in skin colour from the ethnic majority in Poland. In October 2024, during a Nations League match against Portugal, two Black players debuted for the Polish national team: Maxi Oyedele from Legia Warsaw and the previously mentioned Michael Ameyaw. Their roles in shaping attitudes towards more openness and diversity, as well as challenging exclusionary tendencies within Polish society, could be unprecedented. In the coming years, further call-ups of players who, while possessing Polish citizenship, represent different ethnicities and cultural contexts are anticipated. This is a natural consequence of two ongoing migration waves: Poles moving to Western Europe after 2004 (whose children, future representatives of the country, are already being born outside of Poland) and individuals arriving in Poland today. These are factors that will undoubtedly provoke discussions, possibly even adverse reactions, particularly from right-wing football fans who frequently engage in racist and xenophobic manifestations. The increasing presence of non-White players will likely rise in Polish football due to migration processes and may result in a cyclical return to historical patterns. At the beginning of the new millennium, the presence of Olisadebe elicited significant racist reactions; currently, this topic is becoming even more pertinent, albeit on an incomparably larger scale.

This scale will also present a significant challenge for Polish football authorities and clubs, which have so far done little to address the aforementioned problems. To become a truly inclusive country within the realm of football, Polish authorities must be more proactive in promoting diversity and tolerance, and more vocal and assertive in condemning pathological behaviours.

References

Antecki, D. and Łuciów, D. (2013) "Ścigają internetową nienawiść do piłkarza" [They are pursuing online hate towards the footballer], *Gazeta Wyborcza*, 13th March, p. 27.

Burski, J. and Woźniak, W. (2021) "The sociopolitical roots of antisemitism among football fandom: the real absence and imagined presence of Jews in polish football", in Schüler-Springorum, S. and Brunssen, P. (Eds.), *Discrimination in football: antisemitism and beyond*, Abingdon: Routledge.

Dmowski, S. (2013) "Geographical typology of European football rivalries", *Soccer & Society*, 14(3), pp. 331–343.

Doidge, M. (2017) "Racism and European football", in Nauright, J. and Wiggins, D.K. (Eds.), *Routledge handbook of sport, race and ethnicity*, London: Routledge.

Ferriter, M. (2017) "The anthropology of race and ethnicity in sport: unfolding the map", in Nauright, J. and Wiggins, D.K. (Eds.), *Routledge handbook of sport, race and ethnicity*, London: Routledge.

Grodecki, M. (2023) "Performative nationalism in Polish football stadiums and fans' views and attitudes: evidence from quantitative research", *International Review for the Sociology of Sport*, 58(5), pp. 783–808.

Jałowiecki, B. and Szczepański, M. (2007) "Dziedzictwo polskich regionów" [The heritage of Polish regions], in Kojder, A. (Ed.), *Jedna Polska? Dawne i nowe zróżnicowania społeczne* [One Poland? Old and new social stratifications], Wrocław: WAM.

Kołodziej, D. (2022) "Gdy odrzucił banana, sędzia pokazał mu żółtą kartkę. To nie zaczęło się na polskich stadionach wczoraj" [When he threw away the banana, the referee showed him a yellow card. This did not start in Polish stadiums yesterday]. Available: <https://przegladsportowy.onet.pl/pilka-nozna/puchar-polski/to-nie-zaczelo-sie-wczoraj-na-polskich-stadionach-problem-trwa-od-lat/f8xskx5> [accessed on 18th September 2024].

Kossakowski, R. (2021) *Hooligans, ultras, activist: Polish football fandom in sociological perspective*, Cham: Palgrave Macmillan.

Kossakowski, R., Antonowicz, D. and Jakubowska, H. (2022) "'Partners', 'mothers', and 'tomboys': female football fans in the structural trap of assigned roles in Poland", *Soccer & Society*, 22(3), pp. 271–284.

Kossakowski, R., Nosal, P. and Woźniak, W. (2020) *Politics, ideology and football fandom: the transformation of modern Poland*, Abingdon: Routledge.

Kossakowski, R., Szlendak, T. and Antonowicz, D. (2018) "Polish ultras in the post-socialist transformation", *Sport in Society*, 21(6), pp. 854–869.

Łodziński, S. and Nowicka, E. (2023) "Postawy narodowego inkluzywizmu w społeczeństwie polskim" [Attitudes towards national inclusiveness in Polish society], *Studia Socjologiczne*, 2(249), pp. 5–29.

Messner, M. (2004) "Homosociality", in Kimmel, A. and Aronson, A. (Eds.), *Men and masculinities: a social, cultural and historical encyclopedia, vol. I*, Santa Barbara: ABC-CLIO.

Pawlak, P. (2024) "Dość katorg. Rozmowa z Jarosławem Pieprzycą" [Enough of the hard labour. Interview with Jarosław Pieprzyca], *Piłka Noe‚na*, 10th September, pp. 12–13.

PZPN (2021) "The announcement of Polish Football Association regarding "Black Lives Matter" initiative". Available: <https://pzpn.pl/en/association/news/2021-03-31/the-announcement-of-polish-football-association-regarding-black-lives-matter-initiative> [accessed on 14th October 2024].

Wójcik, P. (2023) "Za rządów PiS do Polski przybyła rekordowa liczba migrantów, ale mamy tee‚ złe informacje" [A record number of migrants have arrived in Poland under the Law and Justice government, but we also have bad news]. Available: <https://krytykapolityczna.pl/kraj/za-rzadow-pis-do-polski-przybyla-rekordowa-liczba-migrantow-ale-mamy-tez-zle-informacje/> [accessed on 18th September 2024].

Chapter 9

Portugal

Making sense of and tackling racism in football

Sofia Neves, Joana Topa, Janete Borges, Estefânia Silva, Ariana Correia and Mafalda Ferreira

There is little doubt about the far-reaching socio-economic, political and cultural significance of sports in everyday life of modern societies, as they facilitate community cohesion and offer a framework for social engagement, sociability and stress relief (Ronkainen, 2023). Fostering healthy lifestyles, interpersonal, communal, and institutional relationships and contributing to knowledge and competencies that are transferable to other domains of social life, sport is an important and versatile field for human development (Eather, Wade, Pankowiak et al., 2023). Despite the well-documented positive effects of sport, including health, integration, inclusivity, sociability and the promotion of cultural exchange (Dowling, 2024), it can also be a source of conflicts, divisions, discrimination, oppression and violence (Jeanes and Lucas, 2022). Football is one of the sports where, in particular, racism, xenophobia, sexism, and homophobia affect athletes, negatively impacting not only their performance but also their well-being (Cable, Kilvington and Mottershead, 2022). In societies where racism is widespread, the likelihood of racist manifestations in football is higher (Kassimeris, Lawrence and Pipini, 2022).

Article 13 of the Portuguese Constitution clearly reflects the principles of the Human Rights Act and states that all citizens are equal before the law and have the same social dignity (Official Gazzete n.º 86/1976, Serie I, 1976-04-10). The same article affirms that no one is privileged, favoured, injured, denied any rights, or exempt from social duties based on ancestry, sex, race, language, area of origin, religion, political or ideological convictions, education, economic situation, social condition, or sexual orientation. And yet, human rights violations continue to persist in Portuguese society.

As a former coloniser of some African (Gonçalves, 2021), Asian and South American territories, Portugal still faces challenges related to the treatment of non-White people, including the realm of football. Stigmas, stereotypes and prejudices largely affecting non-White people often result in direct or indirect forms of aggression ranging from psychological to physical attacks. Manifestations of racist attitudes against non-White athletes are not rare inside and outside the football grounds, which demonstrates that racism continues to be

DOI: 10.4324/9781003495970-9
This chapter has been made available under a CC-BY-NC-SA 4.0 license.

a pervasive problem in wider Portuguese society, as well as in this popular sport (Kassimeris, Lawrence and Pipini, 2022).

The socio-historical context

Racism is thoroughly interwoven with the political, social, and cultural past of Portugal, which for almost 600 years had the status of an empire (1414–1999). The heritage of colonialism, in the nineteenth and twentieth centuries, labour exploitation and the transatlantic slave trade still echo today in Portuguese society and continue to shape beliefs, attitudes and behaviours that reinforce systemic and structural inequalities (Coelho, 1998).

The imperial discourse in the twentieth century is closely linked to the country's fascist program and Antonio Salazar, who ran the dictatorship for most of its time from 1926 to 1974. It focused on 'racial' nationalism (Neves, 2023), which supports the concept of lusotropicalism, which is best explained as

> the idea of a special skill that Portuguese ("luso") people have for establishing peaceful and harmonious relations with other peoples and for mingling with people from the tropics, an absence of prejudice among the Portuguese, and their ability to adapt to the tropics.
> (Valentim and Heleno, 2018, p. 34)

From the fifteenth and sixteenth centuries, Portuguese maritime expansion established and strengthened contacts between the Portuguese people and other communities across different continents, which led to the emergence of a colonialist philosophy. Despite being responsible for the trade of millions of slaves, the discourses regarding the Portuguese maritime expansion, symbolically known as *Descobrimentos* (Discoveries), glorified these events, praised bravery as a national identity trait, and massively downplayed the experience and suffering of the colonised (Bastos and Castelo, 2024; Valentim and Heleno, 2018).

Nonetheless, in the late nineteenth century, Portugal suffered from severe economic problems, exposing an underdeveloped country that did not recognise the opportunities of the industrial revolution but was rather tied to rurality. As a consequence, poverty, unemployment, illiteracy and broad social discontent were widespread (Ferraz de Matos, 2019; Sobral, 2004). At the beginning of the twentieth century, a national strategy for overseas migration was developed, especially directed at Angola and Mozambique, to assist colonial administration services and a policy to attract labour to meet technical, industrial and commercial demands was pursued. It reached its peak in the post-Second World War years (Castelo, 2009).

The heterogeneity of the colonial societies led to asymmetrical power dynamics, legitimised through an ethnocentric and condescending lens, and fuelled lusotropicalism narratives (Peralta and Frangella, 2012). Subsequently, these were adopted and adapted by the Portuguese regime and widely disseminated in the 1950s, 1960s and 1970s, until the decolonisation process (Bastos and Castelo, 2024). In 1961, the Government sponsored the publication of a book entitled *The Portuguese and the Tropics* in several languages. It became a key source for other textbooks, films, radio programs and official interventions, advocating Portuguese colonialism as benign, non-exploitative, humane and non-racist. Notions of the "empire" and "colonial" were cut out of that narrative. They were replaced with imagery of a "multi-racial nation" across the continents. The colonies were described as not being areas over which a foreign nation maintains control, subjugates the native population and exploits their land and resources but as parts of a singular nation that extended from Minho in Northern Portugal to distant Timor in Southeast Asia (Bastos and Castelo, 2024; Valentim and Heleno, 2018).

The Portuguese Empire's dominance in the former colonies, such as Mozambique, Cape Verde, São Tomé and Príncipe, Guinea-Bissau, Brazil and Angola, along with the process of decolonisation, contributed, among other factors, to the persistence of prejudices against non-White people, specifically those of African descent, as several studies have shown (Ponte and Sousa, 2017; Abrantes and Roldão, 2019; Vala, Brito and Lopes, 2015). In a memorandum authored by the Council of Europe Commissioner for Human Rights (2021, p. 1), concerns about the "increasing level of racism and the persistence of related discrimination in the country" [Portugal] were raised. Similarly, a very recent study by the European Commission (2023) shows that six in ten European respondents from the 27 European Union Member States reveal discrimination based on ethnic origin is prevalent in their country. Percentages range from 27% to 82%, with 59% of the Portuguese participants responding affirmatively. Regarding discrimination based on skin colour, percentages overall range from 22% to 78%. Portugal's 61% sit comfortably at the upper end of this scale. In the same year, data from Portugal's National Institute of Statistics (INE, 2023) revealed that 10.5% of all discriminatory incidents occurred within sporting contexts and that, in general, the geographical origin, ethnic group and skin colour of the people affected were the primary contributory factors. Even though manifestations of racism are now different from those during the period of colonialism (Casquilho-Martins, Belchior-Rocha and Alves, 2022), and significant advances regarding people's rights have been made, new challenges at the national and European levels have emerged in the last decades. As far-right movements and political parties are growing in Europe, including Portugal, racist, sexist, anti-Islamic, anti-Roma, anti-Africans, anti-immigrant, anti-refugees and anti-LGBTI (lesbian, gay, bisexual, trans and intersex) discourses have become more explicit and louder (Council of Europe, 2023; Krzyẹanowski, 2020). In Portugal, the far-right, populist political party CHEGA has gained considerable support in society, becoming the third largest political force in the Parliament since the general elections in March 2024. Africans, immigrants, members of the LGBTI community and Roma people are singled out as threats to Portugal's national traditions, culture and identity and feature prominently in the hate speeches of prominent CHEGA members (Garcia-Jaramillo, Santos and Fernandes-Jesus, 2023).

Important legal parameters

Racism, rooted in discrimination based on 'racial' and ethnic characteristics, has multifaceted social implications (Casquilho-Martins, Belchior-Rocha and Alves, 2022). Aware of the need to eradicate racism, in 2021, the Portuguese Government (2021) launched the first National Plan to Combat Racism and Discrimination (2021–2025). Following the principles of deconstructing and dismantling stereotypes, coordination, integrated governance and territorialisation, combined with intervention in order to fight various, and sometimes overlapping, inequalities, the Plan defined ten areas of intervention,[1] sport being one of them. Among other measures, the Plan aims to "promote the implementation of initiatives to combat hate speech and discrimination at sports events to sports organisers" (2021, p. 134). In 2023, the Observatory on Hate Speech, Racism and Xenophobia was created to collect and disseminate information and knowledge on racism, xenophobia and discrimination (European Commission, 2024).

Besides the public policies, the Portuguese Penal Code (Official Gazette n.º 63/1995, Decree-Law No. 48/95) punishes racism and discrimination with a prison sentence of six months to five years (article No. 240). In 2007, the Law was amended, reversing the burden of proof in crimes motivated by race, ethnicity, skin-colour, citizenship, ancestry and place of origin (Official Gazzete n.º 170/2007, Law No. 59/2007). In 2024, the Law was changed again, expanding the discrimination factors and also punishing those who founded or established an organisation or developed propaganda activities that incite or encourage discrimination, hatred or violence against a person or group of people based on their ethnic-racial origin, national or religious origin, colour, nationality, ancestry, territory of origin, language, sex, sexual orientation, gender identity or expression, or sexual characteristics, physical or mental disability (Official Gazzete n.º 10/2024, Serie I, 2024-01-15). The Portuguese Labour Code also establishes the Right to equality in terms of access to employment and in the workplace (Official Gazzete n.º 30/2009, Law No. 7/2009). Violations of this law can be considered minor or very serious, depending on the violation of the provisions.

Although racism is an object of criminal penalisation, figures on the prevalence of racism in Portugal do not exist, and data on racist incidents are dispersed. The Annual Report of Internal Security (ISS, 2024) indicates that in 2023 police authorities recorded 367 crimes against cultural identity and personal integrity, accounting for 0.10% of the country's total crime rate. These categories of crimes, where racism is included, are among the least recorded, which may reflect a social devaluation of the importance of such issues.

The Authority for Preventing and Combating Violent Behaviour in Sports (APCVD) is a state-run service under the government's remit for sport, which aims to prevent and oversee violations of the legal parameters for safety and combating racism, xenophobia, and intolerance in sports events and venues (Regulatory Decree No. 10/2018).

Of the 2,525 incidents recorded throughout the 2022/23 season in Portugal's First League of Football, *Primeira Liga*, the main type of incidents reported involved possession and/or use of pyrotechnic devices, with 1,806 cases recorded (71.95%). Sixteen cases of incitement of violence, racism, xenophobia, and intolerance were recorded, contrasting with 78 that occurred in the previous season. Fifty cases led to criminal convictions of the perpetrators (The Public Security Police and the Authority for Preventing and Combating Violent Behaviour in Sports, 2023).

Investigating racism in Portuguese football: some selected data

Currently, in Portugal, as in most countries that are signatories to the Universal Declaration of Human Rights, open racism and other forms of discrimination of individuals of certain social and/or ethnic groups are subject to public prosecution. Nevertheless, violence, xenophobia and more general expressions of intolerance (European Union Agency for Fundamental Rights, 2021), in particular manifestations of discriminatory behaviour persist in several areas, with football being one of the contexts where manifestations are frequent and very pronounced.

Because of the increasing mediatisation of racist incidents involving non-White footballers and driven by the desire to understand how 'race' intersects with other forms of discrimination, such as gender and sexual orientation, the first National Study on Racism in Football in Portugal was conducted in 2021 (Neves, Topa, Borges et al., 2023).[2] Besides determining the frequency and characteristics of racism, through observation, and experiences of different actors, other forms of discrimination were also investigated, in particular sexism and homophobia. Moreover, mechanisms for the (often unsuccessful) resolution of racist cases, and measures to prevent and combat racism in football in Portugal, were analysed. This pioneering study employed a quantitative approach, using an online 28-question questionnaire.

The sample was recruited online and comprised 1.681 participants aged between 13 and 61 years; 456 saw themselves as women and 1.221 as men. Almost 25% of participants are football fans, 20% are coaches, 16.5% are amateur athletes, 11.7% are members of the refereeing team, 8.6% are sports managers, 5.5% are parents, 3.4% are journalists, 3% are sports agents, 2.6% are staff members, for example, doctors or working in communication,

2% are professional athletes, and 2% are other members of the technical teams.

The perception of the existence of racism in football in Portugal was referred to by 60% of the participants, mainly females, amateur athletes and younger participants, with more than 90% considering that the main victims are male athletes. Most respondents aged 40 or older (62.6%) stated that there is no racism in Portuguese football. This considerable gender-based difference might suggest that females and youth are, due to a greater awareness of social inequalities and vulnerabilities, more sensitive towards discriminatory practices, which is possibly the result of their own experiences as marginalised groups. Furthermore, they appear to be more committed to social justice, and antiracist and anti-sexist initiatives and actions, which might contribute to a more informed understanding of what factors promote the risk of being exposed to social discrimination or even oppression (Rabelo and Cortina, 2019). Amateur athletes considered football in Portugal to be racist, as they are often the primary victims. Most of those amateur and also professional athletes who reported to have suffered or witnessed racist attitudes or behaviour had been affected on multiple occasions.

Older people may recognise racism less clearly because they may have a narrower view of what constitutes racist behaviour, which is very likely influenced by the cultural and social norms of their time, in particular their upbringing and education. Women's football has less media coverage and is therefore less visible on a global scale. That also applies to Portugal. There is also less academic research undertaken into women's football (Gredin, Okholm Kryger, McCall et al., 2023; Okholm Kryger, Wang, Mehta et al., 2021). Furthermore, as media reports about racism often involved men, it is no surprise that both women and men identified male athletes as the main victims. However, it is interesting to note that although both males and females identified male athletes as the primary victims of racism, women were more likely to also recognise female athletes and other female actors, such as female coaches, and technical staff as targets. Making sense of how racism targets, affects and is recognised by different groups certainly requires a more detailed understanding of individuals' social identities, personal experiences, background and upbringing.

Those who publicly display racist attitudes and engage in discriminatory behaviour in Portuguese football are primarily individual fans and larger groups of fans such as those organised in clubs. Racism occurs predominantly during the games in the grounds. There, the football culture is characterised by an environment of tensions in which fans, for example, through their chanting regularly reproduce racial stereotypes (Cleland and Cashmore, 2016). They tend to engage in abusive conduct towards rival clubs and players, with elements of hate speech gaining popularity in the last decades (Miranda, Gouveia, Di Fátima et al., 2023). As Chovanec (2023) has pointed out "football-related racist discourse simultaneously generates and is embedded in the broader public and private discourses about football and racism, both in the media and elsewhere" (p. 943).

Skin colour is one of the major factors triggering racist discrimination, especially among football fans, both amateur and professional athletes, and younger individuals. Among participants under 18, skin colour was cited as the primary reason for discrimination (72.3%), followed by ethnicity (53.8%), gender (46.8%), sexual orientation/gender identity (45.1%), and disability (43.9%). Similarly, in the 19- to 24-year-old age group, skin colour featured as the main factor (71.5%), followed by ethnicity and gender (both 64.9%), sexual orientation/gender identity (55.8%), and nationality (49.1%). For participants aged between 25 and 39, skin colour continued to be the primary reason for discrimination (55.5%), followed closely by sexual orientation/gender identity (53.1%), gender (52.3%), ethnicity (50.5%), and disability (43.2%). In contrast, among those aged 40 and over, sexual orientation and gender identity emerged as the most prevalent factors (43.4%), followed by gender (40.4%), ethnicity (39.3%), disability (38.1%), and skin colour (36.1%). Thus, it seems that as the age of the participants increases, skin colour as a reason for discrimination becomes less important, while sexual and gender identity becomes more prominent.

Three-quarters of the women in our study considered that gender is a key source for discrimination in football, whereas half of the men referred to skin colour. In all categories, higher percentages of women, in comparison to men, showed an awareness of discriminatory practices. These findings highlight the multifaceted nature of discrimination, where 'race', gender and other forms of identity construction intersect and often lead to individuals' experiences of discrimination, violence, exclusion, and, when compounded, marginalisation.

Back, Crabbe and Solomos (2001) suggested that there are seven types of racial discrimination in football. This categorisation can also be applied to the situation in Portugal as the following examples demonstrate

- In February 2024, Chiquinho, a midfielder playing for FC Famalicão, reported being subjected to racist insults during a game in Faro, Algarve. The referee interrupted the match for five minutes and the police managed to identify the racist abuser, a 53-year-old man, who was later punished and banned from entering sports venues for two years.
- In August 2023, the Brazilian Otávio (Ataide da Silva), a FC Famalicão player, criticised the referee after the game against Sporting CP for not sending off Viktor Gyökeres after a second bookable foul. That angered Sporting CP fans who subsequently inundated Otávio's Instagram account with racist insults such as "Slave", "Monkey", "F***ing Black", and "Go back to the jungle".
- In the aftermath of the match between FC Porto and FC Famalicão in May 2023, Pepe, the captain of Porto and Portugal's national team, filed a complaint. According to Pepe, the Argentinian midfielder Santiago Colombatto had called him a *mono* (monkey) which he considered to be a racist

insult. Pepe criticised the referee who apparently observed the incident but did not take any action. Colombatto was later acquitted, as one of his teammates testified that he had called Pepe *boludo*, idiot.
- In February 2020, Moussa Marega, then a player for FC Porto, took a stand against racism during a match against Vitória de Guimarães. Marega scored a goal and celebrated it by pointing to his skin, a gesture emphasising pride in his identity and heritage. This was in response to persistent racist abuse from the stands, which had included monkey chants and other slurs. Some fans even threw chairs and objects at him. Despite being the victim of such abuse, Marega received a yellow card. As the hostile environment intensified, Marega ultimately decided to leave the pitch, visibly frustrated by the lack of support from officials and deeply affected by the racist abuse. This incident sparked a widespread debate in Portugal about racism in football, the responsibility of referees and clubs to protect players, and the need for stronger anti-racism measures in the sport.

Taking the aforementioned exemplary incidents into consideration, it is no surprise that 73% of women identified verbal attacks such as racist insults and slurs as the most common manifestations of racism in football in Portugal, followed by psychological violence, for example, intimidation (41.2%), social violence, such as spreading malicious rumours (16.2%), physical violence including beating, kicking, punching, etc. (11.6%), and sexual violence ranging from unconsented touching to rape (4.2%). Half of the male sample (49.6%) confirmed that observation. Second in this list is psychological violence (27.9%), followed by social violence (10.8%), physical violence (6.1%) and sexual violence (1.6%).

Like other forms of discrimination and violence affecting people from socially vulnerable groups, racism is explained by the participants of our investigation as having different types of manifestations resulting in multiple forms of victimisation (DeKeseredy, Pritchard, Stoneberg et al., 2022).

Female participants in our study most frequently associated racism in football with sexual violence, highlighting their greater vulnerability to gender-based violence. Along with racist experiences, female football players, as well as coaches and referees, are more likely to be exposed to gendered micro-aggressions, and being psychologically, physically, and sexually assaulted (Drury, Stride, Fitzgerald et al., 2022; Fenton, Ahmed, Hardey et al., 2023).

There is little doubt that football remains a male-dominated sport that exhibits, celebrates, and reinforces very traditional forms of hegemonic masculinity (Glynn and Brown, 2023). This concept has been widely used, debated, and refined (Connell and Messerschmidt, 2005). It refers to a culturally idealised performance of manhood, in both a personal and a collective project, that reproduces male dominance over women and other men, often from minority groups. The results of our study show that participants view sexual orientation, gender identity, and non-compliance with the principle of non-hetero-cisnormativity as significant risk factors that may trigger discrimination in football. That corroborates other studies that analysed the intersection between racism, homophobia, and sexism (Dixon, 2020).

In the last years, there have been some significant shifts in how racist and homophobic attitudes and messages are communicated and shared. Nowadays, digital contexts, specifically social media, play a substantial role as they constitute an open, easily accessible, and anonymous field for several forms of general and targeted discrimination. These range from racist and xenophobic discourses to homophobic and misogynistic narratives. Equally diverse are the ways these discriminatory dispositions are expressed. They range from subtle micro-aggressions that are frequently normalised, to humorous discourses that perversely entertain the audience and/or more sophisticated othering processes and dehumanising narratives contributing to the stigmatisation of racialised, gay, non-Christian players (Cleland, Magrath and Kian, 2018; Glynn and Brown, 2023). Due to the advance of modern information technologies and the polarisation of politics, in particular the growing popularity of far-right ideas, social networks provide ample opportunities to disseminate discriminatory sentiments and hate speech directed at individuals and groups, threatening their well-being (Cable, Kilvington and Mottershead, 2022; Kassimeris, Lawrence and Pipini, 2022). Having said this, due to its systemic matrix, racist attitudes and practices are not always conscious, neither explicit nor always visible. They manifest themselves in many diverse ways including prejudice and overt bias, stereotyping or racial profiling, but also through micro-aggressions, amongst others (Santos, Santos, Kearns et al., 2024).

Direct and/or vicarious verbal assaults, as a form of hate speech, result in several traumas. Some studies have found an association between being exposed to racist hate speech and discrimination and experiencing psychological distress among people of colour (Moody, Tobin and Erving, 2022).

Preventative strategies and measures to combat racism in football

Our study revealed a widespread consensus regarding the inadequate responses to racism within Portuguese football, with only 17.2% of the men and 13.2% of the female participants believing that the problems were tackled adequately. The participants mentioned that three main factors were responsible for the inadequacy of responses: First, the depreciation of the issue's severity, noted by 58.8% of women and 36% of men; second, the lack of reporting to relevant authorities, indicated by 33.3% of women and 20.1% of men; and finally, the continuation of a prevailing culture of racism in Portuguese society, acknowledged by 31.6% of women and 15.1% of men. The overwhelming scepticism shown by the participants highlights the systemic barriers to effectively tackling racism, as institutional responses fail to address the roots and causes of the problem and do not provide meaningful solutions to the various forms of discrimination in the world of Portuguese football.

Nearly 13% of the female respondents and about 11% of the men considered that Portuguese laws are insufficient to handle racism in football. To prevent and combat racism in football, 70.8% and 69.3% of women and 45.4% and 45.7% of men, respectively, identified the punishment of fans and the investment in continuous education as the most effective measures. Our investigation also exposed major difficulties concerning the effective application of laws and policies aiming to eradicate racism in sports, particularly in football. Despite the existence of laws and policies addressing racism in football, participants considered that they still are insufficient or ineffective, resulting in low conviction rates.

After FIFA's "Good Practice Guide on Diversity and Anti-Discrimination" (2015) and UNESCO's "Kazan Action Plan" (2017), the Portuguese Football Federation (FPF) launched a platform named "Football for All" in 2021. It aims to provide a tool for all stakeholders to report discriminatory incidents and manifestations based on 'race', ethnicity, nationality, religion, identity or sexual orientation, political and ideological beliefs, economic status or other factors.

Considering incidents of discrimination both on and off the field, football clubs often endeavour to preserve a favourable public image and tend to downplay the activities of deviant fans, for example, hooligans, and shifting the blame for such events to wider society, thereby employing a strategy to evade their accountability (Kassimeris, Lawrence and Pipini, 2022).

In addition, numerous civil society organisations, such as *SOS Racismo*, have been crucial in fieldwork, closely engaging with victims, providing active support, developing awareness campaigns, and advocating for policy reforms. So far, the fight against racism and other forms of discrimination in the world of Portuguese football has not been very successful. A concerted effort involving governmental and non-governmental organisations, local authorities, sports federations and clubs, athletes, coaches, referees, supporters' groups, the media and others is urgently needed.

Summary

Football is more than just a popular and exciting sport, as it is embedded in, and often reflects, social, cultural and political values of the host society. This chapter focused on Portugal, a country that is marked by a racist cultural heritage, with football mirroring persistent propensities to discriminate against people of colour, women, and ethnic and sexual minorities. Racist, xenophobic, sexist and homophobic chants and slogans are still common in many Portuguese stadiums. Some of these receive extensive media coverage and public condemnation.

Although the results of the aforementioned empirical study cannot be generalised, they offer interesting insights into the intersection of different axes of discrimination and the relationships between different stakeholders in the world of Portuguese football, for example, players, clubs and fans. According to our investigation, racism in football is widely perceived to be a prevalent problem that affects primarily, but not exclusively, male athletes. Individuals and organised groups of fans are the principal perpetrators, and verbal abuse, through chants and slogans, is the most frequent form of racist behaviour. Skin colour is the main trigger for racism. Therefore, non-white players as well as migrants continue to be frequent targets of racism. And yet, reports of racist incidents to police authorities and subsequent criminal convictions remain scarce in Portugal, which may reflect not only a reluctance and/or inability to identify racist practices but also legal and/or procedural challenges pursuing such charges.

Gender, ethnicity, sexual orientation, gender identity, and disability also appear to be significant risk factors. Thus, alongside racism, other forms of discrimination, such as sexism, xenophobia, homophobia, and transphobia, can be observed in various football settings. Members of the LGBTI community and women continue to be frequent targets, with gender, sexual orientation and gender identity overlapping with other forms of discrimination.

The EU Anti-Racism Action Plan 2020–2025 urges member states to recognise and encourage diversity, fairness, and equality in sports at institutional and societal levels. These principles could constitute an ideal basis for a holistic approach and successful initiatives in Portugal to promote equal treatment and prevent and combat racism and discrimination.

It was beyond the scope of this book chapter to list, describe and evaluate the various policies, strategies, projects and initiatives that aim to fight the aforementioned discriminatory practices in Portuguese football. Instead, we prefer to offer some guiding principles that need to frame that battle in order to make it more effective. By doing this, we implicitly identify some of the weaknesses of the contemporary approaches that are obvious to knowledgeable and critical observers of Portugal's football scene.

Recommendations

Despite several but largely uncoordinated efforts made by the Portuguese government as well as non-governmental organisations to prevent and combat racism and other forms of discrimination in football, discriminatory behaviours persist and are easily identifiable within Portuguese football. Therefore, developing a holistic approach and implementing policies through grassroots initiatives that actively oppose racism, sexism, xenophobia, homophobia, transphobia and other discriminatory practices is essential for embracing diversity. It is crucial to develop effective policies that lead to practices and, for instance promote bias-free language, and tackle subtle and blatant forms discrimination while emphasising culturally aware leadership strategies (Cooper, Newton, Klein et al., 2020). These efforts need to be in line with, and guided by EU and other international legal and policy frameworks, that promote diversity and non-discrimination and combat hate crimes and hate speech. Furthermore, victims' rights should be fully recognised and applied, and racist acts must be effectively penalised. The fight against racism must be institutionalised in governmental agencies and coordinated with civil society organisations, and educational institutions. Ultimately, we suggest that the focus needs to be on three major dimensions: education, in general, vocational training of key stakeholders in the world of sport, and establishing a differentiated legal framework that includes a clear set of policies and, for example, introduces systematic monitoring and evaluation procedures.

With regard to education, both formal and informal strategies need to be further developed and adopted. Educational institutions, including elementary and secondary schools as well as universities, should incorporate multicultural education into their curricula to foster an appreciation for diversity, a culture of tolerance and acceptance among children from an early age (Buiskool and Giannetto, 2021). Educational programs centred on Human Rights and intersectionality approaches would be most suitable to disseminate information about the harmful consequences of racism in sports. Issues, such as structural racism, also need to be addressed as the underrepresentation of historically marginalised groups, for example, in leadership roles within football organisations offers a useful example to demonstrate what racism is and how it is manifested (Cooper, Newton, Klein et al., 2020).

Likewise, community efforts, social initiatives and activist groups like *Black Lives Matter* that promote cultural dialogue may be able to contribute through their work to a reduction of racist remarks and actions inside and outside football games (Buiskool et al., 2021).

To increase the willingness to report racist incidents to police authorities or other organisations such as APCVD or FPF, and speed up investigations of racist incidents, information on how to report such incidents should be disseminated, especially among men and people older than 40 years. Thus, building coalitions against racism in sports by encouraging fans and football clubs to adopt charters with anti-racism clauses and creating a good practice award for combating racism and racial discrimination in sports is urgent (ECRI, 2024). The establishment and dissemination of detailed codes of conduct in football, implemented from the early stages of training, via internal and external channels, may also foster a culture of solidarity among athletes and other sports stakeholders.

As part of the coaching activities for key stakeholders in the world of sport, awareness-raising campaigns regarding diversity and inclusion, concerning the destructive nature of racism, are crucial in educating athletes, fans, sports actors and members of civil society. Using social media channels could be a powerful strategy to capture the youth's attention and involve them in preventing and combating racism and other forms of discrimination in Portuguese football.

UNESCO suggests increasing the training of athletes, coaches, referees and other technical staff on sports violence prevention, with the help of innovative technologies for presenting topics on violence and discrimination to children and adolescents, thus providing them with skills for handling incidents, in partnership and interaction with parents, should be a priority (UNESCO, 2023).

Additionally, there is an urgent need to educate the police forces on how to best handle racist events inside and outside sports stadiums in conjunction with local security staff.

Regarding the existing legal frameworks and policies, a critical review of current laws and policies is needed to ensure that these capture the increasingly complex and differentiated matrix of victims and perpetrators. For example, the likelihood of being exposed to racism or other forms of discrimination depends on various social characteristics. Recognising the links between risk factors and victimisation will underpin prevention initiatives and allow them to target the most vulnerable people. It goes without saying that any changes should be evidence-based.

Furthermore, it would be important to establish monitoring and evaluation processes to assess the effectiveness and impact of existing strategies, projects, and initiatives. A critical evaluation of the National Plan to Combat Racism and Discrimination (2021–2025) will certainly provide insightful indicators of which measures have been more impactful than others. Education, training programs, and legal and policy measures, while considering effectiveness and impacts, could be adjusted based on such monitoring and evaluation.

In addition, existing data on racism need to be merged into a common database, so that its manifestations, characteristics, dynamics, causes and repercussions can be fully analysed to ensure that future policy making is evidence-based. Right now, we can only see the tip of the iceberg. The fact that statistical figures on racism, in general, are dispersed, makes it difficult to map the size of the phenomenon. The iceberg metaphor obviously implies that the visible part is only a small portion of the whole. The iceberg's base, much larger and unseen, represents, amongst others, systemic and structural racism, that is closely linked to power and privilege in Portuguese society. Racism in Portuguese society and football is, of course, embedded in the country's social structures. These underpin deep-rooted beliefs and practices that (re)produce oppression to people of colour (Braveman, Arkin, Proctor et al., 2022).

Notes

1 Governance, information and knowledge for a non-discriminatory society; Education and Culture; Higher Education; Labour and Employment; Housing; Health and Social Welfare; Justice, Security and Rights; Participation and Representation; Sport; Means of Communication and the Digital.

2 More details of this study can be found in Neves, S., Topa, J., Borges, J. and Silva, E. (2023) "Racism in football in Portugal: perceptions of multiple actors", *Social Sciences*, 12(3), p. 165.

References

Abrantes, P. and Roldão, C. (2019) "The (mis)education of African descendants in Portugal: towards vocational traps?", *Portuguese Journal of Social Science*, 18(1), pp. 27–55.

Back, L., Crabbe, T. and Solomos, J. (2001) *The changing face of football. Racism, identity and multiculture in the English game*, Oxford: Berg Publishers.

Bastos, C. and Castelo, C. (2024) "Lusotropicalismo", in *Oxford research encyclopedia of African history*. Available: <https://oxfordre.com/africanhistory/view/10.1093/acrefore/9780190277734.001.0001/acrefore-9780190277734-e-1486> [accessed on 14th September 2024].

Braveman, P., Arkin, E., Proctor, D., Kauh, T. and Holme, N. (2022) "Systemic and structural racism: definitions, examples, health damages, and approaches to dismantling", *Health Affairs*, 41(2), pp. 171–178.

Buiskool, B and Giannetto, A. (2021) *The role of culture, education, media and sport in the fight against racism – policy recommendations Concomitant expertise for INI report*, European Parliament. Available: <https://www.europarl.europa.eu/RegData/etudes/BRIE/2021/690911/IPOL_BRI(2021)690911_EN.pdf> [accessed on 14th September 2024].

Cable, J., Kilvington, D. and Mottershead, G. (2022) "Racist behaviour is interfering with the game: exploring football fans online responses to accusations of racism in football", *Soccer & Society*, 23(8), pp. 880–893.

Casquilho-Martins, I., Belchior-Rocha, H. and Alves, D.R. (2022) "Racial and ethnic discrimination in Portugal in times of pandemic crisis", *Social Sciences*, 11(5), Article 184.

Castelo, C. (2009) "Migração ultramarina: contradições e constrangimentos" [Overseas migration: contradictions and constraints], *Ler História*, 56, pp. 69–82.

Chovanec, J. (2023) "'Bigger than football': racist talk on and off the soccer pitch", *Soccer & Society*, 24(7), pp. 942–957.

Cleland, J. and Cashmore, E. (2016) "Football fans' views of racism in British football", *International Review for the Sociology of Sport*, 51(1), pp. 27–43.

Cleland, J., Magrath, R. and Kian, E. (2018) "The internet as a site of decreasing cultural homophobia in association football: an online response by fans to the coming out of Thomas Hitzlsperger", *Men and Masculinities*, 21(1), pp. 91–111.

Coelho, J.N. (1998) "On the border': some notes on football and national identity in Portugal", in Brown, A. (Eds.), *Fanatics! power, identity and fandom in football*, London: Routledge.

Connell, R.W. and Messerschmidt, J.W. (2005) "Hegemonic masculinity: rethinking the concept", *Gender & Society*, 19(6), pp. 829–859.

Cooper, J., Newton, A., Klein, M. and Jolly, S. (2020) "A call for culturally responsive transformational leadership in college sport: an anti-ism approach for achieving equity and inclusion", *Frontiers in Sociology*, 5(65), DOI: 10.3389/fsoc.2020.00065.

Council of Europe (CE) (2023) *The challenge of far-right ideology to democracy and human rights in Europe*. CE. Available: <https://rm.coe.int/the-challenge-of-far-right-ideology-to-democracy-and-human-rights-in-e/1680ac86d0> [accessed on 24th September 2024].

Council of Europe Commissioner for Human Rights (2021) *Memorandum on combating racism and violence against women in Portugal*. Council of Europe. Available:

<https://rm.coe.int/memorandum-on-combating-racism-and-violence-against-women-in-portugal-/1680a1b977> [accessed on 24th September 2024].

DeKeseredy, W.S., Pritchard, A.J., Stoneberg, D.M. and Nolan, J. (2022) "Racial/ethnic variations in the polyvictimization of college women: results from a large-scale campus climate survey", *Journal of Ethnicity in Criminal Justice*, 20(3), pp. 191–208. https://doi.org/10.1080/15377938.2022.2092575

Dixon, K. (2020) "Sexual abuse and masculine cultures: reflections on the British Football Scandal of 2016", in Magrath, J., Cleland, R. and Anderson, E. (Eds.), *The Palgrave handbook of masculinity and sport*, London: Palgrave Macmillan.

Dowling, F. (2024) "Is sport's 'gateway for inclusion' on the latch for ethnic minorities? A discourse analysis of sport policy for inclusion and integration", *International Review for the Sociology of Sport*, 59(2), pp. 239–257.

Drury, S., Stride, A., Fitzgerald, H. and Pylypiuk, L. (2022) "I'm a referee, not a female referee: the experiences of women involved in football as coaches and referees", *Frontiers in Sports and Active Living*, 3, DOI: 10.3389/fspor.2021.789321.

Eather, N., Wade, L., Pankowiak, A. and Eime, R. (2023) "The impact of sports participation on mental health and social outcomes in adults: a systematic review and the 'Mental Health through Sport' conceptual model", *Systematic Reviews*, 12(102), DOI: 10.1186/s13643-023-02264-8.

European Union Agency for Fundamental Rights (2021) *Fundamental rights report 2021*, European Union. Available: <https://fra.europa.eu/sites/default/files/fra_uploads/fra-2021-fundamental-rights-report-2021_en.pdf> [accessed on 23rd August 2024].

European Commission (2023) *Special Eurobarometer 535: discrimination in the European Union*. European Union. Available: <https://data.europa.eu/data/datasets/s2972_99_2_sp535_eng?locale=en> [accessed on 23rd August 2024].

European Commission (2024) *Country report: non-discrimination transposition and implementation at the national level of Council Directives 2000/43 and 2000/78 – Portugal*. European Union. Available: <https://www.migpolgroup.com/wp-content/uploads/2024/08/Portugal.pdf> [accessed on 9th September 2024].

European Commission Against Racism and Intolerance (ECRI) (2024) *Racism and discrimination against black persons/people of African descent*. Council of Europe. Available: <http://rm.coe.int/0900001680aef79b> [accessed on 22nd September 2024].

Fenton, A., Ahmed, W., Hardey, M., Boardman, R. and Kavanagh, E. (2023) "Women's football subculture of misogyny: the escalation to online gender-based violence", *European Sport Management Quarterly*, 24(6), pp. 1215–1237.

Ferraz de Matos, P. (2019) "Racial and social prejudice in the colonial empire issues raised by miscegenation in Portugal (late nineteenth to mid-twentieth centuries)", *Anthropological Journal of European Culture*, 28(2), pp. 23–44.

Garcia-Jaramillo, D., Santos, T.R. and Fernandes-Jesus, M. (2023) "'Not wanting to see it is hypocrisy, it's denying what is obvious': far-right discriminatory discourses mobilised as common sense", *Journal of Community & Applied Social Psychology*, 33(6), pp. 1413–1425.

Glynn, E. and Brown, D.H.K. (2023) "Discrimination on football Twitter: the role of humour in the othering of minorities", *Sport in Society*, 26(8), pp. 1432–1454.

Gonçalves, M. (2021) "The scramble for Africa reloaded? Portugal, European colonial claims and the distribution of colonies in the 1930s", *Contemporary European History*, 30(1), pp. 2–15.

Gredin, N.V., Okholm Kryger, K., McCall, A., Solstad, B.E., Torstveit, M.K., Massey, A. and Ivarsson, A. (2023) "Psychology research in women's soccer: a scoping review", *Science and Medicine in Football*, pp. 1–11, DOI: 10.1080/24733938.2023.2285962.

Instituto Nacional de Estatística (INE) (2023) *Inquérito às condições de vida, origens e trajetórias da população residente-2023* [Survey on the living conditions, origins and trajectories of the resident population-2023], Lisboa: INE. Available: <https://www.ine.pt/ngt_server/attachfileu.jsp?look_parentBoui=643800069&att_display=n&att_download=y> [accessed on 15th September 2024].

Internal Security System (ISS) (2024) *The annual report of internal security: 2023*, Lisbon: ISS. Available: <https://www.portugal.gov.pt/download-ficheiros/ficheiro.aspxv=%3d%3dBQAAAB%2bLCAAAAAAABAAzNDEyNgEApqka1wUAAAA%3d> [accessed on 2nd August 2024].

Jeanes, R. and Lucas, R. (2022) "Sport, social exclusion, and discrimination", in Wenner, L.A. (Ed.), *The Oxford handbook of sport and society*, Oxford: Oxford University Press.

Kassimeris, C., Lawrence, S. and Pipini, M. (2022) "Racism in football", *Soccer & Society*, 23(8), pp. 824–833. https://doi.org/10.1080/14660970.2022.2109799

Krzyeanowski, M. (2020) "Discursive shifts and the normalisation of racism: imaginaries of immigration, moral panics and the discourse of contemporary right-wing populism", *Social Semiotics*, 30(4), pp. 503–527.

Miranda, S., Gouveia, C., Di Fátima, B. and Antunes, A.C. (2023) "Hate speech on social media: behaviour of Portuguese football fans on Facebook", *Soccer & Society*, 25(1), pp. 76–91.

Moody, M.D., Thomas Tobin, C.S. and Erving, C.L. (2022) "Vicarious experiences of major discrimination and psychological distress among Black men and women", *Society and Mental Health*, 12(3), pp. 175–194.

Neves, J.M. (2023) "Portuguese race' and empire", *Social Identities*, 29(5), pp. 498–515.

Neves, S., Topa, J., Borges, J. and Silva, E. (2023) "Racism in football in Portugal: perceptions of multiple actors", *Social Sciences*, 12(3), p. 165.

Official Gazzete n.º 10/2024, Serie I, 2024-01-15. Law n.º 4/2024, 15th January. Available: <https://diariodarepublica.pt/dr/detalhe/diario-republica/10-2024-836604890> [accessed on 9th September 2024].

Official Gazzete n.º 30/2009, Serie I, 2009-02-12. Law n.º 7/2009. Available: <https://diariodarepublica.pt/dr/legislacao-consolidada/lei/2009-34546475-211390860> [accessed on 21st August 2024].

Official Gazzete n.º 63/1995, Serie I-A 1995-03-15. Decree-Law n.º 48/95. Available: <https://diariodarepublica.pt/dr/legislacao-consolidada/decreto-lei/1995-34437675-836759596> [accessed on 9th September 2024].

Official Gazzete n.º 86/1976, Serie I, 1976-04-10. Decree of Approval of the Constitution Available: <https://diariodarepublica.pt/dr/legislacao-consolidada/decreto-aprovacao-constituicao/1976-34520775-50453575> [accessed on 2nd September 2024].

Official Gazzete n.º 170/2007, Serie I 2007-09-04. Law n.º 59/2007, 4th September. Available: <https://diariodarepublica.pt/dr/detalhe/lei/59-2007-640142> [accessed on 1st September 2024].

Okholm Kryger, K., Wang, A., Mehta, R., Impellizzeri, F.M., Massey, A. and McCall, A. (2021) "Research on women's football: a scoping review", *Science and Medicine in Football*, 6(5), pp. 549–558.

Peralta, E. and Frangella, S. (2012) "Portugal and the empire: discourses and practices on race and gender", in Hipfl, B. and Loftsdóttir, K. (Eds.), *Teaching "race" with a gendered edge*, Budapest: Central European University Press.

Ponte e Sousa, P. (2017) "A identidade nacional portuguesa e as relações externas com as ex-colónias portuguesas: da descolonização ao diálogo multilateral" [Portuguese national identity and external relations with Portugal's former colonies: from decolonisation to multilateral dialogue], *Conjuntura Austral*, 8(39–40), pp. 44–64.

Portuguese Government (2021) *National plan to combat racism and discrimination 2021–2025*. Portuguese Government. Available: <https://www.portugal.gov.pt/download-ficheiros/ficheiro.aspx?v=%3d%3dBQAAAB%2bLCAAAAAAABAAzND I3NgYAMqHeagUAAAA%3d> [accessed on 12th September 2024].

The Public Security Police and the Authority for Preventing and Combating Violent Behavior in Sports (2023) *Report on the analysis of violence associated with sports – Sports season 2022–2023*, Lisbon: The Authority for Preventing and Combating Violent Behavior in Sports. Available: <https://www.apcvd.gov.pt/wp-content/uploads/2023/12/RAViD-Epoca-2022-2023_Epoca-2022-23.pdf> [accessed on 10th August 2024].

Rabelo, V.C. and Cortina, L.M. (2019) "Two sides of the same coin: gender harassment and heterosexist harassment in LGBQ+ work lives", *Violence and Victims*, 34(5), pp. 724–743.

Regulatory Decree n.º 10/2018, of October 3. *Creates the authority for preventing and combating violence in sport*. Available: <https://diariodarepublica.pt/dr/detalhe/decreto-regulamentar/10-2018-116587910> [accessed on 7th September 2024].

Ronkainen, N. (2023) "Sport creates value sports activities as part of a meaningful life?", *Current Issues in Sport Science (CISS)*, 8(2), p. 4.

Santos, G.L., Santos, V.G., Kearns, C., Sinclair, G., Black, J., Doidge, M., Fletcher, T., Kilvington, D., Endo, P. T., Liston, K. and Lynn, T. (2024) "Kicking prejudice: large language models for racism classification in football discourse on social media", *Advanced Information Systems Engineering Lecture Notes in Computer Science*, 14663, pp. 547–562.

Sobral, J.M. (2004) "O Norte, o Sul, a raça, a nação – representações da identidade nacional portuguesa (séculos XIX-XX)" [The North, the South, the race, the nation – Representations of Portuguese national identity (19th–20th centuries)], *Análise Social*, 39(171), pp. 255–284.

UNESCO (2023) *Fighting racism and discrimination: a UNESCO toolkit*, Paris: UNESCO. Available: <https://unesdoc.unesco.org/ark:/48223/pf0000387454> [accessed on 3rd August 2024].

Vala, J., Brito, R. and Lopes, D. (2015) *Expressões dos Racismos em Portugal* [Expressions of racism in Portugal], Lisboa: ICS. Available: <https://repositorio.ul.pt/bitstream/10451/22539/1/ICS_JVala_Racismos_LAN.pdf> [accessed on 24th September 2024].

Valentim, J.P. and Heleno, A.M. (2018) "Luso-tropicalism as a social representation in Portuguese society: variations and anchoring", *International Journal of Intercultural Relations*, 62, pp. 34–42.

Chapter 10

Scotland

Sectarianism as racism in football?
The cut and thrust of an ongoing debate

Alan Bairner and Stuart Whigham

The history of Scottish football has been punctuated by regular episodes of verbal abuse and not infrequent outbursts of violence, primarily, but not exclusively, associated with the rivalry between Glasgow's two biggest football clubs, Celtic and Rangers. These events have traditionally been characterised as sectarian and as evidence of persistent religious bigotry. In Scotland, the term "sectarianism" is generally used to describe the continuous ethnic, political and religious rivalries and tensions between Protestants and Catholics although these terms are no longer necessarily linked to regular church attendance. More recently, however, the debate has moved on with some researchers preferring to use the word "racism" to describe the anti-Irishness directed at Celtic Football Club and its followers and others contending that the word "racism" is inappropriate in this particular context. Meanwhile, legislators and Police Scotland have sought ways to tackle the problem regardless of what terminology is used.

This chapter assesses the use of the term "racism" rather than "sectarianism" in relation to Scottish football and, specifically the rivalry between the so-called "Old Firm" clubs. In order to contextualise this debate, the chapter commences with an account of the degree to which sectarianism has shaped Scottish society and football across time, with a consideration of the shifting dynamics in contrasting periods. Attention then turns to the ways in which these broader developments have, in turn, influenced the specific ethno-religious, political and ideological associations of each club's support base across time, respectively. This approach thus facilitates consideration of the broader context within which an assessment of the debate of whether or not the ongoing blight of sectarianism in Scottish society can be usefully re-framed as a matter of racism.

Historical sectarianism in Scottish football

As Bairner (1994, 1996) has argued, considering the lack of congruence between sporting nationalism and political nationalism in Scotland, it was safer for many Scots to display sporting nationalism in response to the internal

DOI: 10.4324/9781003495970-10

This chapter has been made available under a CC-BY-NC-SA 4.0 license.

divisions within Scotland along ethno-religious, regional and political lines. However, the ethno-religious demographics within the Scottish society have undoubtedly framed much of the discussion on the politics of Scottish football, and in particular, the controversy around the expression of "sectarian" political identities.

Although sectarianism has been argued to be a declining issue in Scottish society and sport, the historic polarisation between the oppositional religious, political and ethnic attachments of the "Old Firm" clubs of Celtic and Rangers means that these divides have not been eradicated (Bairner, 2001; Bradley, 2013; Flint and Kelly, 2013; Kelly, 2011). Past academic studies on these divides have thus stressed that the existence of ethnic, sectarian and 'racial' discrimination undermine any notions of a singular Scottish identity (Bairner, 1994; Bradley, 1995; Boyle and Haynes, 2009; Dimeo and Finn, 2001; Finn, 1991a, 1991b; Horne, 1995; Kowalski, 2004).

As Kowalski argues "[f]ootball, the so-called 'national game', still provides an important focus for the perpetuation of the sectarian divisions that have marred Scotland since the second half of the nineteenth century" (2004, p. 73), and sectarianism has therefore been a common topic in academic reflections on Scottish sport and society. Bairner (1994) contended that the hegemonic position of the Glaswegian clubs of Rangers FC and Celtic FC due to their association with Protestantism and Catholicism, respectively, epitomised the interconnection between sectarianism and support for Scottish football club teams. For Bairner, both clubs have been able to attract supporters from outside the immediate geographic proximity of their home city of Glasgow, drawing supporters from the surrounding West Coast area of Scotland (despite a number of other football clubs in the West Coast) and other areas of Scotland due to the religious and political connotations of each club – in a way that other clubs in Scottish football have been unable to replicate. Furthermore, both clubs also attract extensive support from other international contexts such as Northern Ireland/Ulster, the Republic of Ireland and North America.

Although similar arguments have been made regarding the quasi-religious affiliations to other Scottish football clubs historically, such as in the case of Hibernian FC and Heart of Midlothian FC in Edinburgh, most academic analyses have conceded that the contemporary influence of sectarianism on these clubs is not evidenced to the same extent as in the 'Old Firm' rivalry (Holt, 1989; Kowalski, 2004; Kelly, 2007a, 2007b, 2013; Kelly and Bairner, 2018).

Contemporary sectarianism in Scottish football and Scottish politics

The issue of sectarianism in Scottish football and wider society has prompted legislative action by the Scottish Government, led at the time by the Scottish National Party (SNP). This resulted in the introduction of the Offensive Behaviour at Football and Threatening Communications (Scotland) Act 2012

(Crawford, 2013; Davis, 2013; Flint and Kelly, 2013; Rosie, 2013; Waiton, 2013). Flint and Kelly (2013, p. 3) identified the major catalyst for the introduction of this bill as:

> the so-called 'shame game' between Celtic and Rangers. . . . This match, played on 2 March 2011, resulted in thirty-four fans being arrested inside the stadium, three Celtic players booked, seven Rangers players booked, three Rangers players sent off, managers Ally McCoist and Neil Lennon squaring up to one another at the final whistle and widespread public condemnation from politicians, journalists and football officials.

This 'shame game' was accompanied by other events in Scottish football related to sectarianism during the same period, including incidents involving threatening devices and messages sent in the mail to Celtic fans and officials, controversies regarding refereeing decisions and actions, a physical assault on Celtic manager Neil Lennon by a Heart of Midlothian fan, and disciplinary action by UEFA against both Rangers and Celtic for discriminatory songs in European fixtures (Flint and Kelly, 2013; Flint and Powell, 2014; Rosie, 2013).

In the belief that the existing legislation to deal with offensive and/or threatening behaviour in football was inadequate, the SNP Government proposed and successfully passed the new legislation (Crawford, 2013). However, both the content of the Bill and the process of its passing drew significant criticism from opposition political parties, sections of the Scottish media, the general public and academics (BBC News, 2011a, 2011b; Crawford, 2013; Flint and Powell, 2014; Waiton, 2013, 2014; Walker, 2012). As a leading critic of the legislation, Waiton (2013) suggested that the passing of this Act was symptomatic of an 'anti-sectarian industry' in Scotland which had resulted in elite control over what it means to be 'tolerant' in contemporary Scottish society. Waiton (2013, p. 99) argues that

> anti-sectarianism, within this context, is no longer fundamentally about challenging religious (or political) sect-like behaviour but is part of a wider framework of psychic protection, where everybody, but especially those defined as 'vulnerable groups', is protected from emotional hurt, that is from being offended.

For Waiton and other academics who support his position (Crawford, 2013), this has led to the demonisation of football fans who wish to express their cultural and ethno-religious identity freely. They also argue that the Act had ironically led to intolerance towards such individuals and groups and, ultimately, resulted in restrictions on their freedom of speech. Although other academics adopted more cautious positions on the relative merits and drawbacks of the Act (Flint and Kelly, 2013; Rosie, 2013), Celtic FC released an official club statement demanding a formal review of the "unhelpful and counter-productive Act" (Celtic Football Club, 2014), thereby highlighting the difficulties faced by governmental policymakers when intervening politically within the domain of sport.

The ongoing controversy surrounding the Offensive Behaviour at Football Act therefore led to a sustained public and political campaign to repeal the Act. Following the 2016 Scottish Parliament election, which saw the SNP lose its parliamentary majority, the opposition parties voted to revoke the Act in March 2018 (BBC, 2018). However, given that parties from across the political divide accepted that sectarianism remained a problem in Scottish society, despite their opposition to the nature of the Act per se, it was apparent that the decline of sectarianism in Scotland was still too slow to refute concerns about its impact on society.

Contemporary sectarianism – Scottish football and the 2014 independence referendum

These potential impacts of sectarianism in contemporary Scottish society also played out in the constitutional debates during the Scottish independence referendum of 2014. Despite the failure of the pro-independence SNP to achieve sufficient electoral support for Scottish independence and the serious decline in its electoral performance at the 2024 General Election, the prospect of Scottish independence remains salient within Scottish and British politics (Dalle Mulle, 2016; Ichijo, 2009; Leith and Soule, 2011; Mycock, 2012). Given that the ethno-religious, socio-economic and political stratification of supporters of Celtic and Rangers still have to be linked to their personal voting dispositions (Armstrong, 2014; Bissett and McKillop, 2014; Bradley, 1997, 2013; Giulianotti, 2007; Kelly, 2007a, 2013; Walker, 2014, 2016), it was unsurprising that speculation emerged regarding the impact of footballing loyalties on voting preferences in the 2014 referendum despite its relatively marginal status within the constitutional debate (Jarvie, 2017; Whigham, Kelly and Bairner, 2021; Whigham and May, 2017). In this light, as part of the ongoing opinion polls before the referendum took place in September 2014, a Panelbase opinion poll (see Table 10.1) commissioned in May 2014 by the Wings Over Scotland website presented data on the independence referendum voting preferences simultaneously of Scottish football fans (Wings Over Scotland, 2014a, 2014b).

The only major deviation from the average voting trend (46.3% favoured Scottish independence, while 53.7% preferred to stay in the Union) was the significant difference in the voting intentions of Aberdeen fans (only 25.8% in favour and 74.2% against), in terms of discrepancies based on the assumptions made in past academic analysis of the politics of Scottish football. The most interesting results were the voting intentions of Rangers and Celtic fans. Given the aforementioned associations between Rangers and expressions of Britishness, Conservativism and unionism (Bairner, 1994; Bissett and

Table 10.1 Scottish independence referendum voting intentions by Scottish football club support (Wings Over Scotland, 2014a, 2014b)

Club	"Yes" Vote Intention	%	"No" Vote Intention	%
Rangers	63	52.5%	57	47.5%
Celtic	50	54.3%	42	45.7%
Aberdeen	8	25.8%	23	74.2%
Hearts	14	48.3%	15	51.7%
Hibs	8	47.1%	9	52.9%
Dundee United	8	47.1%	9	52.9%
Other	60	50.0%	60	50.0%
No interest	165	42.7%	221	57.3%
Total	376	46.3%	436	53.7%

McKillop, 2014; Bradley, 2013; Flint and Kelly, 2013; Holt, 1989; Kowalski, 2004), and Celtic's historical association with the political "left", the Labour Party, and republican sympathies (Bradley, 1998; McDougall, 2013; Walker, 2014), it was surprising that the two Glasgow clubs represented the only "Yes" supporting clubs in this opinion poll, which obviously challenges some of the traditional political stereotypes. It is therefore more than appropriate and also timely to consider the degree to which the respective stereotypes of the "Old Firm' clubs" fans, as outlined earlier, continue to hold true in the fluid political climate of contemporary Scotland.

Rangers

Historically, Rangers FC and their supporters have commonly been associated with Protestantism, Orangeism,[1] Conservativism, loyalism (in relation to the Irish and Northern Irish political context) and unionism (in relation to Scotland's constitutional status) (Bairner, 1994; Bissett and McKillop, 2014; Bradley, 2013; Flint and Kelly, 2013; Holt, 1989; Kowalski, 2004; Whigham, Kelly and Bairner, 2021). It has therefore been argued that the club's symbolism has shaped Scottish society and politics outside of the domain of football, given the oppositional religious, political and ethnic attachments of Rangers and their rivals, Celtic (Bairner, 2001; Bradley, 2013; Flint and Kelly, 2013; Walker, 2014). However, some disagreement remains regarding the extent of their impact. Notwithstanding this caveat, Bradley (2013, p. 67) argues that Rangers historically became:

> a symbol of a number of dominant, privileged and institutional features of Scottish-British life, particularly in terms of allegiances and affinities with royalty, empire, unionism, freemasonry and Protestantism, prov[ing] highly attractive to Ulster-Scots in Scotland's central belt.

Turning attention to the issue of whether these historical associations persist for Rangers supporters in the current political context in Scotland, with specific reference to attitudes towards demands for Scottish independence, recent analyses have questioned the validity of the historic stereotypes of Rangers fans. For example, in their introduction to their edited collection "Born Under the Union Flag: Rangers, Britain and Scottish Independence", Bissett and McKillop (2014, p. 19) argue that

> It is often taken for granted, by combatants on both sides of the independence debate, that a Rangers fan will or should be a dyed-in-the-wool Unionist, whose No vote is a foregone conclusion. No doubt there are many such Rangers fans. But there are also many who intend to vote Yes, just as there are supporters of Celtic, Aberdeen, Hibs, Dundee United and Hearts who intend to vote No. While no one would wish to portray Rangers supporters as paragons of virtue, lazy stereotypes can also surround the club.

Similar arguments are made elsewhere in the same collection by fellow contributors, with Richardson (2014, p. 25) suggesting that while

> the Rangers fan base taken as a whole may lean more towards Better Together than Yes Scotland, I know many fans who are strongly committed to independence . . . the idea of the right-wing, Unionist Rangers fan is simply not borne out by the political landscape of Scotland over the last 20 to 30 years.

Duff (2014, p. 110) put forward a more differentiated view:

> Odd as it may seem, I know of many independence-supporting Rangers fans who see no contradiction in associating themselves with the British flag at games whilst simultaneously supporting the breakup of the United Kingdom. They consider the Union Jack to be part of their identity as a Rangers fan, not part of their national identity. For most football fans, the culture that surrounds the match day experience can be packed away at the end of the 90 minutes and kept locked up in the understairs cupboard until the next match.

Therefore, although the historic attachments of Rangers to Protestantism, Orangeism, Conservativism, loyalism and unionism are deemed to still have a part to play in the contemporary era for some supporters, the shifting political climate in Scottish politics more broadly is argued to have impacted upon the Rangers fan base, undermining the "lazy stereotypes" of the club highlighted by Bissett and McKillop (2014).

Celtic

In the case of Celtic FC, Bradley (1995) suggests the club's symbolic position for Irish Catholic immigrants in Scotland – a section of Scottish society that perceives itself as a victim of prejudice, sectarianism and, more recently, racism – has been central in cementing the popularity of Celtic. For Bradley, the establishment of Celtic, and before that of Hibernian Football Club in Edinburgh, allowed integration of the Irish Catholic community into the football culture of Scotland, an important step given the importance of football within the domain of Scottish society, especially for males. The resultant integration process has been argued to be in stark contrast with the sporting culture found in the Republic of Ireland. There, the formation of the Gaelic Athletic Association and its strategy of promoting a distinct Irish sporting culture centred on Gaelic games and pastimes, in opposition to so-called foreign games including association football (Bairner, 2002; Bradley, 1998, 2007; Jarvie, 1993; Jarvie and Walker, 1994; Sugden and Bairner, 1993). Others have outlined numerous examples of historic discrimination against this section of the Scottish population within Scottish football and Scottish society in a wider sense, resulting from the connection between Celtic and issues of ethnic and ethno-religious identity associated with Irishness, Catholicism and republicanism (Dimeo and Finn, 2001; Finn, 1991a, 1991b; Horne, 1995).

However, as is the case for Rangers, it has been advocated by some that the historic political associations of Celtic have softened. For example, Celtic supporters have been argued to have a stronger affinity with the Labour Party in comparison with fans of other Scottish football clubs, as well as left-leaning political and ideological tendencies (Bradley, 1998; McDougall, 2013; Walker, 2016). With regard to the matter of Scottish independence, Walker (2014, p. 38) observed

> Leading Celtic figures, such as past Chairmen John Reid and Michael Kelly, and current director Brian Wilson, are amongst the most prominent anti-independence commentators and this reflects enduring cynicism to Scottish Nationalism within the Labour Party that has traditionally drawn such strong support from the Catholic (of Irish descent) community in Scotland.

Given the conflict between the unionist position of the Scottish Labour Party and the republican ideology associated with Celtic's symbolic position in Scottish society, the constitutional debate in Scotland during the period of the Scottish independence referendum of 2014 resulted in an ideological dilemma for Celtic supporters. Allied to the decline in the fortunes of the Labour Party in Scotland (until their recent recovery in the 2024 UK general election), the rise of the SNP to power and the growth of political nationalism have been linked to numerous Celtic fans switching their political allegiances to the SNP and the cause of Scottish independence (Tomkins, 2014; Walker, 2014; Whigham, Kelly and Bairner, 2021).

On sectarianism and racism in contemporary Scottish football

As outlined earlier, the shifting dynamics of the ethno-religious and political allegiances of each club means that it would clearly be foolish to use football club support as a proxy or predictor for identifying an individual's political preferences. It would be equally rash to completely dismiss the notion that an individual's affiliation and identification with a football club may have some role in their cultural and political socialisation. Furthermore, whether racism, as opposed to sectarianism and bigotry, is a factor in contemporary Scottish society is open to debate. In light of this, attention now turns to examining the shifting nature of the political and ethno-religious attachments of each club to consider their relevance to the ongoing debate.

According to McBride, "the Irish . . . tend to be neglected in academic work on race and racism in Britain" (2018, p. 69). Thus, "the common-sense explanation of sectarianism marginalises claims of the Irish as an ethnic minority and a racialised group, and the 'equivalence' frame which focuses on 'Protestant-Catholic relations' crucially neglects the historic unequal power relations" (McBride, 2018, p. 89). Does this mean then that we can replace the word "sectarianism" with "racism" in discussions about the biggest, and arguably most insidious, football rivalry in Scotland?

The 1978 UNESCO Declaration on Race defines racism as "a theory claiming the intrinsic superiority of racial or ethnic groups which would give to some the right to dominate or even eliminate others, presumed inferior, or basing value judgments on racial differences" (cited in De Benoist, 1999, p. 13). However, as De Benoist (1999, p. 11) argues, "Today the word 'racism' has so many contradictory meanings that it takes on the aura of a *myth* and is, therefore, difficult to define". Thus, "because of a certain affinity, 'racism' can be used as the correlate of a whole series of other terms: fascism, the extreme Right, ant-Semitism, sexism, etc." (De Benoist, 1999, p. 11) and even become synonymous with phobias of any "Other, e.g., ageism, misogyny, anti-young, anti-police, anti-workers, anti-married people, etc." (De Benoist, 1999, p. 32). This was not always the case. As Grosfoguel (2016, p. 10) asserts, "since colonial times color racism has been the dominant marker of racism in most parts of the world". He concedes, however, that the colour of one's skin "is not the only or exclusive form of racist marker". Thus, "in the colonial history of Ireland, the British constructed their racial superiority over the Irish, not through the marker of skin color, but rather through a religious marker" (p. 11). As a consequence, "what appeared at first glance to be a religious conflict between Protestants and Catholics was in fact a racial/colonial conflict" (p. 11).

It is this conflict that, according to some scholars from Finn (1991a, 1991b) onwards, was exported to Scotland and took root with the arrival of thousands of Irish Catholic immigrants in the nineteenth century. They were met with racist prejudice and discrimination in a country which had undergone an extensive reformation of the Christian religion. The result, according to McBride (2018), has been that "in relation to Scotland, sectarianism and racism are not two separate phenomena" (p. 69). McBride (2018) further argues that "Irish Catholics historically were a racialised group which suffered structural discrimination and societal prejudice" (p. 89). Elsewhere, she claims that "understanding sectarianism as a modality of racism, which as Miles and Brown (2003) argue is inextricably bound up with nationalism, emphasises the need to consider the impact of historical colonial relations between Britain and Ireland" (McBride 2022, p. 352). This is supported by Reid (2013) who writes that "the ethno-religious bigotry experienced by the Irish in Scotland is a particular form of racism that is Scotland's national demon" (p. 230).

According to Nazir, James, Abdurahman et al., however, "The relationship (if any) between sectarianism and racism is complex" (2022, p. 788). It should also be noted that McBride agrees that, although sectarianism is certainly a contested term, "it is equally contentious to talk about anti-Irishness in Scotland as a type of racism" (2018, p. 71). One wonders, indeed, whether the racism, if that is what it is best described as, which is evidenced in football rivalry and reflected in the wider society is actually bi-directional with Celtic fans represented not only as victims but as morally superior not only to Rangers fans but also to Scottish Protestants, a majority of whom are no longer religious in a meaningful sense, or, more accurately perhaps Scots without an Irish catholic heritage. The implication is that it is they alone who are able to identify with oppressed peoples around the world, most strikingly and laudably, the Palestinians. There is a danger that this could turn into an essentialist belief about the virtues of the Irish in this regard, which can be easily refuted by consideration of the Irish American experience, also a product of large-scale immigration in the nineteenth century.

Racism and the Irish

According to Rolston (2003), there was no doubt that, upon their arrival in America, "the Irish Catholics were feared and despised for much the same reasons as before . . . their poverty, their tendency to political rebellion and, perhaps most importantly of all, their Catholicism" (p. 44). Another commentator, writing in the Celtic fanzine *Not the View*, noted that "anti-Catholic prejudice has deep roots in America and has only in recent decades begun to fade away" (Tirnaog, 2023, p. 28).

However, "when hostility between black and white did erupt, it resulted from the Irish setting out on the road to upward mobility" (Rolston, 2003, p. 45). Ignatiev (2009, p. 70) argues that "while the white skin made the Irish eligible for membership of the white race, it did not guarantee their admission; they had to earn it" (in opposition to no less a figure than Daniel O'Connell and to the nationalist and republican movement in Ireland itself). For example, the Irish nationalist Young Irelander John Mitchel, while in America, defended slavery. He was excused for doing so by Arthur Griffith, who founded the Irish political party Sinn Féin in 1905. He wrote in the introduction to *Jail Journal*, Mitchel's memoirs, "Even his views on Negro-slavery have been deprecatingly excused, as if excuse is needed for an Irish nationalist declining to hold the Negro his peer in right" (cited in Rolston, 2003, p. 50). Representatives of the Irish community even insisted that "they were enlisting to fight in the Civil War to defend the Union, but not to free the slaves" (Rolston, 2003, p. 46). In such ways did "the Catholic Irish eventually come to establish their "white" credentials . . ." (Rolston, 2003, p. 47).

Racist attitudes also became apparent in American sport, most notably in the city of Boston. Thus, the Boston Red Sox, a baseball team, "hampered by a pronounced strain of racism invoked by ownership and management as well as by the city, whose liberal credo towards freedom and equality of opportunity for all races throughout most of the nineteenth century became badly eroded" (Barney and Barney, 2007, p. 2). The General Managers at the time were Eddie Collins and Joe Cronin, both with Irish heritage, Collins in County Cork and Cronin with roots in County Killarney (Railton, 2024).

This is not to deny that "supporters of clubs like Celtic have a long history of struggling against oppression" (Banal, 2023, p. 8). But this description does not necessarily apply to all supporters of Celtic and what is meant, one wonders, by the phrase "clubs like Celtic"? Presumably, Rangers is not one of these. Indeed, in the words of Tirnaog (2023), "I wonder if there is a support in British football with less self-awareness than some of those who follow Rangers" (p. 27). The writer goes on, "it's almost as if anti-Catholic bigotry is the last acceptable prejudice" (p. 29). The clarion call of "We are the People" so beloved by many Rangers supporters is a demonstration of supposed superiority, perhaps even an implication that others are inferior human beings or not even human at all (see Shirlow and McGovern, 1997). Nevertheless, might it not be possible that anti-Protestant bigotry, or perhaps more accurately, anti-Scottishness exists in sections of the Celtic fan base? Furthermore, it should not be forgotten that Celtic supporters were implicated in what was one of the most blatant incontestable examples of racism in Scottish football, which happened almost 40 years ago.

By the time he signed for Rangers in 1987, Mark Walters, a Black footballer, had already experienced the racism that had infected the grounds of many English football clubs in that era. However, Walters (2018) recalls, "if I thought the abuse I had suffered in England was bad, it was about to fly off the scale when I joined Rangers" (p. 115). Prior to making his debut at Celtic Park, home to the other half of the "Old Firm", according to Walters, "the abuse started the moment we got off the team bus" (p. 116). Despite losing the game, Walters was "singled out for the type of stick I had never experienced before" (p. 116). During the game, he started to think, "Hang on a second, I've just run a metre inside that line and there is a scary array of missiles that have been thrown at me. . . . Probably the scariest items were the darts, as they could've taken my eye out" (p. 117). For the sake of balance, it should be added that by his own admission, Walters was treated even worse by fans of Heart of Midlothian. He writes, "if I thought the scenes at Celtic Park were bad, then what I endured at Tynecastle – both on and off the park – was ten times worse" (p. 119). He goes on, "the fall-out from that game brought the subject of racism in football – a problem Scotland apparently didn't know had – to a head and the following day the papers went to town on the subject" (p. 121). It is ironic that, as we have seen, numerous commentators have argued that the fans of one of the teams most implicated in these seems are themselves the victims of racism.

It is true that the behaviour of some Celtic fans towards Mark Walters was condemned by many, perhaps most, of the others. Speaking on their behalf, Tirnaog (2023) wrote, "The treatment of Rangers player Mark Walters that day was as disgraceful as it was unacceptable" (p. 27). He continued, "racism has no place in any decent society and perhaps it was all the more depressing that it occurred at the home of Celtic, a club which has faced many barriers and much discrimination in its history" (pp. 27–28) and ended, "it was a wake up call to all who follow Celtic and indeed to the wider Scottish society that we weren't immune to the sort of racism that was so prevalent in England at the time" (p. 29).

Conclusion

There is certainly no denying that Britain has a history of racist stereotyping of the Irish (de Nie, 2004). It is also undeniable that Irish Catholics suffered discrimination in a variety of areas of Scottish society into the second half of the twentieth century. However, it is widely accepted, although certainly not by all, that discrimination of this type has all but disappeared (Devine and Rosie, 2020), transferred perhaps to more recent immigrants whose arrival in Ireland itself has also prompted a rise in racism (Gusciute, Mühlau and Layte, 2022; Cannon and Murphy, 2024). This is not to deny that bigotry and sectarianism are still to be found in Scotland. A considerable amount of which is directed towards those of Irish Catholic heritage and, above all, people associated with Celtic FC. Indeed, as has been articulated earlier, the ethno-religious and political fracture lines in Scottish society are still contended to shape the contours of life for many Scots, both within the context of sport and society more broadly. It is to argue, however, that the terms that have been used in the past to situate the rivalry between Celtic and Rangers and the implications of that rivalry are still apposite. To introduce the concept of racism into the debate is arguably to make more than they deserve of the rhetorical and, sadly, on occasions violent excesses in which the fans of these clubs engage. It also runs the risk of diminishing the power of the word when used to describe the treatment of truly oppressed people.

Note

1 Orangeism is the principles and practices of the Orange Order, a Protestant organisation that supports the supremacy of Protestantism in the Republic of Ireland, Northern Ireland and Scotland.

References

Armstrong, C. (2014) "The man's for turning: how a unionist became pro-independence", in Bissett, A. and McKillop, A. (Eds.), *Born under a union flag: rangers, Britain and Scottish independence*, Edinburgh: Luath Press.

Bairner, A. (1994) "Football and the idea of Scotland", in Jarvie, G. and Walker, G. (Eds.), *Scottish sport in the making of the nation: ninety minute patriots?*, Leicester: Leicester University Press.

Bairner, A. (1996) "Sportive nationalism and nationalist politics: a comparative analysis of Scotland, the Republic of Ireland, and Sweden", *Journal of Sport and Social Issues*, 20(3), pp. 314–334.

Bairner, A. (2001) *Sport, nationalism and globalization: European and North American perspectives*, Albany, NY: State University of New York Press.

Bairner, A. (2002) "Sport and the politics of Irish Nationalism: the struggle for Ireland's sporting soul", in Neuheiser, J. and Wolff, S. (Eds.), *Breakthrough to peace? The impact of the Good Friday agreement on Northern Ireland*, New York: Berghahn.

Banal, J.B. (2023) "The greatest blot that has ever soiled Scottish football", *Not the View*, 294, 25th November, pp. 4–9.

Barney, R.K. and Barney, D.E. (2007) ""Get those niggers off the field!": racial integration and the real curse in the history of the Boston Red Sox", *NINE: A Journal of Baseball History and Culture*, 16(1), pp. 1–9.

BBC (2018) "MSPs vote to repeal football bigotry law", *BBC News*, 15th March. Available <https://www.bbc.co.uk/news/uk-scotland-scotland-politics-43405134> [accessed on 7th November 2024].

BBC News (2011a) "Parties urge SNP to 'think again' over bigotry bill", *BBC News*, 3rd November. Available <http://www.bbc.co.uk/news/uk-scotland-scotland-politics-15561485> [accessed on 7th November 2024].

BBC News (2011b) "Anti-bigot laws passed by the Scottish Parliament", *BBC News*, 14th December. Available <http://www.bbc.co.uk/news/uk-scotland-scotland-politics-16138683> [accessed on 7th November 2024].

Bissett, A. and McKillop, A. (2014) "Introduction", in Bissett, A. and McKillop, A. (Eds.), *Born under a union flag: rangers, Britain and Scottish independence*, Edinburgh: Luath Press.

Boyle, R. and Haynes, R. (2009) *Power play: sport, the media and popular culture*, Edinburgh: Edinburgh University Press.

Bradley, J. (1995) *Ethnic and religious identity in modern Scotland: culture, politics and football*, Aldershot: Avebury.

Bradley, J. (1997) "Political, religious and cultural identities: the undercurrents of Scottish football", *Politics*, 17(1), pp. 25–32.

Bradley, J. (1998) "'We shall not be moved'! Mere sport, mere songs? A talk of Scottish football", in Brown, A. (Ed.), *Fanatics: power, identity and fandom in football*, London: Routledge.

Bradley, J. (2007) *The Gaelic Athletic Association and Irishness in Scotland: history, ethnicity, politics, culture and identity*, Edinburgh: Argyll Publishing.
Bradley, J. (2013) "History and memory in Scottish football", in Flint, J. and Kelly, J. (Eds.), *Bigotry, football and Scotland*, Edinburgh: Edinburgh University Press.
Cannon, B. and Murphy, S. (2024) "'We're not right-wing or racist but. . .': far-right myth and distributive conflict in asylum seeker related protest in the Republic of Ireland, November 2022–July 2023", *Irish Journal of Sociology*, 32(1–2), pp. 225–234.
Celtic Football Club (2014) *Celtic football club statement*, 4th March. Available <https://www.celticfc.com/news/5529> [accessed on 13th November 2024].
Crawford, J. (2013) "The politics of anti-sectarianism", in Flint, J. and Kelly, J. (Eds.), *Bigotry, football and Scotland*, Edinburgh: Edinburgh University Press.
Dalle Mulle, E. (2016) "New trends in justifications for national self-determination: evidence from Scotland and Flanders", *Ethnopolitics*, 15(2), pp. 211–229.
Davis, P. (2013) "Hegemonic fandom and the red herring of sectarianism", in Flint, J. and Kelly, J. (Eds.), *Bigotry, football and Scotland*, Edinburgh: Edinburgh University Press.
De Benoist, A. (1999) "What is racism?", *Telos*, 114, pp. 11–48.
de Nie, M. (2004) *The eternal paddy: Irish identity and the British press, 1798–1882*, Madison: University of Wisconsin Press.
Devine, T.M. and Rosie, M. (2020) "The rise and fall of anti-Catholicism in Scotland", in Gheeraert-Graffeuille, C. and Vaughan, G. (Eds.), *Anti-Catholicism in Britain and Ireland, 1600–2000: Histories of the sacred and secular, 1700–2000*, Basingstoke: Palgrave Macmillan.
Dimeo, P. and Finn, G.P.T. (2001) "Racism, national identity and Scottish football", in McDonald, I. and Carrington, B. (Eds.), *'Race', sport and British society*, London: Routledge.
Duff, I. (2014) "Things don't look so different from south of the border", in Bissett, A. and McKillop, A. (Eds.), *Born under a union flag: rangers, Britain and Scottish independence*, Edinburgh: Luath Press.
Finn, G.P.T. (1991a) "Racism, religion and social prejudice: Irish Catholic clubs, soccer and Scottish society – I the historical roots of prejudice", *International Journal of the History of Sport*, 8(1), pp. 72–95.
Finn, G.P.T. (1991b) "Racism, religion and social prejudice: Irish Catholic clubs, soccer and Scottish society – II social identities and conspiracy theories", *International Journal of the History of Sport*, 8(3), pp. 370–397.
Flint, J. and Kelly, J. (2013) "Football and bigotry in Scotland", in Flint, J. and Kelly, J. (Eds.), *Bigotry, football and Scotland*, Edinburgh: Edinburgh University Press.
Flint, J. and Powell, J. (2014) "'We've got the equivalent of Passchendaele': sectarianism, football and urban disorder in Scotland", in Hopkins, M. and Treadwell, J. (Eds.), *Football hooliganism, fan behaviour and crime: contemporary issues*, Basingstoke: Palgrave Macmillan.
Giulianotti, R. (2007) "Popular culture, social identities, and internal/external cultural politics: the case of Rangers supporters in Scottish football", *Identities*, 14(3), pp. 257–284.
Grosfoguel, R. (2016) "What is racism?", *Journal of World-Systems Research*, 22(1), pp. 9–15.
Gusciute, E., Mühlau, P. and Layte, R. (2022) "One hundred thousand welcomes? Economic threat and anti-immigration sentiment in Ireland", *Ethnic and Racial Studies*, 45(5), pp. 829–850.
Holt, R. (1989) *Sport and the British: a modern history*, Oxford: Oxford University Press.
Horne, J. (1995) "Racism, sectarianism and football in Scotland", *Scottish Affairs*, 12, pp. 27–51.

Ichijo, A. (2009) "Sovereignty and nationalism in the twenty-first century: the Scottish case", *Ethnopolitics*, 8(2), pp. 155–172.
Ignatiev, N. (2009) *How the Irish became white*, London: Routledge.
Jarvie, G. (1993) "Sport, nationalism and cultural identity", in Allison, L. (Ed.), *The changing politics of sport*, Manchester: Manchester University Press.
Jarvie, G. (2017) "Sport, the 2014 Commonwealth Games and the Scottish referendum", in Bairner, A., Kelly, J. and Lee, J.W. (Eds.), *The Routledge handbook of sport and politics*, London: Routledge.
Jarvie, G. and Walker, G. (1994) "Ninety minute patriots? Scottish sport in the making of the nation", in Jarvie, G. and Walker, G. (Eds.), *Scottish sport in the making of the nation: ninety minute patriots?*, Leicester: Leicester University Press.
Kelly, J. (2007a) *Flowers of Scotland? A sociological analysis of national identities: Rugby union and association football in Scotland*. Unpublished PhD Thesis. Loughborough University.
Kelly, J. (2007b) "Hibernian football club: the forgotten Irish?", *Sport in Society*, 10(3), pp. 514–536.
Kelly, J. (2011) "'Sectarianism' and Scottish football: critical reflections on dominant discourse and press commentary", *International Review for the Sociology of Sport*, 46(4), pp. 418–435.
Kelly, J. (2013) "Is football bigotry confined to the west of Scotland? The Heart of Midlothian and Hibernian rivalry", in Flint, J. and Kelly, J. (Eds.), *Bigotry, football and Scotland*, Edinburgh: Edinburgh University Press.
Kelly, J. and Bairner, A. (2018) "The 'talk o' the toon'? An examination of the Heart of Midlothian and Hibernian football rivalry in Edinburgh, Scotland", *Soccer & Society*, 19(5–6), pp. 657–672.
Kowalski, R. (2004) "'Cry for us, Argentina': sport and national identity in late twentieth-century Scotland", in Smith, A. and Porter, D. (Eds.), *Sport and national identity in the post-war world*, London: Routledge.
Leith, M.S. and Soule, D.P. J. (2011) *Political discourse and national identity in Scotland*, Edinburgh: Edinburgh University Press.
McBride, M. (2018) "The contemporary position of Irish Catholics in Scotland", in Davidson, N., Liinpää, M., McBride, M. and Virdee, S. (Eds.), *No problem here: understanding racism in Scotland*, Edinburgh: Luath Press.
McBride, M. (2022) "Nationalism and "sectarianism" in contemporary Scotland", *Ethnic and Racial Studies*, 45(16), pp. 335–358.
McDougall, W. (2013) "Kicking from the left: the friendship of Celtic and FC St. Pauli supporters", *Soccer & Society*, 14(2), pp. 230–245.
Miles, R. and Brown, M. (2003) *Racism*, New York: Routledge.
Mycock, A. (2012) "SNP, identity and citizenship: re-imagining state and nation", *National Identities*, 14(1), pp. 53–69.
Nazir, T., James, K., Abdurahman, M. and Al-Khazraji, H.S. (2022) "Pakistani support for Glasgow's Old Firm football clubs", *Soccer & Society*, 23(7), pp. 784–804.
Railton, B. (2024) "Considering history: The Boston Celtics and the city's history of race and sports", *The Saturday Evening Post*, 24th June.
Reid, I.A. (2013) "Just a wind-up? Ethnicity, religion and prejudice in Scottish football-related comedy", *International Review for the Sociology of Sport*, 50(2), pp. 227–245.
Richardson, G. (2014) "A hand-wringer's tale", in Bissett, A. and McKillop, A. (Eds.), *Born under a union flag: rangers, Britain and Scottish independence*, Edinburgh: Luath Press.
Rolston, B. (2003) "Bringing it all back home: Irish emigration and racism", *Race and Class*, 45(2), pp. 39–53.

Rosie, M. (2013) "Outside the hothouse: perspectives beyond the old firm", in Flint, J. and Kelly, J. (Eds.), *Bigotry, football and Scotland*, Edinburgh: Edinburgh University Press.

Shirlow, P. and McGovern, M. (Eds.) (1997) Who are 'the people'? Unionism, protestantism and loyalism in Northern Ireland, London: Pluto Press.

Sugden, J. and Bairner, A. (1993) *Sport, sectarianism and society in a divided Ireland*, Leicester: Leicester University Press.

Tirnaog (2023) "The last acceptable prejudice", *Not the View*, 292, 16th September, pp. 27–29.

Tomkins, A. (2014) "Foreword", in Bissett, A. and McKillop, A. (Eds.), *Born under a union flag: rangers, Britain and Scottish independence*, Edinburgh: Luath Press.

Waiton, S. (2013) "The new sectarians", in Flint, J. and Kelly, J. (Eds.), *Bigotry, football and Scotland*, Edinburgh: Edinburgh University Press.

Waiton, S. (2014) "Football fans in an age of intolerance", in Hopkins, M. and Treadwell, J. (Eds.), *Football hooliganism, fan behaviour and crime: contemporary issues*, Basingstoke: Palgrave Macmillan.

Walker, G. (2012) "Scotland's sectarianism problem: Irish answers?", *The Political Quarterly*, 83(2), pp. 374–383.

Walker, G. (2014) "From darlings to pariahs: Rangers and Scottish national pride", in Bissett, A. and McKillop, A. (Eds.), *Born under a union flag: rangers, Britain and Scottish independence*, Edinburgh: Luath Press.

Walker, G. (2016) *The labour party in Scotland: religion, the Union, and the Irish dimension*, London: Palgrave Macmillan.

Walters, M. with J. Holmes (2018) *Wingin' it*, Worthing: Pitch Publishing.

Whigham, S., Kelly, J. and Bairner, A. (2021) "'Politics and football fandom in post-'indyref' Scotland: nationalism, unionism and stereotypes of 'the Old Firm'", *British Politics*, 16(4), pp. 414–435.

Whigham, S. and May, A. (2017) "'Sport for yes?': the role of sporting issues in pro-independence political discourse during the Scottish independence referendum campaign", *International Journal of Sport Policy and Politics*, 9(3), pp. 557–572.

Wings Over Scotland (2014a) "An opportunist strike", *Wings Over Scotland*, 20th May. Available <https://wingsoverscotland.com/an-opportunist-strike/> [accessed on 7th November 2024].

Wings Over Scotland (2014b) "Panelbase opinion poll – 21st May 2014", *Wings Over Scotland*. Available <https://wingsoverscotland.com/wp-content/uploads/WingsPoll4-May2014.pdf> [accessed on 7th November 2024].

Chapter 11

Spain

Understanding and fighting racism in football: A story of ignorance and half-heartedness

Ramón Llopis-Goig

The prevalence of racism and xenophobia in contemporary Spanish society is in stark contrast to the expectations expressed just a decade ago when many social researchers described the situation in Spain as "unique" and "tranquil", due to the degree of acceptance and welcoming afforded to the immigrant population (Arango, 2015). However, unemployment, economic instability, growing social inequality and progressive impoverishment of the middle class caused by various financial crises in recent years, alongside growing ideological polarisation and the penetration of far-right political parties into Spanish institutions are shaking the foundations of a society which, for a long time, felt immune to the viruses of racism and xenophobia. Michel Wieviorka was not wrong when, 30 years ago, he cautioned that regardless of the future evolution of European society, there was a high probability that it would feel increasingly tempted by, and drawn to, racism (Wieviorka, 1995).

The mass media relatively often reports racist and xenophobic incidents that usually take place inside football stadiums. Coverage and follow-up of such events are substantially more extensive and detailed when well-known teams and high-profile, famous players are involved. The scant attention given to this issue by Spanish social scientists, however, is surprising. Outputs on this topic only come from a limited number of researchers from different academic disciplines who deal with this issue on an occasional but not necessarily consistent basis. The first publications that should be mentioned here sought to describe and analyse specific incidents and examine the main characteristics of racist and xenophobic manifestations (Durán, 2006; Durán and Jiménez, 2006; Viñas, 2006; Durán and Pardo, 2008; Llopis-Goig, 2009; Rodríguez-Moya, 2012). Others assessed the initiatives and counter-measures that were developed and used to tackle these issues (Viñas and Spaaij, 2006; Llopis-Goig, 2013), alongside critical evaluations of relevant legal frameworks and regulations (Ríos, 2014, 2016; Rodríguez-Monserrat, 2015). Subsequently, analyses of concrete episodes were published such as those that, for example, affected Dani Alves (Rodríguez-Moya, 2015), Mouctar Diakhaby (Martín, Buitrago and Beltrán, 2022) and, more recently, Vinícius Júnior (Soriano, Botton, Burgés et al., 2023; Villar, Sánchez and Pulido, 2024).

DOI: 10.4324/9781003495970-11
This chapter has been made available under a CC-BY-NC-SA 4.0 license.

This chapter intends, firstly, to provide a general overview of the evolution of racism and xenophobia and discuss, in more detail, recent manifestations of these phenomena in Spanish football. Secondly, it aims to uncover the main initiatives introduced to tackle these forms of discrimination which have been promoted through governmental agencies and by the bodies responsible for the management and governance of football. In order to address these two objectives, the chapter is divided into four parts. Following the introduction, the next part offers some historical insights with particular reference to the period between 2004 and 2006 as that is the time period that paved the way for the approval of a law that frames the fight against racism and xenophobia in sport. Next, the most important forms of racist and xenophobic manifestations as well as current developments are presented. The following section touches on those initiatives rolled out by the sporting organisations themselves to tackle this type of discriminatory behaviour. The chapter concludes with some critical reflections that focus on the main barriers that prevent racism and xenophobia in the world of Spanish football to be eradicated.

Historical background and evolution

During the first half of the 20th century, the absence of racist and/or xenophobic manifestations was notable as well as obvious and self-evident as there were no foreign players in Spanish football. LaLiga was created in 1928 and until 1933 the participation of foreign footballers was not allowed, except for those who had previously played in the Spanish Cup or in regional tournaments. There are no reports of racism or xenophobia in these first decades. In fact, having a Black footballer amongst their ranks was considered to be a mark of distinction for football clubs. On several occasions, the press and supporters gave foreign players nicknames without the intention of denigrating them (Rodríguez-Moya, 2012). It is not known whether those given nicknames interpreted them in the same, non-derogatory way. Often, these nicknames alluded to their place of origin. The first recorded racist incident affected the Moroccan footballer Ben Barek, known as *la Perla Negra*, the Black Pearl. Gonzalo Suarez chronicled a match between Atlético de Madrid and Sevilla in 1951, in which the Moroccan scored the goal that made the former league champions. Suarez reported that a supporter, who had previously tried to attack Ben Barek, shouted at him in a threatening tone whilst being arrested by the Civil Guard: "Don't come back to Seville, Black piece of shit, because we'll kill you!" (Girard, 2006, p. 83).

The presence of Black footballers and players with different ethnic and/or cultural backgrounds started to become more evident in Spanish football in the late 1970s. In reality, this was nothing really new given that, since the early 1970s, the signing of players from South American countries with native legal status (*oriundos*) had become a widespread practice. As they were considered to be 'natives', they were not registered as foreigners. Most of them were able to demonstrate that they had some sort of – even if distant – familial link with a Spaniard. This flexible interpretation of the rules surrounding the concept of citizenship led to an increase in the number of *native foreigners* in the squads of Spanish clubs.

Racist incidents started to occur more frequently from the beginning of the 1980s. This had a lot to do with the proliferation of the so-called *ultras* or 'radical fan groups' that took place during this same period. Although these distinctive groups of football supporters initially distanced themselves from ideological positions, by the end of the 1980s, they had become radicalised and had started to embrace extremist ideologies, most notably through the inclusion of right-leaning skinheads (Viñas and Spaaij, 2006). The emergence of violent and racist behaviour of these groups was underpinned by an ideological mix of exacerbated patriotism and (biological) racism. Beyond their ideological connotations, the *ultras* or radical fan groups created spaces for young people where marginality, youth gangs and gratuitous violence converged (Viñas, 2024). Alhaji Momodo (Gambia), Rui Manuel Jordao (Angola), Gilberto Silva (Honduras), Carlos Guerini (Argentina), Carlos Gómez Monteiro Pitinho (Brazil) and Luiz Edmundo Pereira (Brazil) were all victims of racist incidents during this period. Two significant cases pertained to the English footballer Laurie Cunningham, who, in the first half of the 1980s, played for Real Madrid and Sporting Gijon, and the RCD Espanyol goalkeeper Thomas N'Kono. Both were frequently abused with racist and xenophobic insults by the supporters of rival teams. Paradoxically, the adoption of racist and xenophobic behaviour was often an imitation of the behaviour of English hooligans and Italian *ultras* (Viñas, 2024).

What had been, up until that time, isolated manifestations, became more regular occurrences during the 1990s with racism starting to be considered a social issue of growing significance. Ezaki Badou, Mallorca's Moroccan goalkeeper, became the first foreign footballer in 1990 to recognise that he was frequently insulted by supporters and that this was commonplace in more than a few football grounds. Other victims of racist attacks during this same decade were Real Sociedad's English player Dalian Atkinson, Sporting Gijon's Nigerian striker Rashid Yekini and Real Madrid's Freddy Rincón. Other victims of these attacks included coaches such as the Argentinian Jorge Valdano, the Portuguese Artur Jorge and the Colombian Francisco Maturana.

During that time, public concern regarding racist outbreaks increased, and there was a growing social awareness of this issue. The Dutch coach Guus Hiddink, for example, insisted on the removal of various flags and banners carrying Nazi imagery and symbols displayed by supporters of his then team, Valencia CF, at the start of a match against Albacete in 1992.

Following the Bosman ruling by the European Court of Justice in 1995, the influx of foreign players into professional Spanish football increased significantly. During the 1996/97 season, almost 150 foreign players were recruited from more than 35 different countries. "People of colour" were coming into professional football, whilst, at the same time, they were also signed up by lower-level teams. This coincided with significant demographic shifts in Spanish society. In 1997, the flow of immigration exceeded that of emigration for the first time. Within this context, a strong increase in racist and xenophobic incidents perpetrated by small groups of politically radical football supporters was notable. These groups were often linked to organisations that subscribed to neo-Nazi ideology, although the reality was much more complex. Their discriminatory attitudes and practices must be seen as a way of channelling and expressing their disapproval with and anger caused by the arrival of immigrants. Police arrests in response to various disturbances at the beginning of the 21st century exposed the multi-layered links between radical football supporters and neo-Nazis (Ibarra, 2006). This connection confirmed the suspicion that racist and xenophobic incidents were often executed by radical groups, who constituted the epicentre of discriminatory behaviour in football grounds. This led to the essentially implicit conclusion that racism and xenophobia were not an issue for Spanish society as a whole. Instead, the blame was shifted to those right-wing groups who were committed to and promoted radical right-wing ideas, largely in response to the considerable social and demographic changes taking place in the country. Increased societal tolerance for insults and verbal aggression in football stadiums also helped to obscure the seriousness of the problem.

Football supporters who committed such insults and verbal aggression did, of course, not consider them to be such acts. Instead, for them, such behaviour was no more than a combination of relief, jokes and banter through which they sought to provoke rival teams and their supporters.

Nevertheless, that kind of simplistic interpretation of fan behaviour started to change considerably following a spiral of racist incidents that took place between 2004 and 2006. There was a very notable surge in verbal racist and xenophobic insults, monkey chants, the throwing of peanuts and bananas, and the use of racist slogans and symbols. These incidents received extensive media coverage and their impact went far beyond the world of sport. To a large extent, the increased visibility of racist and xenophobic manifestations contributed towards raising awareness within Spanish society regarding the severity of the issue. There is little doubt that it also had a significant impact on the passing of the Law against Violence, Racism, Xenophobia and Intolerance in Sport in 2007 (Law 19/2007, 11th July). The purpose of this law was to re-organise the existing legal and regulatory framework and broaden its scope to cover the racist, xenophobic and intolerant behaviours that had become prevalent at the beginning of the new millennium. Previous legal documents had defined racist, xenophobic or intolerant acts as any statement, gesture or insult that supposes a threat, insult or vexation towards another person due to their 'racial', ethnic, geographic or social origin, or due to their religion, convictions, disability, sexual orientation or identity, gender expression or sexual characteristics. In addition to statements, gestures and insults, there is also mention of the uttering of chants and sounds or brandishing of slogans that seek to harm individuals' dignity or create an intimidating, humiliating or offensive environment, in addition to the waving of banners, flags, symbols or other signs which could contain discriminatory messages for the same reasons.

One of the most notable incidents during this time period pertains to the controversy surrounding the behaviour of the Spanish national team coach, Luís Aragonés. He intended to motivate José Antonio Reyes through racist remarks about the player's teammate, at the time at Arsenal FC, the Frenchman Thierry Henry. During a training session on 6 October 2004, Aragonés allegedly said to Reyes: "tell that Black, I am better than you! Black piece of shit, I am better than you!". Outrage about Aragonés' attitudes and behaviour increased during a press conference, prior to a friendly match between Spain and England, which was played five weeks following the remarks at the Santiago Bernabéu stadium. In response to questions from British journalists, Luís Aragonés raged against British colonialism instead of reflecting on his previous actions. The second episode occurred during the aforementioned friendly match between Spain and England, in which a large proportion of the crowd used racist insults and chants towards Black English footballers. In addition to local radical fan groups, a considerable section of the general crowd also imitated gestures and sounds characteristic of primates. These incidents resounded far beyond the world of sport. The British Prime Minister, Tony Blair, publicly expressed his disapproval and urged the Spanish government and football authorities to take appropriate measures to avoid further racist episodes in stadiums.

Immersed in generalised feelings of impunity, racist insults continued to be heard and seen in numerous football games afterwards. What previously had been considered to be behaviours inherent to politically radical groups was now becoming a type of "perverse fashion" that attracted and drew in a large number of supporters attending football stadiums. Subsequently, supporters in other Spanish cities vented their racist attitudes and abused, for example, Mohammad Sissoko (Valencia CF), Roberto Carlos (Real Madrid), Ronaldinho (FC Barcelona), Carlos Kameni (RCD Espanyol), Assunçao (Betis), Richard Morales (CA Osasuna), Daniel Kome (Getafe CF), Paulo Wanchope (Málaga CF), Félix Ettien (Levante UD) and Edwin Congo (Levante UD). This wave of explicit racism also affected Black footballers who played outside the top division (Viñas, 2006). Far from alarmist exaggerations, racism had quickly become an undeniable problem in Spanish football with the culprits, being not only the members of a few radical fan groups but also large sections of its wider following.

Manifestations of racism and xenophobia continued and reached a preliminary climax on 26 February 2006 when the Cameroonian FC Barcelona player, Samuel Eto'o, threatened the referee to walk off the pitch, should the racist chants and insults from Real Zaragoza supporters not stop. That incident marked a turning point with regard to public awareness in Spain.

Recent developments

The spiral of xenophobic and racist incidents alluded to in the previous section highlighted the need for a strong response by the Spanish political authorities. It led to a number of governmental actions and initiatives and culminated in the passing of the *Law against Violence, Racism, Xenophobia and Intolerance in Sport in 2007* (Law 19/2007, 11th July). At the same time, the Professional Football National League (LaLiga) and The Spanish Football Association (RFEF) tightened security measures, introduced harsher penalties and rolled out awareness-raising initiatives. Nonetheless, racist incidents continued and the list of affected football players has considerably grown since then. The most notorious cases reported by the mass media in recent years involved Pierre Webó (RCD Mallorca), Sinama Pongolle (Athletic Madrid), Alberto Quintero (FC Cartagena), Achille Emaná (Real Betis), Kalu Uche (UD Almeria), Paulao (Real Betis), Allan Nyom (Granada), Marcelo Vieira (Real Madrid), Dani Alves (FC Barcelona), Pape Diop (Levante UD), Jefferson Lerma (Levante UD), Iñaki Williams (Athletic Bilbao), Samuel Umtiti (FC Barcelona), Vinicius Tanque (Athletic Baleares), Mujaid Sadick (Deportivo de la Coruña), Mouctar Diakhaby (Valencia CF), Vinícius Júnior (Real Madrid), Eder Militao (Real Madrid) and Nico Williams (Athletic Bilbao). However, this lengthy list only constitutes the tip of the iceberg. In fact, it is much longer and also includes players in the non-professional lower echelons.

Footballers of African and Latin American descent are the main victims, although they are not the only ones. Along with these groups, Muslims and Gypsies are also the target, but to a much lesser extent, especially the latter, as they are also significantly less present in football. These attacks have increased in recent years, particularly on social networks and among young people. In addition to public manifestations, other subtler forms of discrimination exist that are often rooted in unconscious prejudices and are just as harmful and reprehensible. Victims of racism and xenophobia are most frequently the players of rival teams and, to a lesser extent, coaches. Racist attacks also occur against players of the very team supported by the perpetrators, although this is not commonplace. Indeed, one of the arguments most often used by the abusers as evidence that they are in fact not racist is that they accept players of the same descent or with the same skin colour who play for their own team.

The most common racist manifestations continue to be verbal insults. Such insults occur as much during professional football matches as they are detectable during semi-professional and amateur football matches, including regional categories and the lower leagues (youth, junior, etc.). Fairly often, racist insults are used inflammatorily by supporters of one team in order to support their own players. Assaults are often repeated throughout a match and tend to occur when the vilified player walks towards the bench, goes to take a throw-in or approaches the crowd in order to give away their jersey. There are also stadiums in which racist aggression manifests itself as whistling en masse from the crowd every time the vilified player touches the ball. There have also been cases of humiliations, threats and insults that continued even after the end of a game.

One of the most common manifestations of racism in Spanish football grounds continues to be monkey noises, accompanied by gestures mimicking primates and the throwing of peanuts or bananas. It is also fairly common to hear racist chants that use popular melodies to which offensive and abusive lyrics are added. But the racist abuse does not end there. As in many other countries, social media have become another popular vehicle to communicate racist content and engage in hate campaigns. Some 'football fans' go through even more trouble to display their dislike, disregard and/or hatred of others. In January 2023, an effigy dressed in Real Madrid's Vinicius Junior's jersey was hung by the neck from a motorway bridge near the club's training ground shortly before the team's match against Atletico Madrid. A few months later, four men were arrested for this hate crime. According to several media outlets, three of the suspects were members of Atletico Madrid's *ultra*-scene.

In the aftermath of noticeable racist abuse in Spanish football grounds, in particularly in high-profile matches, there appears to be – what Max Weber would call – an ideal-typical sequence of subsequent events. A retrospective reconstruction based on the combination of events from several such incidents may reveal a distinctive blueprint which could be reduced to the following ten stages:

Stage 1: The visible and/or audible manifestation of racism.
Stage 2: The temporary pausing of the game by the referee.
Stage 3: The disapproval of any form of discriminatory behaviour, in particular racism, through the stadium's PR system.
Stage 4: The vilified player confronting the perpetrator(s) and/or vehemently urging the referee to take action.
Stage 5: Expulsion of the player in question due to his/her outrage and subsequent unrestrained behaviour on the pitch.
Stage 6: His/her team mates leaving the pitch to express their solidarity and later return when faced with the threat of having three points deducted.
Stage 7: Home and/or away club condemning the racist abuse and declaring their solidarity with the targeted player(s).
Stage 8: Local, regional and/or national politicians expressing their dismay while also confirming that they will continue to tackle racism in football wholeheartedly.
Stage 9: The club of the affected player(s) and/or other stakeholders announcing that they are going to file complaints with the relevant authorities.
Stage 10: The State Commission against Violence, Racism, Xenophobia and Intolerance in Sport, which comprises the Supreme Sports Council (CSD), the Ministry of the Interior, the Spanish police, the *Guardia Civil*, the state attorney's office, RFEF, and LaLiga, will study and investigate the case.

Available statistical data, for example, from the annual reports of the "State Commission against Violence, Racism, Xenophobia and Intolerance in Sport" (CEVXRID), reveal that as of the 2004/05 season and up until the 2010/11 season, professional football experienced a marked increase in sanctions imposed due to racism or xenophobia. In the 2011/12 season, there was a sharp drop in sanctions which continued in the following season. In the 2013/14 season, this figure, once again, increased almost to previous levels, although numbers then started to reduce steadily from this time until reaching a low of only three sanctions in the 2018/19 season. The last seasons show a return to higher figures, especially in the 2021/22 and even more in the 2022/23 season. Obviously, the 2020/21 season was exceptional due to the restrictions imposed in response to the SARS-CoV-2 pandemic which meant that a large number of matches had to be played behind closed doors. With regard to non-professional football, recorded figures are lower and more consistent. Proportionally, cases of racism and xenophobia in both settings – professional and non-professional – are always scarce and never exceed four percent, although other types of incidents are more commonplace.

Another pertinent source of data to consider comes from a department created by LaLiga in 2015, the 'Integrity and Security Directorate' (DIS). The number of complaints about racist or xenophobic chants or chants inciting violence handled by the DIS during the 2025/16 season totalled 54. Very similar figures were reported for the following seasons: 2016/17: 56, 2017/18: 63, 2018/19: 53 and 49 in 2019/20. No complaint was filed during the 2020/21 season which was largely due to the absence of spectators caused by the SARS-Cov-2 pandemic. However, during the following season, 2021/22, the figure climbed to 114 (Domínguez, 2023). These figures reflect a similar trend to that in reports published by the CEVXRID.

Finally, it is noteworthy that, whilst those responsible for these incidents are no longer only *ultras* or radical fan groups, these groups have not disappeared from Spanish football. They continue to be active in stadiums and increasingly on social networks. A study conducted in 2015 on existing violent groups in Spain estimated that around 430 groups were operative, of which 47 operated in the football setting (Caballero, 2018).

Preventive, punitive and socio-pedagogical responses

At the end of the 1980s, "SOS Racism" in Spain was conceived in response to the emergence of racist groups and the growth of racist and xenophobic attitudes within the Spanish population. In 1995, it published its first annual report in which it threw light on racist incidents and the spread of neo-fascist ideas in football stadiums (SOS Racismo, 1996). In 1997, it reported the *Ultras Sur* group for a series of graffiti paintings made in the Santiago Bernabeu stadium shortly before an anti-racism charity match that depicted Nazi symbols and racist and xenophobic slogans. In its 2005 report, it reiterated its concern about to the spread of neo-Nazi ideology in stadiums and described the situation of racism in football as serious problem (SOS Racismo, 2005). The Movement against Intolerance (MCI, *Movimiento contra la Intolerancia*) is another very active non-governmental organisation (NGO) that aims to tackle racism and xenophobia. One of its main focuses is sport and, especially, football, as highlighted by its engagement in developing and formulating the aforementioned Law 19/2007. MCI periodically publishes the *Raxen Report* (MCI, 2023a), alongside a series of *Cuadernos de Análisis* (Analytical Journals). One of these was recently dedicated to racism and xenophobia in Spanish football (MCI, 2023b). MCI's commitment to fight racism in football is a constant throughout their history. To another extent, *Aficiones Unidas* (Supporters United), the leading football supporters association in Spain, recently collaborated with LaLiga on the development and dissemination of a *Supporters Guide* that strives to promote fair play and harmony.

In recent years, numerous awareness-raising initiatives have been introduced. For example, during the 2014/15 season, LaLiga and the *Asociación de Federaciones de Peñas* (AFEPE, Association of the Federations of Organised Football Fans Groups) rolled out a campaign in the stadiums of first and second division clubs. It comprised the installation of a canvas with an anti-racist slogan on the pitch and public announcements to communicate the punishment of all acts of violence, racism, xenophobia and intolerance. A similar campaign was launched by RFEF, LaLiga and the *Consejo Superior de Deportes*, (CSD, the Supreme Sports Council) in response to racist attacks suffered by the Real Madrid player, Vinícius Júnior, on 21 May 2023 at Mestalla stadium. In addition to players and referees carrying a canvas with anti-racist slogans onto the pitch at the start of the game, the campaign included the use of the hashtag #RacistasFueraDelFútbol (#RacistsOutOfFootball) on social networks and during televised coverage of first and second division matches. The aforementioned entities urged supporters to publicly reject and report any racist incidents or behaviours. Another initiative developed by LaLiga alongside clubs in recent years is the *Dejemos al racismo fuera de juego* campaign (Put Racism Offside). In addition, campaigns that are still being rolled out include first and second division players posing in shirts bearing anti-racist slogans and the display of anti-racist symbols at strategic places inside stadiums and on the captains' armbands.

The 'Integrity and Security Directorate' (DIS), which was created in 2015 as a department of LaLiga, is responsible for supervising first and second division matches. When racist or xenophobic manifestations occur, it activates its internal protocol and reports the events to CEVXRID and the 'Competition Committee' belonging to RFEF (Domínguez, 2023). To this end, DIS examines the information it receives from each game and, if necessary, requests additional information from the "Organisational Control Unit" (UCO) of the National Police whose role has become decisive in recent years given its contribution to the identification of those committing unlawful discriminatory acts. UCO is found in all professional football stadiums where it registers all recordings made from cameras inside the stadium. It is overseen by the National Police and the club's private security manager. When a supporter is identified to be committing racist acts, DIS reports it to CEVXRID, who proposes the corresponding administrative sanction and, should it be deemed appropriate, also initiates proceedings through the legal system. In order to carry out their task, DIS coordinates with the respective club's Chief of Security (a position created by Law Ley 19/2007) and Match Director (a position introduced by LaLiga in 2015) (Domínguez, 2023). The Chief of Security is responsible for private security on matchday and plays a fundamental role in assessing the potential risks of a match, especially with regard to the presence and activities of radical fan groups. They also act as a liaison between the club and the National Police, which is responsible for public security. The police liaison role is also filled by a member of the Security Forces, usually the Security Coordinator. His/her role is to direct and organise the police presence whose primary task is to guarantee the safe running of the sporting event and coordinate the "Organisational Control Unit" (UCO). The Match Director, on the other hand, is responsible for the application of the measures established to tackle and report acts of intolerance and discrimination (Domínguez, 2023).

In the 2022/23 season, LaLiga unveiled new forms of reporting racist and other forms of intolerant and discriminatory behaviour, for example, via email, a Telegram channel and a webpage. The same season saw the placing of anti-racist posters in stadiums and stickers on supporters' seats conveying awareness-raising messages and a QR code. The QR code enabled racist acts observed in the stadium to be reported through a dedicated communication channel set up by LaLiga. The following year, LaLiga created the LALIGAVS, an online platform, to increase the visibility of those initiatives that clubs had developed to tackle racist, discriminatory or humiliating behaviour. Amongst the prevention, awareness-raising and practical initiatives housed on this platform, the campaign #1voiceVSRACISM stands out. This initiative was launched on the 'International Day for the Elimination of Racial Discrimination' and introduced a hymn against racism to be sung in stadiums. Another notable initiative pertains to the educational project *Futura Afición* (Fans of the Future), delivered by the LaLiga Foundation since the 2015/16 season. This project focuses on primary schools and grassroots levels at LaLiga clubs. Its aim is to promote fair play, integrity and respect. Since its inception, 819 schools have participated in the project, 160 organisations have been involved in extracurricular activities, and 58 projects were dedicated to vulnerable groups. So far, a total of 84,776 boys and girls took part. Equally noteworthy is a podcast series that provides chats and conversations with players, coaches and other professionals from the world of football who address issues pertaining to hate speech in sport. Another interesting initiative pertains to the 'Monitor for the Observation of Hate in Sport' (MOOD,

Monitor para la Observación del Odio en el Deporte), that was launched in 2023. MOOD was developed by LaLiga together with two private companies in order to track, monitor, record and analyse conversations on social media that contain racist language and contents. The results of the differentiated semantic analyses of the gathered data, organised by regions, matches, teams, players, fans and other metrics, are available to fans via LaLiga's social media channels. In the initial stages of this project, MOOD is primarily concerned with the issue of racism but intends to widen its fight later and include other forms of intolerant behaviour.

Final reflections

Despite a large number of policies, strategies, initiatives and projects of various kinds from different stakeholders to combat racism, xenophobia and intolerance in Spanish football, the problems have not been eradicated and continue to most noticeable in football grounds. The more extensive and detailed coverage of such events by the mass media may have led to a heightened awareness of the magnitude of these issues. Available empirical data also reveal a worrying increase in such behaviour, although that continues to be nothing more than the tip of the iceberg of unknown dimensions. Nonetheless, it appears that the hidden base of this iceberg has widened over recent years due to socio-demographic, economic and political changes, alongside the emergence of increasingly popular, far-right organisations on Spain's political landscape.

In 2014, Esteban Ibarra published a compendium of legal documents and international recommendations to tackle racism and xenophobia in football. He suggested that since the passing of Law 19/2007, Spain had progressed greatly in the regulatory field and in the context of social awareness. However, he also argued that deficiencies could still be detected in terms of compliance with measures pertaining to the prevention, monitoring, control and punishment of racist and xenophobic behaviours. Examples of this are the expulsion of the perpetrators of racist and violent incidents from stadiums; the inadequate monitoring of fan clubs and updating of their registers and written activity logs by the local football clubs; rigorous imposition of sanctions outlined by the relevant legislation (including the closing of stadiums); and the use of legal channels to deal with any behaviours that could be considered punishable under the Penal Code (MCI, 2014).

Ten years later, the situation is very different, but racist and xenophobic incidents remain frequent. Clubs have certainly become more aware of the severity of the issue but appear to be slow and hesitant when it comes to implement decisive countermeasures. In the past, clubs have shown to be very capable of putting the appropriate measures in place to impede the frequent throwing of cushions or bottles from the stands onto the pitch in order to avoid the sanctions they feared. This demonstrates that imposing draconian sanctions on the clubs as a 'motivational' means is an option that should be seriously considered in order to help eradicating behaviour that does not occur as blatantly or with as much impunity in other spheres of social life as it does in football stadiums.

The view that Spain is nowadays well equipped with legal tools for tackling racism in football stadiums continues to be fairly widespread. However, the question is whether these tools are applied appropriately, consistently and with enough rigour. A clamour of voices indicates that racist and xenophobic incidents cannot go unpunished and must be tackled head on. This is true not only because of the inherent nature of such acts but also because of the enormous social significance and mediated projection integral to football. Within its limited powers, LaLiga has shown to be particularly active and steadfast in the fight against racism and intolerance over recent years. Nonetheless, they have pushed for sanctioning powers to be made available to them in order to be able to act more effectively and impactful. At the present time, sanctions correspond to the RFEF through its "Disciplinary Code" and "Competition Committee" (Instituto Coordenadas, 2023; Fouto, 2023). Currently, LaLiga's ways of intervening are limited to detection and reporting. LaLiga recently requested a series of modifications to Law 19/2007 and the new Sports Law (Law 39/2022), pushing for the right to exercise disciplinary authority and apply measures such as the partial or full closure of sporting facilities, banning of access to supporters and imposing economic sanctions. This goes alongside the adoption of any provisional or precautionary measures deemed to be appropriate.

A key issue in this debate pertains to the cancelling of matches. Law 19/2007 allows for the provisional suspension of games as a measure for restoring legality. The individual bestowed with the power to make such decisions, the referee, can also order the complete or partial evacuation of the stands in which incidents have taken place and, subsequently, restart the game or even terminate the game in extremely serious cases following consultation with the local Security Coordinator. This being said, the existing protocol dictates that referees exhaust all potential avenues before terminating a match. Suspensions of games do not tend to happen and this gives rise to truly double-edged situations. Following a temporary suspension, matches often end up being resumed despite players being inclined to leave the pitch in solidarity with their vilified teammate or as a matter of protest. In accordance with regulations, not returning would lead to the loss of three points which will be allocated to the opposing team. On this basis, preserving the spectacle prevails over solidarity with the victim. In this way, racist abuse not only goes unpunished but, beyond that, the victim may actually be penalised. The lesson learned from this is very clear: racism is an effective weapon for weakening the opponent and does not always have negative consequences for the perpetrator. This represents, therefore, one of the weaknesses of the fight against racism and xenophobia in Spanish football.

Another obstacle in the fight against racism and xenophobia in Spanish football pertains to challenges of classifying these types of acts as hate crimes. The legal system "has been used very cautiously from the outset by the courts" despite the Constitutional Court confirming that "racist and xenophobic discourse has no constitutional support" (Ríos, 2016, p. 51). The reason behind this is clearly related to the need for reputable evidence proving "direct incitement to commit a criminal act that is discriminatory or violent in nature" (Ríos, 2014, p. 18). The aforementioned has, therefore, led to a restrictive interpretation of incitement to hatred (Ríos, 2014). In this regard, there have been occasions on which the Prosecutor's Office has archived complaints of this nature due to the challenge of attributing acts to a single specific person or identifying the sources of such acts. It is safe to assume, however, that this obstacle will slowly but surely be overcome, considering that an increased number of cameras installed in stadiums are nowadays able to capture all seats. On other occasions, racist insults have been deemed to not cross the blurred line into a criminal offense, despite their despicable, offensive and deplorable nature. Specifically, they were not considered to constitute a crime or unlawful act because they took place in the context of an intense and emotionally charged football rivalry, were fleeting, not repetitive and therefore not characterised by the public prosecutors as hate crimes (Sánchez and Herrera, 2023).

Thus, the fight against racism and xenophobia in Spanish football is in need of a stricter application of existing laws. Having said that, it will not be enough to eradicate the issue. It will also be necessary for Spanish society, as a whole, to assume responsibility and stop denying its existence and underestimate or play down the harm it causes to its victims. Expressions of racism and xenophobia that can be tackled with the help of legal tools are those that are manifested most visibly inside stadiums. However, these are no more than the tip of the iceberg, which, at its base, comprises a broad repertoire of more subtle expressions that are rooted in cultural and structural conditions and must also be eliminated.

References

Arango, J. (2015) "España. Una experiencia inmigratoria singular" [Spain. A unique immigration experience], in Torres, C. (Ed.), *España 2015. Situación social*, Madrid: CIS.

Caballero, J.R. (2018) "Los Grupos Urbanos Violentos y los delitos de odio" [Violent Urban Groups and Hate Crimes], Generalitat de Cataluña. *Centre d'Estudis Jurídics i Formació Especialitzada*. Available: <https://repositori.justicia.gencat.cat/handle/20.500.14226/321> [accessed on 15th July 2024].

Domínguez, D. (2023) "La batalla de LaLiga contra el racismo. Así actúa el protocolo de denuncias" [LaLiga's battle against racism. This is how the complaints protocol works], *El País*, 25th May. Available: <https://elpais.com/deportes/eslaliga/2023-05-25/la-batalla-de-laliga-contra-el-racismo-asi-actua-el-protocolo-de-denuncias.html> [accessed on 9th July 2024].

Durán, J. (2006) "Racismo y deporte" [Racism and sport], *Estudios sobre Ciencias del Deporte*, 47, pp. 138–159.

Durán, J. and Jiménez, P. J. (2006) "Fútbol y racismo: un problema científico y social" [Football and racism: a scientific and social problem], *Revista Internacional de Ciencias del Deporte*, 2(3), pp. 68–94.

Durán, J. and Pardo, R. (2008) "Racismo en el fútbol español (1ª y 2ª división). Temporadas 2004/05 y 2005/06" [Racism in Spanish football (1st and 2nd division). Seasons 2004/05 and 2005/06], *Revista Internacional de Ciencias del Deporte*, 12(4), pp. 85–100.

Fouto, I. (2023) "LaLiga no tiene competencias para sancionar actos racistas" [LaLiga does not have the power to sanction racist acts], *Iusport.com*, 7th January. Available: <https://iusport.com/art/121688/laliga-no-tiene-competencia-para-sancionar-actos-racistas> [accessed on 12th November 2024].

Girard, M. (2006) "No despertéis a la serpiente dormida en la hierba" [Don't wake the sleeping snake in the grass], *El País*, 24th June, p. 83.

Ibarra, E. (2006) "Cantera en las gradas ultras" [Youth squads in the ultras stands], *El País*, 12th March, p. 17.

Instituto Coordenadas (2023) *El Instituto Coordenadas destaca las actuaciones de LaLiga para perseguir los actos de racismo que se producen en el fútbol español* [The Coordenadas Institute highlights LaLiga's actions to prosecute acts of racism in Spanish football]. Available: <https://www.institutocoordenadascom/es/analisis/instituto-coordenadas-destaca-actuaciones-laliga-perseguir-actos-racismo-se-producen-en-futbol-espanol_20214_102.html> [accessed on 15th November 2024].

Llopis-Goig, R. (2009) "Racism and xenophobia in Spanish Football: facts, reactions and policies", *Physical Culture and Sport: Studies and Research*, XLVII, pp. 35–43.

Llopis-Goig, R. (2013) "Racism, xenophobia and intolerance in Spanish football: evolution and responses from the government and the civil society", *Soccer and Society*, 14(2), pp. 262–276.

Martín, A., Buitrago, A. and Beltrán, A.M. (2022) "Fútbol, racismo y Twitter. Disección del discurso del odio en el caso Diakhaby" [Football, racism and Twitter. Dissecting hate speech in the Diakhaby case], *Razón y Palabra*, 26(113), pp. 123–139.

MCI (2014) *Contra el Racismo y la Intolerancia en el fútbol. Recomendaciones internacionales y legislación* [Against Racism and Intolerance in Football. International recommendations and legislation], Madrid: Movimiento contra la Intolerancia.

MCI (2023a) *Informe Raxen. Especial 2023. Racismo, Xenofobia, Antisemitismo, Islamofobia, Neofascismo, Totalitarismo y otras manifestaciones de Intolerancia a través de los hechos* [Raxen report. Special Edition 2023. Racism, xenophobia, anti-semitism, Islamophobia, neo-fascism, totalitarianism and other manifestations of intolerance through facts], Madrid: Movimiento contra la Intolerancia.

MCI (2023b) *Stop a la violencia, el racismo, la xenofobia y la intolerancia en el deporte* [Stop violence, racism, xenophobia and intolerance in sport], Madrid: Cuadernos de Análisis, 81, Movimiento contra la Intolerancia.

Ríos, J.M. (2014) "Incitación al odio, derecho penal y deporte" [Hate speech, criminal law and sport], *Revista Electrónica de Ciencia Penal y Criminología*, 16(15), pp. 1–27.

Ríos, J.M. (2016) "Las sombras del deporte. De la violencia exógena a la incitación al odio" [The shadows of sport. From exogenous violence to incitement of hatred], *Revista Inclusiones*, 3(2), pp. 28–57.

Rodríguez-Montserrat, M. (2015) "La eficacia normativa de la Ley 19/2007, de 11 de julio, contra la Violencia, el Racismo, la Xenofobia y la intolerancia en el deporte" [The regulatory effectiveness of Law 19/2007, of 11 July, against Violence, Racism, Xenophobia and intolerance in sport], *Fair Play. Revista de Filosofía, Ética y Derecho del Deporte*, 3(2), pp. 47–65.

Rodríguez-Moya, S. (2012) *Tarjeta negra al racismo* [Black card to racism], Madrid: Editorial Fragua.
Rodríguez-Moya, S. (2015) *Mordisco al racismo* [A bite at racism], Almería: Círculo Rojo.
Sánchez, G. and Herrera, E. (2023) "Los obstáculos para frenar el racismo en el fútbol. De los límites de la vía penal a la falta de protocolos claros" [Obstacles to stopping racism in football. From the limits of criminal proceedings to the lack of clear protocols], *eldiario.es*, 23rd May. Available: <https://www.eldiario.es/desalambre/obstaculos-frenar-racismo-futbol-espanol-limites-via-penal-falta-protocolos-claros_1_10227950.html> [accessed on 3rd July 2024].
Soriano, R.M., Botton, L., Burgés, A. and Granda, L. (2023) *Racismo y xenofobia en las redes sociales digitales en España. Caso Vinicius y caso Badalona* [Racism and xenophobia in digital social networks in Spain. The Vinicius case and the Badalona case], Murcia: Fundación Cepaim. Available: <https://www.cepaim.org/wp-content/uploads/2024/03/Estudio-de-casos-Racismo-y-Xenofobia-EMCIE-2023.pdf> [accessed on 19th July 2024].
SOS Racismo (1996) *Informe Anual sobre el Racismo en el Estado español 1995* [Annual Report on Racism in the Spanish State 1995], Donostia: Tercera Prensa-Hirugarren Prentsa S. L.
SOS Racismo (2005) *Informe Anual sobre el Racismo en el Estado español 2005* [Annual Report on Racism in the Spanish State 2005], Barcelona: Icaria Editorial.
Villar, E., Sánchez, M.A. and Pulido, J. (2024) "El tratamiento del racismo en la prensa deportiva online española. El caso de Vinicius" [The treatment of racism in the Spanish online sports press. The case of Vinicius], *Icono 14. Revista Científica de Comunicación y Tecnologías Emergentes*, 22(2), pp. 1–26.
Viñas, C. (2006) *Toleràncía zero. La violència en el futbol* [Zero tolerance. Violence in football], Barcelona: Angle Editorial.
Viñas, C. (2024) "El racismo en el fútbol español. Una aproximación histórica" [Racism in Spanish football. A historical approach], *Panorama Social*, 40, pp. 67–80.
Viñas, C. and Spaaij, R. (2006) "Medidas y políticas de intervención acerca del racismo y la xenofobia en el fútbol español" [Intervention measures for and policies on racism and xenophobia in Spanish football], *Sistema. Revista de Ciencias Sociales*, 192, pp. 51–76.
Wieviorka, M. (1995) *The arena of racism*, London: Sage.

Chapter 12

Sweden

Swedish society and football at odds with each other – So open, yet so closed

Katarzyna Herd

Immigration and Sweden's changing political landscape

This chapter deals with racism, xenophobia and antisemitism in the world of Swedish football. It is a multi-layered and complex issue shaped by the socio-economic, demographic, cultural and political realities that surround football. Sweden has a history of priding itself on its "open-arms policies" when it comes to migration, welcoming refugees when others closed their borders, for example, in 2015 when more than 160,000 people sought refuge (Migrationsverket, 2023; SCB, 2023). Swedish football, like in other countries, reflects the host society and its culture. By 2023, the number of registered refugees had dropped down to 12,644. Although the numbers of regular immigrants plummeted, Swedish society today represents a multicultural mix of nationalities, ethnicities and religions. However, different kinds of more conservative political discourses have emerged. They are also visible in football. Mike Cole wrote in 1996:

> There is a dialectical relationship between the way we treat people and how we refer to them – a non-positive nomenclature reinforces non-positive thoughts and actions and vice versa. This is the case whether the issues under consideration are social class, gender, disability and special needs, sexuality or, as in our case here, 'race'.
>
> (p. 11)

This dialectic applies well to the intrinsic dichotomies of football, where "us versus them" is the precondition of a competitive game. It produces emotional engagement of the fans and can include racist and/or xenophobic outbursts. In this chapter, after offering some background information, I describe and analyse various forms of discrimination in football that reveal cracks in the polished image of Sweden.

In the recent general elections, the right-wing Swedish Democrat party (SD) came second with 20.54% (Valmyndigheten, 2022). That result came to some as a shock, but in a way, it only confirmed the prominence of some

DOI: 10.4324/9781003495970-12
This chapter has been made available under a CC-BY-NC-SA 4.0 license.

discourses that were long present in Swedish society. A governmental report called *The blue and yellow glasshouse* from 2005 (p. 44) states that

> Sweden's economic boom after the war was complemented by a self-image as a moral superpower. Sweden helped the "third world" and was one of the most vocal critics of apartheid. At the same time, it was implied that such problems did not exist in Sweden.
>
> (SOU 2005:56)

What followed was a denial of problems based on ethnic discrimination such as racism, as the hegemonic narrative continued to perceive and present Sweden as a diverse, fair and righteous country. The aforementioned investigation was ordered to research structural discrimination. When football is taken into consideration, similar mechanisms can be observed. This seemingly open and inclusive space also hosts structural discrimination and is marked by a distinct blindness towards cultural forms of racism. As observed globally, football tends to adapt to the spatial-temporal and societal frames that it occupies. As a result, the metaphor of the mirror image, or reflection, is often used as it is an attractive way to talk about football's relationship with society as whole. The notion of the mirror image was also considered in a UNESCO report about discrimination in football:

> As tempting as the mirror metaphor may be, it is none the less misleading. Football is not a mirror that reflects society as it is. Of course, as an extremely popular and widespread form of mass culture, capable of transcending generations, social classes, ethnic groups and gender in its appeal, it is obviously affected by overarching trends and larger issues that dominate the society in which it is played, watched and talked about by millions. Football is not a mirror of society, but more of a projection screen for images of what individuals and groups think society should be like, for diffuse yearnings and aspirations that are expressed in an emotional manner.
>
> (Ranc and Sonntag, 2015, p. 15)

When asked about problems in Swedish football in 2012 as part of a wider research project about the cultural meaning of football, one person, Alex, who was working for a club, said in comparison to the rest of Europe, Sweden had no problems (21 January 2012). This sentiment has been strong and expressed frequently during my research into Swedish clubs. Certainly, over the years my interviewees listed different issues and areas of concern, for example, police brutality, flares and smoke bombs, acts of hooliganism, or the dreaded artificial turf, one of the biggest headaches in Swedish football (Herd, 2023). Racism, xenophobia, antisemitism or Islamophobia were not mentioned often in interviews, unless specifically brought up by the researcher. Because of the narratives of exceptionalism (Ehn, Frykman and Löfgren, 1993), Sweden has been regarded by scholars as a prime example of a "colour blind" country (Lindberg, 2023, p. 183; Hübinette, 2023). Tobias Hübinette, a researcher in intercultural studies, gives examples of, among others, academic publications that when translated to Swedish lost terms like 'race' as it was considered "negatively charged for Swedish readers" (Hübinette, 2023, p. 15). This can be related to the existence of the National Institute of Racial Biology that operated in the 1920s and 1930s. It was heavily condemned later and marks a shameful page in the Swedish history (Broberg, 1995). Psychiatric institutions were also used as a form of "cleaning" the society from those with perceived problems that would harm the majority (Jönsson and Svensson, 2005). The practice called "race hygiene", embedded in the eugenic movement, and its moral repercussions have been analysed thoroughly (Broberg and Tydén, 1991). Avoiding 'race' discussions can be thus seen as distancing practices from these phenomena.

In this chapter, I focus upon football fans, Swedish as well as ethnic clubs and players. After considering the emergence and social role of ethnic clubs in Swedish society and throwing some light on the related debates about inclusion and exclusion, cultural identity and ethnic differences, I draw on selected examples to show how the various forms of discrimination in Swedish football look like and how they are addressed. For this chapter, eight interviews were conducted with representatives of football clubs and local football associations. They spoke in their official capacity as people working for clubs and discussed various problems and those measures taken to counteract them. Additionally, interviews with football fans and officials, that were conducted earlier, will also be drawn upon as some of them touched on the issues relevant to this chapter. Furthermore, official reports, surveys and newspaper reports were incorporated to provide more varied material. This is then a mix of material typical for an ethnographic approach, where a bricolage of sources is brought to develop a better understanding of the field under investigation (Davies, 2008; Ehn and Löfgren, 2001). The discourse analysis of secondary data allows for providing a broader and more nuanced picture of the existing problems and solutions.

Integration through sport and the contested role of ethnic clubs

Until the end of its amateur phase in 1967, Swedish football could be described as "ethnically homogenous" (Andersson, 2009, p. 400). Yet, immigrant clubs had started to emerge much earlier and were met with a mixed reception. As Torbjörn Andersson pointed out, Jewish clubs that were formed then, like the still-existing IK Makkabi in Stockholm dating from 1933, were not allowed to participate in the official football system because they were for foreigners (2009, p. 400). The perception was similar towards other "immigrant clubs" formed after 1945. They were established due to different migration motives, ranging from labour migrants to political refugees. Italians, Hungarians, Spaniards, Austrians, Greeks and groups from the former Yugoslavia and the Middle East founded their own football clubs in different parts of the country from the 1940s onwards (Andersson, 2009, pp. 400–401). Thus, Sweden has nowadays a plethora of clubs with explicit non-Swedish ethnic and/or national backgrounds. Andersson also reports suspicious attitudes towards these "foreign" clubs that appeared in the media over the decades, as they were often exotified and described as "other". That usually implied non-conformity with Swedish qualities and being rowdy, hot-tempered and more impulsive than the more timid and obedient Swedish population (Andersson, 2009, p. 402). Particularly in the 1960s and 1970s, these teams were described in the press as being different in character than traditional Swedish clubs, indirectly suggesting that they were not rational or logical but rather too emotional and very aggressive. These publications influenced negative attitudes among the public. This characterisation has become more nuanced, and some of the "immigrant clubs" ascended to the highest tier in the Swedish football system, gaining support and attracting fans, namely Syrianska FC, Assyriska FF and Dalkurd FF. Syrians and Assyrians are groups of Christians from the Middle East, escaping prosecutions and repressions from 1960s onwards. Both groups are estimated at about 150,000 people in Sweden (Lundgren, 2017). The first of around 100,000 Kurds arrived in Sweden in the 1960s (Alakom, 2007). Once climbing up the football ladder, these clubs would often become more "Swedish" stressing their open character. Right now, in the Stockholm region, administrated by the Stockholm Football Association (Stockholms Fotbollförbund, 2004), there are 362 football clubs listed, with a vast number of diaspora clubs, representing groups from Afghanistan (Afghanska FF), Italy (AC Azzurri), Argentina (Argentinska Stockholm FF), Croatia (FC Croatia Stockholm), Iran (Parsian IF), Serbia (Srbija FF) and the Middle East (Syrianska FC and Assyriska BK). Some of them are based on the members' ethnicities, others on their nationalities. There are also clubs established by fans of already existing foreign clubs. Carl, one of the interviewed persons, said, "The Italian immigrants that were fans of Juventus established a club called Juventus in Västerås", a town in central Sweden (16 September 2024).

The attitudes towards these clubs are mixed. Sara, reflecting on the role of Syrianska FC, said, "Well spontaneously thinking, it is positive, you can create a space for yourself, and it is not just ethnic Swedish, you can feel comfortable and heard" (9 February 2024). Another interviewee, Ben, was less enthusiastic: "I do understand them, but for example, Assyriska, they are like small national teams, and that is not so inclusive. When you focus on specific ethnicities it is not so inclusive, it is counter-productive" (5 February 2024). This is an example of the paradoxical nature of football. These clubs represent specific ethnicities and/or nationalities and making them visible is a positive development. But they might also be viewed as excluding others and even perpetuating old conflicts and grievances that were transferred together with migrants. Although many of these ethnic clubs play in the lower leagues, occasionally they are the first stepping stones for future stars. Zlatan Ibrahimović, for example, spent the first years of his young playing career with Malmö BI (1989–1991) and FBK Balkan (1991–1995) before joining Malmö FF in 1995. FBK Balkan was founded in 1962 by Yugoslav immigrants.

Dalkurd FF is an interesting contemporary case. Its name is a compound. The first part refers to Dalarna, a region in Sweden, where the "founding father" of the Swedish modern state, Gustav Vasa, also known as Gösta Eriksson comes from. He led a rebellion against the Danish King Christian II and became the founder of the Vasa dynasty. His flight from Danish soldiers through the Dalarna region has a mythical status in Swedish historical discourses (Lagerqvist and Åberg, 1993). The "Kurd" element refers to the Kurdish diaspora that has a long and strong presence in Sweden (Duarte Dias, 2024; Alakom, 2005). The club was established in Borlänge, Dalarna, in 2004 and sky-rocketed to the second highest division, the *Superettan*, in 2018. Its achievements were widely praised, and the members' ethnic background was considered to be an enrichment, adding an extra dimension to an otherwise very Swedish club (Duarte Dias, 2020, 2024). This should be viewed in the context of Sweden having a long history of supporting different ethnic and/or national groups fighting for independence and accepting a variety of political refugees (Byström and Frohnert, 2017). However, the Dalkurd club moved first to Gävle, where it played for two years, and then to Uppsala, where it has been based since 2020 (Duarte Dias, 2020). This created friction with the teams already existing in these cities, Gefle IF and IK Sirius, respectively, and prompted questions about the local identity and footing of Dalkurd.

Swedish football has been praised for its local character and traditions. Many fans and officials stress those as key features (Herd, 2018). The idea of moving a club has been controversial and is extremely rare. One of my interviewees, Ben, who works for a Stockholm-based club, was very critical of the very existence of clubs such as Dalkurd. In his opinion, it was not necessary to establish "ethnic" clubs as the local patriotism should be the most important factor. He questioned the identity of the club and referred to their relocation. As he put it, "They are the Kurds from Dalarna, and now they play in Uppsala. Like what is the 'Dal' and what is the 'Kurd' bit there actually?" (5 February 2024). Tiago Duarte Dias' analysis of Dalkurd FF suggests that the Kurdish identity was used intentionally to establish rivalries. That, in turn, would help them to position themselves as a Swedish team. Duarte Dias shows that having enemies or rivalries would prove that Dalkurd FF was a worthy opponent, sitting firmly in the Swedish football system. This becomes additionally complicated when other "ethnic" clubs are taken into consideration. As Duarte Dias explains, some fans wanted to downplay animosities between Dalkurd and, for instance Syrianska FC. Instead, rivalries with traditional Swedish clubs like IK Sirius were considered desirable (Duarte Dias, 2024).

Another example of an ethnic club is the aforementioned IK Makkabi in Stockholm, one of the three Jewish sport clubs in Sweden. IK Makkabi is the biggest. It goes back to the pre-World War II tradition of Jewish Makkabi clubs in major European cities, such as Vienna (Austria) or Helsinki (Finland). Sam, an official representing Makkabi, mentioned that sometimes their players are advised to hide their religious identity for protection: "We tell them not to say out loud that they are Jewish, for example, when they play in different clubs in Stockholm. That can spark trouble. You never know" (2 February 2024). One of the specific problems surrounding Jewish clubs is that many of the other ethnic clubs in Sweden have roots in the Middle East and sometimes regard Makkabi as an Israeli team, which, of course, they are not. Sam also mentioned in the interview that incidents affect primarily the male team but not the women's. He stated that the club could not face just any opponent without contemplating their stance on Israel. Every season, there is a discussion of the composition of the lower leagues and which teams IK Makkabi would prefer to avoid (2 February 2024). The interview with Sam happened after the Hamas attack on 7 October 2023 and the subsequent armed conflict in the region. He appreciated that one of the Iranian clubs had contacted them and offered a friendly match to make a symbolic and public statement against marginalisation and prejudice.

This mix of diasporas and ethnicities is a reminder that old conflicts are difficult to eradicate, and some of the prejudice and judgement can cement a group identity in a struggle against "the other". Carl, representing the district's Football Association, commented on the diaspora clubs:

> I worked in one district in another city, and there were five of these diaspora clubs in one geographic area, and we thought they could cooperate to make a stronger football scene, but they refused. . . . On one hand it is good, there is a stronger feeling of belonging, sharing the roots, and people can be themselves . . . but on the other hand it can alienate, and it contrasts with the traditional Swedish clubs that represent your area, your district. It is complicated.
>
> (16 September 2024)

When asked about antisemitism, Ben, one of the interviewed officials, commented that they do not focus on this specific type of problem, but rather work on issues such as employment, physical health, and inequalities when it comes to access to physical activities (5 February 2024). Another official, Sara, expressed similar sentiments when asked about the issue of antisemitism:

> We discuss religious freedom, but there is not much talk about Judaism. Though we have many players with Muslim heritage, and it is not a problem at all. You can have traditional clothes and be open about it.
>
> (9 February 2024)

Certainly, Sweden never had a substantial Jewish population, but the Hamas attack on 7 October 2023, and the following war triggered not only pro-Palestinian marches but also a flood of antisemitic sentiments. Even a political party who prides itself on its work against racism, *Vänsterpartiet* (The Left Party), was confronted with members sharing hateful conspiracy theories about Judaism (Hamdan and Ivarsson, 2024). Some commented that the relatively new electoral base of the party, with roots in the Middle East, can have antisemitic components (Wennblad, 2024). Sam, from IK Makkabi, mentioned that one person who had made antisemitic online comments also used a logo that stated "Fight racism" as a profile picture. This paradoxical behaviour hints at conflicts and grievances that go far beyond the football world. Sam thought that the football officials were not doing enough, even though, in his opinion, it was not football's task to decrease antisemitism, as it just signals developments in a society (2 February 2024). Still, the issues presented here confirm and exemplify the findings already published in the 2004 government report. There continues to be an enduring denial that these kinds of problems, for example, antisemitism, exist.

Swedish clubs and football fans

There is a general consensus that Swedish football has come a long way since the 1990s, when fans would openly chant racist insults on the stands (Carlsson, 2016). Many of my interviewees pointed to that period as the worst in terms of disorderly crowd behaviour. During the 1990s, Swedish football turned fully professional, foreign players enriched the domestic football scene, and ethnic diversity started to be more visible on football pitches. Just like in other European leagues the influx of, for example, African players, triggered monkey noises, the throwing of bananas, explicit racist slurs and provocative, discriminatory banners in stadiums. But some fans and supporter organisations were quick to react and started to tackle the issue. Their work is widely considered to be a success. One of the interviewees, Daniel, remembered a Malmö FF's fan initiative: "You should remember why MFF support even started: in late 80s early 90s we had problems with racism and the right wing. Then MFF support managed to clean it up, which was brilliant" (5 April 2013). Another big club from Stockholm, AIK, was aware of the racism problems in the past. David, working for AIK, also pointed towards the fans playing a crucial role in combatting the problem:

> [W]hen the club started to sign players with foreign background and so the supporters themselves put their foot down and were like we cannot have racism here and now . . . we don't see that much racism these days in the stadium. It was almost as if it was organized in the beginning of 1990s. But now it is gone, thankfully. And I think it has a lot to do with what our

club has done, and it has had effect on the stands as well. I think there is an article written in *Aftonbladet* [Swedish evening newspaper] about AIKs stands and that AIK has the most successful integration project in Sweden. Because people come here with dramatically different backgrounds, so it is a real mix of people, poor and rich, people who are completely Swedish and not at all, and people with all possible political views. And they can share the same stand and be the same in some 90 minutes plus.

(5 March 2015)

This sentiment is common. However, some of the behaviour of fans is ambiguous. One of the best-known controversies is linked to another Stockholm club, Djurgårdens IF, which translates to animal park. The club was originally established on former royal hunting grounds. The nickname used sometimes by Djurgården fans is *Aporna*, the monkeys. This iconography was used by Djurgården supporters when they displayed a huge banner during a derby match against AIK in 2023. A massive King Kong–like figure was presented on the stands and generated admiration across the football world (e.g. Reddit, 2023). However, such a depiction as well as monkey noises and the throwing of bananas, the fans argue, is not racist, just an insult directed at the other club. Furthermore, jokes and chants spiked with 'racial' content directed at specific clubs have also been observed. Again, fans are aware of the grey zone between being racist and using banter in order to insult their opponents to the best of their abilities. This phenomenon can best be explained by a concept of reflexive anti-reflexivity developed by the sociologist Keith Khan-Harris, which can be succinctly summarised as "knowing better but deciding not to know" (2006, p. 145). In other words, there is an awareness of how certain behaviour is likely to be seen, but the actors decide to ignore that knowledge. Jonathan, a former hooligan, claimed that racism and the use of racist chants is often a by-product of the bonding process within a fan group and a means of establishing clear boundaries between us and them:

I don't think it is about racism; it is about being in a group, connecting to something. And after a while you start to accept what they say, even if you didn't from the beginning. And if it leads to fighting . . . some people learn to like it. Most violent football supporters are not really violent; some . . . most grow up and grow out of it.

(21 March 2013)

Although about 20 years old, similar reflections and insights can be found in one of the best-known hooligan autobiographies in Sweden. Johan Höglund, the author, claims that groups of supporters would fight gangs of immigrant youth not because of their migrant background but because they were simply interested in fighting (2005). As sociologist Aage Radmann indicates, making sense of, and acquiring a sort of, social and cultural capital and street credibility through violence is a common trait in hooligan biographies (2015). Here, again, the racist element is downplayed in favour of a different explanation. Höglund suggested that a sense of belonging, finding a place in a group and fitting in, which sometimes would require fighting, were more important factors for the group's cohesion than discriminatory attitudes.

It seems that such (hooligan) behaviour is now part of a distant past but in 2024 a scandal shook the Swedish football world when an online conversation involving hooligans and a well-known football player were revealed to the public as the chats had a "strong antisemitic content" (Stenquist and Wagner, 2024). The player himself did not post anything antisemitic and after the initial investigation all allegations against him remained unsubstantiated. However, these kinds of chats show that racism and antisemitism continue to be lingering, although nowadays well hidden, for example, in encrypted messaging apps.

In 2022, a student project focused on the experiences of coaches and revealed some serious problems. According to the coaches, racist incidents still happen quite openly. For example, young players are confronted with racist jargon from parents, referees or other coaches, and discriminatory comments are very pronounced at the junior levels of football (Johnson, 2022). It does not come as a surprise that even though there are plenty of meaningful declarations and well-intended intentions, 'racial' abuse continues to occur in various football environments. Although much has been done and the worst manifestations of racist behaviour have disappeared, some forms of discrimination still exist. This paradox or contradiction is not unique to Sweden. The multi-layered world of football is expected to be a part of, and contribute to, various integration and informal educational processes. Yet, at the same time, the realm of football provides a fertile ground for breeding and displaying various forms of discriminatory behaviours, in particular manifestations of racism (Ranc and Sonntag, 2015, pp. 16–17).

As stated by several authors, racism in Sweden often has cultural connotation and is part of the institutional fabrics but not exclusively (Hübinette, Hörnfeldt, Farahani et al., 2012; Scott, 2015; Lindberg, 2023). There is a fundamental understanding that systemic racism exists within the official structures. Comparative examinations of leadership positions and board memberships in Swedish football were done in 2015 and 2024. The results from 2015 were rather bleak, as men born in Sweden dominated the official structures and held most of the powerful positions. When comparing to 2024, the number of women had slightly increased, though not many were holding leadership positions. The lack of ethnic diversity continued to be very much the same. One news channel succinctly summarised the report:

> The skewed distribution is even more noticeable when national origin is considered. Among the 723 entries, there are more (18 people) with the

first name Anders than those who were born outside Scandinavia, which is 17 (the same number of people named Peter who sit on boards in Swedish elite football). Board representatives who were born outside of Scandinavia make up just over two percent of the total number of decision makers, and there is only one person who is a chairman [sic] in Swedish elite football, that is Peyman Rezapour in Bollstanäs in the elite topflight. One out of 93 is just over a percent. It is a number that is also not in good agreement with society in general. In 2023, 18 percent were born outside Scandinavia (including Finland and Iceland), according to Statistics Sweden. Within SvFF's [*Svenska Fotbollsförbundet*, the Swedish Football Association] various boards and committees, there are only two people who were born outside of Scandinavia.

(Sunberg, 2024)

Certainly, these results stand in sharp contrast to the diversity among players or supporters. Ben, one of my interviewees, commented on the issue as well:

You have everything in football, like in a society. For most of it, the management is Swedish and white. On the pitch, absolutely, there is diversity. And in different sports too, you don't have to have a norm-specific name.

(5 February 2024)

Those working with football are aware that the clubs can build bridges, bring people together, evoke emotions and create a sense of inclusion. However, feelings can run high and abuse can occur. One of my interviewees, Carl, who works for a regional Football Association when asked about racist incidents said, "Well, I heard the n-word from the stands, for example, to a player on the pitch. That person was expelled, but it became quite heated" (16 September 2024).

Commenting further on 'racial' abuse from the stands, Carl speculated that it comes from sudden frustration and a lack of knowledge and education. Respect, inclusion and understanding should, in his opinion, come from home, and addressing these issues through social, educational and cultural institutions might not work, if there are contradictory messages in the home environment. Swedes have a long and successful history of organising themselves in clubs and associations (*förening*). As a governmental report about integration from 2004 stated, "Folk movements and associational life play an important role in Swedish society" (Bengtsson, 2004, p. 3). The report further suggests that integration would work better, if migrants become more included and active in the association life, such as football clubs. Carl, who has been quoted earlier, subscribed to that view, saying that awareness of the association life and its importance would be beneficial for the integration process.

Players: subjects of a racialised gaze

Like other European leagues, Sweden has an extensive mix of nationalities and ethnicities on the football field, prompting critical discussions about local patriotism and belonging while also welcoming talents from all over the world in order to secure titles. Additionally, there is a notion that

> the game can act as a dual catalyst for integration: first, at the professional level, where the sport may serve as a model of successful multi-racialism/multi-culturalism for society as a whole, and second, at the amateur level, where the game can help promote social harmony by bringing together people from different races, ethnicities, and cultures.
>
> (Scott, 2015, p. 2)

One of my interviewees, Carl, mentioned that he witnessed young players in a team with players predominantly from Middle Eastern countries being exposed to Islamophobic slur during a match (16 September 2024). The experiences of players with a foreign background, particularly from African countries, were researched by Carl-Gustaf Scott (2015) and Emy Lindberg (2023). Scott focused on male footballers in Sweden and studied the nexus between immigration and integration. He raises an important point about open and covert racism:

> the reduction of overt displays of prejudice in the stands does not necessarily signify that racism as such has been eradicated from the sport. In fact, in some ways, this development may even be detrimental in that it has created a false sense of complacency that this situation has now been totally remedied.
>
> (Scott, 2015, p. 135)

Scott argues that 'race', culture and religion became more visible in abusive discourses (2015, pp. 135–136). Lindberg underpins her thesis with the concept of "hegemonic whiteness" that is prevalent in Swedish society (2023, pp. 183–184). Her study of Ghanaian footballers playing in Sweden showed that they had experienced both old and new forms of racism, that is traditional derogatory verbal comments, insults and chants from the stands but also more modern online hate. Lindberg concludes that "within the performance industry and economic business of football, Ghanaian, African, and black players are understood and objectified through a racialized gaze and discourse" (2023, p. 230).

The experience of a racialised gaze, objectification, resentment and discriminatory treatment is not limited to locally and/or nationally known players. Two of Sweden's most successful footballers, Zlatan Ibrahimović and Henrik Larsson, openly discussed racism they experienced in their life spans, especially during their childhood. In 2024, Larsson was interviewed by *The Guardian*, a high-quality British daily newspaper, where he stated that he is not really feeling Swedish, and that he felt accepted in the society once he proved himself on the pitch. In his own words, "When you're nothing, you don't matter. When you're something, you're part of this society. Then people forget where you're from, what your race is" (Butler, 2024). His views resonated in the Swedish press, with many newspapers commenting on Larsson's words. According to Carl, in the football world, Zlatan Ibrahimović's suggestion that foreigners need to work three times as hard as native citizens is quite widespread (16 September 2024).

Another internationally well-known Swedish player is Jimmy Durmaz, born to Assyrian parents. In 2018, the Swedish national team united behind Durmaz after he had been the target of racist online abuse subsequent to the 1–2 defeat to Germany in the World Cup finals. He was inundated with 'racial' slurs, as his foul let to a free kick for Germany who then scored the winning goal in extra time (Christenson, 2018). After the match Durmaz, and his family, received hateful messages, insults and threats (Sveriges Radio, 2018). Some commentators mentioned that Durmaz had not experienced such abuse after winning matches. This appears to be a common practice and part of the process of othering, which in this case involves identifying a guilty party and showing them that they are not belonging to the majority group. The ethnic background is often used as a marker for otherness and as means to vilify the other. My interviewee, Carl, was very aware of this mechanism, "There is this norm, and if you come from outside, and you make one mistake then you will know it. They must do more to prove themselves. It is also something the leadership should address in a club. Like how we see individual players and what we expect of them and why" (16 September 2024). The aforementioned case of Jimmy Durmaz also provoked a strong reaction of his teammates. After delivering a message against racism, the Swedish squad joined Durmaz and collectively shouted "F*** racism!" before returning to their training session.

Tackling discrimination in Swedish football

As the UNESCO report authored by David Ranc and Albrecht Sonntag (2015) suggested, recent decades saw a plethora of legislations and policies, on international and national levels, that are put into place to prevent discriminatory behaviour (p. 35). In the world of football, regional, national and international governing bodies have developed their own tools to fight discrimination. The Swedish Football Association (*Svenska Fotbollsförbundet*, SvFF) has worked continuously on these issues. In 2023, a strategic plan was developed focusing on sustainable development. It includes action points against racism and discrimination and is aligned with UEFA's objectives and the UN's 17 global goals for sustainable development (Waldheim, 2023), thus framing them as parts of a bigger social project. SvFF's overreaching goal is to clean football from any expressions of discrimination by 2030. In order to do so, SvFF lists several current initiatives to tackle racism:

1) *Reboot* is an initiative that helps people who are outside the labour market and wish to find to employment;
2) *A better way* aims to improve the conditions for playing football in socio-economically vulnerable areas;
3) *Everyone is different – different is good* is designed to support associations that work on projects that promote gender equality and inclusion;
4) *Street soccer* wishes to facilitate different ways of playing street football and generate measurable public health effects;
5) *Representative* refers to a scheme which enables an appointed representative to follow up serious incidents, for example, racist attacks (Waldheim, 2023, p. 22).

Even more important is the work done on district levels, by clubs and through local projects. A few club officials I interviewed pointed to initiatives in their clubs that were designed to foster integration and counteract racism. For instance, traditional and well-established clubs, like Malmö FF in southern Sweden and Hammarby IF in Stockholm, ran initiatives that focused on social integration through work and employment. It involved organising meetings between unemployed members of the local community, who have difficulties in the job market, with possible employers. Hammarby IF runs an initiative called *Samhällsmatch* (community match), which is responsible for several events and activities. For instance, they work on establishing trust between the police force and youths or having meetings to pair those "who are far away from the labour market" (Samhällsmatchen, 2024), which is a diplomatic way of saying that they do not meet the demands of the labour market. This involves persons with non-Swedish background and different ethnic roots. Steady employment is considered the key element of successful integration. Malmö FF operates a similar initiative called *Karriärakademin* (Career Academy) that offers contacts between individuals seeking jobs and the club's business partners (MFF Karriärakademin, 2024). Malmö FF has also cooperated with Malmö municipality in creating and facilitating "Primary School Football Against Racism", which is manifested in a football tournament for 12-year-olds with the theme "Give Racism the Red Card" (Malmö Stad, 2023). Furthermore, the club hosts an annual event under the same theme, which is widespread in the European football world and is meant to combat racism and other forms of discrimination in social and cultural environments, increase awareness on diversity, foster social and ethnic cohesion and reduce discriminatory practices.

The aforementioned examples derive from the big clubs in Sweden, but many, regardless of scale, try to be visible in their local communities through activities that foster integration and fight discrimination. Ben observed that "before, we were just a few with such initiatives, now there is many more" (5 February 2024). It shows a trend where the football clubs feel a need to be more active in, and engage with, their local community. To quote Ben again, "Nowadays you must do it. It is almost a demand. Many sponsors are vocal about it. Like cool if you win, but what can you do" (5 February 2024).

The push for assuming more social responsibility recognises the social power football has and its influential position in Swedish society, but it might also be connected to the shady past that still lingers in the collective memories. Many people I talked to suggested that it was not too long ago one would hear openly racist comments or chants in the football context in Sweden.

There is also a lot of proactive and preventive work being done at the school level as the aforementioned co-operation of Malmö FF with local schools has already demonstrated. Several of my interviewees, for example, Carl, stressed the importance of educational measures outside the world of football, as values and beliefs are shaped there and then brought into football.

Conclusion

This chapter has explored key questions about the relationship between football and immigration, integration, exclusion, racism and xenophobia against the context of contemporary Swedish society. Sweden is internationally well-known and highly regarded for its openness, economic stability, high quality of life, an extensive welfare system and a long history of immigration. However, the reality is more complex as, for example, the growth of far-right sentiments and attitudes, embodied by the rise of the Sweden Democrats (SD), has shown.

Several of my interviewees expressed a sense of relief that the behaviour of football crowds had considerably improved over the last two decades, and manifestations of racism and xenophobia are nowadays rare occurrences. Although they do not appear to be a major problem in football grounds, there is an increased amount of online abuse. As Lindberg pointed out (2023), 'racial' discrimination towards players happens increasingly online rather than in the stadiums. Swedish football clubs seem to have adopted the view that discrimination appearing in the context of the game is connected to broader social developments and often stems from inequalities and ignorance. In short, football is seen in Sweden as a tool to fight racism that derives from other social contexts rather than the cause of these issues.

In addition to cooperating with educational institutions, football clubs often focus their efforts on socio-economic inequalities and employment as key factors that may help tackle different social problems, including racism and discrimination. Football is generally understood to have a strong and influential presence in local communities, thus able to have a positive impact. Several of my interviewees, who work in the football industry, support this approach and argue that those factors outside the world of football need to be addressed as they are the likely causes for discrimination and exclusionary attitudes, and ultimately the reasons for racist outbreaks. As a result, various efforts are made outside the football sphere, with the game only serving as a mediator and the clubs as an organisational framework. Football clubs arrange job markets or career days by tapping into their extensive networks of, for example, sponsors, suppliers and business partners and hope to build connections with those who have difficulties finding steady employment. This strategy is strongly connected to the traditional role of associations in Swedish society that promotes grass-roots engagement. Following the logic of one of my interviewees, Carl, all these efforts help to create a stable and safe environment for, for example, young players and fans, and would in turn reduce discrimination and abuse. In Sweden, efforts to tackle racism are combined with exceptionalism – an idea that this country knows better and can teach others.

In the wake of the multiple efforts already undertaken or currently underway, it might feel that most of the work has already been done. However, the minimal amount of 'racial' abuse that happens in Swedish football grounds does not mean that the issue is under control. There is, for example, little doubt that the management of football, in particular the governing bodies, continue to lack diversity.

References

Alakom, R. (2007) *Kurderna. Fyrtio år i Sverige (1965–2005)* [The Kurds. Forty years in Sweden (1965–2005)], Stockholm: Serkland.

Andersson, T. (2009) "Immigrant teams in Sweden and the case of Assyriska FF", *Soccer & Society*, 10(3–4), pp. 398–417.

Bengtsson, B. (2004) "Föreningsliv, makt och integration – ett inledande perspektiv", in Westholm, A., Borevi, K. and Strömblad, P. (Eds.), *Föreningsliv, makt och integration. Rapport från Integrationspolitiska maktutredningens forskningsprogram* [Association life, power and integration. Report from the Integration Policy Inquiry's Research Program]. Regeringskansliet, Justitiedepartamentet. Ds 2004: 49. Available: <https://www.regeringen.se/contentassets/f37d5f12007049f19009dbad6a47f43c/foreningsliv-makt-och-integration-del-1/> [accessed on 29th August 2024].

Broberg, G. (1995) *Statlig rasforskning: en historik över Rasbiologiska institutet* [National racial research: a history of the Institute of Racial Biology], Lund: Ugglan Lund University.

Broberg, G. and Tydén, M. (1991) *Oönskade i folkhemmet. Rashygien och sterilisering I Sverige* [Unwanted in the people's home. Racial hygiene and sterilization in Sweden], Stockholm: Gidlunds Bokförlag.

Butler, M. (2024) "Henrik Larsson: 'I have 106 caps for Sweden but I see myself as foreign'", *The Guardian*, 3rd March. Available: <https://www.theguardian.com/football/2024/mar/03/henrik-larsson-i-have-106-caps-for-sweden-but-i-see-myself-as-foreign> [accessed on 5th May 2024].

Byström, M. and Frohnert, P. (2017) *Invandringens historia – från "folkhemmet" till dagens Sverige* [The history of immigration – from the "the people's home" to today's Sweden]. Kunskapsöversikt: 2017:5. Available: <file:///C:/Users/kult-kyh/Work%

20Folders/Downloads/delmi-kunskaps%C3%B6versikt-2017_5.pdf> [accessed on 13th September 2024].

Carlsson, C. (2016) "Omtvistat om rasism i svensk fotboll" [Controversial about racism in Swedish football]. *Centrum för Idrottsforskning* [Center for Sport Studies]. Available: <https://www.idrottsforskning.se/omtvistat-om-rasism-i-svensk-fotboll/> [accessed on 2nd June 2024].

Christenson, M. (2018) "Sweden squad rally behind midfielder Jimmy Durmaz after racial abuse online", *The Guardian*, 24th June. Available: <https://www.theguardian.com/football/2018/jun/24/sweden-jimmy-durmaz-racial-abuse-germany-free-kick> [accessed on 11th November 2024].

Cole, M. (1996) "'Race', racism and nomenclature: a conceptual analysis", in Merkel, U. and Tokarski, W. (Eds.), *Racism and xenophobia in European football*, Aachen: Meyer & Meyer Verlag.

Davies, C.A. (2008) *Reflexive ethnography. A guide to researching selves and others*, Oxon and New York: Routledge.

Duarte Dias, T. (2020) "Dalkurd FF: being an Uppsala club during a pandemic", *Cadernos de Campo* (São Paulo), 29, pp. 105–113.

Duarte Dias, T. (2024) "Inserting Kurdishness within Swedish football", *Soccer & Society*, 25(3), pp. 321–332.

Ehn, B., Frykman, J. and Löfgren, O. (1993) *Försvenskningen av Sverige: det nationellas förvandlingar* [The Swedization of Sweden: the transformation of the national], Stockholm: Natur & Kultur.

Ehn, B. and Löfgren, O. (2001) *Kulturanalyser* [Cultural Analyses], Malmö: Gleerups Utbildning.

Hamdan, I. and Ivarsson, D. (2024) "V-politiker sprider judehat och hyllar terrorister" [The Left Party politicians spread Jew hatred and praise terrorists], *Sydsvenskan*, 29th August. Available: <https://www.sydsvenskan.se/artikel/v-politiker-sprider-judehat-och-hyllar-terrorister/> [accessed on 11th September 2024].

Herd, K. (2018) *"We can make new history here". Rituals of producing history in Swedish football clubs*, Lund: Lund Studies in Arts and Cultural Sciences.

Herd, K. (2023) "Pitch fever: Swedish football and the politics of grass", in Alpan, B., Sonntag, A. and Herd, K. (Eds.), *The political football stadium: identity discourses and power struggles*, Springer Nature, pp. 151–170.

Höglund, J. (2005) *En av grabbarna: En berättelse inifrån brödraskapet Firman Boys* [One of the boys: a story from inside the Brotherhood of Firman Boys], Stockholm: MMG Books AB.

Hübinette, T. (2023) *Den svenska färgblindheten* [The Swedish colour blindness], Stockholm: Verbal förlag.

Hübinette, T., Hörnfeldt, H., Farahani F. and León Rosales, R. (2012) *Om ras och vithet i det samtida Sverige* [About race and whiteness in contemporary Sweden], Botkyrka: Mångkulturellt centrum.

Johnson, K.B. (2022) *Racism in Football Sweden: from the coaches' perspective. Msc in Sport Science: Sport in Society*, Malmö: Malmö University, Department of Sport Science.

Jönsson, L.-E. and Svensson, B. (2005) *I industrisamhällets slagskugga. Om problematiska kulturarv* [In the shadow of an industrial society. About problematic cultural heritage], Stockholm: Carlsson.

Khan-Harris, K. (2006) *Extreme metal: Music and culture on the edge*, Oxford: Berg.

Lagerqvist, L. and Åberg, N. (1993) *Gustav Eriksson (Vasa) i Dalarna 1520–1521: minnen, myter och monument* [Gustav Eriksson (Vasa) in Dalarna 1520–1521: memories, myths and monuments], Stockholm: Vincent.

Lindberg, E. (2023) *Dream machine. An ethnography of football migration between Ghana and Sweden*, Uppsala: Uppsala University.

Lundgren, S. (2017) *Assyrierna. Femtio år i Sverige* [The Assyrians. Fifty years in Sweden], Södertälje: Nineveh Press.

Malmö Stad: *Grudskolefotboll mot rasismer certifieras av LUCS* [Malmö City: Primary school football against racism is certified by LUCS]. (2023) Malmö city, 13th October. Available: <https://malmo.se/Aktuellt/Artiklar-Malmo-stad/2023-10-13-Grundskolefotboll-mot-rasismer-certifieras-av-LUCS.html> [accessed on 6th November 2024].

MFF Karriärakademin [MFF Career Academy]. Malmö FF. Available: <https://www.mff.se/karriarakademin/> [accessed on 24th September 2024].

Migrationsverket [The Swedish Migration Agency]. (2023) *Migrationsverket svarar: Vilka är det som kommer till Sverige – och varför?* [The Swedish Migration Agency answers: Who are coming to Sweden – and why?]. Available: <https://www.migrationsverket.se/OmMigrationsverket/Pressrum/Nyhetsarkiv/Nyhetsarkiv-2023/2023-10-20-Migrationsverket-svarar--Vilka-ar-det-som-kommer-till-Sverige---och-varfor.html> [accessed on 19th September 2024].

Radmann, A. (2015) "Hit and tell – Swedish hooligan narratives", *Sport in Society*, 18(2), pp. 202–218.

Ranc, D. and Sonntag, A. (2015) *Colour? What colour? Report on the fight against discrimination and racism in football*, UNESCO Publishing. Available: <file:///C:/Users/kult-kyh/Work%20Folders/Downloads/235721eng-1.pdf> [accessed on 11th May 2024].

Reddit. (2023) *Djurgården fans with a cool King Kong-inspired TIFO*. Available: <https://www.reddit.com/r/soccer/comments/16so0qm/djurg%C3%A5rden_fans_with_a_cool_king_konginspired_tifo/?rdt=56513> [accessed on 21st September 2024].

Samhällsmatchen [The Society Match]. "Rekryteringsträff" [The Recruitment Hit]. Available: <https://samhallsmatchen.se/projekt/rekryteringstraff/> [accessed on 28th September 2024].

Scott, C.-G. (2015) *African footballers in Sweden. Race, immigration, and integration in the age of globalization*, Basingstoke: Palgrave Macmillan.

SOU 2005:56 (2005) *Det blågula glashuset – strukturell diskriminering i Sverige. Betänkande av Utredningen om strukturell diskriminering på grund av etnisk eller religiös tillhörighet* [The blue and yellow glasshouse – structural discrimination in Sweden. Report of the Investigation into structural discrimination based on ethnic or religious affiliation]. Available: <https://www.regeringen.se/rattsliga-dokument/statens-offentliga-utredningar/2005/06/sou-200556/> [accessed on 5th September 2024].

Statistikmyndigheten SCB [The Statistical Authority]. (2023) *Asylsökande i Sverige* [Asylum Seekers in Sweden]. Available: <https://www.scb.se/hitta-statistik/sverige-i-siffror/manniskorna-i-sverige/asylsokande-i-sverige/> [accessed on 15th August 2024].

Stenquist, V. and Wagner, M. (2024) "Pontus Jansson tar avstånd från chattar med 'starkt antisemitiskt innehåll'" [Pontus Jansson distances himself from chats with "strong antisemitic content"]. *Aftonbladet*, 6th June. Available: <https://www.aftonbladet.se/sportbladet/a/EypdlP/pontus-jansson-tar-avstand-fran-chattar-med-starkt-antisemitiskt-innehall> [accessed on 15th August 2024].

Stockholms Fotbollförbund [Stockholm Football Association] (2004) "Våra föreningar" [Our clubs], Available: <https://www.stff.se/tavling/vara-foreningar/> [accessed on 4th September 2024].

Sunberg, A. (2024) "Svenska männen styr svenska fotbollen – väldigt få utrikesfödda" [Swedish men run Swedish football – very few foreign-born], *TV4*, 6th May. Available: <https://www.tv4.se/artikel/2vSyvGcYBOLBtF2JLEnpap/svenska-maennen-styr-svenska-fotbollen-vaeldigt-fa-utrikesfoedda> [accessed on 3rd September 2024].

Sveriges Radio [Swedish Radio]. (2018) *Sveriges spelare Jimmy Durmaz fick rasistiskt hat efter matchen* [Sweden's player Jimmy Durmaz received racist hate after the match]. Available: <https://sverigesradio.se/artikel/6983789> [accessed on 18th August 2024].

Valmyndigheten [The Electoral Authority]. (2022) *Valresultat* [Election Results]. Available: <https://www.val.se/valresultat/riksdag-region-och-kommun/2022/valresultat.html> [accessed on 24th May 2024].

Waldheim, C. (2023) "SvFFs hållbarhetsstrategi: Nationalsporten – för alla överallt" [SvFF's sustainability strategy: The national sport – for everyone everywhere]. *Svenska Fotbollsförbundet*. Available: <https://svff.svenskfotboll.se/4a8eb4/globalassets/svff/bilderblock/arkiv/2023/2310/svff_hallbarhetsstrategi_2023_10_13.pdf> [accessed on 16th November 2024].

Wennblad, P. (2024) "Vänsterpartiet har inte råd att tappa Israelhatarna" [The Left Party cannot afford to lose the Israel haters], *Svenska Dagbladet*, 4th September. Available: <https://www.svd.se/a/mP53E0/vansterpartiet-har-inte-rad-att-tappa-israelhatarna> [accessed on 11th September 2024].

Chapter 13

Europe (I)
Supranational political and policy responses to racism and discrimination in football

Christos Kassimeris

As various forms of discrimination, in particular racism, continue to blemish the game of football, the European Union (EU), Council of Europe (CoE), the Union of European Football Associations (UEFA), and the Football Against Racism in Europe (FARE) network have all become involved in combating racism in football, albeit not in a concerted effort. While all have repeatedly been issuing anti-racism resolutions, the two political entities have been mostly preoccupied with policy-making and legislative measures, UEFA has been keener on experimenting with disciplinary action, and FARE is more accustomed to campaigning. This chapter will, therefore, attempt an evaluation of their contribution in the fight against racism in European football.

All four organisations appear to be dedicated to tackling racism in European football (and society by extension) and have voiced their concerns through a series of declarations, resolutions and related statements. In a roadmap entitled "UEFA's position on Article 165 of the Lisbon Treaty", in Section 4, under the heading "Fostering cooperation with third countries and the competent international organisations," it states that "UEFA invites the European Commission, the Council of the EU and the Member states to strengthen and organise national initiatives to promote the fight against racism and violence in sport, and to work together systematically, with other international bodies, such as the Council of Europe, to secure these objectives" (UEFA, 2010, p. 12).

Despite UEFA's call for action and the very sensible suggestion to work together in a concerted effort, the four organisations examined here have all clearly failed to do so. Institutionally, it is, of course, UEFA that is primarily responsible for tackling racism in football. However, the phenomenon that is racial discrimination necessitates a more rigorous and holistic approach. It needs to include political entities for issuing relevant legislation, in collaboration with organisations such as FARE for collecting football-related information as well as awareness-raising campaigns.

DOI: 10.4324/9781003495970-13

This chapter has been made available under a CC-BY-NC-SA 4.0 license.

The Council of Europe (CoE)

"If you want to know what action the Committee of Ministers has taken on a particular topic" (CoE Council of Europe, 2014, Committee of Ministers), the webpage of the Council of Europe's decision-making body reads, one needs only choose from a number of different types of documents of adopted texts, such as decisions, declarations, treaties, and recommendations. The plethora of texts available reveals copious amounts of information on a range of several interrelated topics. However, examining the content alone of those texts is not merely as significant as determining the actual impact of any such action taken by the Committee of Ministers and the Council of Europe. Recommendations, for instance, are not binding to member states, even though the Committee of Ministers retains the right to ask governments "to inform it of the action taken by them with regard to such recommendations" as per Article 15.b of the Statute of the Council of Europe (Council of Europe, 2001, p. 3).

One such recommendation was adopted by the Committee of Ministers on 18 July 2001. It focuses on the prevention of racism, xenophobia and racial intolerance in sport. Yet racism in sport, particularly football, is a phenomenon that spans over several decades and has affected several European countries (Blecking, 1993; Jarvie, 1991; Maguire, 1988; Merkel and Tokarski, 1996; Williams, 1992). Therefore, it should have attracted the attention of the Council of Europe at a much earlier stage. The recommendation suggested that "the governments of member states adopt effective policies and measures aimed at preventing and combating racist, xenophobic, discriminatory and intolerant behaviour in all sports and in particular football" (CoE, 2001, p. 1). Besides providing a brief definition of the term "racism", the recommendation outlined the essence of shared responsibilities among all pertinent stakeholders, emphasised the significance of international cooperation, and underlined the importance of legislative measures and their proper implementation. Though acknowledging the fact that such legislation already existed in the majority of its member states, the resolution stated that "special legislative measures should be taken to deal with the issue of racism in sport", further proposing that "legal measures on combating racism in sport could be introduced into the existing body of legislation, for example, in the penal code. Such measures could also be adopted as part of a specific sports law, the law concerning the fight against violence in sport or the law relating to a particular sport, for example football" (CoE, 2001, p. 2). The example of football is, of course, intentional, since football is known to attract huge, and sometimes disorderly, crowds. Before the arrival of modern technologies such as CCTV, nowadays necessary for identifying perpetrators, football grounds offered a high degree of anonymity that allowed much room for collective anti-social behaviour of the thousands of football fans occupying the terraces.

The resolution also highlighted the need for national legislation to "proscribe as criminal offences all types of acts (flaunting of banners or symbols) or words (insults or chanting), committed or uttered at sporting events such as to incite violence or other discriminatory behaviour against racial, ethnic or religious groups or members of those groups on the grounds that they belong to such a group", and "provide for strict penalties for racist acts committed in sports arenas. In addition, other non-penal sanctions such as exclusion or banning from stadiums should be provided for". To increase the effectiveness of all relevant legislative measures, "proceedings should automatically be brought for all racist acts" (CoE, 2001, p. 2). With regard to the implementation of legislative measures, co-operation among all relevant parties (e.g. the police force, public courts, match and competition organisers, stadium management, club managers, stewards, fans and related non-governmental organisations) was considered vital. Equally important was the use of surveillance technologies such as CCTV for identifying racist offenders, proper training for police officers and stewards, and the establishment of a database for sharing relevant information. Interestingly, the resolution also noted that "actions that have been taken against those who have engaged in racist behaviour should be given appropriate publicity" (CoE, 2001, p. 3). Such measures, the resolution continued, should be supported by social and educational initiatives to address the issue of racism in sport, particularly football; condemn racist behaviour of all forms; adopt anti-racism policies; educate players, coaches, and fans; urge match-day ticket holders to refrain from racist conduct; make relevant announcements through the PA system, and ban the distribution of all racist material both in and around stadiums. At national level, governments, local authorities, and sports organisations should promote the principle of inclusion, whereas at international level, increased police co-operation at international matches was considered imperative.

The Council of Europe's recommendation, nevertheless, failed to address the issue of racism in football with effect. It appears that the key messages and recommendations did not reach the addressees, given that all four organisations discussed herein issued a number of similar declarations in the years to follow, the Council of Europe included. During this time, political conditions in Europe changed considerably, as populism, ultra-nationalism, and anti-Europeanism came to the fore, in response to matters related to the Eurozone crisis, migration, and European Union affairs. For instance, the Council of Europe, as per Resolution 2276, adopted by the Parliamentary Assembly in 2019, not only condemns discrimination of all forms, it also explicitly stresses that "the danger posed by populists and other ideologues attempting to manipulate sports supporters for electoral and political gain should be prevented and countered". Having realised the impact of football in societies across the continent, the Council of Europe signed, in 2018, memorandums of understanding with UEFA and the *Fédération internationale de football association* (FIFA) in order "to promote human rights, integrity, good governance and non-discrimination in football" (CoE, 2020, p. 26). The fact that racism in European football continues to tarnish the popular game, given the number of racist incidents during the recent EURO competition in Germany (see below), indicates that the two memorandums of understanding had and have little impact. Evidently, the ongoing atrocities in Ukraine and the Middle East (in reference to human rights), the issue of a President's term limits at both FIFA and UEFA (with regard to good governance), and the numerous racist incidents recorded at football matches ever since (relating to non-discrimination in football) clearly render the two memorandums insufficient.

Within the same context, the Parliamentary Assembly called the member states of the Council of Europe to "promote research and data collection on hate speech and hate crime in the sports environment", probably ignoring the difficulty in precisely defining what constitutes a hate crime, as well as the fact that many incidents are not officially reported. The member states were also asked to "integrate into their national plans or strategies against hate speech and hate crime specific measures to address these issues in the sports environment", even though the said measures already exist in most of the CoE's member states but are probably rarely implemented. Furthermore, they were urged to "strengthen co-operation with sports organisations in areas relevant to hatred and intolerance" (CoE, 2020, p. 26), hoping that such co-operation would materialise into concrete action and not be limited to the narrow scope of merely signing a relevant memorandum of understanding.

The Parliamentary Assembly also called on its member states to "ensure that reporting mechanisms are available for victims of hate speech and discrimination in the sports environment", a measure that probably exists in most, if not all, member states. However, "incidents of discrimination and racist and xenophobic crimes are often not reported to the authorities" (de Groot, 2024, p. 6). Calling on the Council of Europe's member states to "combat impunity by ensuring consistent implementation of existing administrative and criminal sanctions for hate speech in the sports environment and making use of the technologies currently available in sports grounds to identify perpetrators" probably has limited effect too. In Cyprus, for instance, during a match that took place in February 2020, a Black player left the pitch in protest of having been called "a 'slave' by players and fans of the opponent team" (CoE, 2023, p. 16). Subsequently, "the referee interrupted the match, not on account of racist abuse, but on the ground that the victim's teammates walked off the field. Furthermore, the police initially denied that there was a racist motive" (CoE, 2023, p. 18). The CoE's recommendation continued by calling on the member states to "conduct awareness-raising campaigns targeting the general public on the dangers posed by hate speech" and "integrate sports ethics into school curricula", with both measures being more feasible to implement. It also "encourage[d] media to provide pluralistic, unbiased information on athletes, particularly those most exposed to hatred, and their performance, and to report accurately and without bias on hate speech incidents and hate crimes" (CoE, 2020, p. 27). On one occasion, however, several English media outlets were criticised for making use of Bukayo Saka's photo following England's defeat in a friendly match against Iceland, held at Wembley Stadium in June 2024 (BBC, 2024a). To remind the reader, Saka was one of three Black players who was racially abused, largely on social media, for missing a penalty in the EURO 2020 final against Italy.

The Parliamentary Assembly also "calls on sports federations and other sports organisations to: integrate equality and non-discrimination into their activities and promote democratic values; prevent and combat hate speech and, to this end, strengthen co-operation with supporters' clubs, civil society organisations, the media and educational institutions; appoint outstanding athletes as "ambassadors for equality and non-discrimination"; require all players to formally commit to refraining from hate speech and manifestations of hatred and intolerance; provide all players and staff members with training on how to identify, prevent and counter hate speech and intolerance; promote educational programmes for sports supporters and fan clubs in order to prevent hate speech in stadiums during matches" (CoE, 2020, p. 27). Such ethical recommendations, when properly delivered and implemented, can, of course, generate a fertile base for tackling racism and other forms of discrimination in football more effectively. Two of the key points here are the promotion of democratic values and the role of education. Safeguarding democracy, as the cornerstone of European civilisation, would help preserve the essence of a pluralistic society; making good use of education would allow every person to make a valuable contribution to society. After all, sport, democracy and education hold the key to equality, equity and inclusiveness.

The European Union

The legal framework against discrimination within the European Union (EU) is primarily based on Articles 2 and 3 of the Treaty on European Union, as well as Articles 10, 19 and 67 (3) of the Treaty on the Functioning of the EU. The Charter of Fundamental Rights of the EU, too, reiterates the principles of non-discrimination and equality. It is noteworthy that the first legal instrument at EU level prohibiting discrimination on either 'racial' or ethnic origin was the Racial Equality Directive, adopted in 2000. The Framework Decision on Combating Racism and Xenophobia (2008) is yet another legal act stating that any form of 'racial' discrimination is prohibited and punishable across the EU. As regard to European football, more than 140 Members of the European Parliament wrote to UEFA in 2019

> calling for 'urgent action' against racism and discrimination in the wake of an incident during a match in the Netherlands. While the lawmakers acknowledged the work done by the body to tackle racism and discrimination – including through the so-called 'three-step procedure' under which referees can halt a game if there is a racist incident inside a

stadium and, if the perpetrator persists, abandon the match – they argued that much more needs to be done.
(European Parliamentary Research Service, 2021, p. 3)

Prompting the MEPs' response was a racist incident that took place during a second division match between FC Den Bosch and Excelsior Rotterdam where fans of the former racially abused Ahmad Mendes Moreira of the opposition. The match was only temporarily stopped, as per the three-step protocol (see below), and ended in a 3–3 draw with Moreira scoring one of his team's goals. The following weekend the two top divisions in Holland decided to suspend playing for a minute right after kick-off to protest against racism.

The above follows from a European Parliament declaration (2006) on tackling racism in football, in the aftermath of a number of racist incidents across Europe, which stressed that the game's popularity "offers a new opportunity to tackle racism" (European Parliament, 2006). The declaration stated that the European Parliament condemns all forms of racism in football, commended the work of UEFA and FARE in their attempts to tackle racism in football, and called on all pertinent actors and stakeholders such as associations, leagues, clubs, players and staff to adhere to UEFA's ten-point plan (see below). It also urged UEFA and other governing bodies to empower referees, deliver severe sanctions for offenders, and instructed its "President to forward this declaration, together with the names of the signatories, to the Council, the Commission, the governments of the Member States and UEFA" (European Parliament, 2006).

Evidently, the declaration failed to transpire into concrete action and, instead, called on football governing bodies, competition organisers, clubs and even supporters to act. The first four points of the declaration merit little attention for they are limited to condemning racism (*cliché*), commending the "excellent" work of UEFA and FARE (see the relevant sections below for a different evaluation), and, generally, calling on every pertinent party to take action. Empowering referees (Point 5) by asking UEFA and other competition organisers to ensure that the former have the option to stop and even abandon a football match carries much significance. However, only very few matches have indeed been abandoned, including the Champions League fixture between Paris Saint-Germain and Istanbul Basaksehir in December 2020. Imposing sanctions (Point 6) on national football associations and clubs has been implemented more often; however, neither a partial stadium closure nor a substantial fine seems to have contributed much to eliminating racism from football. Perhaps, one tangible contribution of the European Union amounts to the European Commission helping set up FARE in 2001.

Union of European Football Associations

On 15 December 2005, at its meeting in Nyon, the Union of European Football Associations (UEFA) Executive Committee issued a declaration against racism, condemning any form of discrimination in European football.

Racism in football was perceived as a top priority for the European football governing body, calling all stakeholders and other parties to act against racial discrimination. More specifically, the declaration urged "the national associations, leagues and clubs to be proactive by applying the UEFA ten-point plan" and "endorses and urges support for the written declaration on tackling racism in football issued by MEPs at the European Parliament on 9 December 2005" (UEFA, 2006). As the governing body of European football, UEFA has over the years developed a range of tools and measures dedicated to the elimination of racism in football, but its efforts have yet to be crowned with success.

As per Article 2 of the Statutes (2024) of UEFA, the objectives of the European football governing body include the promotion of football across the continent "in a spirit of peace, understanding and fair play, without any discrimination on account of politics, gender, religion, race or any other reason" (UEFA, 2024c). Addressing racial discrimination in particular, Article 7 (par. 7) stipulates that

> Member Associations shall implement an effective policy aimed at eradicating racism and any other forms of discrimination from football and apply a regulatory framework providing that any such behaviour is strictly sanctioned, including, in particular, by means of serious suspensions for players and officials, as well as partial and full stadium closures if supporters engage in racist behaviour.
>
> (UEFA, 2024c)

Croatia's Josip Simunic was banned for 10 official matches and missed the 2014 FIFA World Cup for "leading a pro-Nazi chant with fans" (AP News, 2013), three Valencia fans were sentenced to jail for racially abusing Real Madrid's Vinícius Júnior (France 24, 2024), and several stadiums have faced restrictions on fan attendance (UEFA, Stadium bans), yet racism in European football persists.

In a similar context, Article 14, Racism and other discriminatory conduct, of the UEFA Disciplinary Regulations (2024b) states that a ten-match ban is issued when any entity or person "insults the human dignity of a person or group of persons", a partial stadium closure or a ban on selling tickets to its away supporters is delivered in case "one or more of a member association or club's supporters engage" in racist behaviour, which may be extended to playing "matches behind closed doors, a stadium closure, the forfeiting of a match, the deduction of points and/or disqualification from the competition", and should the match be suspended by the referee "the match may be declared forfeit" (UEFA, 2024b).

Again, partial stadium closures, playing behind closed doors or fining clubs and associations have not produced any noticeable results. Deducting points or eliminating a national association or club from a competition, on the other hand, are rarely considered an option; at international level, only Croatia has been punished with a one-point deduction, during the qualifying stage for EURO 2016, but still qualified for the tournament in France. And while the impact of such a severe penalty would be impossible to estimate, to suggest that the fan base would probably refrain from similar discriminatory practices in the future would not be entirely irrational. Considering the likely consequences for national associations and clubs, their officials would be forced to take immediate action by banning racist fans and act pre-emptively in forthcoming matches in order to avoid further sanctions. Forfeiting a match, though available as an option, has never really been considered. In January 2024, two incidents on the same weekend – one in Italy (AC Milan v. Udinese) and one in England (Sheffield Wednesday v. Coventry) – prompted FIFA president Gianni Infantino to state that "we have to implement an automatic forfeit for the team whose fans have committed racism and caused the match to be abandoned" (BBC, 2024a).

Considering that the above measures failed to curb racism in European football, UEFA issued the *Football Sustainability Strategy 2030* (2021), which combines "ambition and realism, outlining a 10-year journey and keeping in mind what UEFA can *realistically* do through its strong platform [emphasis added]" (UEFA, 2021, p. 6). Among other things, it was designed to "prevent and fight all forms of racial discrimination in the football environment, from grassroots to the elite professional level", with the ambition to "eradicate racism in all its forms on and around the pitch across European football" by 2030. To facilitate its ambitious strategy,

> UEFA conducts a review to further improve existing systems for reporting racism and racial discrimination across European football. Consequently, it ensures systems are developed and accessible to support victims. Furthermore, the structures and communications around the investigation and sanctioning of discrimination cases will be strengthened. Lastly, discriminatory actions and management procedures within stadiums as well as UEFA online platforms will be identified.

Existing initiatives include

> Consultation and dialogue through an independent UEFA anti-discrimination working group; Match observer scheme implementation within club and major national team competitions; Control, Ethics and Disciplinary Body ruling on all disciplinary, ethical and other matters that fall within its competence under UEFA's statutes and regulations; Relationship building with global institutions in view of developing joint actions in the fight against discrimination; Campaigns to promote UEFA's vision that everyone should be able to enjoy football.
>
> (UEFA, 2021, p. 32)

What UEFA considers an aspirational target with regard to anti-racism is "Zero racist incidents across all UEFA events and collaboratively across European football by 2030" (UEFA, 2021, p. 49).

Setting 2030 as a target for the elimination of racism across all UEFA events is probably anything but realistic. During the early stages of EURO 2024, UEFA identified 17 games as being affected and "sanctioned seven of the 24 competing countries . . . because of racist or discriminatory behaviour by their fans" (Stone, 2024). That the penalties delivered were a combination of fines and bans on selling tickets to their next UEFA away match clearly indicates that UEFA is more willing to discipline its member associations by means of imposing punishments of a financial nature rather than adopting a more severe stance against racial discrimination. Two of the nations concerned, Georgia and Slovenia, advanced to the knockout stages as two of the best third-placed teams in the group stage. Had UEFA decided to either eliminate them from the competition or, at least, impose a points deduction, neither one of them would have featured in the first knockout round.

The *UEFA Safety and Security Regulations* (2019) recommend that the match organiser, the police officer in charge of the match and the local safety and security officers collaborate to prevent racist behaviour and, should such action arise, intervene by means of either making use of the public address system or removing related offensive people and/or material. Certainly, one of the most important tools in tackling racial discrimination in European football is UEFA's *Ten-Point Plan on Racism*, announced on 10 October 2002. It includes the following action points:

1. Issue a statement saying the club will not tolerate racism or sectarianism, spelling out the action it will take against those engaged in racist or sectarian chanting. The statement should be printed in all match programmes and displayed permanently and prominently around the ground.
2. Make public address announcements condemning racist chanting at matches.
3. Make it a condition for season ticket holders that they do not take part in racist abuse.
4. Take action to prevent the sale of racist literature inside and around the ground.
5. Take disciplinary action against players who engage in racial abuse.
6. Contact other clubs to make sure they understand the club's policy on racism.
7. Encourage a common strategy between stewards and police for dealing with racist abuse.
8. Remove all racist graffiti from the ground as a matter of urgency.

9. Adopt an equal opportunities policy in relation to employment and service provision.
10. Work with all other groups and agencies, such as the players union, supporters and schools, voluntary organisations, youth clubs, sponsors, local authorities, local business and police, to develop pro-active programmes and make progress to raise awareness of campaigning to eliminate racial abuse and discrimination.

(UEFA, 2019, p. 27)

Although, at first sight, this appears to be a sensible action plan, there are a number of concerns. A first major weakness of the *Ten-Point Plan on Racism* is that it is addressed to clubs. Football is a valuable commodity and taking firm action against any form of discrimination would devalue their own product and its reputation by means of inviting unwelcome, negative attention by the (social) media and beyond, thus affecting a club's image and, quite possibly, its financial gains. Even if clubs were prepared to acknowledge the presence of racial discrimination within the game of football,

> the need to maintain a positive public profile encourages them to deny that racism is a feature of their club – or if it is, then it is one caused by extremist hooligan outsiders who are not 'real football fans.' Collectively this leads to a situation whereby there is a broad consensus that racism exists within the sport, and yet an equally widespread insistence that the difficulties are primarily elsewhere – somebody else's concern.
>
> (Garland and Rowe, 2001, p. 190)

The more seasoned readers may recall that football clubs and authorities also claimed that hooliganism was not really their problem to deal with but society's concern. Secondly, the majority of the issues raised by the *Ten-Point Plan on Racism* mostly concern a club's internal policies and regulations and while issuing anti-racism statements, making public address announcements, preventing the sale of racist literature, removing racist graffiti, raising awareness against racism, and improving employment provisions should not require the allocation of any significant resources. However, even if implemented, it is unlikely that they will have any significant impact. Perhaps item 5 could have a more direct impact on eliminating racism from football, if properly applied. When Enzo Fernandez of Chelsea posted on his Instagram personal account in July 2024 a video singing a racist song with his Argentina teammates, his club announced that an internal disciplinary procedure would be instigated. Eventually, they decided not to take any action against him after the player, first, apologised and, then, donated to an anti-discrimination charity (Aarons, 2024).

More significant, perhaps, is the three-step protocol, outlined in the *Guidelines for Match Officials in cases of Racist Behaviour in Football Stadiums*, approved by UEFA's Executive Committee in July 2009.

1 Stop the match in case of serious racist incidents

   a. When the referee becomes aware (in particular if he [sic] is informed by the UEFA match delegate through the fourth official) of racist behaviour (especially racist chants, insults and screams, banners, etc.) and if, in his [sic] opinion, this racist behaviour is of a strong magnitude and intensity, he [sic] shall, in application of Law 5 of the Game, stop the match and ask for an announcement to be made over the public address system (in the languages of both teams) requesting the public to immediately stop such racist behaviour.
   b. The match may resume only after the announcement has been made.

2 Suspend the match in case of serious racist incidents

   a. If the racist behaviour does not cease once the game has restarted (i.e. step 1 was ineffective), the referee shall suspend the match for a reasonable time period (e.g. 5 to 10 minutes) and request the teams to go to the dressing rooms. The UEFA match delegate shall, through the fourth official, assist the referee in determining whether the racist behaviour has ceased following step 1.
   b. During this time period, the referee shall again ask for an announcement to be made over the public address system requesting the public to immediately stop such racist behaviour and warning them that this may even result in the match being abandoned.
   c. During this suspension, the referee shall consult with the UEFA match delegate, the UEFA security officer and the relevant police and stadium and security authorities on the possible next steps, in particular the possibility to abandon the match.

3 Abandon the match in case of serious racist incidents

   a. If the racist behaviour does not cease after the game has restarted (i.e. step 2 was ineffective), the referee shall, as a very last resort, definitively abandon the match. The UEFA match delegate shall, through the fourth official, assist the referee in determining whether the racist behaviour has ceased following step 2.
   b. However, any decision by the referee to abandon a match in such circumstances shall only be taken after all other possible measures have been implemented and the impact of abandoning the match on the security of the players and the public has been assessed by means of a full and extensive consultation with the UEFA match delegate, the UEFA security officer and the relevant police and stadium security authorities.

> In principle, abandoning the match is subject to the agreement of all parties involved.
>
> (UEFA, 2019, p. 29)

The three-step protocol was first applied in October 2019 during England's game against Bulgaria in Sofia, when the match was twice halted by the referee following racist chanting directed at England's Black players. Step 3 was never applied, prompting UEFA's mild response to the incident, since Bulgaria were given a one-match stadium ban and a €75,000 fine. As is designed, the three-step protocol allows much room for any group of organised fans to resort to racist behaviour aiming to halt the match twice and, therefore, interrupt the flow of the game and influence the opposition's performance. In other words, the three-step protocol allows fans to freely express their racist beliefs until they receive a second warning and, still, evade punishment.

Echoing UEFA's *Statutes* is the *European Football United Against Racism* resolution, unanimously adopted by UEFA's Congress on 24 May 2013. The resolution reiterated UEFA's zero tolerance to racism and urged the European football governing body and its member associations "to re-double their efforts to eradicate racism from football" and impose "stricter sanctions", while "Referees should stop, suspend or even abandon a match if racist incidents occur". Players or team staff "found guilty of racist conduct must be suspended for at least ten matches", whereas in the event of supporters engaging in racist behaviour the penalty for supporters is a ban from attending future matches and for clubs and national teams a partial stadium closure for a first offence and a full stadium closure and a fine for a second offence. The resolution also called for the need to carry out awareness programs and ended stating that "UEFA is fully committed to these strong sanctioning and awareness policies and all national associations support the implementation of similar policies" (UEFA, 2019, p. 28). In the case of the match between England and Bulgaria, as per UEFA's resolution, the Bulgarian Football Union was sanctioned with a full stadium closure and a financial penalty since it was only Bulgaria's second offence. Obviously, the resolution's main weakness is that it fails to address the possibility of multiple offences. In the event of a third offence, would a national association face a point deduction or even elimination from the competition?

UEFA's other official documents aiming at tackling racism include Article 7 (*Respect for opponents*) and Article 10 (*Behaviour of spectators*) of the *UEFA Fair Play Regulations* (2015) that consider racial discrimination as a negative attitude (UEFA, 2015, pp. 7–8). Similarly, Article 5 (*Guiding principles*) of the *UEFA Equipment Regulations* (2022) states that "No item falling under the scope of these regulations may offend common decency or transmit political, religious or racial messages" (UEFA, 2022, p. 16). Finally, Article 29

(*Anti-racism*) of the *UEFA Club Licensing and Financial Sustainability Regulations* (2024), too, addresses the same issue in that "The licence applicant must establish and implement a policy to tackle racism and to guarantee that all the licence applicant's policies, programmes and practices are exercised without discrimination of any kind" (UEFA, 2024a, p. 26). A more recent instrument in UEFA's campaign against racial discrimination – though not solely focused on racism alone – is the OUTRAGED toolkit, a six-episode documentary launched in December 2020 to share the experiences and thoughts of 38 players, coaches, referees, officials, and others related to the game of football in yet another attempt to tackle all forms of discrimination in sport (UEFA, 2020, p. 8).

Football Against Racism in Europe

Football Against Racism in Europe (FARE) is a network comprising some 150 members from about 40 European countries, as well as associates in the United States, South Africa and Brazil, all aiming to tackle discrimination in football. FARE's mission is to "achieve equality and social inclusion through the power of football", and its key objectives including "Tackle, prevent, respond to and encourage action against discrimination at all levels of football across Europe; Raise awareness about the integrative potential of football and use it as a tool for social equality; Undertake activities to empower and build capacity of marginalised and discriminated groups; Give a voice to those combating discrimination in football". Supporting FARE's initiatives includes "Hosting international events and conferences; Producing best practice guides and educational materials; Organising pan-European and international campaigns, including the Football People action weeks; Delivering activities at international football competitions; Monitoring matches and reporting discrimination" (FARE, *About us*).

One of FARE's most exciting initiatives is the "Football People" campaign over the course of a two-week period, as more than 150,000 people in some 50 countries "organise and participate in events and activities to bring about social change" (FARE, *Football people*). Another important initiative is the "Observer scheme," allowing

> to better understand the scope of the problem, collect evidence and conduct an analysis, and call for responsible action by governing bodies. The data collected is used to focus stakeholder attention on particular problems and incidents, and stimulate a debate on measures to tackle the problem on the part of NGOs, fans, clubs and governing bodies.

The observer scheme is focused on international football matches across Europe, not domestic leagues, and the matches that are monitored are selected on a previous evaluation of their risk potential for discriminatory conduct. Unlike football's governing bodies, FARE does not have the authority to issue sanctions (FARE, *Observer scheme*). Finally, "Campaigning against discrimination and promoting an inclusive environment for everyone, both in football and society, is an essential element of the Fare work programme" (FARE, *Campaigns*).

FARE works closely with UEFA and human rights organisations to help eliminate racism from football. They, too, recognise the threat posed by those fans who find far-right ideas and ideologies attractive. The *Guide to Discriminatory Practices in European Football* (FARE, 2021) booklet provides an insightful display of those fans' practices inside stadiums and depicts a vast range of discriminatory symbols, flags and banners to illustrate the extent of racist discrimination in European football. Relevant discriminatory manifestations "include verbal and symbolic abuse of Black and ethnic minority players and fans, the display of far-right and neo-Nazi symbols" (FARE, 2021, p. 6). Some of the more common racist displays include: Blackface (FARE, 2021, p. 6), slant-eyed gesture (FARE, 2021, p. 7), gorilla/monkey words (FARE, 2021, p. 7), monkey noises/gestures (FARE, 2021, p. 8), the N-word (FARE, 2021, p. 7), far-right signs and symbols (FARE, 2021, p. 10), the Swastika (FARE, 2021, p. 10), references to Ku Klux Klan (FARE, 2021, p. 11) and White Power/White Pride (FARE, 2021, p. 11), antisemitic banners (FARE, 2021, p. 44), and Islamophobic messages (FARE, 2021, p. 45). On the whole, "Fare focuses on advancing the social inclusion of marginalised and disenfranchised groups while engaging policy makers, governing bodies and the wider public in the process" (FARE, 2021, p. 4) and is present at most of football's mega events, such as the UEFA EURO competition, the FIFA World Cup and the FIFA Confederations Cup.

Conclusion

There is little doubt that the four organisations discussed earlier have employed different tactics and tools in their efforts to eliminate racism from football, yet it is more than obvious that their responses to racial discrimination lack efficacy. While UEFA is more concerned with devising disciplinary measures, the Council of Europe and the European Union are focused on legislating, and FARE's efforts are limited to educational campaigning. Although all four organisations have publicly denounced racism in football and urged all pertinent actors to take action, the sheer absence of a coordinated effort is a major concern. The fact that the official documents presented herein raised the issue of racism in football at the turn of the century does not suggest that it is a recent phenomenon. To the contrary, it offers convincing evidence that racial discrimination in football had long been overlooked.

Since FARE's overall contribution is restricted to activities designed to raise awareness of racial discrimination in football and collect relevant information, the responsibility for implementing those measures (and penalties) intended to curb the phenomenon of racism in football rests with the Council of Europe, the European Union, and UEFA. The latter is, obviously, more suitable for delivering penalties, however, it is not certain that it is equally adept to realise the urgency of the matter or sympathise with the victims of racial abuse. In a photo (UEFA, 2024d) portraying the 20 members of the UEFA Executive Committee, the only non-white person is Nasser Al-Khelaifi. Given that the chairman and CEO of Paris Saint-Germain Football Club became a member of the UEFA Executive Committee after being elected by the European Club Association, the Executive Committee could well have an all-white composition. Likewise, the Secretary General of the Council of Europe, his deputy, and almost all members of the Committee of Ministers – except for the representative of the United Kingdom – are also white. Ursula von der Leyen's team of new European commissioners that she introduced to the press in September 2024 certainly contained a significant number of women but continues to lack ethnic diversity. Senior EU policymakers appear to pay attention to gender equality, and more recently also to the inclusion of members of the LGBTQ+ community but continue to struggle with the principle of ethnic diversity. Perhaps, it is this lack of diversity at crucial junctures of power in Europe that epitomises the failure of all three organisations to address effectively the issue of racism in European football and society more generally.

References

Aarons, E. (2024) "Chelsea take no action against Enzo Fernández after charity donation", *The Guardian*, 30th July. Available: <https://www.theguardian.com/football/article/2024/jul/30/chelsea-take-no-action-against-enzo-fernandez-charity-racist-song> [accessed on 17th July 2024].
AP News (2013) "Simunic banned for 10 games for pro-Nazi chant", 16th December. Available: <https://apnews.com/simunic-banned-for-10-games-for-pro-nazi-chant-78f4d198cd7a4067acb9b0962ffae9ac> [accessed on 17th July 2024].
BBC (2024a) "Bukayo Saka: media coverage criticised after England defeat", 10th June. Available: <https://www.bbc.com/sport/football/articles/c888v0lwxy2o> [accessed on 17th July 2024].
BBC (2024b) "Football racism: Forfeit matches when fans are racist – Fifa's Infantino", 21st January. Available: <https://www.bbc.com/sport/football/68046422> [accessed on 12th June 2024].
Blecking, D. (1993) "Sport and ethnic minorities in Germany", in Laine, L. (Ed.), *On the fringes of sport*, St. Augustin: Academia, pp. 149–155.
Council of Europe (1949) *Statute of the Council of Europe*, London.
Council of Europe (2001) *Committee of Ministers, recommendation on the prevention of racism, xenophobia and racial intolerance in sport* (2001/6). Available: <https://search.coe.int/cm/Pages/result_details.aspx?ObjectId=09000016804fcf3b> [accessed on 11th November 2024].
Council of Europe (2014) *Committee of Ministers*. Available: <https://www.coe.int/en/web/cm/documents> [accessed on 5th June 2016].
Council of Europe (2020) *Racism, intolerance, hate speech: a compilation of texts adopted by the Parliamentary Assembly of the Council of Europe*.

Council of Europe (2023) *ECRI report on cyprus*. Available: <https://rm.coe.int/ecri-6th-report-on-cyprus/1680aa6876> [accessed 10th November 2024].

de Groot, D. (2024) *Briefing: EU legislation and policies to address racial and ethnic discrimination*, European Parliamentary Research Service.

European Parliament (2006) *Declaration of the European Parliament on tackling racism in football*, P6_TA(2006)0080.

European Parliamentary Research Service (2021) *Briefing: fighting discrimination in sport*, by Ivana Katsarova, European Union.

FARE. *About us*. Available: <https://farenet.org/about-fare> [accessed on 17th May 2024].

FARE. *Campaigns*. Available: <https://farenet.org/our-work/campaigns> [accessed on 17th May 2024].

FARE. *Football people weeks of action*. Available: <https://farenet.org/our-work/football-people-action-weeks> [accessed on 17th May 2024].

FARE. *Observer scheme*. Available: <https://farenet.org/fare-observer-scheme> [accessed on 17th May 2024].

FARE (2021) *Guide to discriminatory practices in European football*, London.

France 24 (2024) "Spanish court sentences three Valencia fans to jail for racism against Real Madrid star", 10th June. Available: <https://www.france24.com/en/live-news/20240610-fans-get-8-months-jail-for-racism-targeting-real-madrid-s-vinicius> [accessed on 12th June 2024].

Garland, J. and Rowe, M. (2001) *Racism and anti-racism in football*, Basingstoke and New York: Palgrave.

Jarvie, G. (1991) *Sport, racism and ethnicity*, London: Palmer Press.

Maguire, J.A. (1988) "Race and position assignment in English Soccer: a preliminary analysis of ethnicity and sport in Britain", *Sociology of Sport Journal*, 5(3), pp. 257–2690.

Merkel, U. and Tokarski, W. (1996) *Racism and xenophobia in European football*, Aachen: Meyer and Meyer.

Stone, S. (2024) "Uefa sanctions seven nations for racist chants", *BBC*, 24th July. Available: <https://www.bbc.com/sport/football/articles/cgerp2d5pn5o> [accessed on 5th August 2024].

UEFA (2006) *Executive committee declaration against racism*, Nyon: UEFA.

UEFA (2010) *UEFA's position on Article 165 of the Lisbon Treaty*, Nyon: UEFA.

UEFA (2015) *Fair play regulations*, Nyon: UEFA.

UEFA (2019) *Safety and security regulations*, Nyon: UEFA.

UEFA (2020) *Outraged toolkit*, Nyon: UEFA.

UEFA (2021) *Football sustainability strategy 2030*, Nyon: UEFA.

UEFA (2022) *Equipment regulations*, Nyon: UEFA.

UEFA (2024a) *Club licensing and financial sustainability regulations*, Nyon: UEFA.

UEFA (2024b) *Disciplinary regulations*, Nyon: UEFA.

UEFA (2024c) *Statutes, rules of procedure of the UEFA congress regulations governing the implementation of the UEFA statutes*, Nyon: UEFA.

UEFA (2024d) *The UEFA Executive Committee on 8 February 2024 following the 48th Congress*. Available: <https://editorial.uefa.com/resources/028a-1a220416777e-8ac026bfd3b9-1000/format/wide1/48th_uefa_ordinary_congress_-_meeting.jpeg?imwidth=2048> [accessed on 11th September 2024].

UEFA. "Stadium bans". Available: <https://www.uefa.com/running-competitions/disciplinary/stadium-bans/> [accessed on 13th June 2024].

Williams, J. (1992) *Lick my boots: racism in English football*, Leicester: Sir Norman Chester Centre for Football Research.

Chapter 14

Europe (II)

Comparative observations:
Commonalities and differences

Udo Merkel

Although the focus of this book is on racism, xenophobia, antisemitism, Islamophobia and other forms of discrimination in the complex and multi-layered world of European football, it is also about a disconcerting mystery. While the world of football is ethnically one of the most diverse segments of European society and culture and has frequently been praised for its power to bring people together and contribute to various integration processes, the aforementioned forms of discrimination continue to constitute serious problems in the world of recreational, amateur, professional and international football and clearly contradict the expectation of building bridges and uniting people.

This book is not able to solve this fundamental enigma, but it aspires to offer a better and more differentiated understanding of the discriminatory manifestations and the counter-measures taken to combat them. In order to achieve this, the book pursues three main objectives: First, it aims to offer a large number of detailed European country case studies that all examine racism, xenophobia, antisemitism, Islamophobia and other forms of discrimination, as well as overlaps, in football. Methodologically, territorial definitions of modern societies have become increasingly problematic due to the powerful and ongoing globalisation process that is responsible for the growing interconnectedness and interdependence of modern societies all over the world. And yet, the world of football continues to be strictly organised along national lines with each country governing their affairs independently in co-operation with, and under the guidance of, UEFA and FIFA. Centrally involved in the national management of football are, of course, the respective national governing bodies. Second, this book also intends to outline and critically evaluate selected policies, strategies, campaigns, initiatives, measures and actions that have been developed and taken by different stakeholders to remedy the aforementioned issues. Third, it endeavours to cautiously compare and contrast the findings of the previous chapters in order to identify, explain and critically evaluate commonalities and differences as well as, possibly, detect European trends and tendencies. The latter is addressed in this final, concluding chapter.

Cross-cultural, comparative research is nowadays an undeniable element of many mainstream social-scientific disciplines. Such studies are helpful due

DOI: 10.4324/9781003495970-14

This chapter has been made available under a CC-BY-NC-SA 4.0 license.

to the ongoing globalisation process, in general, and the European integration process, in particular. They offer countries and governments opportunities to learn from each other, facilitate socio-economic, political and cultural co-operation, avoid re-inventing the wheel and support professionals involved in policy development at all kinds of different levels. In addition, cross-national comparative studies are not only useful in understanding others but also one's own society and culture. Therefore, they help to develop a critical consciousness and increase our sensitivity towards our own socio-economic, cultural, and political structures that we generally perceive as given, stable and unchangeable.

Cross-national comparative studies are, of course, only sensible and pragmatic, if the countries and objects under investigation share a large number of equivalencies. In other words, in all the countries covered in this book, football is played according to the same rules, overseen by governing bodies, and organised in more or less the same way in a pyramid system with clubs being the standard organisational unit. Furthermore, football is the most popular spectator sport in most European countries with hundreds of thousands of passionate fans filling stadiums every weekend and millions watching the matches on television or online. It is also noteworthy that almost all authors of the individual case studies felt that it was important to alert the readers to two significant and influential contexts that most European countries share: the ethnically, culturally and nationally diverse composition of the respective societies, largely caused by several migration waves in the aftermath of the Second World War, and the increasing popularity and rise of far-right, populist ideas, movements, organisations and political parties. Although the latter is a complex phenomenon and the result of several interconnected reasons and developments, one of these appears to be the steady influx of migrants into Europe that has caused widespread fears about the loss of a genuine, home-grown, homogenous, national culture, or way of life, in several countries. On its own, that is an insufficient explanation of the various discriminatory phenomena that the previous chapters have dealt with. However, combined with discussions about the rise, reconstruction and renewal of nationalism in Europe, there is some truth in such an approach. After all, one of the oldest strategies of constructing and forging a community involves identifying and labelling those who are not part of it. That kind of exclusion inevitably promotes internal social cohesion and causes tensions and conflicts with other groups.

This concluding chapter is organised according to selected stakeholders in the large and complex world of football. Stakeholders are individuals, groups and organisations that have a vested interest in, an impact on, are affected by, and/or shape, in this case, the game of football through their attitudes and actions. The most important stakeholders that have been mentioned in the previous chapters are the performers (players, coaches and match officials), the spectators, the local clubs, national and international governing bodies, and nation-states and their governments. Although local people, for example, those living in the vicinity of football grounds, owners of teams and/or venues, security forces, as well as sponsors, investors and the media are also influential stakeholders, they will be ignored in this final chapter as they did not play a significant role in the previous accounts.

The performers: players, coaches and match officials

Manifestations and targets of racism, xenophobia, antisemitism and/or Islamophobia in football vary from country to country and depend on the ethnic composition and socio-political situation of the respective society and its football culture. However, there are several commonalities. Primary targets tend to be individuals or small groups of players, particularly those with a different skin colour, occasionally match officials, coaches, the fans of the rival team and, less frequently, clubs as a whole, particularly those that have some kind of Jewish heritage. Due to the differential media coverage, we know more about high-profile, male targets in the top European leagues, although male, recreational and amateur players as well as women are also affected. In particular, the chapters on England and France have shown how, for example, the Islamic code of conduct that requires modesty in dress contradicts the high visibility of women's bodies in sport, which is part of the Western secular sport culture. Female athletes wearing a *hijab*, are, of course, visibly different and in many cases, do not comply with the requirements of explicitly secular states (France) and/or the regulations of national and international governing bodies. The *hijab* ban in some countries and sports is also a prime example of the intersectionality of gender discrimination and Islamophobia, or in other words, gendered anti-Muslim racism.

Abuse occurs at football matches as well as online. While the former is open and detectable, the latter is usually anonymous and difficult to trace. Without having to repeat any of the verbal, visual and symbolic manifestations or online messages, they all have in common that they express rejection, discrimination, bigotry, and, in many cases, hatred. That also applies to the rare incidents in which players abuse other players, for example, from the opposing team or reveal discriminatory attitudes online (Italy and Sweden). The identification and labelling of others as distinctively different and outsiders is often combined with the notion of exclusion from the majority ethnic, religious and/or national group.

In the past, affected players often suffered in silence, kept quiet and did not reach out for support. The notable and memorable exception is Eric Cantona. In 1995, the Frenchman, while playing for Manchester United, literally tried to kick xenophobia out of football. He jumped over a fence and attacked a Crystal Palace fan with a kung-fu kick after he had verbally abused Cantona on the grounds of his national origins. Today, more and more players go public with their complaints, share their suffering, call on relevant organisations for support and action, confront the perpetrators, take legal action and use social media platforms to voice their frustration and anger. Prime examples of such more confident and assertive reactions are Raheem Sterling in England, Antonio Rüdiger in Germany, Mario Balotelli in Italy, Samuel Eto'o and Vinícius Júnior in Spain, and Jimmy Durmaz (and his fellow national team members) in Sweden. In France, Kylian Mbappé, Jules Koundé and Marcus Thuram even attempted to dissuade people from voting for the divisive policies of the far-right in the parliamentary elections in 2024. Unlike in North-America where we have repeatedly witnessed athletes of various kinds of sports challenging, defying and resisting discriminatory politics and politicians, most notably Colin Kaepernick, who ignited a national debate over racial injustice that quickly spread to other countries, Mbappé, Koundé and Thuram constitute a welcome exception in Europe. Ten years before, in 2014, Brazilian Dani Alves, playing for Barcelona FC, reacted more humorously, and equally provocatively, to a banana thrown at him by a Villarreal FC fan. He took a bite before taking a corner. (The fan was later banned for life and the club was fined €12,000 by the Spanish football federation.)

Several chapters (England, Germany, France, the Netherlands, Poland, and Sweden) have explicitly mentioned the link between national identity discourses (Smith, 1991), nationalism and racist, xenophobic, antisemitic and Islamophobic abuse of selected players. They appear to not fit into what some sections of fans believe constitutes the genuine national community. It is no longer sufficient for one to hold the same passport to be a fellow citizen. They also need to be *native* and of the same "soil". In particular racism operates through nationalism. Hans Kohn's (2005) differentiation between ethnic and civic nationalism may be invoked here to make sense of the contested role of, for example, Black players in traditionally White national teams. The former refers to a shared ethnic identity of the citizens of a nation-state, while the latter reflects a shared sense of culture, government and political rights. Kohn's approach is rooted in Friedrich Meineke's (1970) distinction between *Staatsnation* (state nation) and *Kulturnation* (culture nation) that he developed at the beginning of the 20th century. In particular, the accounts for France, the Netherlands and Poland show that ethnic nationalism is more popular among football fans as Black players do not qualify for membership in a national community that has traditionally been White. While the latter are considered to be the true representatives of an ethnic nation that is defined by blood ties, language and religion, Black and foreign players can be linked to what constitutes a civic nation and are frequently viewed as inauthentic or ungenuine representatives.

Several chapters in this book (England, France, Germany, Poland and Sweden) touched upon the practice of scapegoating. It is about singling out an individual or small group of individuals that are made responsible for not achieving a desired outcome and are, for example, blamed for the defeat of one's favourite football team. Quite frequently, it is the coach, usually after a long spell of disappointing results; on other occasions, these can even be outstanding players of one's own team such as the previously mentioned Jimmy Durmaz in Sweden, Youssoufa Moukoko and Jessic Ngankam in Germany, and Marcus Rashford, Jordan Sancho and Bukayo Saka in England. All of them received a torrent of, primarily online, vicious racist abuse and became the scapegoats of their respective teams after they had been defeated in different competitions. Black French players were treated in a very similar hostile way after they failed to meet the public's expectations in 2010. Ten years later, *Kylian Mbappé* became a prime target after missing a penalty. When Mesut Özil retired from international football in 2018, he blamed the racist abuse by fans and officials, as well as being made a scapegoat for Germany's early exit from the 2018 FIFA World Cup for his resignation. The aforementioned abuse and scapegoating of Black and Muslim players convincingly show that recognition as bona fide fellow citizens and inclusion into the civic life of the nation does not only depend on their skin colour and religious orientation but also on how well they perform as footballers.

Referees are also popular (alleged) culprits, who tend to be accused of bias and are frequently reviled as frauds, crooks, robbers, scoundrels and, for example, labelled as Jews in Germany, regardless of their spiritual preferences. *"Jude"*, in this context, is intended to be an insult based on and perpetuating the mythical belief that Jews have been responsible for many of the problems that humans have suffered throughout history, from various plagues to modern global economic crises.

The chapters on England, Germany, France, Poland, Spain and Sweden also touch on the notion of double-standards which also seems to exist in other football contexts. After Turkey's victory over Austria during the EURO 2024, the Turkish player Merih Demiral was suspended for two matches. He had celebrated his team's success by forming the "Grey Wolves Salute" with his fingers, which is a symbol linked to the country's far-right movement. Since similar incidents, in which players had used highly controversial symbols of national and/or political significance, were not even investigated, let alone punished, some critical commentators viewed this as a double standard that displayed an anti-Turkish attitude in European officials. The aforementioned English, German, French and Swedish players being scapegoated after their respective teams' defeats represent another variation in the application of double standards. In case of success, they are part of the in-group; in case of failure, they are moved to the out-group. Several years ago, Mesut Özil felt like he was treated like a German after a victory of the German national side, but like an immigrant after a defeat. Furthermore, Sweden's Zlatan Ibrahimovic´ suggested some time ago that foreigners (and members of other ethnic minority groups) need to work much harder as they are held to higher standards. They appear to have a considerably smaller margin of error and tend to be judged more harshly.

Players of foreign descent with dual nationality are increasingly aware of these mechanisms and, as suggested in the chapter on France, take this into account when deciding which national team to play for. In addition to the French team, there were another 38 French-born players in action at the 2022 FIFA World Cup in Qatar. Thirty-four played for African countries, including Cameroon, Morocco, Senegal, and Tunisia. The Moroccan squad stood out in this context as more than half of its team members (14 out of 26) were foreign-born players from Belgium, France, Italy, the Netherlands and Spain. Footballers opting to play for the country of their cultural roots rather than their country of birth raises a complex set of interrelated and critical questions about integration, inclusion, discrimination and identity.

When considering the role of coaches or managers, an inconsistent and contradictory picture emerges. In the early 1990s, the Dutch coach Guus Hiddink insisted on the removal of various flags and banners with Nazi images and symbols displayed by supporters of his then-team, Valencia CF. Almost ten years later, in 2004, Luis Aragonés, at the time Spain's national team coach, was accused of racism when, in an attempt to motivate former Arsenal striker José Antonio Reyes, he referred to his teammate, Thierry Henry, in racist terms. In 2008, Chelsea FC's new manager, the Israeli Avram Grant, became the target of vile antisemitic abuse. The chapter on Spain identifies several Latin-American coaches as targets of xenophobic attacks. In 2011, Laurent Blanc, then in charge of the French national team, discussed the introduction of a limit on the number of Black and Arab players with members of the French Football Federation. Much more recently, in 2023, John Yems, the former Crawley Town manager in England, was banned from football for three years for using discriminatory, racist and Islamophobic language. Although not discussed in previous chapters, three of football's most famous and successful managers, the Italian Carlo Ancelotti, the Catalan Pep Guardiola and the German Jürgen Klopp, have repeatedly spoken out very openly about the problem, condemning racism in football, recognising that it is a wider societal problem and called on the relevant authorities to take tougher measures. More importantly, however, several chapters in this collection (England, the Netherlands and Sweden) specifically point out the glaring lack of Black managers in the top positions of their respective countries. At the end of the 2023/24 season, there were only two Black managers in France's Ligue 1, one in Italy's Serie A, and none in the top divisions of Spain and Germany. That obviously raises the question whether there is a bias in the recruitment process. Such blatant lack of diversity is also observable in, and very likely related to, the composition of boardrooms in European football, an issue that will be addressed below.

The spectators

If we look at European football from a bird's eye view and take into account the descriptions and analyses of the previous chapters that have sought to make sense of various national football audiences and their ideological proximity to, relationship and engagement with, racism, xenophobia, antisemitism and Islamophobia, it is possible to cautiously identify five distinctive groups:

1) **The reactionaries**: Die-hard members and/or sympathisers of far-right movements, organisations, and/or parties who reject traditional liberal ideas, values, and principles such as open-mindedness, tolerance, political equality and equal rights, and openly express their superior, hostile and discriminatory attitudes, frequently grounded in a nation-first stance, in and outside football grounds;
2) **The collaborators**: Unorganised football fans and some sections of the *ultras* who are committed to, and celebrate, an exclusionary sense of (ethnic) nationalism almost exclusively in football grounds, which includes humiliation and vilification of those players that are different;
3) **The associates**: Subcultural groups who employ racist, xenophobic, antisemitic and/or Islamophobic discourses for bonding purposes and use the display of discriminatory attitudes as markers of difference in order to nurture cohesion through social connections within the group;
4) **The entourage**: Spectators, who on certain occasions, feel attracted to, are drawn into, and participate in the display of racist, xenophobic, antisemitic and/or Islamophobic attitudes due to the appeal of the aforementioned highly visible and vocal groups;
5) **The activists:** Those rebellious fans who do not hold and disapprove of the public display of, racist, xenophobic, antisemitic and/or Islamophobic attitudes and are actively involved in the fight against these forms of deviant behaviour.

These five groups are *ideal-types* in a Weberian sense. According to Max Weber (1968, pp. 3–26), they are useful analytical tools and explanatory devices. They are simple reconstructions of observable realities that deliberately ignore details and also overlook links, overlaps and connections between these different groups. The first four groups of this model are actively involved in the process of "Othering", which, in the context of football, involves discrimination and vilification. The main differences of the first four groups are the intensity, depth and ferocity of their racist, xenophobic, antisemitic and Islamophobic convictions and how these affect their views of the world and everyday lives.

As mentioned in the introductory chapter and confirmed in several of the country case studies (England, France, Germany, the Netherlands, Poland, Portugal and Sweden) Europe's far-right is characterised by ideological positions that prioritise the ethnic nation and disregard the values of all those who do not belong to what they perceive to be the genuine nation. This disdain of Others typically results in racism, xenophobia, antisemitism and Islamophobia which we find in both everyday life and at all different levels in football. There is little doubt that both are somehow related and there appears to be a broad consensus that the latter is, at least, a reflection of the former. Others go further and argue that the language of prejudice, intolerance and discrimination of the far-right has spilled over into the world of football, particularly in countries with far-right governments.

Scapegoating minority communities and blaming them for a wide variety of problems is a popular strategy of far-right politics as that process provides simple and straight-forward answers to often complex and complicated questions. This is also true in the world of football, where fans often blame members of minority groups for failures. Emile Durkheim (1995) introduced the notion of scapegoating to sociology at the beginning of the 20th century. He suggested that the construction of scapegoats is a social phenomenon inherent to modern societies, involves the arbitrary placement of blame on (usually vulnerable, weak, less powerful, peripheral and/or minority) individuals and/or small distinctive groups and helps to maintain social cohesion and order. In the aftermath of events that generate negative emotional responses of the in-group, such as anxiety, disappointment or fear, members of this group blame others, that is the out-group, for the experience. This applies, of course, to defeats in football where the fans' default position is that their team is superior to their opponents which will inevitably lead to a victory. Defeats therefore pose a significant threat to this core belief of the in-group, which subsequently assigns responsibility and blame to members of the out-group. Ultimately, scapegoating promotes division, hostility and exclusion of those who become its targets. As such, it is a detrimental social practice that is also popular in many European discourses about migration as particularly the chapter on Italy has convincingly demonstrated. The chapter on England has shown that the heterogeneous group of male Muslims are often portrayed as terrorists who pose a threat to the British way of life. Despite evidence to the contrary, immigrants are frequently blamed for several socio-economic problems, for example, unemployment and crime. In both chapters, on England and Italy, the perceived threat and fear of minorities play a significant role. In Europe, the scapegoating of Jews dates back to ancient times and early Christianity. As a minority, they were frequently persecuted, and prejudice was a pervasive part of European history.

Such a long-term developmental account does not offer a comprehensive or convincing explanation for the deviant phenomena this book is dealing with. But it points to some continuities and makes a useful contribution. So, does acknowledging that five countries included in this anthology, Britain, France, the Netherlands, Portugal and Spain, used to be colonial empires. They subjugated other nations and their territory, took political control, exploited their resources and often forced their native language and cultural values on the suppressed people. Furthermore, and very relevant for this book, was the tendency of the colonisers to view the colonised as socially and culturally inferior. Although the lengthy process of decolonialisation came to an end in the third quarter of the 20th century, colonial nostalgia, in particular discourses of 'racial' thinking, continue to influence European societies to varying degrees. The chapter on Portugal addressed this issue in greater detail.

Andrei Markovits and Lars Rensmann (2010) point out that the more contemporary globalisation of football, in general, and the cosmopolitan composition of the majority of professional European teams, in particular, stands in stark contrast to the make-up of the fan base that is not as diverse as the group of players on the pitch. Consequently, what we are witnessing is a typical Othering process, a form of counter-cosmopolitanism (Appiah, 2007, pp. 137–153), as the ethnic and national diversity of the teams constitutes a threat to the relative homogeneity of the fans and their sense of identity. Counter-cosmopolitanism is a defensive reaction to profound cultural changes in both society and football that tend to challenge existing identity narratives.

Although the first four groups have featured most prominently in the previous country case studies, fans of the fifth group, the activists, who are involved in anti-discriminatory activities, exist in all European countries. They are a timely reminder that not all fans are *the problem*. Quite the opposite: those who exhibit and engage in discriminatory, abusive and threatening behaviour constitute a minority. On the other hand, in many European countries, fans were, and often continue to be, responsible for alerting and putting pressure on other stakeholders to take notice and action in order to combat various forms of discrimination. They use(d) banners, T-shirts, balloons, leaflets, fan magazines and fanzines to make a public stance and campaign against racism and other forms of discrimination. Some of the more organised groups have systematically lobbied their local football clubs and authorities to take responsibility and be more proactive opposing racism, for example, through permanently displaying banners in stadiums with unequivocal statements condemning racism and other forms of discrimination.

While discriminatory chants in football grounds have a long history, online abuse is a relatively recent but already widespread phenomenon that the chapters on England, France, Germany, the Netherlands, Poland, Portugal, Spain and Sweden explicitly mention. It appears that abuse on social media has grown considerably in many European countries as the internet has become a popular arena for obsessive fandom and is frequently used as a fertile ground for political interest groups. Messages containing derogatory, threatening, intimidating, harassing and/or humiliating contents are either about or directed at specific players and teams (Vidgen and Williams, 2022). The anonymity of the digital space encourages the creation and spread of distorted and controversial narratives about supposed opponents, minority groups, scapegoats and others. Players' extensive use of social media as a marketing tool makes them accessible to the wider public who can post racist abuse anonymously. But it is not only Black male footballers who are targeted. Female footballers and other sportswomen are also plighted by online abuse that is often sexist and homophobic in nature.

Local clubs

Football clubs are like wheel hubs in the complex and multi-layered world of football and constitute important institutions of civic society. These organisations provide people with opportunities to participate in competitive and/or recreational physical activities, socialise with others, and learn a large number of social skills, democratic principles and political practices. They are also sources of local identity and pride. It is therefore no surprise that almost all chapters have examined the role of football clubs in various contexts, in particular as anchors for minority groups, selected targets for discriminatory and offensive attacks, and as driving forces and intermediaries of anti-discriminatory campaigns. Furthermore, several chapters noted a lack of diversity in high-profile coaching positions and in powerful management roles.

Most European countries host diaspora football clubs. They were initially established to serve a particular national, ethnic or religious community outside of their home country; nowadays, most of the clubs' membership is no longer exclusively diasporic. They vary widely in age, size, support, finances and following. What they all have in common, however, is a distinct cultural heritage and identity that reflects their original national, ethnic, and/or religious roots. The chapters on Germany, Scotland and Sweden have explicitly and in great detail dealt with these clubs. But there are many more in other countries, for example, in Andorra (FC Lusitanos, founded in 1999 by Portuguese immigrants), Denmark (Vatanspor, established in 1989 by Turkish migrants), England (Indian Gymkhana Club, set up in 1916, initially as a cricket club and is rooted in London's Indian community) and the Netherlands (Amsterdam Gençler Birliği, founded in 1982 by Turkish migrants), to name just a few. Maccabi sport and football clubs exist all over the world. They are part of the Jewish sports movement that aims to preserve Jewish heritage, foster the personal development of its members, promote healthy life styles, and offer as sense of community and pride.

Without doubt, two of the oldest and best-known diaspora football clubs play in Scotland's top division. In 1875, members of the Irish community set up Hibernian FC in Edinburgh, Scotland's capital. The Irish heritage of Hibernian FC is reflected in the name (Latin for Ireland), colours (the shirt's green colour is usually accompanied by white sleeves and shorts) and badge of the club. Celtic FC was set up in 1887 as a charity to alleviate the poverty facing the thousands of Irish immigrants in Glasgow's East End. Furthermore, Celtic FC was central to the identity of Glasgow's immigrant Catholic community. Green and white also dominate the club's logo, with a four-leaf shamrock added. Nowadays, both clubs attract support that goes far beyond their original mission. That applies to most diaspora football teams whose membership criteria tend to be much more open than the name of the club often suggests.

The key question that has been raised for many years in the sociology of sport and, implicitly or explicitly, by various authors in this book also remains unanswered in the wider European context: Do football clubs that have distinctive national, ethnic, and/or religious origins and links to specific communities increase the socio-cultural isolation of their members or do they actually help to strengthen the self-awareness and self-confidence of the minorities concerned "and, thus promote interaction with, as well as participation in, the culture of the majority ethnic group" (Merkel, Sombert and Tokarski, 1996, p. 160)? However, there is no doubt that these clubs attract criticism and, in some cases, abusive behaviour.

The very obvious Jewish connection of Maccabi clubs tends to be a catalyst for antisemitic abuse (Germany, the Netherlands and Sweden). Antisemitic chants are particularly pronounced in matches that involve Ajax Amsterdam, Austria Vienna, Bayern Munich, Cracovia Football Club (Poland) and Tottenham Hotspur (London). These clubs have had some Jewish connections in the past, either through their location in predominantly Jewish areas, for example, Tottenham in North London, or because several of their directors were Jewish. Bayern Munich, for example, was labelled a "Jewish club" by the Nazi authorities in the 1930s when both president and manager were Jewish. However, none of these five clubs are explicitly Jewish organisations, nor do the clubs' identities or brands incorporate Jewish markers. They may have attracted a broad Jewish fan base in the past and even nowadays some Tottenham supporters – despite lacking religious links – refer to themselves as "Yids" or the "Yid Army", an extremely derogatory and offensive term describing a Jewish person. However, overall, this connection has become rather tenuous. Nevertheless, some Tottenham fans maintain a Jewish identity, and the Israeli flag continues to be a popular prop in the team's football ground. The situation is similar in the Dutch capital, where Ajax's home ground, the De Meer Stadium, was, until the 1990s, geographically right in the heart of the large Jewish community. The club also had a number of Jewish leaders and players. Like Tottenham players and fans, Ajax supporters and their team also frequently face antisemitic abuse from other fan groups, often including evocations of the Holocaust combined with neo-Nazi slogans. The self-proclaimed Jewishness of the Ajax and Tottenham supporters, in fact, also defies antisemitism. The football grounds of these clubs have become spaces for negotiating and challenging the meaning of Jewishness and antisemitism in contemporary European society (Brunssen, 2023). However, that is a complicated and sometimes even contradictory process. In November 2024, Ajax Amsterdam played Maccabi Tel Aviv in the European League. The match was marred by unprecedented levels of violence on the streets of the Dutch capital between Israeli fans and pro-Palestinian demonstrators, which, apparently, included Ajax fans and hooligans.

In addition to describing and analysing racism, xenophobia, antisemitism and Islamophobia in football, all chapters have, to varying extents, also outlined and critically evaluated selected policies, strategies, campaigns, initiatives, measures and actions that have been developed and taken by different stakeholders to combat the aforementioned behavioural patterns. There is little doubt that football clubs play a vital role here, as they operate at the grassroots level, are able to engage with fans and other stakeholders, and influence the atmosphere in their stadiums. Permanent anti-racist banners and messages on hoardings can nowadays be seen in many grounds across Europe. While the poorer, usually smaller local amateur clubs appear to struggle to engage in anti-discriminatory campaigns due to their modest resources, professional clubs have the means to engage in a number of activities over extended periods of time. And yet, there is a dilemma as promoting and engaging with anti-discriminatory campaigns implies that the product they are selling, football, is "faulty". That is certainly one of the reasons why some chapters have mentioned that some professional clubs have not been very enthusiastic and forthcoming. Others suggested that sponsors have increasingly stressed that they wish clubs to take their Corporate Social Responsibility (CSR) seriously. On several occasions, it was the impetus and pressure of local fans who persuaded clubs to take action.

In the previous chapters, a large number of specific programs and initiatives that local clubs have implemented have been mentioned. Typically, the overarching framework, rationale and objectives have been developed by state institutions and/or the relevant football associations, which also provide various forms of (limited) financial and practical support. The actual activities usually involve publicly expressing an anti-discriminatory stance, showing solidarity with the victims, promoting tolerance, inclusion and diversity, raising awareness, publishing anti-discrimination policies, stadium bans for convicted perpetrators, and a range of educational initiatives, in-house and with external agencies such as educational establishments. Although technological advances, such as the widespread use of CCTV systems in stadiums, have enhanced surveillance capabilities, with dedicated police control rooms monitoring all activities and disturbances, some clubs also encourage spectators to monitor and report discriminatory incidents. This obviously requires the collaboration with national law enforcement agencies in order persecute the perpetrators.

Polish and Swedish clubs appear to be quite different. While the former show very little enthusiasm to tackle racism and hardly get involved, the latter's overall strategy is very different. Swedish clubs focus on the socio-economic conditions of poorer and/or unemployed fans as racism, xenophobia, anti-semitism and Islamophobia are no longer considered to be major problems in Swedish football.

Most of the aforementioned efforts have been geared towards changing attitudes among, and behaviour of, fans. That, of course, is not a simple task, particularly when racism remains institutionalised in the sport itself. While many clubs have implemented measures to combat the abuse of players, the lack of diversity in powerful positions such as in the boardrooms of football clubs does not appear to be on their radar. The chapters on the Netherlands and Sweden have clearly identified this shortcoming. It has also been argued that the absence of minority members in senior management and coaching roles is usually not understood as the outcome of discriminatory attitudes and (biased recruitment) practices but is simply acknowledged as a lack of diversity.

National and international governing bodies

The role and efforts of the European Union (EU), the Council of Europe (CoE), the Union of European Football Associations (UEFA), and the Football Against Racism in Europe network (FARE) have been outlined, analysed and critically evaluated in great detail in the previous chapter. All of these supra-national organisations oppose racism, xenophobia, antisemitism and Islamophobia and have developed distinctive policies and strategies to combat the various forms of discrimination in football. Unfortunately, their success has been limited, partly due to a lack of coordination. Despite this, FARE appears to be the most hands-on organisation that provides a variety of tools and resources for individuals, groups and organisations.

The national governing bodies of sport such as the various football associations, or federations, in Europe, are responsible for governing, managing and administering a specific physical activity on a national scale. That involves developing and promoting the sport, establishing, implementing and overseeing health and safety measures, nurturing the grassroots level, strategic planning and financial management. One other key task is to enforce rules and regulations in order to maintain fair play and integrity, and uphold ethical standards. It is the referee and his/her assistants who represent the governing body on the pitch and are responsible for carrying out this task. Both the national football associations and match officials have been mentioned in all country case studies, except for Scotland, as they play important roles in the punishment of deviant behaviour and the promotion of inclusion in football.

The following episode reveals the complexity and controversial nature of penalising those involved in racism during a competitive match, in this case in Spain's third division: In April 2024, Rayo Majadahonda FC's Senegalese goalkeeper, Cheikh Kane Sarr, was sent off for entering the stands to confront a rival fan who had racially abused him. His teammates followed him to the locker rooms and refused to finish the match, causing the match to be abandoned. Sarr, subsequently, received a two-match ban. The team was punished with a 3–0 defeat and a deduction of three points. The club had to pay a fine of €3,006. Opponent Sestao River Club was fined €6,001 and ordered to play two home games behind closed doors. The dual punishments of both teams as well as perpetrator and victim, obviously raise some tricky questions about the way referees and the national football associations deal with these kinds of situations. In the aforementioned case, Sarr's teammates' sense of unequivocal solidarity meant that the game had to be abandoned. There are, however, plenty of occasions where players – due to racist abuse of one of their teammates – walk off the pitch and return, after a few minutes, in order to avoid being penalised for their action. This short-lived, symbolic display of solidarity is rather half-hearted but understandable, considering the commercial parameters and financial pressures of modern professional football. The latter may also be the reason why referees appear to be rather reluctant to abandon matches, although the previously mentioned revised protocols allow them to do so under certain conditions. The chapters on Italy, the Netherlands, Poland, Portugal and Spain have, to varying extents, dealt with this dilemma and speculated that referees may be overwhelmed by the additional task to recognise and react appropriately to racist, xenophobic, antisemitic and/or Islamophobic abuse. Many do not mention such incidents in their match reports.

Three further key themes emerge from the different country case studies. Firstly, the attitudes and commitments of the various football associations to the fight of racism, xenophobia, antisemitism and Islamophobia vary widely across Europe. Secondly, many of football's governing bodies are primarily concerned with their own moral positioning and focus on public relations activities. Thirdly, there is an undeniable lack of diversity in the upper echelons of many football associations.

There appear to be considerable differences in the way the umbrella bodies of football in Europe respond to racism, xenophobia, antisemitism and Islamophobia on and off the pitch. While a few appear to be indifferent and do very little, several football associations take their responsibility seriously. They strive to educate fans and the general public in the hope of creating alliances against the various forms of discrimination, provide tools, funds and resources, offer training programmes and advice, and are proactive. Some of them have developed anti-racism charters that contain a set of fundamental anti-discriminatory principles, encouraged individual clubs to adopt these, to display them in their grounds and urge others to comply with them. For example, after decades of intermittent attention, the Royal Dutch Football Association, in conjunction with the national government, appears to have developed a rather thorough and detailed action plan against racism and discrimination in both the recreational and professional segments of the sport. However, the previous chapters have also shown that some national football authorities in Europe do not always pull their weight in the way one would expect, often reacting late, intervening slowly and sometimes lacking conviction.

Considering all the anti-discrimination activities of football associations that have been mentioned in the previous chapters, a rather complex and, occasionally, confusing picture emerges. There is little doubt that the main concern of football associations is to position themselves publicly as advocates of diversity and inclusion and to improve the image and reputation of the sport. For that purpose, they tend to largely draw on symbolic gestures, slogans and mottos. They also dedicate special days or weeks as occasions to address the various forms of discrimination. Although these campaigns and activities may raise awareness among other stakeholders, they tend to be superficial, media-effective gestures that do not address the deep-rooted causes and systemic issues. One might even suggest that such a superficial engagement with racism and other forms of discrimination is caused by a lack of genuine interest in fundamental change. While these activities appear to align with broader efforts, for critical observers they come across as tokenism. Furthermore, one-off events convey a sense that the issue is peripheral and minor rather than significant and serious. As fleeting performances, they are unlikely to initiate meaningful change.

National football associations do not seem to realise that fighting racism, xenophobia, antisemitism, Islamophobia and other forms of discrimination is actually in their own interest. Ultimately, it allows them to draw on a larger pool of players when selecting the best for their national teams. In Belgium and the Netherlands, for example, Moroccans are an integral part of both countries' football scenes, in the leagues, the academies and the national youth teams. And yet, the team sheets of the senior national squads of both countries hardly feature any players of Moroccan descent. Although they are eligible as they hold passports from Morocco and their country of residence, many of them opt(ed) to play for the North African country. Footballers inevitably make choices that are based on personal circumstances and factors. However, their sense of national identity, experiences of integration and/or discrimination in their countries of birth and the intensity of ties to the motherland of their family also prove to be very important. At the World Cup in Qatar, in 2022, Morocco's team made history as they were the first African and Arab team ever reaching the semi-finals.

As previously mentioned in the context of local clubs, there is also a lack of diversity in powerful positions of the national football associations. Members of minority ethnic groups are absent from board rooms and therefore unable to participate in important decision-making processes. Although this has been noted by several governing bodies, they do not see any connection to discriminatory practices, although biased recruitment processes are very likely at the heart of this problem. The introduction of the "Rooney Rule" was only mentioned in the chapter on the Netherlands. It requires the interviewing of potential candidates from minority groups for top (leadership) positions. This has become standard practice in many high-profile global organisations as they recognise that a workforce comprising a mix of people with different cultural backgrounds, gender, experience, and socio-economic status is highly valuable. Having said that, inclusion and diversity is not just about numbers. Rather, it is about an organisation's culture, which is defined by assumptions, beliefs, norms, and values held by its members and their corresponding socio-cultural practices.

Nation-states and their governments

Almost all country case studies have, to different degrees, examined the role and involvement of nation-states and national governments in the general management of football in conjunction with the respective governing body of this popular sport and as providers of laws that prohibits and, if necessary, punishes deviant behaviour in football environments. That is no surprise as in most European societies the connection between sport, in general, and local and national governments is rather close. Although the nature and extent of governmental involvement varies from country to country, there is a long list of domestic and international reasons, which comprises desirable outcomes and benefits, that explain this almost symbiotic relationship.

The expectation that sport, in general, and football, in particular, has the potential to bring people together, build bridges between different social and/or ethnic groups, contributes to the social cohesion of a local community or even whole society, and underpins identity formation processes is of particular significance for nation-states (Sugden and Bairner, 2000). All of these benefits assume that this sport is inclusive and able to integrate people of different backgrounds. However, the reality, as shown in the previous chapters, is rather bleak as football also provides a stage for the public display of divisive, for example, racist, xenophobic, antisemitic and Islamophobic attitudes. There is plenty of evidence that football frequently causes, reinforces and exacerbates tensions, conflicts and various kinds of divisions. Throughout this book, in particular in the chapters on England, Germany, the Netherlands and Sweden, there has been a disconcerting tension between inclusion and exclusion, diversity and homogeneity, multi- and monoculturalism.

As a popular community activity football teams, clubs and matches also offer opportunities to experience a sense of local, regional and national identity. Successful teams are sources for prestige and esteem, and active participation has educational, health and fitness benefits. Competitions promote dominant socio-economic principles and cultural values, and successful national teams can even be used as a foreign policy tool to improve a country's reputation and increase its soft power (Nye, 2004). The latter refers the ability of countries to attract and persuade others. While hard power is based on a country's military or economic power, soft power derives from the attractiveness of the cultural industry, ideological foundations, political ideals, and policies of a country. Having a successful national football team and hosting mega sports events such as the FIFA World Cup (Sugden and Tomlinson, 1994) can make significant contributions to the production of soft power. However, being linked to, and associated with, an explicitly racist, xenophobic, antisemitic and/or Islamophobic football culture is detrimental for the soft power of a country and, occasionally, even leads to international political tensions. Brazil's president, Luiz Inácio Lula da Silva, and several of his cabinet ministers publicly expressed their concern about the treatment of Vinícius Júnior and the inaction of the Spanish authorities after the Brazilian player was repeatedly the victim of racist insults.

France seems to be aware of the opportunities football offers to strengthen its soft power and has been quite successful in sporting terms. The men's team has won the FIFA World Cup and the UEFA European Championships twice. The country hosted the World Cup twice and the European Championships three times. Most recently, Paris staged the Olympic Games. And yet, the country's international sporting reputation has been seriously tarnished by its dogmatic insistence on being a secular state. Despite France's motto and key principles, *Liberty, Equality, Fraternity*, and the country's declared commitment to inclusion, the neutrality and secular nature of the state prohibits the wearing of religious outfits in public. That, for example, prevents Muslim girls and women, who usually wear a *hijab*, from taking part in sport. Although this ban is discriminatory and violates international human rights obligations, in particular the entitlement of people to freely manifest their identity, religion or belief in private and in public, the French football federation (and other sport governing bodies) enforce this ban. Furthermore, French referees do not interrupt matches during Ramadan to allow Muslim players, who fast during the day, to eat and drink, which has become a common practice in lots of countries. In the context of this book, this is a rather unusual case as most nation-states and their governments in Europe are keen to promote a positive image of the country through successful athletes and team and hosting international sports events.

The chapters on France, Germany, the Netherlands, Portugal, Spain and Sweden are very explicit about the use of sport, in general, and football, in particular, to advance the integration of minority groups, although their understandings of the key concept, integration, appears to differ. The governments in these countries are usually motivated by the desire to improve social relations and many of them are also actively involved in fighting discrimination in the world of sport. What sets them apart is the point at which they began to take the problems in their respective football environments seriously. While governmental involvement in Spain already commenced in 2007, the Portuguese government presented its comprehensive strategy to fight racism and discrimination in 2021. One of the ten areas of intervention is the world of sport. Although the authors of these country case studies also criticised and expressed their concern about several aspects of the governmental policies and strategies, there is little doubt that some governments are taking the issue seriously.

State organisations, in particular the security forces and courts, are centrally involved in the prosecution of perpetrators. Under European law, any speech that expresses hate or encourages violence towards a person or group of people is illegal. That includes certain forms of racism and xenophobia, that is hatred based on 'race', skin colour, descent, national or ethnic origins, religious preferences and sexual orientation. All of these acts have harmful impacts on the individual victims or groups of victims but also on society as a whole. Although the legal parameters are relatively clear, the actual prosecution of perpetrators appears to be rather difficult and many ultimately remain unpunished, very often due to the lack of unequivocal evidence.

Summary

There is little doubt that racism, xenophobia, antisemitism and Islamophobia are socially constructed attitudes and forms of behaviour that cause fear, harm, anxieties, tensions and conflicts. To varying extents, they are deeply rooted in the past, for example, in the colonial empires of Britain, France, the Netherlands, Portugal and Spain as well as the long history of scapegoating Jewish people, and the medieval anti-Islamic and anti-Muslim sentiment propagated by the Christian Church. They are also deeply rooted in the contemporary fabric of European societies. They do not exist in a vacuum and therefore are best understood in their specific demographic, socio-historical, economic, political and cultural contexts. Although the essence of all four phenomena is the same, there are notable national variations in terms of the actual manifestations, targets, perpetrators, the way the abuse is communicated, counter-measures and media treatment. Racist, xenophobic, antisemitic and Islamophobic abuse is primarily directed at players, occasionally at other fans, match officials and clubs as a whole if they are considered to be representatives of specific minorities. However, although the public display of such discriminatory attitudes is frequent, often involves individuals and/or small groups, it is certainly not as organised as violent hooligan encounters in the past. Racist, xenophobic, antisemitic and Islamophobic attitudes are also very likely the cause for the blatant absence of ethnic minorities, in particular Black coaches and the lack of diversity in senior management positions in clubs and governing bodies. The vast majority of the previous chapters have focused on the experiences of Black sportsmen. There is an urgent need to add a (feminist) gender dimension to these discussions and, ultimately, pay more attention to the intersectionality of various forms of discrimination.

The factors that have been considered in this book as they appear to contribute to the deviant behaviour of some football fans in the 21st century are: far-reaching socio-demographic and rapid political changes and governmental socio-economic policies throughout the last two decades; the structural and cultural changes that have occurred in many European societies due to increased migration, in particular the changing ethnic, national and religious composition and contours of many European societies; the massive growth of deliberate misinformation and fake news, in particular those that promote conspiracy theories, hate speech, violent extremism, and mistrust in democratic organisations and processes; the increasing social, economic, political and cultural uncertainty caused by the powerful globalisation process, far-reaching technological advances and rapid societal transformations; and, last but not least, the steady rise of far-right ideologies, groups, organisations and political parties in Europe. At this point, it is impossible to clearly outline the extent to which any of these factors can be attributed to central causal status.

Despite the absence of a widespread, media-orchestrated moral panic, there is pressure on clubs, governing bodies, and national governments to take remedial action. The days of denying the existence of the aforementioned problems are certainly over. While many clubs are taking their responsibility very seriously, often driven by an increasing commitment to CSR and pressure from sponsors and fan groups, several of the country case studies in this book convey a sense that the national football associations wish to be seen as proactive but rely largely on token-gestures. Although several engage in a variety of awareness-raising activities, many of these come across as half-hearted, undifferentiated and not necessarily fully thought-through campaigns. Few, if any, of the remedial initiatives – ranging from persuasion to punishment – have, so far, succeeded in eradicating racism, xenophobia, antisemitism and Islamophobia.

The introduction of more intensive policing, simplified reporting mechanisms and CCTV surveillance systems inside football stadia probably played a part in driving the problems on to the various social media platforms that offer the perpetrators anonymity. Fighting online hate requires government intervention on an international scale, and drastic action from social media companies in collaboration with law enforcement agencies. However, that is not an easy task as many online trolls and abusers are based around the world, many using fake accounts.

Most of the aforementioned measures focus on eradicating the verbal and/or written abuse, that is on words. However, they do not address the hostile ideological underpinning of such chants and social media posts, the attitudes that lay at the heart of these and are becoming more popular and widespread, as demonstrated by the steady rise of the far-right in many European countries.

Given the longevity of racism, xenophobia, antisemitism and Islamophobia in European football and the normalising of far-right ideas in many European countries, which has made discriminatory attitudes and practices respectable, I struggle to be optimistic about the future. What European football needs is a much more comprehensive and coordinated strategy (and, of course, action) that also tackles the absence of non-White managers, coaches, and board members in order to dismantle structural and institutional racism. Only then, it will be possible to achieve meaningful change.

I hope, at the very least, this anthology has helped the readers to better understand that these forms of deviant behaviour are complex and deeply rooted social phenomena that – despite some minor and a few major differences – blight the experience of football in several European countries.

References

Appiah, K.A. (2007) *Cosmopolitanism*, New York: W.W. Norton.
Brunssen, P. (2023) *The making of "jew clubs": performing Jewishness and antisemitism in European soccer and fan cultures*, Ann Arbor: Michigan University.
Durkheim, É. (1995) *The elementary forms of the religious life*, New York: Free Press.
Kohn, H. (2005) *The idea of nationalism: a study in its origins and background*, London: Routledge.
Markovits, A.S. and Rensmann, L. (2010) *Gaming the world: how sports are reshaping global politics and culture*, Princeton: Princeton University Press.
Meineke, F. (1970) *Cosmopolitanism and the national state*, Princeton: Princeton Legacy Library.
Merkel, U., Sombert, K. and Tokarski, W. (1996) "Football, racism and xenophobia in Germany: 50 years later – here we go again?", in Merkel, U. and Tokarski, W. (Eds.), *Racism and xenophobia in European football*, Aachen: Meyer and Meyer.
Nye, J. (2004) *Soft power – the means to success in world politics*, New York: Public Affairs.
Smith, A. (1991) *National identity*, London: Penguin Books.
Sugden, J. and Bairner, A. (2000) *Sport in divided societies*, Aachen: Meyer and Meyer.
Sugden, J. and Tomlinson, A. (1994) *Hosts and champions: soccer cultures, national identities and the USA World Cup*, Aldershot: Arena Ashgate.
Vidgen, B. and Williams, A.R. (2022) "Nearly 70% of premier league footballers are abused on Twitter – we used an AI to sift through millions of tweets", *The Conversation*, 12th August. Available: <https://theconversation.com/nearly-70-of-premier-league-footballers-are-abused-on-twitter-we-used-an-ai-to-sift-through-millions-of-tweets-188317> [accessed on 15th March 2024].
Weber, M. (1968) *Economy and society: an outline of interpretative sociology*, New York: Bedminster Press.

Index

abuse: antisemitic 98, 227, 232; racial 37, 46, 97, 196, 197, 202, 214–215, 220; racist 64, 77, 108–109, 118, 135, 147–148, 179, 184, 209, 214, 226, 230
activism 37
Africa 7, 9, 14, 26, 56–58, 61–62, 77, 95, 100, 110–113, 117, 119, 145–146, 178, 190, 198, 222, 224, 233
AIK 194–195
Ajax Amsterdam 17, 113–114, 232
anti-Irish sentiment 158, 166
anti-Muslim 8, 12, 14, 27, 37–38, 40–41, 44–48, 50, 72, 75, 77, 79, 224, 239
anti-racist 81, 98, 101–102, 136, 138, 181, 181–182
antisemitism xii, 1, 2, 3–5, 7–10, 16–17, 27, 44, 72, 80–82, 98, 111, 113, 188–189, 193–194, 196, 222, 224, 228, 232–236, 239–240
Arsenal FC 177
AS Roma FC 97–98
assimilation 72–73, 81, 85, 114–115
Assyriska FF 191
attitudes xii, 5, 11–12, 15, 21–22, 27, 37–38, 45, 50, 67, 74, 77–78, 94, 136, 138, 141–142, 146, 149, 163, 167, 176–177, 180, 191, 196, 201–202, 223–224, 228, 233, 234–235, 237, 239–240
audience 73, 83, 149, 227
Austria Vienna 232
awareness raising 48, 66, 78, 152, 178, 181, 206, 209, 240

banlieue 11, 57–59, 62, 54
banter 43, 80, 176, 195

Bayern Munich FC 2, 232
Barcelona FC 177–178, 225
Belgium 227, 236
Black player(s) 1, 24–25, 42, 65, 77, 98, 113–114, 134–135, 138, 198, 209–210, 217, 225
British Asian 29, 37, 42, 45, 49–50
Britishness 161
Bundesliga 77, 85
Burnley FC 47

campaign(s) 14, 46–50, 66, 77–78, 83, 95, 98, 101, 116–117, 132, 135–137, 150, 152, 161, 179, 181–182, 206, 209, 213, 214, 218–219, 222, 230–233, 236, 240
Catholicism 129, 159, 164, 166
celebration(s) 26, 56–57, 79, 125
Celtic FC 158–168
Chelsea FC 44, 215, 227
Christianity 111, 132, 229
citizenship 7, 11, 16, 25, 40, 54–55, 60, 67, 114, 125, 127, 129, 135–136, 138, 144, 175
civil society 85, 150, 152, 210
club(s): diaspora 168, 191, 193; ethnic 74, 76, 190, 192–193
colonialism 20, 26, 39, 142–143, 177
community: local 96, 103, 200–201, 237; Muslim 82; national 104, 225
conspiracy 8, 14, 81–82, 170, 194, 239
cooperation 206–207
coordination 144, 234
Corporate Social Responsibility (CSR) 78, 201, 233
Council of Europe 143, 206–207, 219–220, 234

Index   243

Cracovia FC 133, 232
crime 3, 6, 27, 44, 49, 80, 95–96, 99, 144, 145, 152, 179, 185, 209–210, 229

Dalkurd FF 191–192
decolonisation 43
democratic 12, 15, 25, 74, 83, 126, 131, 210, 231, 239
Den Bosch FC 108, 211
disability 24, 75, 144, 147, 151, 176, 188
discourse(s) 10–15, 19–21, 24, 26, 26, 28, 36–45, 48–50, 54–55, 63, 71, 75, 79, 95–96, 100, 104, 110–111, 115, 120–121, 126, 142–143, 146–147, 149, 185, 188–190, 192, 198, 225, 228–229
discrimination: ethnic 189; racist 47, 77, 147, 219; territorial 94, 99, 100–101, 103–104; xenophobic 24
diversity 2, 43, 48–49, 54–56, 60, 63, 71, 83, 85–86, 102, 108–110, 113–114, 116, 118–120, 126, 136, 138–139, 150–152, 194, 196–197, 200, 202, 220, 227, 230–231, 233, 235–239
Djurgårdens IF 195
double standard 79, 226
dress code 9, 38, 50

education 19, 28, 39, 58, 66, 73, 83–86, 117–118, 141, 146, 150, 152–153, 182, 196–197, 201, 208, 210, 218–219
Ekstraklasa 125, 128
employment 12, 73, 96, 130, 142, 144, 173, 193, 200–202, 215, 229, 231
English Premier League 29, 43, 47, 97
ethnicity 4, 23, 27–28, 79, 109, 111, 115, 144, 147, 150–151
EURO 2024 79
European Union (EU) 1, 7, 128, 143, 145, 206, 208, 210–211, 219–220, 234
Excelsior Rotterdam FC 108, 211
exclusion 1, 7, 8, 26, 65, 67, 71, 76, 81, 104, 115–116, 119, 121, 133, 138, 147, 190, 201–202, 208, 223–224, 228–229, 237
executive board(s) 77–78, 113, 117, 196–197, 227, 233

Famalicão FC 147
fan culture(s) 37, 41, 43, 45–46, 49–50, 82, 126
fans 1–3, 15, 17, 27, 37, 42–50, 57, 71, 78–80, 83, 97–99, 101, 103–104, 108, 111, 113, 119, 125, 128, 130–138, 145–148, 150–152, 160–168, 179, 181–183, 188, 190–195, 202, 207–220, 223–235, 239
fanzines 230
FARE (Football Against Racism in Europe) 136, 206, 211, 218–219
far-right 7–17, 56–59, 62–65, 67, 73, 77, 79, 95, 98, 103, 120, 134, 135, 143, 149, 173, 183, 201, 219, 223, 225–226, 228–229, 240
fascism 95, 98, 130, 135, 165
fear 6–8, 10, 16, 26, 38, 96, 98, 100, 104, 134, 223, 229, 239, 256
FIFA (Fédération Internationale de Football Association) 37, 43, 45, 54, 56, 61, 63, 66, 84, 102, 116, 150, 208, 212–213, 219, 222, 226–227, 237–238
football: amateur 1, 17, 36, 48, 54, 65, 71, 76–78, 83–85, 109, 112–113, 117, 119, 145–147, 178, 190, 198, 222, 224, 233; club(s) 3, 17, 27, 43, 46–48, 50, 60, 72–78, 80, 82–85, 97–101, 103, 112–113, 116–117, 119, 125–126, 128, 130–134, 135–137, 139, 146, 148, 150–152, 158, 174–175, 179, 181–184, 189–197, 199–202, 211–215, 217–218, 223–225, 230–236, 239–240; grassroots 1, 37, 42–43, 45–46, 48–50, 102–103, 108, 131, 151, 182, 213, 233–234; manager 16, 24–25, 37, 42, 48, 61, 63, 113–114, 145, 167, 208, 227, 232, 240; professional 1, 2, 17, 29, 36–37, 42–44, 46–50, 65, 71, 76–80, 83, 85, 102, 108–109, 112–114, 117, 119, 175, 178, 180, 182, 194, 198, 213, 222, 235; team(s) 16, 24, 27, 42–43, 54, 56–66, 71–72, 76–77, 79–80, 84–85, 93–94, 97–98, 101–103, 108, 111–114, 116–117, 125–127, 134–138, 147, 159, 173, 175–179, 183–184, 191–193, 198–199, 209, 214, 216–217, 224–227, 229–232, 234, 236–238

foreigner(s) 5, 6, 10, 12, 16, 26, 59, 61, 63, 65, 72, 85, 127–129, 132, 134–135, 138, 174–175, 190, 194, 198–199, 225–227
French Football Federation (FFF) 59–66
Frenchness 62–63

Gastarbeiter 9, 72
gender(ed) 11, 21, 27–28, 40, 42–43, 50, 71, 75, 102, 109, 121, 132–133, 145–151, 176, 188–189, 200, 212, 220, 224, 236, 239
German Football Association (DFB) 71, 73–77, 80, 84–85
Glasgow 158–162
globalisation 20, 222–223, 230, 240
governing body/bodies 41, 44, 47–49, 60, 66, 74, 104, 119, 121, 126, 137, 199, 202, 211–212, 217–219, 222–224, 234–240

hate speech 22, 144, 146, 149, 152, 182, 209–210, 239
Heart of Midlothian FC 159–160, 168
Hibernian FC 159, 164, 231
hijab 9–10, 38, 40, 43, 66, 224, 238
homophobia 28, 66, 83, 141, 145, 149, 151
hooliganism 3, 189, 215
hostility 8, 27, 36–38, 45, 59, 75, 83, 166, 229
Human Rights 15, 75, 141, 145, 152, 208–209, 219, 238

identity: construction 147; cultural 144; ethnic 4, 129, 225; local 192, 231; national 25–26, 104, 126–127, 129, 142, 163, 225, 236–237; religious 160, 164, 193
ideology 8, 21, 25, 80, 130–134, 164, 176, 181
IK Makkabi FC 190–194, 225
inclusion 49, 78, 102–103, 109, 114, 116–117, 120–121, 128, 135, 152, 175, 190, 197, 200, 208, 218–220, 226–227, 233–238
integration 11, 16, 39–40, 46, 54, 67, 71–74, 77, 79, 81, 84–85, 109, 114, 120, 141, 164, 190, 195–198, 200–201, 222–223, 227, 236, 238
Inter Milan FC 92, 93, 97, 99, 101
intersectionality 10, 21, 27, 75, 82, 85, 152, 224, 239

Israel 8, 17, 41, 47, 81–82, 193
Italian Football Federation (FIGC) 97–98, 101, 103
Italianness 104

Jew(ish) 5, 7–8, 27, 80–82, 113, 127, 131, 133, 190, 194, 224, 226, 229, 231–232
jokes 22, 109, 112, 176, 195
Juventus FC 98–99, 191–192

knowledge 23, 25, 28, 38–39, 98, 102, 129, 131, 141, 144, 195, 197

LaLiga 178–185
Lech Poznań FC 132
Lechia Gdańsk FC 125, 133, 135, 138
Legia Warsaw FC 132, 135, 138
legal framework 3, 152, 173, 210
legislation 12, 26, 118, 133, 160, 183, 199, 206–207
Leicester City FC 46
LGBT (Lesbian, Gay, Bisexual and Transgendered) 40, 47, 133
LGBTI (Lesbian, Gay, Bisexual, Transgendered and Intersex) 143–144, 151
LGBTQ (Lesbian, Gay, Bisexual, Transgendered and Queer) 13, 132
LGBTQI+ (Lesbian, Gay, Bisexual, Transgendered, Queer and Intersex) 109, 117, 220
Liverpool FC 27, 44, 46, 50
ŁKS Łódź FC 130–133
loyalty 67, 79

Maccabi 17, 82, 231–232
Malmö FF 192, 194, 200–201
management 24, 78, 118, 167, 174, 197, 202, 208, 213, 222, 231, 234, 239
Manchester City FC 49
Manchester United FC 62, 224
manifestation(s) 1, 2, 6, 8, 21, 26, 36–41, 46–48, 50, 71, 76–77, 80, 92–93, 97, 103–104, 112, 117, 126–127, 131–132, 137, 139, 141, 143, 145, 148, 150, 153, 173–179, 181, 196, 202, 210, 216, 219, 222, 224
marginal 21–29, 126, 130, 130, 146–147, 152, 161, 165, 175, 193, 218–219

Marseille FC 65
masculinity 76, 82, 130, 148
media: coverage 46, 80, 119, 146, 150, 176, 224; discourse 36, 41, 44
migrant(s) 1, 7, 9, 11–15, 26, 55, 61, 72–74, 79, 81, 94–97, 100, 102–104, 110–115, 118, 128, 132, 138, 143, 143, 151, 164, 166, 168, 173, 176, 188, 190–192, 195, 199, 223, 226, 229, 231
Middle East 17, 72, 81–82, 110, 191, 193–194, 198, 209
migration 7, 9–17, 20, 26, 39, 72–74, 94–96, 100, 109–113, 119, 127, 8, 136, 138–139, 142, 166, 176, 188, 191, 198, 201, 208, 223, 229, 239
minority/ies 11, 13, 29, 55, 109, 111–112, 115, 118–121, 126, 133, 135, 148, 150, 165, 219, 226, 229–234, 236, 238–239
monitoring 36, 76, 81, 83, 85, 116, 118, 137, 152–153, 183, 218, 233
Morocco 110–111, 227, 238

Napoli FC 92–93, 97
national: government 116, 119, 235, 237, 240; identity 25–26, 104, 126–127, 129, 142, 163, 225, 236–237; team 2, 56, 59–62, 64–65, 72, 77, 79, 85, 94, 108, 111, 114, 125–127, 135–136, 138, 147, 177, 191, 199, 213, 225, 227, 236
nationalism 25, 56, 125, 134, 142, 158, 164, 166, 208, 223, 225, 228
nationality 23, 25, 60, 75, 131, 135, 137, 144, 147, 150, 226
nation-state(s) 8, 15, 25–26, 40, 55, 104, 127, 138, 224–225, 237–238
neo-Nazi(s) 77, 176, 181, 219, 232
Newcastle United FC 43, 49
nomenclature 1, 3, 188
norms and values 8, 132, 236

Online 1, 43, 46–47, 50, 117–118, 125, 145, 182, 194, 196, 198–199, 201, 213, 223–224, 226, 230, 240
orientalism 37–39, 50

Palermo FC 103
Paris Olympics 2024 10
participation 49, 61, 64, 67, 74, 103, 109, 115, 120–121, 174, 232, 237

patriotism 63, 175, 192, 198
Piast Gliwice FC 125, 138
polarisation 73, 121, 149, 159, 173
police 42, 57, 97, 133, 144, 147, 151–152, 158, 165, 176, 179, 181–182, 189, 200, 208–209, 214, 216, 233
Polishness 129
politics 19, 25–26, 41, 55, 63, 80, 82, 95, 103–104, 120, 133, 149, 159, 161–163, 212, 225, 229
Polish Football Association (PZPN) 126, 136–137
Polonia Gdańsk FC 134–135
Porto FC 147–148
positional segregation 114
power relations 21, 25, 165
propaganda 12, 25, 59, 144
protest 40, 58, 65, 97, 130, 133–134, 184, 209, 211
protocol 181, 184, 211, 216–217, 184, 209, 211
public discourse(s) 10, 13, 71, 75, 95, 110

quota(s) 10, 13, 71, 75, 95, 110

racialization 111
racism: biological 175; cultural 5, 21, 24, 27; individual 23–24; institutional 28, 108, 113, 118, 240; structural 25–26, 152–153; systemic 4, 21, 196
Raków Częstochowa FC 125
Rangers FC 158–168
Real Madrid FC 1, 175, 177–179, 181, 212
recommendation(s) 83, 119, 151, 183, 207–210
referee(s) 1, 43, 66, 71, 76, 81, 83–84, 93–94, 97, 99, 112, 117, 125, 133, 138, 145, 147–148, 150, 153, 177, 179, 181, 184, 196, 209–212, 216–218, 226, 234–235, 238
refugee(s) 1, 11, 13–14, 26, 72–74, 95–96, 103, 125, 132, 143, 188, 191–192
resistance 11, 13, 21, 28
right-wing extremism 14, 75, 80, 85–86
rivalry 98, 101, 125, 158–159, 165–168

Rooney rule 118, 236
Royal Dutch Football Federation (KNVB) 109, 112, 116, 118–119
Ruch Chorzów FC 127, 130, 134–153

sanction(s) 84, 101, 137, 180, 182–184, 208–209, 211, 213, 217, 219
scapegoat(s) 1, 8, 61, 65, 81, 130, 225–226, 229–230, 239
Schalke 04 77–78
Second World War 9, 80, 100, 110, 127, 131, 142, 223
secularism 10, 27, 45, 49, 55, 66, 81, 224, 238
Serie A 93, 101, 103, 227
sexism 28, 76, 82–83, 102, 109, 141, 149–151, 176, 239
sexual orientation 21, 141, 144–145, 147, 149–151, 176, 239
Śląsk Wrocław FC 132, 134
skin colour 4, 38, 59, 75, 110, 117, 120, 125, 129, 135, 137–138, 143–144, 147, 151, 178, 229, 238
skinheads 130, 175
social class 38, 127, 188–189
socialism 131
social media 27, 37, 44, 46–47, 64, 76–77, 112, 149, 152, 179, 183, 210, 215, 225, 230, 240
social relations 27–29, 127, 238
South America 111, 141, 174
Soviet Union 110, 127, 129
Spanish Football Association (RFEF) 178–179, 184
spectators 6, 27, 29, 71, 84, 94, 117, 180, 217, 223, 227–228, 233
sponsor(s) 1, 83, 201–202, 215, 224, 233, 240
SS Lazio FC 2, 26, 97–98
stakeholder(s) 2, 3, 37, 47, 50, 83, 85, 108, 115, 150–152, 179, 183, 207, 211–212, 218, 222–223, 230, 233, 236
stereotype(s) 6, 21–25
Stockholm 42, 48, 50, 59, 61, 72, 99, 100, 113–115, 141, 144, 146, 162–163, 190, 193–195
strategies 2, 3, 14, 48, 71, 73, 78, 109, 118, 133, 149, 151–153, 183, 209, 222–223, 232, 234, 238
subculture(s) 130–131
Swedish Football Association (SvFF) 197, 199, 200

symbol(s) 2, 7, 16, 40–41, 47, 54–55, 63, 67, 79, 97, 116, 130–131, 134, 162, 175–177, 180–181, 193, 208, 219, 226–227
Syrianska FC 191–192

territory 144, 229
terrorist(s) 2, 36, 39–40, 43–44, 64, 85, 229
threat 6, 8, 10, 12–13, 15, 27, 36, 39–41, 44–45, 47, 82, 120, 144, 176, 179, 199, 219, 229–230
Tottenham Hotspurs FC 27, 232
tradition(s) 10, 19, 56, 110, 114–115, 144, 192
Turkey 16, 72, 79, 100–101, 226

Udinese FC 101, 213
UEFA (Union of European Football Associations) 1, 16, 77, 79, 132, 136–138, 160, 199, 206, 207, 210–219, 234, 238
Ukraine 128, 132, 209
ultras 72, 97–98, 101–102, 125, 132–136, 175, 180, 228
UNESCO 20, 150, 153, 165, 189, 199
United States 4, 26, 28, 100, 218

Valencia CF 175, 177–178, 212, 227
victims 2, 25, 40, 50, 83, 99, 109, 118, 146, 150, 152–153, 166, 168–169, 175, 178, 185, 209, 213, 220, 233, 239
vilification 6, 50, 101, 135, 228
violence 1, 7, 45, 78, 83–84, 114, 126, 130, 136, 141, 144–145, 147–148, 153, 158, 175–176, 178–181, 196, 206

West Ham FC 44
whiteness 4, 28, 45, 111, 198
Widzew FC 131, 133
woman/women 1, 9–11, 17, 19, 39–40, 42–43, 49–50, 54, 72, 74, 102–104, 113, 118–119, 132, 134, 145–151, 193, 196, 220, 224, 230, 238
World Cup: Brazil 2014 61; France 1998 54, 56–57, 63; Germany 2006 58; Qatar 2022 37, 45, 64, 116, 228, 236; Russia 2018 63, 79, 226; South Africa 2010 59–61

Zagłębie Lubin FC 132

For Product Safety Concerns and Information please contact our
EU representative GPSR@taylorandfrancis.com Taylor & Francis
Verlag GmbH, Kaufingerstraße 24, 80331 München, Germany